DARKENING
MIRRORS

I can't help thinking this book cd be benefitted by Occam's Razor.
Too much hiding behind "complexity."

DARKENING MIRRORS

IMPERIAL REPRESENTATION
IN DEPRESSION-ERA
AFRICAN AMERICAN
PERFORMANCE

Stephanie Leigh Batiste

DUKE UNIVERSITY PRESS
Durham & London 2011

© 2011 DUKE UNIVERSITY PRESS

All rights reserved. Printed in the United

States of America on acid-free paper ∞

Designed by Amy Ruth Buchanan

Typeset in Arno Pro by Tseng Information Systems, Inc.

Library of Congress Cataloging-in-Publication Data

appear on the last printed page of this book.

For Ernest & Louque

CONTENTS

....

PROLOGUE

Au uses "complexity" a lot.

The "darkening mirrors" of the title derives from a memory, a personal experience of the uncanny. One summer at the amusement park at the county fair, I unwittingly followed my sister into a cruel maze of tall cubicles with mirrors covering every side, a House of Mirrors. Each closed room provided endless reflections of the self. I saw my clothes, my face, the skin on my hand repeated over and over again in the walls around me. When I touched the mirror, my fingerprint was invisible directly behind my hand but discernable in smaller and smaller versions behind itself a million miles deep into the two-dimensional surface in front of me, behind me, and at my sides. And again and again in each succeeding room. Looking farther into the mirror showed more of the same and the same with a difference, as refracted images from other mirrors volleyed my lanky body back and forth in a different pose from an opposing angle — my arm in the way of my shirt here, but not there — over and over again, faster into forever. It took more pressure than my eight-year-old body could apply to move the one secret wall in each cubicle that would deposit you into the next mirrored room in the maze. In a tired moment I slumped and lifted my chin toward the ceiling, noticed the bright bare bulb high above my head, and immediately became aware of the impact should that light go out. Those glimmering mirrors that seemed filled with endless images would go black, empty. The perplexing, ungraspable infinity would vanish. The possibility was both terrifying and comforting. I could be stuck in the darkness, taunted by reflections of myself all around that I couldn't even see, but then at least I wouldn't have to look at them anymore. I peered harder, farther back into the most distant image I could perceive in this visual echo of myself, trying to determine if there was ever a point where I disappeared, if at some point deep within that chasm of myself everything went black. The mirrors seemed less powerful, more controllable when their fullness also carried the potential of an ultimate emptiness-darkness or disappearance. Despite the staring and searching, I still wanted to get the hell out of there. I ran into my sister in one of those glass boxes, and together we pushed our way out into the welcome dull heat of the broad afternoon.

"Darkening mirrors" act as both a conceptual and a metaphorical framework for this study and its implications. The little girl, the subject/agent (and, in some sense, the object, a cultural product herself) in the House of Mirrors operates in my study as a metaphor for the African American performers and performances of the 1930s. The girl seems stuck in an endless process of looking that is both chosen and accidental. The possibility of changing rooms provides a sense of escape, though the shift primarily offers a repetition of the previous experience with a change. More effective in achieving a sense of agency is her awareness of the process and investigation of its operation—her realization of its bottomless, receding, pyrrhic depth and her contact with the mirrors' flatness, falsity, and inscrutability. The receding images really go no farther than their distance from the opposing mirror, even as the mirrors' tiniest representation is not visible owing to its extreme distance. Even when lit the mirrors reflect invisibility in their apparent fullness. Rejection of the images and the process invoked by the mirrors might occur if the light, the mechanism of their propagation, were extinguished, affecting a cessation of looking and, further, of the possibility of reflection. Yet within the desire to extinguish the look is a sense of loss of self that is accompanied by a sinking awareness of the possibility that the image does not really disappear, but merely waits for the application of more light— that is, a promise of more looking and more production of images to be seen. The proliferation of images' contradictory reflections that shift with the physical and looking position of the subject fail to offer truth or clarity. Inescapable and unreal, reflection becomes an absorbing, dizzying trap affected only by the movement, awareness, and sometimes collective pushing by the subjects. Looking, shifting, changing, examining, redirecting, refusing, collective pushing—all become modes of repeating and resisting imperial structures of representation.

My sense of darkening mirrors as a conceptual model is grounded in postcolonial race theory. The metaphorical and historical weight of the black Atlantic has impacted the theory and methodology of this study in profound ways through its particular contemplation of black identity in the West. Paul Gilroy poses the question of black peoples' problematical relationship to Western epistemologies of identity and knowledge, global capitalism, the substance of white supremacy, and forms of "democratic" power.[1] The black Atlantic describes the trade of bodies, goods, and ideologies that fueled the engines of modernism and modernity and created "blackness" as a capitalist and democratic cipher of otherness. As was the concept of blackness itself, so were diasporic populations' identities born out of this matrix of industry, capital, commerce, white supremacy, exploitation, hatred, and abuse, so thickly (step)child to this matrix that it seems impossible to imagine a material blackness as *in but not of* the imperial operations that brought it into being. This book addresses the substance and consequences of that inheritance by pinpointing black peoples' use of representational structures that sustained the imperial project, and how black people changed those structures. New generations of black people in new places inherit, adopt, assimilate, and act out new ways of being from ancestral, colonial, and indigenous forces as well as the bubbling circumstances of history. Cultures of those "traded" bodies repeat and reinvent old ways, forging new expressions encompassed within new national boundaries and traditions.

I focus on performance in the Unites States as a cultural node of the black Atlantic. Performances, like music and literature, are a production of identities and desires resulting from the complex process of history. Outside of a purely historical process, diaspora operates as a kind of vision and materializes as an activity of intercultural recognition and exchange. Blacks' American identity is an insular national articulation of the black Atlantic. Black performance serves as evidence of Fanon's vision of national culture as a local push for black freedom. These performances predate Senghor's philosophy of Negritude, which promoted the hope that even a local push for black freedom might loosen the bonds of oppression everywhere. Thus this insularity that seems to reify national boundaries can serve as one step in developing transnational black identities.

I am particularly interested in the specific metaphorical quality of dark water. I imagine the deep powerful force that moved ships across space as a reflective substance that traps, reflects, and refracts light—images, ideologies, sensibilities, a dynamic mirror grasping and returning distorted images of the cargo on its surface. Gilroy's image of the black Atlantic became powerfully trapped in my imagination because of its resonance with the memory of standing enclosed in that succession of small, mirrored rooms. The "black Atlantic" serves not merely to name a literal means of transportation, the bodies it transported, their movement, their conditions, and its justifications, but also as a symbolic purveyor of ideology, culture, and knowledge. This diasporic Atlantic is easily analogized to waters of the Caribbean and Pacific in their contiguous relationships to an imperial United States. Notions of dark and deep reflection serve as a corrective. They acknowledge and redress the ways "seeing" as a means to access knowledge fails to recognize "meanings that are masked, camouflaged, indirect, embedded, or hidden in context," meanings that are in motion and invisible, like deep currents in dark water.[2] *Deep currents ARE visible w/ the proper means of observation*

The performances and performers in my study activate and appropriate representations that articulate power. They are bodies actively reflecting, reflecting upon, and enacting both dominant and alternative cultural ideologies. Their images and activities provide insight into, perhaps reflections of the many locations and inflections of black subjectivity and national identity. In these representations black cultural producers depict black and other nonwhite cultures and spaces. The multiple reflections of self in the face of the "other," and vice versa (as the other seems to peer out of one's own skin), in the deployment of representations of cultural power create a palimpsest of identities, disidentifications, and activisms that demonstrates the deep complexity of black Americans' national identities. In fact what is signified by notions of "other" and "self," theoretical and material locations central to postcolonial studies, becomes unstable as the conditions of nation and race force complicated and conflicting allegiances across both categories. The performances are creations, reflections, projections, desires, and protests that signal the texture of the subjects' racial, cultural, and national visions of self. The metaphor of darkening mirrors refers to these everdeepening creations and reflections of black identity, particularly given their manifestation of the often racist and damaging terms by which dominant and colonial national identities get established. As certain national and racial identities become clear, others cloud; new identities get

If they are invisible, who can see them or use them?

Identities as they try to + :. distinct from actual persons.

PROLOGUE

created that incorporate, use, and change previous ones, all in relationship to one another. "Darkening" refers to the participation of people traditionally understood as "dark" in the formation of their own identities through imagination of internal belonging and oceanic crossing. It invokes a process or sense of envelopment, if not doom, in the ubiquitous effects of power, and simultaneously a sense of hope for a future where such thick, instrumental, and infinite reflection becomes so full as to become ineffectual—the mirrors darkened, possibility reborn. The performative sites of endless reflection, the darkening mirrors of this study, are many: the entrapping discourses themselves—primitivism, expansion and its very *west*erliness, orientalism, and ethnographic representation; the imaginative process of representation within racialized and racist discourses; and the media that transmit the image and image making, the stage, the screen, and the performing body. Performative systems act as a house of mirrors, a visual sound chamber, as it were, where bodies, performances, discourses, and the technologies involved volley meaning in endless reverberations of images.

What emerges through the symbolics of the mirror and blackness is a story about a particular kind of awareness or desire in African American artists for a dizzying, recursive (and quite paradoxical) form of participation in history, modernity, and the promise and failures of American national identity. "Darkening mirrors" as a conceptual apparatus derives from the complexity of the materials themselves and the way they negotiate identity. These are specific performances by African American historical actors (directors, filmmakers, writers, performers) who cannot avoid being swept up into the larger cultural currents that surround them, currents such as modernism, primitivism, imperialism, nationalism (diasporic and otherwise), individualism, and expansionism. African Americans were very much implicated in the articulation of such various powerful cultural categories as, say, nationalism, yet in mobilizing these discourses and their signifying rubrics, they reveal how spiraling and complex this sort of implication is. The metaphor of the darkening mirror helps us see how African American culture in the 1930s and beyond is (a) reflective in some sense, mimetic of the conflicts and conjunctures around it; (b) organic as it performs its own inherited and developed sense of itself; (c) appropriative, stealing, almost, some of the privileged tropes of imperial domination and in doing so folding over the discourse of imperialism and in the process turning up some new, unacknowledged seams; (d) kinetic in the sense of an active response to stimuli and stimulation of further response; and (e) recursive, turning over again and again in a process of cultural exchange which makes its initial object disappear. African American cultural aspirations exuded a sense of darkening reflection, a sense of the potential fullness of reflection that creates an almost sublime abyss, perhaps the abyss of freedom or solitude or emptiness.

In these various texts and performances, cultural producers with *multiple* forms of agency (some compromised, some not) try to grasp the importance of their own artistic, cultural, and perhaps social powers. The texts are forms of self-reflection and self-definition, while at the same time they are points of mirroring where the concerns and dynamics of the larger culture, which happens also to be their own, act as a starting point for improvisation. The processes of cultural transformation are complex and elusive, and always will be. But the larger hopes and desires that inform this process—the seductions of the mirror and the tain that marks its reflections as unreal—are vivid and concrete.[3] In *Darkening Mirrors* I ask how a specifically African American perspective on mirroring participates in and contests more traditional notions of fictional representation and aesthetics.[4] One answer is that it leads us toward performativity of a particularly complicated sort because of the simultaneous enactment and acting out, manifestation and production of malleable categories of race, nation, and subjectivity through (and as) fictional representation. As black performance invokes the postcolonial and aesthetic concepts of mirroring, mimesis, and mimicry,[5] it also reveals the shortcomings of these models, particularly the hamstrung agency and two-dimensional subjectivity they suggest. These three-dimensional darkening mirrors of representation and performance specifically *produce* culture and identity, an imagined future, at least in part through an evaluative and instrumental positioning of the act (as in activity and also pretense) of reflection and the contents of the repeated image as tools of analysis and innovation. Performativity in this context posits the act of imagination as agentive behavior, especially in its capacity as an enactment of certain desires.[6]

In this book I connect performativity and embodiment to empathy and desire and explore how these create the possibility of change. The performance acts as an embodied commitment to a hypothetical present and a possible future. Take the example of ritual communion,

PROLOGUE

the performers' embodied committing of a symbolic act that affirms faith and articulates hope. Participants repeat the act, like a rehearsal, in the continual approaching of abstract perfection. The repetition suggests a persistent hope in the possibility of change achieved through the repeated playing out of the desired state, in its eventual achievement. In the performances I analyze, actors commit to certain embodied repetitions of experiences and ideas. In their performative acts they take on and convey an empathy with their subjects, whether that empathy is sympathetic or antagonistic. In some instances that imagined connection seems to be about a desire for one's own existence as much as or more than about the other. In the system of acts that constitute these plays, dances, and films, performers reflect a broad desire for the conceptual and material possibilities narrated by the texts, often something slightly, or very, different from their current conditions.

In performance emotion is a key product, part of the aesthetic excess of drama. Part of the production of careful performance is the response elicited in the viewer. Performance space acts as a venue for transformation because of this dynamic characteristic, this transmission of the performative excess of emotion through the performative space.[7] I explore the coexistence of conflicting and competing desires in form, its impact on viewers and participants, and thus its possible effects on the public. The impact of black cultural and artistic performance encompasses the emotional, psychic, and kinetic. Perhaps in this way performance allows us to get at the contours of political significance in black art, seeing its processes as personal, communal, and something other than and in addition to activism.

Participants in performances I analyze, particularly the performers but also the cultures that produce them, imagine and enact, for themselves and their audience members, the performed nature of race and the possibility of power, and sometimes, in the same gesture, the dismantling of structures of power. Stage and screen become metaphors for the condition of race, its very performativity, for blacks in the everyday. The ephemeral nature and repetition of performance operate like memory or fantasy, a repeated enacting of a past and hypothesizing of a future. As a temporary space for imagining past, present, and future the stage and screen provide a moment when audience, performers, and producers can experience pleasure or pain in the transformative and temporarily transformed reality of that reimagined space, with its re-

xvii

imagined conditions of living and artistic hyperboles of emotion and experience. These performers deploy performance space and performative opportunity to reimagine themselves and the world they inherited. One of the primary elements of the aesthetic, racial, and performative excess in *Darkening Mirrors* is a negotiation of power and, certainly, its lack. In the trajectories of time the performances in this study capture for us moments, frames of a people in the process of apprehending racial, political, and national freedom — not necessarily in some progressive or easily observable way but in the uneven, uncontained, messy manner in which competing performances vie for dominance.

So what's the political pt? This is method not argument.

xviii

....

....

ACKNOWLEDGMENTS

I express deep gratitude to the mentors, friends, and colleagues who have inspired me, supported this project, and helped me through its years of creation. I owe special thanks to Melani McAlister and Jennifer Brody, Judith Williams, Tera Hunter, E. Patrick Johnson, Harry Elam Jr., Jonathan Holloway, Daphne Brooks, Gayle Wald, Joe Trotter, Joseph Roach, John Jackson, Rena Fraden, Mike Witmore, Jennifer James, Tanisha Massie, Michele Gates Moresi, Denise Meringolo, Hershini Bhana Young, Terri Francis, Scott Trafton, Shelley Lee, Badia Ahad, Ayanah Moor, Grisha Coleman, Heather Arnet, Jeffrey Williams, Joan Prince, Neil Barclay, David Kaufer, Kristina Straub, Kathy Newman, Jennifer Richeson, Nicole Shelton, Chantal Morgan D'Appuzzo, John Rickford, Vera Grant, Claudine Michel, Julie Carlson, Ingrid Banks, George Lipsitz, Roberto Strongman, Gaye Johnson, Stephanie LeMenager, Laura Helper-Ferris, and Ed Blum. I am grateful for Ken Wissoker's faith in this project and his continual development of brilliant lists in diasporic, cultural, and performance studies, of which I am proud to be a part. You are each so wonderful. I am privileged to know you.

I thank my family, Shelley and Steve Benton, Keith and Vinti Batiste, and Kellie, Tianna, Kenietha, Kyle, Brent, and Lisa, and all my nieces and nephews for your support, humor, diversion, interest in this project, and refreshing lack thereof. Ernest Prescott and Louque have enriched my life immeasurably. This effort is dedicated to you.

Several research assistants helped in myriad ways: Amber Bailey, Jennifer Miller, John Newton, Katie June-Friesen, Melissa Wehler, Amy King, Sheila Mae Liming, and Philip Stephenson. Lydia Balian, Alison

Reed, Jessica Lopez-Lyman, and Shea Kenny helped endlessly with details and logistics. Thanks, too, to Eileen Quam, who assisted with the index.

Fellowships, archives, and organizations that have provided invaluable funding and information include the Center for AfricanAmerican Urban Society and Economics, whose extensive support and encouragement included both grants and friendship, the Carnegie Mellon University Department of English, the Falk Foundation, the Berkman Fund, the fellows and faculty at Stanford University Research Institute for the Comparative Study of Race and Ethnicity, Stanford's African and African American Studies Department, the thinkers at Black Performance Theory, the Women and Theater Program of ATHE, Madeleine Matz and Rosemary Hanes at the Library of Congress Motion Pictures Reading Room, the archivists and staff at the Library of Congress Music and Performance Reading Room, the Margaret Herrick Library of the Motion Pictures Academy, my cohort in The George Washington University American Studies and English Programs, the UCSB Department of English, and the UCSB Department of Black Studies.

An earlier version of chapter 3 was published as "Epaulettes and Leaf Skirts, Warriors and Subversives: Black National Subjectivity in Macbeth and Haiti," *Text and Performance Quarterly* 23, no. 2 (2003), 154–85. An earlier version of portions of chapter 5 was published as "Dunham Possessed: Ethnographic Bodies, Movement, and Transnational Constructions of Blackness," *Journal of Haitian Studies* 13, no. 2 (2007), 8–22.

INTRODUCTION

> Fortunately there are constructive channels opening out into which
> the balked social feelings of the American Negro can flow freely....
> These compensating interests are racial but in a new and enlarged way.
> One is the consciousness of acting as the advance guard of the African
> peoples in their contact with Twentieth Century civilization; the other
> the sense of a mission of rehabilitating the race in world esteem....
> Harlem, as we shall see, is the center of both of these movements; she
> is the home of the Negro's "Zionism." The pulse of the Negro world
> has begun to beat in Harlem.
> —Alain Locke, *The New Negro*, 1925

An exile from Chicago's black urban society strikes out west to become an envied, wealthy rancher in South Dakota. A half-dressed black
American playing a Haitian revolutionary hangs a white American actor
playing a French imperialist with his own belt in a New York play. Dancing to swing music black performers with liner-extended eyes perform a
British play in yellowface makeup. An American actress playing a Jamaican casts a fake voodoo curse on her estranged American half-sister. A
famous tap dancer dressed as an African native in zebra stripes hops
across enormous drums in a song about tom-toms. In instance after instance Depression-era black performance appropriates and manifests
modern imperialist representation. This engagement poses the question
of how African Americans identified with the nation and with power as
second-class citizens in the United States. Broadly defined, this book
focuses on black American cultural and ideological struggles against

Sounds, um, complex.

racism and oppression during the 1930s, as these were embedded within an attempt to define and articulate an inherent Americanness that was also black and to develop a diasporic sensibility that reached beyond national boundaries. For many African Americans in the 1930s, this occurred through the dynamic artifice of performance.

cultural reelements of imperialism

The black performances I analyze participate in representations of imperialism including expansion, primitivism, exoticism, orientalism, ethnographic anthropology, and militarism. They demonstrate a struggle for freedom, dignity, and nationhood through geographies of the body, stage, and screen. I identify performances that were diverse in their types of access to funding and audiences. For example, the performances include plays, operas, and ballets from the Federal Theater as well as small, independent black westerns and dramas from the 1930s and larger budget studio films starring Nina Mae McKinney and Lena Horne. While many performances featured big name stars or directors, they also included large casts of unknown performers, involving the black community as participants as well as spectators. Non-professional international and American "natives" appeared in Dunham's ethnographic films and dances, and in 1938 the Federal Theater hired locals to join as natives of West Indian and Pacific Islands in *Haiti* and *The "Swing" Mikado*. Beyond big budgets and names, this practice drew a black public interested in representations of the rest of the world and their own place in the global community into the literal production and consumption of international connections and of culture and its meanings. Across these

a polymorphous list.

forms imperial representations open myriad discussions of the significance of black property ownership for national belonging, modernist national citizenship, the impact of global movements of peoples and cultures, international affinities and their national consequences, and how difference fuels notions of power and identity. These performances are inevitably linked to issues of embodiment, not only to the symbolic nature of black masculinities and black womanhood, but also to how

another mis-use of "thus".

bodies signify blackness as a cultural, racial, and global category. Thus each imperial performance — be it a western, drama, group or individual dance, song, joke, or comedy sketch — shows a fascination with bodies as well as their literal and symbolic enactments. These diverse modes of performance make up a configuration of representations and cultural products that are engaged implicitly or explicitly with each other — as mirrors of self, of other, of race, of nation, of power.

2

The Depression era was a time of political diversification and radical-ism, yet also a moment of swelling racial violence in the United States. Black performance in movies and Federal Theater plays of the 1930s hovers at a crossroads of experiences, histories, and futures of black popular culture, nationally regulated entertainment, internationalism and the formation of diaspora, assimilationist and nativist trends, the Harlem Renaissance, and the Popular Front.[1] The era saw a virtual ex-plosion of black film production and theatrical activity. Because of the democratic destitution of the populace and the proliferation of political ideologies, from socialism to fascism, this historical moment was rife with political possibility and presented black Americans with an oppor-tunity for creative negotiation of national identity and belonging. Black performance shows African Americans coming to terms with a nation that had both betrayed them and from its foundational creed continu-ally held out the glimmer of a promise of inclusion. Roosevelt's Works Progress Administration supported black artists through the Negro Units of the Federal Theater Project, including black performers but segregating them. The Negro productions performed through the Fed-eral Theater were thus condoned by the federal government and took part in a cultural project of nation building when the United States was in crisis. A black audience had been identified for film, and "all-Negro" race films produced by blacks in interracial combines proliferated dur-ing this period. Yet, films were primarily shown to segregated audiences and followed strict regulations prohibiting the display of miscegenation and interracial violence. During this period of increased cultural produc-tion, black theater, film, and dance as popular culture and representation became central to the performance and restructuring of racial identity.

Darkening Mirrors is critical of two problems of understanding racial identity and power, and thus our approach to liberatory thinking: first, that African Americans as a subaltern population raced by a dominant white population, by virtue of a history of oppression in the U.S., inher-ently and necessarily disidentify with oppressive modes of power; sec-ond, that the disempowerment resultant from racial oppression keeps people from imagining or, more important, enacting themselves as empowered subjects. To assume that African Americans are unable to imagine and enact themselves as empowered subjects promotes a naïve view of power. It denies African Americans a full spectrum of social and cultural agency. It is also quite simply historically inaccurate. My study

3

(handwritten marginalia: 1) that blacks are separate from americans 2) lack of power prevents one from imagining oneself as powerful. (whom the world says that?)

(handwritten note at bottom: NB: She doesn't call out her targets. But her suspicions.)

presents some of the multiple ends of African American imaginations of empowerment through their participation in discourses of imperialism. Given their concern with power, the cultural performances I examine matter because they *do* something in the world for the subjects, the audience, and us as critics.[2] The performances experiment with black access to or possession of power to define self and nation and affect change.

I investigate how disempowerment in America combined specifically with an empowered national gaze in American Negro culture. African Americans ironically maintain a national identity that figures them as empowered on the global stage, particularly, but not solely, in relation to diasporic black populations. This work shows how agency shifts positions and how the assumption of empowered perspectives can be part of several projects at once. While it is controversial in cultural studies and in African American studies to claim that colonized people were at times invested in or complicit with power, it is nonetheless true that, as a result of the operation of culture and the ways that humans are caught up in it, there has been no pure state of African American decolonization. Sometimes black American expression and subjectivity, what Houston Baker describes as a "voice crafted out of tight places," developed through consent and complicity with imperial discourses and their effects.[3] Often, however, such consent provided a space for the articulation of more complicated formations of identity, including equality, resistance, superiority, black particularity, and diaspora.

The plays, films, and dances I discuss displayed imperial agency and a profound sense of American inclusion and nationalism on the one hand, and disidentification with America, national subalternity, American racial difference, and diasporic internationalism on the other. African Americans' performative engagements with imperialist discourses reveal an inherent national identification, more like a cultural interpellation, that manifests itself in African Americans' fluency in dominant cultural forms that glorify nation, celebrate modernity, and emphasize the difference of others. The desire for national identification and inclusion appears in the capacity of imperial representations to act as a display of integration and assimilation. Part of blacks' assertion and manifestation of inclusion obtains precisely in the performance of imperial power through which they assume national alterity and national power. These forms represent consent and complicity in American national identity even as performers and performances also express disidentification with national identity in the critique of racism and exclusion that have been the national inheritance of African Americans. African American representation of imperial forms also demonstrates an outward seeking for identity and affiliation with extranational blacks. In some moments African Americans use primitivism, for example, in an imperial manner to establish national belonging, alterity, and representational power. The selfsame performances also engender a position from which international coalitions of disidentification and dissent could be imagined and forged. The absorptive mirrors of performance capture and refract images, deepening and changing the possibilities of racial and national identity in their reflections. Performance becomes a space to imagine and posit a form of blackness that both exploits and transcends national boundaries.

The imperial tone of African Americans' global imaginings took shape amid the race-defining gestures of the Harlem Renaissance. Alain Locke's "The New Negro," the credo of the Harlem Renaissance (1920–40), called for African Americans to demonstrate the artistic and cultural vigor of Negro America, shining their own transformative light on the world and on blacks elsewhere lacking civilization. Locke's *new* formulation of a Negro "city on a hill" was truly urban, secular, modernist, fundamentally Americanist, and imperial. His declaration of Negro energy and power <u>laid the foundation</u> for black American complicity in projects establishing Western superiority in its desire to articulate full inclusion within modern Western civilization. It also defied racist notions that African Americans could not be full Americans. The definition of "the new Negro" as a nationalized American entity developed in specifically Western terms of progress and triumph. The cultural relationship Locke authors in his anthem to Negro culture comprises more than a duality between Negro identity and American identity, that "two-ness" that presses the question of citizenship with its split national and racial visions of the self. Locke swallows this two-ness whole and instrumentally assumes American identity as a necessary precondition of the proclamation he aims at the rest of the world. Layered atop the familiar question of duality, and rather subtly drawn, is the link he asserts between black identity and Western cultural power—an inheritance he claims for black Americans and activates in his call to art. Intellectual and artistic production of the Harlem Renaissance and black internationalism of the Renaissance and Depression eras in their many manifestations

5
....

[handwritten margin note:] But this isn't new — see Crummell's self-labeling as Anglo-African.

[handwritten margin note:] No. Locke's formulation is the end of this way of thinking before foundation & separate black identity / culture — not the beginning.

constituted modes of anticolonial protest against domestic racism and the national boundaries that enforced it. For black thinkers, artists, and performers in the West, Africa developed a symbolic power appropriated in shaping African *America*'s Harlem as a symbol of black freedom and civilization.[4] The new mission of black Americans, however, also inhered an extranational focus that linked American Negro identity to an internationally constituted black race. This outward looking in itself acted out a conflicted desire for power, one that sought to exalt a global blackness yet in a manner that enforced hierarchies of nation, modernity, and representation. This tension between notions of cultural power and blackness, black national and global identity resonated in Negro expression of the Depression era. Imaginations of cultural power akin to Locke's revealing formulation in "The New Negro" are poignantly embodied in the "constructive channel" of African American performance from this period.[5]

In *Darkening Mirrors* I examine Depression-era black stage and screen productions for their express and underlying imperial representations and ideologies, showing that African Americans were involved in American imperial projects on the level of culture.[6] In a cultural moment characterized by racism, poverty, disenfranchisement, and ideological unrest, African American participation in embedded ideologies of U.S. imperial culture became a means of articulating inclusion in and critique of the nation. "The nation" is an "imagined political community" and must "be distinguished, not by [its] falsity/genuineness, but by the style in which [it is] imagined."[7] African Americans' style of imagining nation through performance of imperial codes experimented with what nationhood could mean. The performance of these representations challenged access to and ownership of modes of power through the body and, in doing so, upended assumptions about where power resides and with whom. It also exposed black performance as a persistent African American aesthetic, a mode of both self-definition and cultural expression. Revising notions that black American culture has primarily produced and negotiated conditions of survival, continuity, and resistance, black performance in the 1930s shows that black culture also contained an aggressive current of desire for power.

"Power" in the representational or discursive sense differs from "power" in the material sense. Cultural power differs from political or economic power, but does refer in some ways to the forces of hegemony.

In the context of the United States, all blacks are subject to pervasive forces of white racism. Black performers may wield power over their dark others, or objects of imperial representation, performed through colonial discourse, but this does not necessarily redound to material power over them.

Performance as a creative project of imagining self and community, of theorizing identity on and through the body, its words, and the scenarios it enacts is key in this discussion of cultural power. Staged performances often act as a ritual of nation, national memory, and embodied identification with larger historical and imagined ideas and forces.[8] Performers take on structures of cultural power in their bodies and in the narratives they perform as a means of exploring its dimensions, looking for spaces of manipulation and freedom in a manner far from binary. Part of the experience of cultural power for these historical and stage players lies in the claim that race itself is performative, taking on race as a structure of power, and thereby assuming a hand in producing race and blackness.

Performance calls a broad community into being that results from literal administrative and artistic collaboration and audience spectatorship. Production and performance constitute a representational matrix wherein multiple subjects and perspectives together participate in expression of identity, laying the groundwork not only for productive imagination but for the possibility of change and activism. Manthia Diawara observes that black performance "records the way in which black people, through communicative action, engender themselves within American experience. Black agency here, involves the redefinition of the tools of Americanness. . . . Performance presumes an existing tradition and an individual or group of people who interpret that tradition in front of an audience in such a way that the individual or group of people invent themselves for that audience."[9] In the 1930s that mode of interpretation and invention acted to imagine and put into place autonomous social communities and futures of empowerment.[10] The confluence of large casts, crews, and audiences made these performances collaborative public events. Extant spectator and community perspectives emphasized the cyclical, recursive nature of performances as audiences responded to staged representations.

Films' imagery, plot, and enactment, plays' plots and performances, and archival materials such as photographs, reviews, and production information reveal the nuances of imperial ideologies' role in forming black Americans' sense of nationhood, their national consciousness, and their relationship to ideologies of Western imperial power. I scrutinize and challenge the meanings of African American cultural production without assuming an inherent moral rectitude of black cultural expression that ignores how African Americans have been implicated in configurations of power in ways more complicated than (only) domination or (only) resistance.

Primitivism and Black Modernism

Black performance in the 1930s fits the period of modernism scholars have established for black cultural producers, implicating these representations in the power dynamics of modernist forms. Like many African American theorists, Arnold Rampersad extends the period of modernism for blacks back a bit earlier and forward a bit later than that of mainstream modernism.[11] Blacks, particularly in America, experienced a kind of existential crisis and self-alienation associated with the psychic disillusionment that occurred after the First World War normally associated with modernism much earlier, during the Civil War and its aftermath and as a result of racial terrorism and white supremacy. Rampersad posits a black modernism that began to develop before 1900 and culminated with Langston Hughes rather late in the Harlem Renaissance and into the 1930s. Blacks at the turn of the century recognized race as determinant of "aloneness" in the world, of the "wasteland" of modern society and human possibility.

African Americans' experimentations with identity during this period were emblematic of the political and social possibilities offered by this moment of economic hardship, collective organizing, and politicization of the arts. Primitivism was a part of American and African American expressions of modernism, wherein African American or black bodies signaled the modern.[12] The concerns of modernity for blacks were not, however, restricted to the symbolic use of blackness in its expression. Black performers participated in the production of the modern and were products of its ideologies, not just its symbols. Modernist forms and sensibilities — for instance, investments in grand narratives such as nation and progress inspired by industrialization — accompanied total social disillusionment and self-alienation.[13]

The problematic collision of blackness and modernity manifests itself in the careers of Josephine Baker and Paul Robeson, figures whose early performative work constitutes a kind of prehistory of my book. These star figures were famous for performances on both stage and screen and were aware of the signifying currency of their bodies as figures of the primitive and a developing international modernity. Examples from their careers are emblematic of these symbolic relationships. In *The Emperor Jones* (1935), Robeson as Brutus Jones establishes himself as the despotic king of an unnamed, primitive West Indian island; in *Jericho* (1937) Robeson is again a king and rules a primitive African tribe.[14] Robeson took parts representing Africans in hope of bringing nobility to these characterizations, but also to valorize the special gifts of black people to an overcivilized West. Josephine Baker regularly represented primitive North African colonials and simultaneously irresistible superstars, a representation that darkly mirrored her own rags-to-riches career. One of Baker's most famous numbers is the exotic banana dance, in which she performs topless, her waist adorned in a skirt of yellow bananas. In another famous performance she swings from the perch of a golden bird-cage dressed in feathers. She exudes oversexed, primitive savagery and animalism in the service of colonial fantasies about blackness and at the same time the gorgeous desirability of an uncontained black difference. Robeson's and Baker's performances during this period are poignant examples of constructions of blackness and black otherness performed by African Americans, constructions that the performers often did not control. Well-known images found in their work reflect the limited roles available to blacks and consumed by multiracial viewing publics. In their capacity as American performers who traveled abroad and played black American and non-American black characters in America and abroad, Robeson and Baker crossed performative, national, and racial boundaries in their lives and in their work. Their careers and star status acted as instantiations of a transnational modernity that emerged through embodied blackness.[15]

In one way or another the representations of the era toyed with the concept of black primitivism: who was primitive, who was not, how primitivism seemed to make meaning. Primitivism and exoticism defined the development of Western modernism. Within this structure of primitivism lay tensions over the relationship between blackness, civilization, and modernity; geography and black civilization (that is, where the black primitive existed, if at all); and so, ultimately, black Western citizenship. The notion of primitivism not only negotiated modernity itself, but also pressed the question of black belonging in the modern world. The concept of "the modern" accounted for cultural attainments of ideological values of rationality, consciousness, civilization, and various modes of enlightened autonomy. Modernism acted as a specifically nationalizing force in America, based on iconographic American developments such as industrial technology and jazz.[16] Through concepts of primitivism, blacks and blackness became symbols around which projects of modernism and developments in modern identities congealed. As an icon, blackness defined the new, the cool, the modern.

Blacks and "primitive" blackness were central concepts not only in the development of modern values generally, but also in the ways African Americans themselves constructed and manipulated primitivist modernism in the development of the modern. Black people were conscious of and participants in discourses of the primitive. When the acclaimed singer, actor, activist, and primitive performer Paul Robeson made a case against Western values in distinguishing them from African, Eastern, working-class, and Negro peoples' ways of being, he accepted the basic premise that primitive people and "so-called 'primitive'" societies materially existed.[17] Robeson celebrated the primitive even as he questioned the validity of the title. For him, as for others at the time, primitive qualities included the genius of spontaneity, cultural virility, and creative vitality. The primitive escaped the suicidal corruption of the "peak overhanging an abyss" in an overly intellectualized Western society.[18] The other was not an abject savage, but a manifestation of a claimed past, of brotherhood, of organic inner strength, of power.[19] This is what makes the primitive in the hands of blacks so very slippery — this fascinating recuperation of it in the service of an articulation of civilization and subjectivity. By ignoring the apparent conundrums in black representations of imperialism and the investments in power they imply, we risk perpetuating a naïve view not only of black people but of power itself. Black primitivisms show that ideologies of power rooted in hierarchy and racism can at times coexist with agendas to assert racial equality and black humanity even as the very terms of representation insist upon the opposite.

The force of primitivism in black expressive culture can be seen in the playwright Langston Hughes's treatment of Haiti's revolutionary past.

Scholarly analysis of the play *Emperor of Haiti* demonstrates the tendency to unequivocally recuperate black primitivisms in order to assert diasporic harmonies, a trend from which *Darkening Mirrors* departs. I highlight difference in black performances of blackness to explore the nuances of black imperialist representation. This attention reveals how black subjects positioned blackness itself as symbolic and treated it as a force that described something other than their bodies. Hughes's *Emperor of Haiti* has been interpreted as a straightforward celebration of Haitian experience, yet even Hughes conflates and appropriates black difference and manifests primitivism in ways that scholars have ignored. In an analysis of the play, Helene Keyssar considers the effect of stage directions and theatrical notes signaling drumming and voodoo dances. Her treatment of the script's exotic elements includes several imperialist perspectives: that these drums and voodoo dances act as a "visual diversion," as a reflection of emotional chaos, as "vitally authentic," as definitive of "black" culture in distinguishing it from "white" culture, as combining the past and the present. She finds the primitive elements suggestive of a black power that can control, of the "erotic," and of the "unpredictable, fearsome and mysterious." Keyssar acknowledges a seeming conflict between Western civilization in the play and "symbolic African tribal culture" and interprets this as Hughes's ambivalence about how the cultures mix rather than as evidence of a Western perspective on Hughes's part and an exoticization of Haiti.[20] Her descriptions replicate three separate problems in scholarly analysis that my study attempts to settle: a minimizing of the significance of the voodoo aesthetic as a primitivist aesthetic in black culture; conflating African American, Haitian, African, voodoo, and imaginative black cultures; and describing exotic, imperial performance without identifying it as such and thus passing over its consequences. These oversights simplify diaspora and conflate black identities and differences in a utopian apprehension of a common blackness.

In my exploration of black imperial representations I respect such differences between nations and ethnicities in an attempt to bring out the contours of American blacks' negotiation of differences. In the United States, native and African contact developed broadly in at least three ways, through (a) historical inheritances, (b) fiction, imagination, and appropriation, and (c) lateral cultural contacts resulting from travel and immigration and emigration at various historical moments. These pro-

11

cesses can easily get collapsed in scholarship, their differences erased in black fantasies of diasporic harmonies and traceable origins. Artists and scholars have conflated Africa and black authenticity, West Indian culture and its African origins, as if the West Indies, with supposedly fewer or lesser European contacts, existed unchanged by history, as did a static Africa. In my analysis representation of the West Indies, the presence of drums, other "Africanisms," and certainly voodoo are not assumed to herald a black authenticity whereby politics of appropriation do not come to bear. Instead I problematize these conflations by attending to the layers of appropriation and representation in black primitivism.

Manifestation and Forms of Misdirection: Aspects of Performing Black Identity

For the operation of black expressive culture and race relations, the notion of signifying and metaphors of veiling, masking, hiding, and performing illuminate how multiple levels of meaning coexist in black artistic production. Expressive histories of indirection, signifying, masking, and displacement have become signature elements of a black aesthetic.[21] Through masking and misdirection African Americans have managed to express subjectivity, a sense of their own humanness, and concern about American race relations in theater. Theorists of black identity in the West have used performance constructs to define the nature of blackness in everyday life. What becomes clear is that blackness itself is a performance and poses the opportunity for performance to become a means of constructing identity. Strategies of a performative black masking are suggested by W. E. B. Du Bois's concept of "the veil," articulated in 1899; Paul Laurence Dunbar's concept of "the mask that grins and lies," penned in poetic form in 1908; and, most theatrically, Zora Hurston's formulation in the 1930s whereby African American subjects will sit, a "play thing outside the door" of their mind, true or untrue (at times both), for the outsider other to consume while they watch.[22] The striving for the possibility of full expression in theater and film has been the subject of much scholarship on black theater and film.[23] Obfuscation and misdirection became embedded intentions and thus a part of an ironic structure of black performance. It is in these aesthetic practices that blacks have managed to craft their own meaning.

Paul Gilroy articulates the slipperiness of black expressivity by observing colonized blacks' historical awareness of a constant white audience and the challenges both posed for black creativity:

> The pattern of communication found in the unstable colonial world was governed by radical contingency. The civility of the slaves, the colonised and their descendants remains sly. Their signifyin(g) and shape shifting can still be tactical as well as playful; contestatory as well as compensatory. Creolised creativity entered the arterial system of the modern body politic via the capillaries of popular culture. It made resistance and accommodation into inseparable twins.[24]

Such representations, twinned by simultaneous audiences and signifying, could be stereotypical and "true," imperial and resistant. African American cultural expression historically both incorporated and spoke across and through, in the voice of, in the midst of, and despite a colonialist presence. In the case of primitivism, for instance, gestures of black identity reflected such multiplied cultural positions and desires.

This slipperiness extended beyond the level of production implied in Gilroy's description of signifying and shape shifting. Mediation and multiple meanings also obtain in practices of black spectatorship. Manthia Diawara and Anna Everett assert the position of African Americans as resistant spectators of dominant narratives, particularly filmic narratives of racial identity and white superiority. This resistant gaze also positions blacks spectators to read alternative, subversive, and multiple meanings in *black* performance — that is, to view "signified" reflections of black identities in texts and performances. Diawara demonstrates that a black gaze, in the form of spectators, reviewers, and the public, can be both resistant to and complicit in dominant narratives, at times knowingly and at other times ignorantly.[25] Thus performers and watchers of black performance mutually engage in complex signifying and critical practices at once. This creates the conditions whereby imperial representations, for instance, can be produced and received in ways that manifest and undermine dominant notions of power simultaneously.

Through embodiment and performance, blackness emerges as both lived and symbolic for performers and spectators. Black film and theater operate as forums for performance of identity as signified by the body. African American performance positions bodies "as a foundational ground in relation to which actions gain their meanings."[26] The imagined and performed identities of black subjects can be understood as a cultural construction vulnerable to change, re-formation, and reimagination even as it is performed on and through the seemingly stable material body. Harry Elam elaborates:

> The black performer, visibly marked and read by the audience as "black," enters the stage and negotiates not only the spaces between the stage representation and the social reality but also racial definitions and stereotypes, racial misconceptions, and ambivalences of race. . . . Through the productive ambivalence of the black performer, these racialized meanings can be destabilized and possibly even erased. . . . The black performer can purposefully acknowledge and utilize her ambiguous status — as real person, as theatrical representation, as sociocultural construction — to explore, expose, and even explode definitions of blackness.[27]

Black performers and performance demonstrate the performativity of blackness and have the potential to unravel and challenge pieties and misconceptions around race. Elam highlights the ironically embodied nature of black performative hypothesis and imagination. Thus for black performers the very "blackness" of their bodies becomes a symbolic tool theorizing race and its meaning and place in society. The performing black body is material and metaphorical, real and unreal.

The symbolic nature of blackness becomes eminently clear when one considers black blackface minstrel performers.[28] In black minstrelsy the black facepaint doubly signified the symbolic nature of blackness as a performance trope and racial identity. Annemarie Bean explains that neither race nor gender were "realistic" in black minstrel shows, but were put on for the entertainment of viewers, using stereotype and creative play upon expectations and ideologies of race and gender.[29] Blacks performing in blackface accomplished the same creative play and also the same powerful distancing and othering that obtained in blackface and made blackness and the paint fecund symbols. Even for immigrants who were black minstrels masking became a mode of appropriating American identity and assimilating into African American identities (or perhaps being appropriated into them). Thus the minstrel mask permitted a generalized opportunity for the performance of an Americanist blackness as a nationalist gesture.[30] Black facepaint on black skin doubled blackness and national identity in a manner similar to the ways that imperial representations of black Western subjects multiplied national and racial identities.

Primitivism, exoticism, and other imperial representations operated in a similar manner for black performers without the facepaint. Such performance of an othered, markedly different, and fully constructed culture and identity permitted performers both to embody rejected cultural characteristics and to distance themselves from an identity they demarcated as "not me."[31] Created in most colonial encounters, this othered identity justified the systematic discrimination against and disenfranchisement of the othered population—a population that already inhabited a disempowered position signaled by their very availability for symbolic construction and manipulation. The imperial and nationalist nature of primitivism and exoticism operated as mask, manifestation, and misdirection in African American performances of identities in a manner similar to nationalist blackface minstrel traditions in the United States. Layered upon the symbolic use of blackness, enactments of imperial identities and otherness that included various kinds of "dress-up" and "social construction" themselves *performed* raced, gendered, and national identities as an imaginative structure of metaphor and possibility.[32]

As symbolic constructions of identity some imperial performances act as interventions, whereby performers or performances create a particular argument or idea, and some act as effects, whereby the cultural significations absorb, invoke, and produce meaning as a product of the cultural environment. That is, some performance *does* and some *is.* To borrow from the vernacular where "existence" constitutes a form of action, some performance *be*—making the symbolic real and the real symbolic.

Depression-Era Internationalism: Contradictions and Conformities

The Depression era both continued and transformed trends of the black renaissance of the 1920s. The 1930s was a time of interracial coalition in America as well as black international intraracial coalition. Poverty, labor activism, and communism brought members of different races together around social causes in the United States. African American political imagination did not stop at the borders. Black activists reached across national borders to address and improve living and political conditions of black people around the world. African American leaders supported global anticolonial movements and hoped to bring their effects home.[33]

Performers, artists, writers, and scholars who traveled to Europe, the West Indies, and South America both informed and were informed by this cultural moment. Garveyite ideologies of repatriation to Africa and Du Bois's efforts to activate a black international caucus with broad-based American support influenced discourses of African American national identity in the 1930s. Pan-Africanism and Garveyism sought to unite black people around the world in support of racial justice, liberation, and the support of a colonized and decolonizing Africa.[34] Ethiopia and Haiti loomed large in the African American symbolic and political imagination as examples of black independence and national self-sufficiency. Black Americans contributed as much financial, labor, and military support to Ethiopia in the Italo-Ethiopian War (1935–41) as the U.S. government would allow.[35] African Americans fought fascism alongside communists in the Spanish Civil War in a global black (inter)nationalist extension of the Italo-Ethiopian conflict in an effort to (symbolically) further defend Ethiopia and the world against insidious and ubiquitous forces of fascism.[36] After Japan's rise to imperial status and its efforts to pass a "racial equality clause" through the League of Nations in 1919, the African American press and black nationalist organizations continued to celebrate the Asian nation as "the champion of the darker races" into the 1930s.[37] Delegations of African Americans visited Japan and China during this period, reporting both to be "friendly" to African Americans.[38] Gandhi's nonviolent actions against colonization in India attracted black attention and support, inspiring transnational visits, new activist ideologies, and the institution of international student exchange programs.[39] The Communist Party attracted and sought African American members, encouraging identification across the working classes, with Russia, and with the Soviet Union.[40] The global stage provided a place for African Americans to curry and demonstrate international support. The relationships of international looking became increasingly complex during this period.[41]

Race-based black internationalisms and black Americans' imperial images of national others seem incongruous with such global political developments. Black participation in the pan-African movement and Garveyism coexisted with blacks' enacting a black primitivism. At first this coincidence appears to be an ironic simultaneity of opposing forces of identification and denigration. Rather than constituting a binary dialectic or push-pull effect, however, these forces are connected. Their coexistence shows the ambivalence of black national identity and allegiance. Their seeming contradiction gestures toward the problems possible in a reductive Western perspective of these movements that allows for blacks to exist only on one side of this binary. In a certain sense the ethnonationalist characteristics of primitivism was consistent with Western blacks' sense of themselves as world leaders in the recuperation of global blackness.

African American imperialisms at specific sites of performance demonstrated ambivalence toward experiences of transnationalism. An international perspective, a desire for international unity across and among the world's "darker races," created a situation that would seem to preclude participation in imperialist discourses. Yet contradictions arose. Pan-Africanism was often charged with nativism and elitism. Support of Japan accompanied acrobatic apologetics for the brutal Japanese imperial invasion of China.[42] Class-based domestic squabbles between urban black and Jewish populations in Harlem were exacerbated by German propaganda and precipitated only limited critique among blacks over Germany's imperial designs in Europe during the Depression.[43] Communists in America were seen to undermine racial struggles in the interests of a proletarian agenda.[44] Thus complicated black internationalisms included competing ideologies and agendas.

Such ambivalence in culture and representation finds precedent in African American political and social conversations about imperialism at the turn of the century. When dealing with international issues during the height of U.S. imperialism, black populations in the United States adopted diverse stances toward foreign policy. Sometimes African Americans supported imperial ventures. For instance, national identity was defined and justified by participation in the Mexican-American (1846–48) and Spanish-American (1898) wars that pushed the United States to imperial status. The triumph of the black Buffalo Soldiers who served under Theodore Roosevelt at San Juan Hill were a source of pride and evidence of patriotism, humanity, bravery, and citizenship for African Americans.[45] During the imperial period African Americans engaged in discourses of civilization and uplift that positioned educated, Christian, primarily urban American blacks as civilized leaders in the U.S. and the world. Black literature and rhetoric could echo imperial goals, ideologies, and racisms. As a means of separating American blacks from savage racial others in the empire, blacks relied on a sense of domestic and racial exceptionalism based in their American national identity. In the face of essentialized understandings of race blacks adhered to arguments that linked racial development to the attainment of civilization in the West.[46]

At the same time there was a great degree of protest and discomfort with imperialism that was directly connected to the conditions of African American life and citizenship. Black Americans critiqued global oppression that appeared to them to be rather similar to their own plight as (non)citizens. Empathy, outrage, and a sense of injustice suffused critiques about the spread of American racism through empire and international policy. Outcries from black churches condemned the treatment of Cubans, Haitians, and Filipinos under U.S. occupation.[47] The identification of African Americans with colonized others around the world was not only racial, but also political, as African Americans protested American imperial policies, their concomitant racism, and overall human oppression. Historians have long understood the complexity of African American relationships to imperialism. This sense of history informs my analysis of black performance and representation.

African American awareness of and activity around American imperialisms fostered the spirit of internationalism that fed diasporic movements of the early twentieth century. As a result the 1930s saw a serious rise in black internationalism that increased African American political leverage in a way that would continue to develop through the Second World War and into the civil rights movement. Black internationalism manifested itself as imperial and anti-imperial activity and as a general sensibility and discourse. As such it resonated intranationally and influenced domestic experience. These activities and ambivalent sensibilities left their mark on black cultural representation and performance. Like other historical agents blacks strove, sometimes in intentional ways and sometimes not, sometimes in moral ways and sometimes not, to negotiate the multiple subjectivities that suffused their lives. Black Americans' domestic activism for rights and human dignity also characterized the period. Conditions seemed set for positive change. Burgeoning urban populations were transforming city politics and urban culture and developing influence on local and national politics. Mary McCloud Bethune and Walter White served on F. D. R.'s "Black Cabinet." Their roles heralded a new relevance of blacks' political voice at the highest level in the United States. Political allegiances were divided as Garveyite nationalism challenged American nationalism and as socialist ideals challenged New Deal liberalism. Black people manifested a spectrum of political beliefs, creating the possibility for productive disagreement.[48]

Black expressive traditions have been relevant beyond the shaping of black subjectivities. They have developed and exposed the character of the entire nation. Black "'counterculture' ... defines the core of national culture."[49] The countercultures of black dissent in performance helped to define the nature of citizenship in the United States. Some argue that in this era black expression served a special purpose in the coalescence of American nationhood, indeed of Western identity, in crisis.[50] Black expressive culture was linked to American struggles with the onset of technological modernity, placing African American music and dance at the center of American identity and cultural development between the wars.[51] Black resistance to industrial regimentation and later mastery of "the machine" through rhythm and movement were fundamental to America's ability to cope with the alienation spawned by mechanization and Depression-era poverty. Black performance carried broad consequences for the general meaning and direction of American identity.

Artistic movements in African American communities echoed and defined debates about black racial and national identity. Ideological struggles that characterized the Harlem Renaissance pivoted on the impact and nature of black art and identity.[52] Cultural producers of the Popular Front specifically understood art as politically and socially transformative.[53] Both New Negro and Popular Front movements explored the way theater might define the essence of a people and their sociopolitical strivings. Performance had the potential to forge new racial and national identities. Rena Fraden explains that these debates sought to determine "the proper sort of New Negro and the politically and artistically correct theater that should portray him and her.... [Federal Theater] Negro units were shaped by and responding to ongoing debates about race, art, ideology.... The theater came to seem an appropriate medium for creating new identity, a Negro, or black, or African, or African American, or American identity of resistance and pride during the FTP (Federal Theater Project)."[54]

Negro Federal Theater and Black Film

Black theater and film during this period reveal a black cultural engagement with concepts of nation and structures of modernism. By the 1930s black theater and film had developed broad audiences as well as their own particular style. Experimental theater troupes sprang up and produced plays in libraries, public halls, and churches. Increased Broadway opportunities made stars of many performers. Some gained international audiences based on their stage and screen performances at home and abroad. The Federal Theater Negro Units gave African American dramatists an unprecedented opportunity to practice their craft, hone their skills, and parade their work before mass integrated audiences. For most of early film history, blacks were shut out of or severely handicapped within the industry because of racism, lack of capital, and lack of technological experience.

The Federal Theater Project (FTP) was created in 1935 by the Works Progress Administration to provide work relief to artists, writers, and technicians. The Project also provided a much-needed social and cultural outlet to the American people suffering from the hardships of the Depression. Because of its labor politics, approach to art, and the productions it supported, the Federal Theater constitutes a radical chapter in American cultural history.[55] Hallie Flanagan, the FTP's national director, firmly believed that national theater should be relevant to people's lives and an expression of their own communities. Therefore Federal Theater Units were organized on a regional basis, with units reflecting the makeup and interest of Americans themselves. As such the Federal Theater contained Jewish, Latin, Chinese, and children's units as well as mainstream white units. The most successful nonwhite units, however, were the FTP Negro Units.[56] In the cities where they existed, they grossed greater profits than any of the other units. In New York the plays of the first Negro Unit established by the famous Negro actress Rose McClendon and her handpicked codirector, the white theater director John Houseman, attracted hundreds of thousands of spectators over the project's short life span, from 1935 until 1939.[57] The FTP's active support of minority theater was extraordinary, as was the Project's celebration of its own race and class radicalism.[58]

The FTP provided fantastic new opportunities to minorities in the theater as a result of its left-leaning politics and insisted upon integrated audiences, but its integration was uneven. The FTP still maintained racially segregated units. This level of segregation kept blacks from being offered roles with white troupes. Yet whites performed in black shows, although whites' open expression of racist beliefs lost them roles in black productions.[59] White Americans wrote and directed plays performed by the Negro Units, but not the reverse. Audiences were rigorously not segregated, although performances in multiple venues in different parts of town sometimes resulted in de facto segregation. Thus the FTP Negro Units straddled the line of American racial politics, both reflecting and transgressing separatist mores. Black units partook of and constituted the very grounds of Federal Theater radicalism.

Black film during this period navigated similar difficulties of representation and production. Black filmmakers grappled with myriad challenges in producing a great store of films featuring black storylines and all or majority black casts during this period.[60] Black filmmakers and interracial independents tried to escape "southern darky," domestic, menial, and criminal images in their own films.[61]

The 1930s witnessed the full transition to sound film. Like the visual accomplishments of the blockbuster epic *Birth of a Nation* (1915), this stage of the industry's technical transformation linked blackness to discourses of Americanness and modernity in its first talkie, *The Jazz Singer* (1927). Blacks were emblematic of the shift to modernity, but perennially relegated to its margins. Thus most independent black filmmakers went out of business due to the expense of sound production and the stress of Depression economics. The only survivor was the black independent filmmaker Oscar Micheaux, who eventually supported his Micheaux Film Corporation with white financial backing and production. The all-Negro films analyzed in this study, much like the plays, were produced by interracial combines, including Million Dollar Productions, Dixie National Pictures, Hollywood Productions, and Sack Amusement Company, that catered to "race" audiences during the 1930s.[62] These interracial independents operated in the lucrative space vacated by major Hollywood studios' temporary abandonment of black cast films designed for black audiences.[63] Black moviegoing in the early twentieth century constituted a practice of black modernism whereby black urban populations visualized and experienced modernity as critical viewing communities.[64] All-Negro films of the era met enormous popularity among black audiences, who "un-self-consciously embraced" these nar-

21

rative fantasies of a whites-free, and (socially) racism-free, life.[65] These entertainment films met a public desire for images of black people in black contexts, along with a critique from some arenas for not being socially conscious. They did not fully escape distortions of black life characteristic of racist media representation, but they did avoid some of the socially and representationally violent stereotypes depicted in white and interracial films. By the late 1930s all-black casts appeared in several types of films, including musical revues, migration stories, films about theater and performance, westerns, biblical allegories, and gangster movies. The diversity of black film suggests a continuing demand for portrayals of blacks in the media by a black viewing public. I examine some of these relatively unknown materials for their participation in discourses of identity and power through representations of otherness.

The performances I examine in *Darkening Mirrors* had to negotiate subjection to certain governmental and structural surveillance, regulation, and expressive restriction. Regulatory and spectatorial surveillance of black expressive production existed in both the Federal Theater and all-Negro film productions. The challenge of pleasing the inevitable white audience as well as black ones presented the same difficulty in the medium of film as it did in the theater. The Hays Commission regulated film in a similar manner as the Play Readers Bureau for the Federal Theater in their roles as arbiter of what constituted acceptable representation.[66] While all Federal Theater and film production during this period was subject to this kind of active censorship and surveillance, another, more generalized cultural surveillance of black expression also prevailed. The racist representational structure in the United States historically condoned racist stereotypes of blacks in popular culture. Artists struggled to communicate black stories that would ring true to black American experiences and not offend federal or white sensibilities or violate tricky antimiscegenation laws. Marginalized black cultural performance characterized by its own strivings was saddled with the restrictive structure of a white racial regime in a racist society. Thus the representation of black cultural interests and desire was inherently heavily mediated, forcing creative escapes from restriction and complex appropriations of form in reflecting black identities and concerns. Not only the subjects became embattled, but also the very ways they were expressed.

Darkening Mirrors

As black Americans chose or were coerced to look, travel to, and imagine other cultures across expanses of ocean and land, they also imagined, envisioned, and performed various potentialities of their own identities. Their performances became darkening mirrors that reflected cross-cultural contact, creativity, and imperialist construction.

My exploration of African Americans' investment in and resistance to American imperial and expansionist projects through stage and screen performance develops in six topical chapters. In almost every instance these chapters begin by examining the discourses of imperialism and their consequences for black subjects and setting up a theoretical framework for the analysis of primary texts. These analyses consider how historical circumstances shaped black imperial perspectives. Analysis of primary sources illuminates the way black people have engaged with and produced notions of identity and power. The performances reveal how African Americans theorized hierarchy, difference, hybridity, and national belonging through imagination and action.

Chapter 1, "'Harlem Rides the Range': Expansion, Modernity, and Negro Success," shows how blacks' use of images of expansion and notions of open space in film established African American fulfillment of dominant middle-class ideologies. Three films produced over the course of the Depression era demonstrate black uses of expansion to imagine open space and the American West as a template for the articulation of modernity and national inclusion. Modernity acts not as counterculture but as national culture, as blacks both play out and actively argue inclusion in this national condition through its performance.

Chapter 2, "Epaulettes and Leaf Skirts, Warriors and Subversives: Exoticism in the Performance of the Haitian Revolution," focuses on blacks' performances of exotic and primitive otherness that suffuse two plays produced within the Federal Theater that dramatize a single historical event, the Haitian Revolution of 1802. The performance of high modern exoticism in two plays, the "voodoo" *Macbeth* (1936) and *Haiti* (1938), articulates a contradictory mix of imperial sensibilities and radical protest. In these performances diaspora becomes part of a larger antiracist and anticolonial discourse. A black American sense of diaspora also becomes part of a domestic racial and national project.

Chapter 3, "Prisms of Imperial Gaze: Swinging the Negro *Mikado*," explores the significations of orientalism in African Americans' "swing" performance of the British imperial play *The Mikado*. I trace the imperial significance of *The Mikado* as history, legacy, and future in its performance by African Americans. African Americans took on and inhabited the racist structure of the play, claiming it in their own particular way. The use of a loose South Seas aesthetic extends its imperial focus to the Pacific, allowing black cultural performance to mirror American imperial desire. The chapter picks up the thread of "going west," or expansionism, as black performers extend an imperial gaze into the Pacific. The performative extension of an American expansionist vision beyond the West into other national borders recalls turn-of-the-century wars and rewrites subaltern allegiances, solidifying the promise of a twentieth-century American empire.

Chapter 4, "Lens/Body: Anthropology's Methodologies and Spaces of Reflection in Dunham's Diaspora," examines anthropology as a discourse of imperialism and the role of anthropological theory and practice in the formation of black diaspora. Ethnography's process of collection and investigation secured non-Western populations in a hierarchical relationship to civilization. The anthropological discourse that drives the construction of these performances complicates African Americans' searching outward for images of self to inform their creative works. This chapter returns to representation of the black West Indies through a focus on the impact and meaning of anthropological techniques in the research films and Federal Theater ballet made by Katherine Dunham, a highly talented woman who took up typically masculinist negotiations of nation and diaspora. I address questions of power, hybridity, diaspora, and the crossing of black and Western subjectivities through analyses of ethnographic perspective in African American film and narrative dance.

Chapter 5, "Ethnographic Refraction: Exoticism and Diasporic Sisterhood in *The Devil's Daughter*," extends a discussion of the role of ethnographic looking and representation to fictional film. *The Devil's Daughter* (1938) incorporates ideas of expansion and land ownership similar to those explored in the discussion of westerns, while also including wild portrayals of West Indian religion. A drive for authenticity dominates the conceptualization of the film's staged and filmed performances. "Real" dance moves and "real" black performers provide a narrative of origins and racial identity for African Americans. In *The Devil's Daughter* the deployment of ethnographic technique secures a Western perspective while offering utopias of diaspora in a female-gendered representation of sisterhood.

Chapter 6, "No Storm in the Weather: Domestic Bliss and African American Performance," explores the collision between typically resistant black performative expressions and their mainstream appropriation in a Hollywood musical poised to recuperate American blacks as citizens. *Stormy Weather*'s insistent modernism as a display of inclusion ultimately celebrates patriotism and establishes domestic belonging. The film's classic performances constitute a nostalgic journey through black style that exposes the symbolic nature of such performance genres as soft shoe and modern tap. In its revue of performance modes, *Stormy Weather* positions performance itself to critique and reshape the meanings of performance forms such as primitivism.

For African Americans in the 1930s, movement into, across, and from the center of power was both ideological and cultural as they manifested and transformed imperial modes of expression. African American performers used, made, and reproduced imperial identity even as they contested, changed, and undermined it. Their deployment of imperial forms in performance traversed genres of performance and embodiment, committing the performers to negotiations of national belonging, transnational desire, racial symbolics, and the operation of power.

1

....

"HARLEM RIDES THE RANGE"

Expansion, Modernity, and Negro Success

Since the American West was white, black manipulation of western representation had to contend with absolute material exclusion and ideological racism. Meanings of modernity, masculinity, and expansion wrapped up in American idealization of the frontier and wilderness required reevaluation for blacks, as they signified both a structural and ideological complicity in imperial projects and also a complicated, culturally resistant representation of cultural desires for inclusion and equality. Given the radical exclusion of African Americans from mainstream society and its dreams of freedom and expansion, it seemed overly hopeful, if not radical, for blacks to participate in imaginative appropriations of open lands, a material process from which they had been excluded in American history except, for the most part, as bound labor. Blacks' recuperation of an imagined American West in richly visual and narrative ways intervenes in this history of exclusion, participating in nationalist discourses in complicated ways.

Stories that imagine the West tell about American national identity and imperial desire in a relatively bare way, lauding American expansion through impressive shots of wild woods, vast plains, and broad deserts. These illustrations of national abundance justify for the viewer a nostalgic participation in the military conquest and genocidal "glory" inherent in the expansion of U.S. borders and the settlement of the wilderness. The images and narratives celebrate stoic toil and determination, as if the "empty" land itself yearns for human discipline.[1] Imaginative and physical appropriations of the West, open space, and nature stand in as signifiers of cultural and material power. In dominant iconography of the West, the landscape invited the inscription of new lives and desires. A harsh environment served as a reflection of the internal mettle of the men who tamed it, rugged, strong, reliable, and enduring. Everything western opposed eastern industrialized culture, with its teeming crowds, overcivility, alienated labor, and mixed multitudes of immigrants and Negroes. The West was pure and regenerative. Imaginations of the West rebelled against industrialization, thus rejecting the city, yet also mourned the loss of a dying frontier, symbolized in the death and disappearance of native people who were both noble savages and dangerous enemies. The West was quintessentially American, xenophobically so, representing the solidity of white nationhood.[2] The solidification of national identity in western films occurred with the redundant triumph of acquiring land and autonomy in what was already nationally claimed space. Repeating conquest and domestication in film enacted a commemorative celebration of national expansion.[3] Notions of the frontier have continued to serve as fertile ground for the imagination of American identities in cultural production.[4]

In films produced in the 1930s African Americans imagine a fruitful, tamed, accessible West. Like other Americans imagining the frontier, African Americans sought opportunity, self-definition, and a sense of spatial, economic, and national power.[5] Through a performative consent to the idea of expansion, African Americans expressed concerns about the constitution of nation and community and also posited the fact and the terms of their own inclusion. Through participation in the imperial structures of imagining the West, African Americans readily avowed the acquisition of property and capital as part of a national project, albeit their own, as opposed to a reflection of the natural order. In this way the films unabashedly manifest the economic stakes and cultural consequences of imperialism and its imaginings.

In this chapter I look at three very different African American films produced over a ten-year period during the Depression era: a travel film, a drama, and a western. They demonstrate an ongoing and diverse African American engagement with this major symbolic discourse of American identity. African Americans' assertions and representations of westward motion show a clear identification with a peculiarly American romanticizing of open space, untamed nature, rugged manhood, and individual wealth. Enacting a particular change on these concepts, these representations idealize natural space and the West to establish a sense of black community—rather than individualism—characterized by sophistication, technological modernity, and constant cultural trade with black urban life. African American representations of western domestication are distinctive in their maintenance of a constant balance between "closed" urban spaces and "open" westerly ones. Urban performance styles, bodies, technologies, and identities emphasize the constant exchange and geographical interconnectedness of black culture. These films visualize a geography of African American national belonging that reorients black life in the United States from trajectories of south-to-north and rural-to-urban to a relationship between *urban* and *west*, forcing typical meanings of expansion to reverberate in the construction of black national identity.

The promotional film for an African American resort titled *A Pictorial View of Idlewild, Michigan* (1927) uses the impulse to travel to promote black cultural normativity and fluency in national symbols and values. Images of the West in Oscar Micheaux's first talkie, *The Exile*, dramatize the American dream of landownership and upward mobility while also positing racial equality as part of an ideal community. The musical western *Two-Gun Man from Harlem*, one of four formulaic westerns produced in the late 1930s and starring the singer Herbert Jeffrey, performs these themes as well as a compulsive cross-germination between city and frontier communities.[6] In the first film, *A Pictorial View of Idlewild, Michigan*, the visual inducement to travel positions the Midwest, the original western frontier, as open space outside of the city that is available for domestication and discovery.[7] In all the films the experience of seeing becomes part of the journey of transformation for the viewer as much as the journey west transforms the characters. All of the films imagine great prosperity in a time of national deprivation. The films discussed in this chapter are not all westerns with the familiar plot structure of "good versus evil" and the character of the gun-toting savior. They all, however, enact visual and spatial movement away from the city, toward nature, imagining settlement in an idealized nonurban natural space. In these ways, the production of black images of westward motion and settlement portray an already existing nationalistic expansive spirit as well as a proactive desire to become fully part of the nation.

Instead of rejecting the city and demonizing technology as the tool of amorality in the manner of mainstream representations,[8] black films of the 1930s appropriate the city as important to a black western cultural landscape. The relationship between nature and technology is one of the core oppositions of American modernism.[9] Elements of the city and urban life infiltrate and characterize blacks in nature and on the frontier, displaying modernist concerns and laying claim to the sophistication and cultural excitement of the urban-centered Harlem Renaissance. Through their constant invocation of the city, the films affirm and capitalize on the existence of a defining community necessary for the maintenance of a black identity. For the most part, the ideal community in spaces west excludes whites, creating all-black environments peopled by all-black casts. The idea of open space alone becomes insufficient to define and sustain a sense of community or a sense of an ideal future for blacks in the West. Far from spelling out a location or geographical area, "west" was an ephemeral concept for African Americans that included objectives and notions of freedom more than actual places.[10] The West, then, produces a black identity that is indeed expansionist, escapist, and idealistic, but also communal, rooted, and aggressively self-justifying. The films' imaginative establishment of a black presence in the West asserts an Americanist black national identity on the big screen through discourses of class, urban life, technology, modernism, racial identity, upward mobility, gentility, romance, and gender.

A Pictorial View of Idlewild, Michigan: Modernity, Community, and Middle-Class Civility

In the first moving image of the black-and-white, silent promotional film, *A Pictorial View of Idlewild, Michigan*, produced by the *Chicago Daily News* in 1927, a steam engine rolls into an immaculate station, introducing a clean town with broad, even roads and sturdy buildings.[11] These first images celebrating sleek technologies of motion signal a concern for modernity even as the train then transports the viewer away from the city, away from the station town, to an idyllic nature resort, "Idlewild in its rustic infancy." Not simply a descriptive ad, the visual inducement to travel to open space becomes an expression of modernity through the juxtaposition of civilization, middle-class civility, and technology against nature as a demonstration of national citizenship.[12]

In *Pictorial View* the Midwest figures as a conquerable frontier. The wilderness becomes livable, its natural resources enhanced through their constructive exploitation for leisure by African Americans. *Picto-*

rial View opens with an extended epigraph that introduces the viewer to Idlewild and serves as a prologue for what follows:

> A Pictorial View of Idlewild Summer Resort, Michigan showing its beautiful scenic location in the midst of towering pines and stately oaks; fragrant wildflowers and abundant foliage; pearly lakes and winding river; blue skies and golden sunset.
>
> Idlewild is the National Recreation Center of the best class of colored American people and is destined to be one of the cultural seats of its activity.
>
> Its easy accessibility by means of the many broad hard roads leading to it has brought Idlewild within easy reach of every large city and as a consequence, thousands of people visit there yearly.
>
> Pretty summer cottages and expensive mansions are dotted here and there in an irregular picturesque manner.
>
> Idlewild is rightly named "The Beautiful."

This introduction tantalizes the viewer into spending one day in this spectacular resort, a day ending with a singular "golden sunset." Certain key terms identify major cultural concerns of the film: Idlewild's "national" importance, its visitors as the "*best class* of colored American people," "broad, hard roads," "*irregular* picturesque" beauty, and accessibility from every major urban center. As a space of escape, respite, and renewal, the community offered here is all-black, technologically advanced, and primarily middle class. As an example of Negro accomplishment, Idlewild is a lakefront oasis of health, leisure, convenience, social organization, and hierarchy. The film advertises more than a lovely place for vacationers to visit; it presents an imagined community that serves as a promotion of black advancement and contribution to American society in general. Imbuing the black *community* with civilized urban origins and with the characteristics of individualist American character, black Americans reimagined black national identity in the performance of western belonging and fluency in modernist concerns.

A brief postscript and extraordinary closing image indicate the film's capacity as a justifying narrative for black national citizenship: "The American Colored Citizen has worked and sacrifices to the end that his people may possess a proper measure of life's comforts and enjoyment—Idlewild represents the greatest achievement in this direction that has yet been accomplished and more than justifies Abraham Lincoln's famous proclamation." A portrait of Lincoln fades up and lingers as the film's final image.

The film becomes a message to blacks, boasting of black accomplishments and the availability of leisure, as well as a message to the world. *Pictorial View* proclaims racial pride as if to assert that black people deserve the kind of pleasure Idlewild offers. The great accomplishment of "American Colored Citizens" is the attainment of middle-class standing and a concomitant civilized outlet for leisure. The name of the resort combines two stereotypes often applied to Negroes, "idle" and "wild." It operates both symbolically and ironically, literally communicating the experiential duality offered by the resort. It names a place where vacationers can relax and play, be "idle" and "wild" without the stigma of lacking civility. The closing montage argues for African American inclusion in the body politic. The caption capitalizes "The American Colored Citizen" and names a racialized national citizen as the subject of the film in place of the resort. Holding up work and sacrifice as means of uplift and achievement, African Americans insist upon a strong work ethic and middle-class aspirations. The community offers these qualities as a justification, proof of the rightness of the "famous proclamation" issued by Lincoln in the previous century, freeing enslaved black Americans. The film invokes not only black accomplishment, but also the iconic authority of the martyred president, a symbol of black freedom and enfranchisement as a proclamation of belonging. *Pictorial View* makes the development of Idlewild, a symbol of modernity, labor, "comfort and enjoyment," a "justification" for citizenship and national inclusion established by the Emancipation Proclamation.

The display of taming a vibrant and burgeoning nature accompanies a demonstration of the discipline of the individual and collective body as a further justification of national worth and belonging. The dialectical relationship between technology and nature bespeaks the very essence of modernity's discontents and inherent contradictions.[13] In *Pictorial View* technological advances promote accessibility and achieve the regulation of the wilderness needed for settlement and civilization. Early on, the film inventories various modes of transportation to emphasize accessibility for Idlewild's "thousands of visitors" from "every large city." Positioning the viewer as a virtual visitor and certainly as a potential tourist, the film begins not with the resort itself, but with three shots of a train speeding down the tracks toward, past, and away from the

32

viewer, through forests and over a scenic lake. A caption announcing "Some come by train" is followed by views of the Pacific Railroad line heading steadily toward busy "Baldwin Railroad Station and Gateway to Idlewild." The film figuratively shuttles the visitor through space and time into the world of the film and vacation space of Idlewild, Michigan. Images of transportation technology emphasize the role of film technology in providing a mental vacation. The film is the speeding train. The camera invites, inventories, and transports. Once transported, well-dressed women and children vacationers detrain and walk toward the camera. Fancy new black Fords drive along hard, dry roads to the resort's entrance. The modern roads and cars become part of the resort's appeal: "The wonderful roads encourage many to come by auto." The camerawork throughout is comprehensive and lingering, taking multiple shots of the same person or object for emphasis. A caravan of three cars appears in multiple, repetitive views: entering and leaving town, traversing long roads that set them against a wild country environment, and stopped at Idlewild's fairly elaborate gate of stone and brick pillars. Mental and physical travel becomes quick, exciting, and possible. The obsession with technological modernity resonates in the film's concern with controlled space, physical discipline, social organization, and environmental order.[14]

Idlewild's civic infrastructure affirms its modernity. The resort boasts a large shore-side hotel, hospital, post office, grocery, barber shop, electrical plant, and modern kitchen at the well-planned clubhouse. Idlewild's roads, bridges, and constant construction of cottages signal its self-sufficiency and progress. *Pictorial View* demonstrates how dedicated staff, filmed at their place of work, operate these industrial facilities with care. Images of the best technologies reveal Idlewild to be an operational town that provides access to nature's beauty and restorative properties while maintaining urban conveniences.

The complete filming of the resort's infrastructure indicates more than just pride in the accomplishments of the founders and staff and the technological advancement at Idlewild. Showing the postman opening the post office, the electrician at the generator, community center board members standing together, and the kitchen staff with community children smiling and holding up chickens at the clubhouse kitchen subtly informs visitors that in addition to providing convenience, Idlewild also offers an environment run completely by Negroes and inclusive of all members of the community. The resort, a frontier town begun in 1915, is appealing as a respite from racism offered by the dominant culture. The prospect of denial of services, discrimination, mistreatment, and even violence that faced blacks pursuing a vacation disappears. Once in Idlewild, visitors can also look forward to a vacation from the daily insults of racism in the safe and protective space of an all-colored town.[15] African Americans claim the frontier as a space that offers the possibility of an ideal community.

Life at Idlewild subjects the body, as it does the land, to discipline and regulation. The film promotes sports and leisure activities on its "athletic field that bids fair to become the national center of athletics" and "championship standard tennis court of concrete." The resort's proud athletic director, "Charles A. Wilson, Chicago Attorney," attractive and sharp in a light suit and top hat, is one of three distinguished men who show off these features' evenness and readiness for use. "On the beach," groups of young vacationers dive, sun on the shore, play in the sand, and swim in the lake. Sequences of people hiking, riding horseback, rowing, canoeing, fishing, and gardening demonstrate concerns about the physical health of men and women. At Idlewild visitors can invigorate themselves by filling their free time with any number of enjoyable, physically challenging, and yet relaxing pastimes. Control and discipline of the body through constructive exercises mark civilization. The detailed filming of healthful activity in the natural environment associates black people recreating at Idlewild with the structured, ordered renewal characteristic of civilized societies. Blacks' representation of civilized recreation can be read both as evidence of their modernity and as an attempt to proactively assert inclusion into dominant ideologies of embodied civility. *Pictorial View*'s construction of comfort in the wilderness implicitly juxtaposes physical resilience against the self-alienating, weakening effects of the city and stereotypes of black idleness. Negro bodies are disciplined, but not so much as to be weakened by overcivilization; rugged and natural, but not so much as to be savage.

An elaborate visual balancing of technology, nature, and dignified human presence in the wilderness occurs in a montage of a motorcade, rustic road, and trout stream called the "Père Marquette River." The confluence of road and river appear out of narrative sequence in the film, emphasizing the spectacular character of this visual journey. The montage documents the arrival of the annual pageant's keynote speaker,

William Dean Pickens, after we have already seen his speech. A group of Idlewildians meet Pickens at the Baldwin train station and escort him to the resort in an impressive caravan of ten black Fords, the lead car sporting an American flag. The overstated parade signals patriotism, wealth, organization, and civilized technical advancement.[16] The double appearance of the caravan—at the outset and again in the midst of the sequence celebrating nature—insists upon the centrality of the human presence in the wilderness and amplifies the significance of the industrial and natural images. As the caravan leaves the Baldwin station, *Pictorial View* cuts to the "short scenic route," a rough country road through Idlewild. The montage implies that the caravan drives this path, but it does not. Instead images of the Fords bracket it. The caravan approaches the road and later parks in a clearing. The insinuation that the cars drive this road exposes the ideological nature of the sequence.

Visual techniques blur the line between the technological, civilized, and natural as the camera strives to emphasize the untamed, irregular quality of the natural surroundings even as it maintains connections to civility (an illustrious guest) and technology (shiny new cars). Parallel filming strategies of the rustic road constituting the "short scenic tour" and the meandering Père Marquette River enforce unity between these man-made and natural resort features. The winding "short scenic route" contrasts starkly with the broad flat avenues of Baldwin. Thick woods hug its edges. It is overgrown and rough, with two deep ruts where tires have carved the road through the woods. Eleven separate views inventory the road's straightaways and curves. The road itself, in all its shabby mediocrity, becomes not only a tourist attraction, but also a part of the *natural* landscape, as *Pictorial View* analogizes it to a breathtaking, life-sustaining trout stream. Unlike the more natural stream, however, this hand-cut road lacks a formal or colloquial name, its connection to technology and order thus minimized and its stature as a natural feature implied.

The camera treats "Michigan's Most Beautiful Trout Stream—the Père Marquette River" in the same way as the road. Long shots are taken from either edge, from behind tree branches, and into the shallow stream, as if to show invisible trout beneath its surface. The caption "Countless trout abound in the crystal clear waters and may be seen at play" suggests the easy accessibility of nature's abundance. The camera pans around curves and along the water both upstream and down.

Every picturesque view catches the stream glimmering as sunlight filters through leaves and breezes gently stir the surface of the flowing water. The effect is calming and inviting. Exactly eleven long views of the stream occupy about seven minutes of the hour-long film. The identical approach to the road and river renders them mutually constructing. The shots themselves emphasize irregularity and thus Idlewild's natural, untouched, extra-urban character, even as they absorb space in an application of control. Likewise, in contrast to the naturalized road, a modernized river, used for pleasure and sustenance, is bent to human needs. Both sequences, though long, suggest that there's more to be seen. The inclusion of so many consecutive views to fully represent the road and stream highlights the difficulty of capturing their extensive charm. The thick, rough edges of both demonstrate their untouched beauty, intimating that whether man-made or naturally occurring, the road and river flow seamlessly into the surrounding wilderness.

In the midst of this visual parallel, an elaborate series of shots capture the well-dressed men, women, and children from the caravan taking a hike along the trout stream. As if to immerse them completely in the setting, the film shows them in several stages along the hike. They walk along each bank and cross over the water twice on a natural bridge, a fallen tree, and a man-made rope bridge. The film consistently disrupts a sense of overcivilization through periodic natural views and activity, particularly in this sequence: cars juxtaposed against the country road (that they do not drive); a big dog leaning out of a car window; hikers in high style walking eagerly through the woods. Likewise positioning people and technologies at the core of and as parentheses around natural images creates a sense of human harmony with the wilderness.

Pictorial View inventories Idlewild's civic structure in a manner similar to its display of the resort's technological features. Both the physical and social structure communicate the organization and regularity of a thriving community. A detailed display of the housing stock includes all classes of visitors and residents. Big-city professionals' "expensive mansions" sport second stories, enclosed porches, gazebos, wooden swings, landscaped gardens, and stone-lined paths leading to small private docks. A dignified Mrs. J. O. Morely of Chicago smiles invitingly beneath her archway, on which is painted "Gray Gables, He who Enters here Leaves Care Behind," before retiring indoors. The long focus on her polite welcome contributes to the middle-class sensibility in the

36

film. Quick views of more modest homes (often shown without owner-hosts), vacation cottages under construction by a white builder, and a shotgun house with peeping children and chickens gesture toward less privileged classes. Though filming the different types of homes presents various options for viewers who might purchase real estate, it also communicates a class structure inscribed by the built environment. Nearly all residents face the camera at some time, introducing themselves and the exteriors of their homes, regardless of class. Though the film values middle-class ownership, it carefully includes all residents as full members of the community, strenuously emphasizing community in the face of economic disparity.

This economic organization echoes a regulated social structure visualized through Idlewild's "1927 Chautauqua." A Chautauqua (bearing a Native American name but including no Native American presence) was an event that, in form, celebrated American character in a variety of specifically uplifting entertainments, such as speeches, pageants, and music. A Chautauqua provided a space for self-improvement, informed discussion, and the inculcation of "culture," "uplift," "propriety, decorum, restraint and reason." The form was praised as representing the "highest form of democracy."[17] Events during Idlewild's African American Chautauqua take on special significance through their inclusion in this nation-building tradition. During the pageant *Pictorial View* engages in a celebration of black culture that amounts to a cultural nationalism celebrating professional success, fame, family, literary accomplishment, and beauty. *Pictorial View* records a camera recording the Chautauqua. Here performance and film collide. The camera records the performance event and its audience and becomes both the audience of the pageant and a subject of the film. The camera inventories the filmmaking technology itself. Audience members look into and at the cameras in their midst. The recording process becomes the subject of the black gaze watching the stage show, its filming, and eventually the film.

During the Chautauqua's ceremonies, Idlewild's significant citizens parade before the camera. Intertitles announce the cities from which vacationers and staff hail: Chicago, Detroit, Pittsburgh, Indianapolis, Ironton (Ohio), Fulton (Kentucky), and others. Often combined with notations of career accomplishment, the titles demonstrate the scope of Idlewild's draw, emphasizing its popularity and aura of cosmopolitan sophistication. The Chautauqua provides the opportunity to celebrate individual leaders and special organizations, including "Reverend R. L. Bradby, Pastor of the 2nd Baptist Church of Detroit, Michigan," shown both alone and with his wife and four children; "the Byron Brother's Orchestra," a seven-piece band; four ribbon-bearing "Idlewild Representatives"; the "Kentucky Harmony Singers," one of whom is the "founder of the Housewife Training School at Fulton, KY"; and several other distinguished pairs, lushly dressed in suits, pearls, and fur. The politicos "Dan Jackson: Chicago Politician of National Prominence" (whose name appears three times in the film's captions) and "Dean William Pickens, Field Secretary of the NAACP and Contributing Editor of the Associated Negro Press, author and noted world traveler," receive notice as special guests.[18] Seven separate angles record Pickens's animated keynote speech to an attentive audience. The impressive crowd so dedicated to Idlewild's organizational health bears witness to the distinguished character of the resort.

Pictorial View lingers on the distinguished African American novelist and journalist Charles Chesnutt at the Chautauqua. Chesnutt appears in a sequence with a second young writer, Robert Belton, active in the community as a member of Idlewild's committee of four "Representatives." *Pictorial View* links two generations of black writers by the style in which they wrote, reflecting a major movement in black literary production. Sixty-nine years old at the time of the filming, Chesnutt had been part of the turn-of-the-century intellectual elite and the forefather of black dialect writing.[19] In the early decades of the twentieth century, dialect writing was a controversial aspect of a literary movement that appropriated a folk heritage. Chesnutt's collection of short stories, *The Conjure Woman* (1899), subtly challenged the white writer Joel Chandler Harris's more entrenched and solidly racist "Uncle Remus" dialect stories.[20] His status as a vocal "race man" whose writing about Negro life also critiqued racism made Chesnutt a hero according to the "uplift ideology" of the late nineteenth century.[21] Belton, celebrated in 1927 as "Idlewild's poet" for his poem "'Ef You Want ter Git to Heaben Quick, Jest Go to Idlewild," extolled the resort's beauty in dialect. Belton's work echoed Chesnutt's groundbreaking literary efforts. This heavy-handed visual sequence that shifts from Chesnutt to Belton honors a culturally nationalist literary movement by celebrating its craftsmen. Filming Chesnutt and his literary descendant at the Chautauqua associates the place with the African American intellectual elite and shows pride in African Americans' history of letters. The Idlewild resort community associated itself with racial progress by connecting itself to arts and entertainment and thus renaissance movements under way in New York and other cities.[22]

Pictorial View includes a display of gendered civility that upholds its middle-class claims. In the West the place of women signified a society's degree of civilization. Women appear as often as men in the film's representations as a result of their participation in the resort's civic life. The Chautauqua includes a beauty contest that shows off women's community participation as well as their bodies. Its inclusion in the ceremony, and in the film, constructs a regulating concern for feminine beauty and "proper" conceptions of womanhood. A sequence titled "Selecting Ms. Idlewild" shows four accessorized women in swimsuits and sandals who sashay, hands on hips or poised in the air, past the politely applauding audience. Pride in the beauty of black women's diverse body types and skin tones is significant given mainstream mores that attractiveness required thinness and white skin. Five judges, "prominent society matrons from *seven* states" (my italics), appear in conservative, dropped-waist dresses. These older women stand primly before the camera, the sobriety of their demeanor contrasting starkly with the bathing beauties. The event constructs appropriate roles, not only of behaving but also of looking and being looked at, for older and younger women. The mild exhibitionism of the contestants is pleasurable and safe due to the shield of matronly oversight. The thinnest, youngest looking, and only unmarried contestant, Ms. Maree Weaver, wins, reflecting values of beauty based in youth and sexual availability. As the camera pans down and up the body of the winner, focuses on the prize ring, and finally comes back to her face, Ms. Weaver chats casually with the cameraman. She is both a sexualized visual object and a speaking agent consistent with the image of the "new woman" of the roaring twenties. *Pictorial View* positions women's bodies as symbols of racial civility and gentility in this display of propriety and African American attractiveness.

Idlewild's members include professionals, race leaders, accomplished elite, laboring staff and resort management, literati, responsible matrons, and young attractive ladies. Even when framed by the wilderness, Negro organizational, social, professional, oratory, musical, and literary culture remains intact. The formal events of the Chautauqua not only reveal social organization and civic culture to demonstrate belonging in a modernist nation, but also manifest pride in the presence of notable black figures and the "race" accomplishments they represent. The visual inventory that categorizes technical and natural features of the resort thus also collects and organizes people. The film imposes a visual unity upon these subjects, representing an integrated, perhaps machine-like, community that resolves conflicts between black identity and ideologies of Americanness.

Given mainstream cultural tendencies to associate black people with nature and deny them the possibility of culture and civic virtue, the consistent assertion of civility and structure disrupts stereotypes of savagery or of hopeless subjection to nature. Images of controlled infrastructure, built environment, social structure, human behavior, and bodies reinforce one another. *Pictorial View* confronts the conundrum facing modern man as to the human's position in nature and culture. In the film Negroes assert belonging in both ideological spaces. Historically pathologized in the wild and in the city, African Americans negotiate these issues of modernity to balance technological progress with a desire for the freedom associated with venturing into the wilderness — and the power associated with the accomplishment of both. The mastery of technology and of nature admits marginalized black subjects into discourses of modernity and becomes the film's justification for national inclusion and claims against customary and legal denials of black citizenship.

Pictorial View ends with casual scenes of leisure and extended views of towering transcendent nature. The film's last ten minutes are shot from a rowboat in the middle of Lake Idlewild, detached even from land. As the audience bumps along the waves, the film almost seems to be in color, vivid and bright. In the pristine evening of sparkling sun and floating clouds, a couple out fishing waves at the camera. The man rowing the cameraman's boat smiles as he works. The focus on shimmering water and vast natural views of sky and forest create a sense of serene freedom.

Blacks and the American West

Imagining a pastoral freedom, black western films romantically rewrote the history of persecution blacks experienced on the American frontier during its acquisition and settlement. Black participation in the creation of western settlements was characterized by systematic marginalization and racial terror.[23] Though not typical of a majority of blacks' rural experience, black involvement in western settlement constituted an important part of American history. Blacks used westward movement in the nineteenth century to challenge slave laws and test the extent of their freedom in the United States.[24] The presence and status of blacks moving to and, in some cases, forcibly moved into western territories precipitated violence and legal political battles that led to the Civil War.[25] Though central in multiple military successes and the economically vital border-patrolling practice of cow herding, blacks experienced the nationalization of racial hostility, disenfranchisement, and marginalization in the new territories.[26] In western states as in eastern, legal barriers to full citizenship included restrictive laws on even the tiniest of black communities based on white racial fears. Uneven enforcement of restrictive black laws and community and racial mixing between blacks and Native Americans did permit some freedom and greater opportunity. Nevertheless the expansion of the white population brought steadily increasing restriction of black freedom. Many black westerners, having tried the West as their last hope to escape racism, began to support emigration, and many settled in Mexico.[27] Others organized against slavery and later against racial discrimination in general. With the close of the frontier in the 1890s white Americans codified segregation and extinguished even the slim hope of the West as an avenue for escape.[28] The close coincided with American international expansion in Cuba, the Philippines, Puerto Rico, the Caribbean, and Hawaii. The presence of black anti-imperial activism indicates social organization and remarkable cohesion in communities despite the brutal challenges blacks faced.[29] Black responses to American movement westward and international colonization efforts in the nineteenth century included protest against nationalist racism, increased support of black expatriation to Africa, and protest against imperial action in Cuba and the Philippines.[30]

Such historical experiences, however, typically failed to influence the content of black films involving the West. As a terrain for the imaginative creation of identity, the filmic West allowed blacks to re-create their past and their politics, reimagine the present, and posit a hypothetical future of national belonging in a politically neutral space. The performance of westward settlement and land acquisition in film re-

41

articulates American expansion in a celebration of national identity, yet it also imagines for the first time, from a middle-class perspective of landownership, black dreams of owning a piece of the nation, its ideals, and its future. The films brought into being, for public view and imaginative savor, a self-sufficient community where blacks enjoyed the freedom and pleasures of economic success. During the Depression era only a minute portion of the nation was able to maintain middle-class status. The financial status the films fantasized was as available to blacks as the threadbare promise of national belonging. Given the circumstances, the West proved even more ideologically malleable in the production of black identity than it was for the mainstream.[31]

For African Americans, a symbolic invasion of the West was a dangerous and intricate task whereby multiple layers of entrenched stereotypes and preexisting appropriations of black identity had to be evaded and rescripted. The films carefully balanced rejections of stereotypes of both urban savagery and savagery in nature, that is, of primitivism. Stereotypes of black urban savagery posited African Americans as exhibiting a degenerate lack of civilization and as indivisibly one with nature and the wild, and thus not fit for city life. Yet mainstream constructions recuperated the "man in the wild," discarding a "feminized," urban civility for primitive ruggedness as evidence of strength, virility, national prowess, and global control.[32] Stereotypes of blackness fed constructions of white supremacy because of the way whites othered blacks to give currency to ideologies of noble "savage" *white* manhood and primitivism in general. In characterizing blacks, notions of the savage, primitive, wild, uncivilized, and dangerous were conflated into a bundle of racist imagery that invoked both urban and nonurban environments. African Americans walked a veritable tightrope of representation in establishing a public identity consistent with contemporary narratives of American identity involving "uncivilized space." To maintain balance they cultivated a visual relationship to the city and technology and excluded Native Americans.

To help navigate this territory blacks enacted their own imperial erasure of Native Americans to clear the way for black representation. Contemporary mainstream westerns represented Native Americans as violent, aggressive, and savage, serving as a foreign enemy, though a weak and defeatable one, on the plain against which white communities defined borders and American identity. The stereotype provided a national and racial foil as well as the opportunity for white American victory. In contrast the elision of Native Americans in African American films resisted that trend. The crucial effect of the omission was a mitigation of savagery in the wilderness for blacks. If the role of savage was already occupied ideologically and spatially by stereotyped Native Americans, then the cultural and biological savagery of African Americans could become secondary as they entered a space and symbolic system inhabited by an entrenched and absent "primitive." The stereotype of the vanishing Native dignifies human presence in the wilderness, actually creating a normalized space for blacks to appropriate and inhabit.[33] The primitive slot is filled, facilitating the use of the West as a tapestry for black civility and a new symbolic belonging, such as that seen in *Pictorial View* and *The Exile*.

The Exile: Homesteader Hero

The Exile (1931) was the first talking, feature-length, black commercial film the Micheaux Film Corporation produced.[34] Oscar Micheaux was the premier producer of black films, making and distributing about thirty-five films between 1918 and 1940. *The Exile* weaves a tale of westward motion and settlement that repeats the themes and plots of several of his earliest works. Micheaux's very first movie, *The Homesteader* (1918), and the subsequent *Symbol of the Unconquered* (1920) were based loosely on his autobiography *The Conquest* (1913), which detailed the early part of his life, his ranching exploits on the South Dakota plain, and his romantic foibles.[35] He also wrote a melodramatic novel, a fictional love story based on the same experiences, also called *The Homesteader* (1917).[36] *The Exile* was the fifth incarnation of Micheaux's autobiographical story. This film emphasizes work, honesty, love, and success as the main characters carve a life out of the untamed West. Micheaux positions his own pioneer experience as central to his artistic expression in his insistent multiple tellings of the same story in the development of his craft. Even when times were lean, these themes and images of the West, settlement, and starting anew continued to draw viewers. The West constructed in Micheaux's reincarnations of the settlement story reflects neither black history in the West nor experiences of failing farms, joblessness, continued denial of rights, and segregation in the 1930s, but rather an idealized attainment of wealth and power. *The Exile* premiered in New York at the Lafayette Theater in Harlem. The plot involves the migration of an ambitious young man out of black Chicago to establish his fortune. The hero, Jean Baptist (Stanley Morrell), purchases land in South Dakota, initiating a sequence of romantic dramas that establish the possibility of black success through representations of gender and space. In *The Exile* land availability west of Chicago facilitates the development of the Horatio Alger drama of upward mobility and romance.

True of many black films of the time, *The Exile*'s technique, plot, and performance leave much to be desired. Shots are repetitive and lingering. Images of city streets and picturesque outdoor shots of plains and fields, filmed on location in Chicago and South Dakota, appear in key places, while the film's action occurs indoors against simple sets. The plot is melodramatic and helped along by long segments of text in the form of intertitles, notes, letters, telegrams, and newspaper articles to which actors respond with heightened emotion. Except for the intertitles, the use of written forms of fast and mass communication media interacts with sound technology to underscore the film's modernity. Though a contemporary review applauds the film's "good acting," in actuality the acting is stilted.[37] In many scenes actors demonstrate the meaning of lines and experiences with exaggerated gestures characteristic of silent film acting, where most of these performers would have gained experience. In this sense the actors were performatively unprepared for the consequences of sound in film. Several sequences of a nightclub revue, popular in black film, display the musical skill of a jazz band and the dancing talents of a fair-skinned female chorus. The club performance acts as a defining characteristic of black city life, though the revue contributes little to the action of the film.[38] Despite some of this stiltedness, *The Exile* is one of Micheaux's better films in terms of its production values, camera work, and editing. Though common in Micheaux's own work, the story is unusual in the context of black films of the period. Its use of the latest in sound technology to communicate an epic American tale of upward black mobility made it appealing to audiences. This film uses narratives of westward mobility, western space, middle-class respectability, skin color, and images of regal Ethiopia in an expression of cultural nationalism and national integration.

Immediately the film announces "Negro progress" as one of its operating tenets. With a Negro spiritual rising in the background, *The Exile*'s

1. *The Exile* movie poster.

opening credits boast an "All Negro Cast." Images of Chicago's busy city streets slowly fade out, and, relying on techniques of silent film, intertitles describe the setting and facilitate the plot. The film "is a story of Chicago and the Negro shortly after the close of the World War." Further situating the viewer and acting as an educational prologue of Chicago's history, the following words introduce the scene:

> A mansion, somewhere on the Southside, once the home of a wealthy meat packer, but deserted by heirs who fled, frightened and terrified by the sight of a — seemingly endless stream of Negroes, brought North to supply labor for the demands of war — and moving in this direction, in quest of a place to live! [A mansion situated in the black belt fills the screen.] It is occupied now, however by Edith Duval, a former maid, but since the war, and prosperity, an ambitious "social leader."

The first great migration provides context for a film that replaces that watershed relocation with westward reachings. After the First World War blacks were indeed moving to cities, working in industry, stretching the seams of the segregated Southside and perhaps enjoying a modicum of disposable income, the expenditure of which makes Edith Duval (Eunice Brooks) a prosperous woman. Capitalizing on some of this available cash, Duval has turned the mansion into a club that deteriorates into a gambling den and brothel. Setting the film in about 1918, a tad more than a decade earlier than its actual release in 1931 and the financial crash of 1929, permits a nostalgia for the good old days and the imagination of a certain hope of continued financial success.

The film pairs parallel models of urban and western success in the initial romantic coupling and breakup of Edith and Jean. While Edith stays in the city to develop her nightclub and satisfy her ambition for success, Jean hopes to make a fortune as a rancher in South Dakota. When she refuses to support him, Jean and Edith break up and Jean strikes out west. Three shots of an approaching, passing, and receding train transition the viewer a thousand miles west and five years into the future. The screen fills with images of vast fields and pastures filled with cattle. Men on harvesting equipment drawn by teams of horses and workers stacking hay demonstrate the extent of Jean's wealth and influence. He is the only colored man in town and also the only person successful enough to hire new help. Despite the odds, Jean acquires wealth and opportunity, all seemingly there for the taking.

As Jean's fortunes increase, so do Edith's, but in inverse moral proportion. A telegram Jean receives while on the plain alerts him to the mythic reputation he has earned as a result of his physical and financial distance, and also communicates Edith's rise as queen of Chicago's underworld. She runs card and dice games and a numbers racket and is frequently raided by the police, only to bail out truckloads of her patrons and return them to her joint. The writer of the telegram celebrates Jean's escape from marriage to Edith, who represents urban vice and lack of morality. Although a group of "the best colored people" exists as potential clients in Chicago, Edith's ways have driven them from her club.

Jean's superior moral fiber is established in opposition to Edith's in a scene in which the main characters discuss gender roles. Edith verbally attacks Jean's masculinity in the film, setting him up to assert his own manliness over and against her accusations. When he refuses to stay and join her in converting the club into a speakeasy and racketeering joint, she repeatedly calls him "nothing but a sissy" with clear distaste. She taunts him, calling him a "nice man, goodie man" and "not like other men" for not drinking, staying out late, or kissing her. She challenges his sexuality as a means of humiliation, manipulation, and punishment. Jean protests that he is like other men who choose not to do such things, who choose instead to "maintain a high moral regard for women they love and honor, all women." According to Jean, Edith's desires degrade them both. His strength in denying her demonstrates his upstanding manhood and her degenerate womanhood, setting them up as gendered representations of the influences of the city and the West.

Jean's travels to the frontier allow him to demonstrate the rewards of a rugged determination through which he transforms uncultivated land into a successful farm and cattle ranch. Never seen performing manual labor, but only conducting business and hiring others, Jean accrues an elite status. Thus in contrast to Edith's desires for a hipster, Jean manifests honest strength and determination, cultivating an intact, genteel manhood along with his wheat.[39] His activity and success contribute to the economic and territorial solidifying of national power.

The city acts as the template of black culture, maintaining a balance between civilization and the frontier. It also acts as an oppositional template for the development of Jean's manliness. He must leave the negatively feminized city in order to develop his character and fortune. Women, in the form of dancing dames, gossipy gamblers, and emasculating madams, interfere with the development of the hero's manhood in the city. Thus Jean risks ridicule and failure to try his fortune out west. Two narratives of the city develop, one that demands urban connection in order to maintain black identity and another that draws upon mainstream discourses of urban degeneracy to facilitate the discovery of manhood in the West. Unlike ideologies of genteel middle-class *manhood* that contrasted with a western rugged *masculinity* that was more physical, natural, and less civilized, Jean goes west into the realm of masculinity and becomes more manly.[40] He combines the masculine experience with the traits of manliness, reversing the typical impact of the wilderness on manhood. It is through these representations of male gender identity that the centrality of the urban to black experience gets articulated. Under the influence of the West, Jean develops refined, urban manliness along with quiet strength of character and the ability to survive frontier conditions. The film replaces the vector of black spatial identity from rural, southern farm to northern city (that "endless stream of Negroes brought North") with city to frontier. This geographic and symbolic shift incorporates the conditions that produce both masculinity and manliness, fitting black male gender identity into several traditions at once in order to maintain civility and take advantage of the symbolically invigorating and nationally significant topologies of the rugged West.

The film pits African American freedom and manhood against the influence of a cruel city woman, Jean's former fiancée, who gets her just deserts in the end. A similar dichotomy contrasting bad womanhood against redeemed manhood exists in the relationship between Edith and her new lover, Jango (Carl Mahon), who is from Ethiopia. Edith attacks Jango with verbal taunts that he is worthless and spineless. Jango blames Edith for teaching him "to drink and smoke reefer" and for diverting him from his plans in coming to "this country to become a teacher." Both agree that Edith is responsible for removing Jango's courage, dignity, and resolve. Flaunting his weakness, Edith hands him a gun, challenging him to have the courage to take his own life and prove his worth. Through this symbolic offer of phallic power, Edith shows her own evil, unnatural womanhood and reinforces Jango's lack. Fully emasculated and locked in a verbal and emotional battle with Edith, Jango is unable to decide what to do, until he learns of the crowning of the Abyssinian king. Jilted and contemplating suicide, Jango is immediately inspired to reinvigorate his life and manhood by a glimpse he catches of a news-paper headline announcing the crowning of "Addis Abba, Ras Tafari, who traces his ancestry in an unbroken line, back to King Solomon and the Queen of Sheba . . . Emperor of the oldest Kingdom of the World." Now proud and resolved to return to his country, Jango determines to avenge himself and undo any evil he has committed under Edith's influ-ence by sending her to her grave. His presence makes the development of self-rule and power in Ethiopia relevant to the virility of black urban masculinity. Jango regains pride in himself as well as a sense of deter-mination. With his newfound power, he uses the gun Edith offered him to murder her. The corruption he has acquired in the city plays out in his execution of corrupt justice against corrupt Edith. Jango is unable to successfully create a new self in the way Jean can in the wilderness. Through this tragic turn of events, however, masculine power is restored in urban space. Even though, in a subsequent twist of plot Jean is ar-rested for this murder, black Chicago police ultimately arrest and jail Jango. His fate communicates the inspirational power of global black independence and pride in black nationalism, while the ultimate domi-nance of the domestic system of governance and justice prevails.

In multiple ways the film establishes constant communication, con-nection, and difference between city and western space. The interplay between the spaces replicates imperial relationships of space, distin-guishing the city as a Negro metropole from the West as periphery. The vast distance between city and prairie requires technological media-tion that symbolically collapses the distance between them even as they are contrasted. The two spaces share the technological advances of the telegram and railroad system. Jean maintains an epistolary relationship with Chicago, sending and receiving news. His physical travel occurs by train. Images of the West's endless fields and pastures alongside shots of the city's bustling thoroughfares and house-lined streets accentuate the difference between the spaces. The contrasting spaces become de-fined in relation to each other through these technological connections: the West and open space with its fields, livestock, and different social values is set against the city's corruption, gossip, murder, alcohol, and sex. Yet strangely enough, the city offers Jean refuge when his love life hits trouble in South Dakota. Black neighborhood and club culture re-main a characteristic of black identity and home when the frontier with-holds its romantic promise.

Jean's new spatial foreignness in the city signifies the difference between metropole and periphery. News of Jean's enormous success reaches Chicago. A telegram informs him that a young woman who had been interested in meeting Jean would not "marry an exile (all the colored people call you 'The Exile') and live in the wilderness! Why honey, I wouldn't move that far from State Street with Henry Ford!" The linkage between the wilderness and Jean's rather extreme new name, "the Exile," one who has been forced from or voluntarily quitted his home, indicates the foreignness and difference of Jean's life from that of the city—to the extent that even his great wealth cannot draw love from so far away. The name has an othering effect even as it sets Jean up as a misunderstood adventurer, bravely embarking on a strange journey away from his true home. While Jean's spatial movement and independent spirit stretch the boundaries of possibility for black life, the dominance of urban community as the core of identity remains intact. After all, the epithet defines Jean by what he has left behind. The black urban metropole becomes the center of cultural and political power and knowledge. As the center, it radiates identities and meanings to be carried to or remade in othered spaces. The conception and development of identities in the West always refer to already established knowledge and cultures of the city. The periphery is influenced by the culture of the metropole and yet exists beyond its grasp, presenting the possibility of new cultural formations, signified, in this case, by interracial love and black wealth. Thus the West as periphery becomes a place of experimentation and creative possibility even as, and perhaps because, it exists in relation to black urban spaces.

The Great Migration, which frames the film's opening scenes, took place during the fifteen years after the First World War and meant that most adults had not been born in the cities where they lived.[41] Since the vast majority of blacks in cities had migrated from rural spaces, farming and ranching would not have been foreign to them. This dominant experience also means that the city as the locus of black culture was a relatively new and constructed identity. Establishing the city as a point of origin insists upon the New Negro as a foundational black identity and sets up the possibility for participation in traditional narratives of urban emigration. This reverses the dominant experience of the period. The centrality of the city as home allows African Americans to participate in discourses of the western frontier, imagine self, and construct symbolically usable gender identities. Such constructions cement racial goals and community ideals. In doing so they serve a nationalizing function by imagining new origins, gender roles, and mainstream experiences for black people retroactively as part of a process of expansion.

For blacks, the West and this film also become spaces for the negotiation of racial relationships between black and white. Once Jean has taken advantage of opportunity, he faces the challenge of race hatred in his quest to gain fulfillment and happiness. His chance comes with the film's visual introduction of Agnes Stewart (Nora Newsome), shown alone quietly brushing her hair before a mirror. The camera lens and the mirror doubly record her "whiteness," suggesting the inability of the audience to detect blackness in the Negro actress playing the young white heroine. Jean falls in love with Agnes and begins a romance. Within weeks the interracial couple declare their love for each other in a long scene on a park bench. They kiss and pledge their undying devotion in spite of what the world may bring.[42]

Just prior to the onset of this love affair, three separate conversations about race occur in quick succession in the South Dakota phase of the film. When asked if he is "all colored" by an apparently white ranch hand, Jean responds that he is and explains that all Negroes, even those of "mixed blood," are "all-colored." In the very next scene, the white Scot Stewart, Agnes's father, and Bill Prescott, a white man from Arkansas with a small ranch nearby, discuss the fact that Jean Baptist is the only man in the area rich enough to hire Stewart's son. Prescott observes that this is "funny" since Baptist is a colored man. A shot of Agnes in an interior room dressed in white and again sitting before a mirror appears in the middle of the conversation. These consecutive shots juxtapose the idea of Jean's "funny" coloredness against Agnes's pure white womanhood that is both affirmed and called into question by the mirror. Prescott's statement gives Stewart the opportunity to protest vigorously, asking "What difference does that make?" To Prescott's answer, "A lot to me," Stewart responds, "Well, I'm from Scotland, and to me a man is a man." The two agree to disagree and Prescott leaves on good terms, stating that they can still be friends "in spite of our differences in opinion." Immediately thereafter Stewart enters his daughter's room, where they have a conversation about Baptist's race. Upon learning Jean's race, apparently undetectable to her mirroring eyes, Agnes exclaims, "A colored man? Does that mean he is Negro, Father?" Stewart replies in the affirmative and adds, "That makes no difference," for he "judge[s] a man according to his honesty and ability." Agnes agrees that "that is the only fair way to judge anybody." They hug. Agnes also remarks that when she was in Chicago she noticed that "many Negroes were quite light," as light as her mother in fact. Tripling the question of visibility, Agnes looks in the mirror, at her mother's picture, and then at her own skin. She muses about her own racial identity saying, "I wonder . . . ," and stares intently at the ceiling and wall.

Thus an open environment of acceptance pervades the Stewart household, welcoming the wealthy, colored Jean and his affection for Agnes. Yet the relationship falls apart as the sense of its impossibility weighs on Jean. In a letter to Agnes he confesses to fear of being "snubbed, insulted, and ostracized" and to loving her too much to allow her to suffer all that. Self-sacrificing and noble, Jean buries the temptation to "take [her] in [his] arms and fly to the ends of the earth" and flies, instead, to Chicago.

After Jean's departure Mr. Stewart reveals his "life's secret: that [Agnes's] mother was of Ethiopian extraction." The dependence upon a symbolic Ethiopia in this moment facilitates the union of the two lovers and the film's happy ending. The great love affair can continue due to a small portion of "black blood" in Agnes's veins, redeeming her whiteness and permitting the once fated love affair. Agnes begs her father to bring Jean back to her and collapses in a fit of tears. Thus twice in the film Ethiopia facilitates the development of power, courage, and the potential to trounce evil.

In the vein of imagining black economic and personal success, the film also idealizes the racial possibilities of western space. Racial harmony becomes possible, as does the destruction of racism and color prejudice through metatropes of passing (black passing for white on screen, becoming black again in the plot). Interracial conversations about blackness, race, and acceptance occur peacefully in homes in western space. No declarations against Jean's and Agnes's romance stand. The only overt racist in the film, Prescott, is arrested for stealing cattle shortly after the park bench love scene. Already cast as foolish in the face of Jean's and Agnes's devotion, race-based hatred is dismantled by the arrest. Thus racism becomes associated with poor moral character, dishonesty, and lawlessness.

Stewart, the older man who spouts the racial agenda of equality and content of character, actually favors W. E. B. Du Bois, the face of racial ideologies of equality at this particular historical moment. Stewart's instructive, preacherly conversations are centered in his household, the white household, intimating that it is not just black people who espouse human equality and reject discrimination. Ultimately the death of the black mother redeems that space and love triumphs over racist society. Through her own marriage to the white Scot and her black body and history, she allows the possibility of Jean's and Agnes's marriage. In her absence this black mother serves as a foil for Edith's evil and claims Agnes's sweet innocence for black womanhood. As a result both black and white people are good, loving, and able to overcome race prejudice in South Dakota. The daughter of the white family travels to the city to save and retrieve Jean, bringing the narrative of racial equality into city space before returning to an idyllic and ideologically open West.

The film poses a conundrum in its all-black cast and the representation of an interracial romance. The audience is forced to suspend their disbelief in the racial whiteness of the actors. That is, the film requires the viewer to believe in Prescott and the Stewarts' visible and acted white identity even though they are really Negroes. And yet the fact that they *are* black and can still believably portray white characters upholds the argument that race is meaningless and often invisible. Jean's beige skin color resembles the Stewarts' almost exactly, echoing the sameness asserted by the film's casting and narrative since Jean plays an "all-colored" man. The film "passes" the Stewart family, the ranch hand Bill Prescott, and the only representative of civil authority, a district attorney played by a black man who seems to wear pasty whiteface.

Micheaux's apparent obsession with black bodies looking white in black-and-white on the silver screen creates this narrative of racial acceptance through double passing: black actors passing as whites who actually are black. They are able to verify racial equality through their own signifying bodies. The medium of black-and-white film made the argument for him in the on-screen blurring of racial differences commonly evident in gradations of skin color. In gray-scale it was difficult to distinguish a black person (of a certain hue) from a white person. This characteristic of black-and-white film, combined with Micheaux's penchant for interracial romances saved by a single drop of black blood, titillated and upset white audiences, who would often complain to movie house management during a film that a black man was kissing a white woman.[43] Because of its representation of interracial romance the film was temporarily banned in New York City in 1932. Micheaux manipulated the expectation that his films would deal with issues of race and color in order to support his arguments of uplift and equality.[44] As problematic as it remains in *The Exile* and in other films, using "light, bright" black actors was a means of undermining the sanctity of whiteness. Black bodies became indistinguishable from white on screen. "Blood" and appearance emerged as untrustworthy criteria for determining a person's worth. In this way choices to cast light-skinned blacks, which have been criticized in Micheaux's work as colorist, perform a kind of pride in "race" and black ability through an assertion of equality.[45] Screen representations achieve a coup against race prejudice as one is unable to tell whether a person is or is not black. These visual narratives of racial passing enacted an erasure of difference based upon how bodies of black people appeared on screen and challenged the color line through both technology and plot.[46]

Showing white-looking black bodies in western space also toyed with the image of white settlers in America, using blackness as a symbol thorough which to address white immigration. Black actors played white immigrants, and yet in reality (the promotional materials and opening credits remind us) they were not white. The representation of white immigration through blackness, for instance of a Scot through the body of a black actor, critiques the status of white immigrants. White immigrants become embodied as foreigners, at least to the extent that blacks are considered foreign to or outside of culture within America. Thus the Scot's acceptance of racial equality, evidenced through his marriage to a woman "of Ethiopian extraction" and his willingness to marry his daughter to Baptist, claims white immigrants as equal to blacks. His Scottish origin also manages to name white European immigration without directly invoking the urban hostilities between blacks and specific immigrant groups, such as Italians and Irish, populating the cities. The film overcomes racial difference without having to negotiate race hatred common to urban ghettoes.

The representation of international connections in either spatial extreme in the film — Abyssinia in the city and Scotland in the West — operates instrumentally. Both incarnations of the foreign represent a kind of freedom and autonomy in relation to black identity in America. In addition to interracial idealism enacted through romance on the plain, the influence of freedom in Abyssinia facilitates justice and re-demption in Chicago. Jango's pride in racial nationalism gives him the courage to commit the misogynistic murder of Edith that symbolically returns his manhood and also frees Jean to marry Agnes. Through the murder Jango regains a sense of self and the falsely accused Jean regains his innocence, the associative purity of his bride, and cross-racial accep-tance through his impending marriage to the Scot's daughter. Interna-tional influences on the racial narratives of each space encourage black racial pride and possibility. Jango's resolution to claim his own future and become a man illustrates the inspiring power of Africa. His criminal demise, however, facilitates the domestic story of racial acceptance and assimilation that seem to be the point of the film.

The Exile's romance in the West and its narrative of racial accep-tance are not coincidental, but rather mutually productive. The trope of romance helps feed and establish racial citizenship in the same ways as ambition, upward mobility, outward mobility, and ruggedly genteel masculinity. The success of interracial love and marriage (the Baptists' and the Stewarts') and concomitant themes of acceptance in western space communicate an American desire for national acceptance, where romance stands in for a kind of territorial acquisition. With Jean's "ac-quisition" of Agnes's racially obscure body, he accomplishes racial ac-ceptance and the destruction of prejudice as achievements of westward motion. This romantic achievement symbolizes national desire in its communication through the national iconography of westward motion, settlement, and upward mobility.

In this African American construction of western space, the possi-bility for middle-class wealth and opportunity is only the first assimila-tion narrative the West permits. The second narrative is specifically of racial assimilation, the blurred, untenable nature of the color line, and racial equality. A third assimilation narrative develops when these two characteristics combine. Economic and racial assimilation combined with success and the establishment of true masculinity in the American West constitute the quintessential American dream. Manifesting such inherent symbolic Americanness in desire, imagination, and identity produces an overwhelming assertion of inclusion in all aspects of the national body. The argument for equality and inclusion evolves along-side an insistence upon black racial integrity and autonomy of commu-nity in the hypothesis that these might exist together.

2. Jean Baptiste and Agnes Stewart in *The Exile*.
COURTESY OF THE LIBRARY OF CONGRESS, MOTION PICTURES READING ROOM

Filmmaking as Modernity

The process of blacks making film offers a metacommentary on national belonging, elaborating through form the claims I just made. The very techniques used to make these films emphasize concerns with scientific modernity that construct black identity in each. *Pictorial View*, *The Exile*, and *Two-Gun Man* repeat obsessions with modernity and technological advancement. Procuring images through the modern technologies of the camera activates a process of viewing that asserts control for the filmmaker. The medium of film requires an editorial process of inventorying and arranging that also dominates the recorded object.[47] In narrative film, documentary or otherwise, the arranging of images into a representation of reality serves as a further control that black cultural producers enacted on material objects, bodies, and space.[48] A very basic regulation obtains when collecting, organizing, and watching images. The use of the camera to explore open space and nature bolsters the construction of an empowered perspective by codifying an African American gaze and using the camera to assert visual, narrative, and technological mastery. Part of the process of becoming Western requires filmmakers' mastery of the *form* of the western, its tropes and images. Black films involving western images became formulaic, fictitious in the late 1930s (that is, imagined instead of based on a history, an individual, or an existing community), and visually and narratively similar to mainstream westerns of the same period. The mastery of the western genre in narrative and image over time echoes the assimilationist ethos at the center of these black films.

The tone, content, and visual structure of African American narratives of expansion and settlement assumed rather than asserted a type of national inclusion over the decade of the 1930s. Over time African American symbolics of the American West change from seeking to establish Negro appreciation and habitation of frontier space in early representations to asserting inclusion by failing to question blacks' belonging in that space. This shift takes place through the appropriation of film technique and genre. Much of this assumption, this taking for granted of national identity manifests in appropriations of form as African Americans produced increasingly mainstream and increasingly popular visual texts establishing their presence in the American dream of expansion. Blacks demonstrated the ability to possess, enjoy, and exploit frontier resources on film and to master filmic forms of western appropriation and representation. These films show that blacks in the 1930s already operated ideologically as Americans, even as they proffered images to argue the point. The period's black B westerns perform this formal inclusion most clearly.

Two-Gun Man from Harlem: Generic Mastery and the Cowboy Gangster

In the late 1930s four B westerns made a hit on the big screen. They engaged in ideas and images of expansion and the American West and also had the look and plot structure pioneered by the western. The "Harlem" series closely followed mainstream narrative structures that depicted fully fictional characters and situations.[49] This choice indicates an interest not in excavating the past or representing history, but in taking part in spinning fantastical tales about settlement and success. Stories of individual triumph in settling the West, defending property, forming communities, or escaping and resisting racism are not the subject of black westerns in a generic form. Black westerns are action adventures, in which clear good is pitted against simplistic evil, much like mainstream westerns of the time. Bogle compares the content of the "Harlem" westerns to "Tex Ritter–Gene Autry heroics and exploits."[50] The "Harlem" series had much in common with the popular and plentiful mainstream singing cowboy pictures that played to a cult following in rural areas and urban centers. For the most part the films repeated a basic format. "There was always a singing cowboy with his . . . horse and comic sidekick involved in a situation with some ne'er-do-well businessman who attempted to bilk the local cattlemen/ranchers/citizens out of their cattle/land/oil rights."[51]

Herbert Jeffrey, the actor who played the films' heroes, stated in interviews that he and Spencer Williams, a well-known black actor, wanted to provide black youth with black cowboy images to look up to and to model.[52] The representation of black male gender identity ultimately forged in the films collapsed spatial gender iconography that held the West separate from the city and nationhood separate from blackness. *Harlem on the Prairie* (1938), *Bronze Buckaroo* (1938), *Harlem Rides the Range* (1939), and *Two-Gun Man from Harlem* (1939) each present a mild-mannered singing cowboy who helps execute justice. The construction of the singing cowboy in black representations of open space and expansion in the 1930s most closely manifests a mainstream genre. In this series of black filmic engagements with expansion where urban identity infuses the West, the motif gets fully embodied in Jeffrey's cowboy only in the final film, *Two-Gun Man from Harlem*.[53] Many elements of production remained consistent across the four films. The team mastered a process whereby they created a consistent product and maintained production value and content in multiple efforts. Herbert Jeffrey, a nightclub singer, played the hero in every film. Spencer Williams, an actor and director, acted in each and helped to write some of the screenplays. Flournoy Miller acted in several of the films. Both Williams and Miller participated in writing and production. The actor Clarence Brooks was another regular. All but the last of the movies were made at N. B. Murray's black dude ranch near Victorville, California. The white director and producer Richard C. Kahn was involved in the making of all except *Harlem on the Prairie*. Music and vocals in three of the movies were provided by the Four Tones. Three of the films still exist for screening. *Harlem on the Prairie*, also known as *Bad Man from Harlem*, has been lost.[54] The title under which this lost film was released captures the spirit of the entire series. The films render black urban culture iconic in the logic of a black West.

The "Harlem" westerns adhere to the basic B western's plot, though the black films' comedy and music had their own particular flavor based on black performance styles, the hero had no trouble attracting the girl, and the land in question typically hid some secret valuable natural substance more exotic than oil just under the surface. A man in financial straits trying to keep his land is threatened or killed, leaving his property and pretty young daughter in need of saving from evil developers (also African American). The hero, Bob Blake, saves the day and the girl, helping to discover the truth and restore right. The films feature shootouts, singing and music, a jester sidekick of the black vaudeville type, panoramic views, and lots of good horseback riding in a visual display of vigorous western living. Three of the four titles mention "Harlem," and the new landowner is invariably a noble patriarch who hails from one of the major eastern cities. This character signals a kind of hope in a western future. Along with the urban performance of the sidekick, he maintains a link between black life in the West and urban black communities.

Two-Gun Man from Harlem has the most complex and well-developed version of the scenario just described. A murder for which Blake is framed complicates the plot. In the end Blake wins the girl, saves her land by outwitting the cheater, murderer, and land swindler John Barker (Clarence Brooks), and frees a trapped morally corrupt woman. Blake captures Barker and exposes him as a crook. Virtue triumphs as Blake saves not only the mineral-rich land of the young girl, but also his own good name and the life of Mrs. Steele (Mae Turner), the woman who framed him.[55] Blake's collapsed persona with "the Deacon" from Harlem through most of the film permits the clearest unifying of city and periphery in the films. The figure of Bob Blake becomes the primary terrain through which questions of black possibility in the West are most compellingly performed.

With his white horse, studded saddle, and willingness to joke playfully with his pals, Blake comes off as a regular guy, not a loner, but friendly and helpful. He offers his own help and that of "some of the boys in his outfit" to Mr. Thompson, the ailing rancher. His repartee with Sally Thompson's (Marguerite Witten) little brother, Jimmy, played by Matthew "Stymie" Beard of *Little Rascals* fame, shows Blake

3. *Two-Gun Man from Harlem* movie poster.

to be patient and good-natured. He is a cowboy hero with a sense of community and justice. He helps the disempowered: women, the poor, the elderly, and children. He champions the underdog against exploiters and in his own unassuming, earnest, easy cowboy way shows that good can conquer evil. Bob Blake's persona is genteel, strong, and virile. His clever planning shows through the elaborate trap he creates to expose John Barker and buy off Sally's land with Barker's own money. When necessary, he springs into action, proving he can ride, shoot, and fight like the best of them (see figure 4). In the film's best chase sequence he overtakes the villain on horseback and fights him to the ground in a lengthy hand-to-hand struggle. He shoots the head off a match, set-ting it alight, impressing an adversary and establishing his own (obvi-ously phallic) skill with a gun. A man of relatively few words, he is a skilled, self-sufficient, and generous hero. In his appropriated identity of a Harlem gangster, "the Deacon," Blake's black suit and black cow-boy duds juxtaposed against the light-colored coats and white shirts of Barker's gang subvert the typical western association of white with good and black with bad. Since only black characters exist in "all-colored" pictures, this inversion makes a statement about broader race relations in the U.S. that does not transmit through any other aspect of the all-black film.

Blake leads the audience in a struggle against greed and corruption in newly claimed space, spreading virtue and justice across the plain. The villains are not marauding outlaws but upper-class landowners, bankers, and speculators trying to exploit honest citizens for financial gain. When valuable mineral deposits are discovered on the Thompsons' property, Barker tries to recall the loan and take back the land, a move that would leave the family homeless. Blake's actions protect the right of individual landownership and the belief in upward mobility, doing his part in up-holding liberty and the pursuit of property. Middle-class values support individual access to property and success in *Two-Gun*, while greed and exploitation are denounced. The Jeffrey films side with the little guy in the struggle against corrupt capitalists. Not truly proletarian in this as-pect, the films preserve the sanctity of individual rights, upward mo-bility, and law-abiding citizenship as they also consent to local power structures. No superhero, Blake always helps to restore order and his own "regular cowboy" status at the end by turning the villains over to the sheriff.

4. Movie stills of Bob Blake in *Two-Gun Man from Harlem.* COURTESY OF THE LIBRARY OF CONGRESS, MOTION PICTURES READING ROOM

Most of *Two Gun*'s action occurs while Blake is disguised as a murdering gangster, The Deacon, an identity he picks up while on the run in Harlem. Encouraged by Mrs. Steele to run south of the border in her frame-up for the murder of her husband, Blake instead escapes to the city. For him, deep *urban* space provides escape and renewal. Even as mainstream devices of the West are used to further arguments about national identity and assimilation, black westerns reject complete assimilation of mainstream forms. Unlike in the typical western, a black West requires a referential relationship to an urban metropole. In the central sequence of the film, Blake is shown riding, running, and hitch-hiking, desperately striving to get away from the Arizona desert. He becomes more deeply ensconced in industrial modernity as he travels from horse, to car, to truck, to train, through major metropolitan centers, and finally substantiates his identity with evidence from the mass-produced popular press. Scenes from city streets flash in the background as titles proclaim "Chicago," "New York," and finally "Harlem," the so-called black capital of the world, in large print on the screen. *Two-Gun* provides a virtual tour of iconographic centers of black urban life and culture that ends in Harlem, the urban heartland and spatial antithesis of the West.

The urban and the West combine in Blake's presence and interactions in the stereotypically black urban space of a club in Harlem. Blake appears comfortably settled in Harlem, smoking a cigarette and having a drink. Even though his five-gallon hat stands out, he fits in easily. His inclusion is indicated by his acceptance by one of the club performers, Delores, who flirts with him and also happens to be the girlfriend of a fearsome urban badman, the Deacon. Blake's language is markedly different from the city slang and accents of the clubbers. In fact he compliments Delores by saying that her dancing reminds him of a "heifer full of loco weed." Although he is incorporated into the city scene, his honest innocence sets him apart. Thus he comes to the city and yet is able to maintain his western difference, infusing the city with a bit of the West.

When the Deacon, also played by Herbert Jeffrey, comes into the club his power is indicated in the fearful reaction of the clubbers. Everyone jumps up in fear, nervous that the Deacon's "girl" is flirting with Blake. Rumored to have been a preacher before his first murder, the laconic Deacon speaks in Bible verses. A split screen shows the Deacon and Bob Blake in the same frame as Delores comments on their striking resemblance (see figure 5). The use of new film technology produces an

5. Movie still of Blake, the Deacon, and Dolores in *Two-Gun Man from Harlem*.
COURTESY OF THE LIBRARY OF CONGRESS, MOTION PICTURES READING ROOM

uncanny doubling of East and West as mirror-image characters, played
by the same actor, face each other. The urban center and western out-
post meet, double, and split off as Blake embodies the Deacon's image
and identity and carries it back west. This collapsing of twin identities
and their westward motion bears crucial symbolic weight for the meaning of blackness, space, the West, and power. Ultimately the West operates not as a completely free and open ideological terrain for the imagination of new and specific identities in black discourse, but as a place
that unequivocally requires the urban. Blake's movement insists upon
the presence of blackness in all national spaces and makes blackness
ubiquitous in spatial articulations of power. It is perhaps most clear here
how black cultural production uses blackness symbolically. Signifying
beyond the body of the actor, blackness becomes a spatial principle that
represents civilization and power.

Intent on clearing his name for the murder of Mr. Steele, Blake adopts
the Deacon's identity and goes back to Arizona. His appropriation of the
urban identity performs the hybridity of black spaces and identities as
he literally imports urban identity into western space. Western space
also provides the possibility for city evil to be recuperated and do good,

as the Deacon persona saves the Thompson ranch and exposes the real bad guys. Blake returns home in costume, carrying an article from a New York paper about the mobster as his identification card. A sensational article from a popular print source asserts the value of the press as a means of communication and purveyor of truth in black culture. Urban and western poles meet in the operation of the popular press as evidence to support and bolster the power of Blake's new identity. As the Deacon, Blake "preaches the gun gospel" while singing spirituals and quoting his own homemade Bible verses. Holding both of his lapels most of the time, Blake's Deacon constantly threatens to draw on his interlocutors, as both guns rest just beneath his hands, holstered over his chest under his knee-length black jacket. Blake's machinations as the Deacon coax Barker (the killer and land speculator) and his gang into a trap that foils their evil plans.

Once again urban forms and symbols infuse western life in African American representation. The transportation of a physical body touched by modernity and the city and an urban identity, accomplishes the contact and trade between metropole and periphery that maintains black culture in western space and insists upon the importance of the city to black identity. The western hero escapes to the city, traveling east to find safety in the metropolis. Thus on some level African American representations of the West are not only linked to and supported by representations and infusions of the city, but also refuse to give themselves over to the West as an absolute saving space.

The masculinity represented by Blake's cowboy hero in *Two-Gun* blends characteristics associated with the city, (measured sociability, immorality, and intelligence,) and the range, (rugged physicality, sterling character, and willful independence). With the introduction of the Deacon personality, the origin of various traits gets blurred. The gentility usually associated with the city derives from Blake's western identity. The aura usually associated with the lonesome, desert gunman originates in the city with the donning of the gangster identity. Playing the New York gangster allows for a more austere, removed demeanor, whereas gentle friendliness indicates Blake's true cowboy personality. The New York disguise permits Blake to be more mysterious, fearsome, and cavalier, traits more commonly associated with western masculinities.

Edicts of manhood and masculinity supposedly characteristic of specific places and values implode in this film. Blake is more manly and genteel, while the urban gangster is rugged and cold. Manliness and masculinity are reversed, parallel, and coexistent, creating new models of possibility for black male gender identities. Constructed masculinities associated with place and thus the meanings of certain spaces break down in this film, splitting the mutual construction of place and gender in a representation of nation. If the male body bears the onus of national identification, then *Two-Gun* becomes a figure that brings black urban masculinities to the periphery in a rescripting of the possibilities of nation and its gendered characteristics. This film resists that characteristic of mainstream westerns to construct a certain kind of man to establish national identities and goals only in a certain kind of space. Indeed the blurring of performances of masculinity and of the spatial origins of various characteristics still allows the West to operate as a space of hope and the forefront of possibility, but negates the ideological purity so dependent on clear constructions of male gender roles.

Black performance styles also link the West and the city. The use of live performance within the film bears out the relationship between city space and western space in a manner that shows off the broad scope of black life and experience, even beyond the western periphery. In *Two-Gun*'s opening scene, references to popular city club culture and humor link the western life in the film to popular black culture in the city. The comedian is an implant from the urban revue. Lyrical resemblance to jazz tunes makes western music both familiar and quaint. *Two-Gun* opens with Bob Blake crooning his signature song: "Got my ropes and my saddle, my hat and my gun, *I'm a Happy Cowboy.*" Herbert Jeffrey had been a nightclub singer, and his mellow, smooth urban vocals complicate the country lyrics. He and his backup quartet, the Four Tones, extol the cowboy life.

> You can bet your bottom dollar, you'll never hear me holler
> 'bout my work on the range
> We love to hit the leather, no matter what the weather
> And I know I'll never change
> So when the day is ending with the sun
> A happy cowboy's work is fun!

In contrast to Blake's slow melody, the Four Tones speed up the tune a bit and sing a "zuh zah zu zah zu zey" scat verse. They set the tone for the easy diligence that characterizes cowboy life. Dressed in black clothes with a white scarf and a big white cowboy hat, Blake appears affable and easygoing.

After "Happy Cowboy" ends, Bob and his sidekick, Bill, played by Mantan Moreland, perform a comedic exchange about how Bill can sing only as well as a penguin can fly, but can "cook musical." Bill's chili is just like Cab Calloway's band, "red hot, honey, red hot." He is encouraged to get along and "play a symphony on his pots and pans." As Bob's sidekick and friend, referred to familiarly as "brother," Bill provides comic relief in a vaudeville, almost minstrel tradition. In the "Harlem" series the sidekick is either a gullible "coon" or, as in *Two-Gun*, a wise co-conspirator. Bill fulfills a very urban performative stereotype of minstrel jester that seems out of place in the context of the western.

The Harlem club scene includes a bucket player who tap-dances and blows a kazoo, stringing beats together into a jazz piece. The pretty young dancer Delores performs a short series of hip and shoulder slips and gyrations to a drum-heavy swing tune before she begins to flirt with Blake. A quartet sings a scat harmony. When the bass player says, "Yeah. Gimme somma' that Ethiopian melody," the group sings a rendition of the previous song in a West African tongue, repeating two lines in call-and-response style between the bass and a falsetto soprano. Throughout a member of the Deacon's gang provides comic relief, sitting at the bar peppering the show with jokes told to a table of spectators.

The club scene samples various aspects of black urban performance culture: a folk performer using unsophisticated implements, a sensual dancer of popular moves, and a smooth, melodious, multilingual, gospel-style quartet, each exhibiting different talents than those of the Four Tones, who sang prairie harmonies at the beginning of the film. Each also demonstrates a respect for various performative origins: the folk, the church, the city, and, significantly, Ethiopia. The extranarrative performances themselves perform work of identification in the film as they signify and invoke specific African American styles. The performances connect the West to the city and the city to other locations of black cultural development, creating a web of locations and experiences that insist upon the diversity and specificity of black culture even as it engages and infiltrates the west. In the urban club, while Bob Blake reflects himself as the Deacon, black culture of the West is reflected against modern sensual jazz dance, multinational diversity encapsulated in the black barber shop quartet that sings Ethiopian melodies, and a street musician who has commandeered buckets and other quotidian items for his one-man band. This relationship has its analogue in *The Exile*, in Jango's urban black nationalist masculinization inspired by an insurgent Ethiopia paired with Jean's manly triumphs on the plain. Both spaces expand as reflecting black frontiers of urban modernity, international blackness, and domestic expansion.

It is not just the music, genteel masculinity, cars, and trains that communicate a concern with modernity typically associated with industry and urban space. In each of the "Harlem" series films, a valuable hidden mineral increases the fortune of the poor transported landowner. While gold represents monetary fortune in the first film, the substances providing wealth in later movies are uranium and radium, rare materials highly valued in a modernized society for their use and not just their trade value. Western space becomes a place for the extension and fulfillment of modernist development and possibility through access to important minerals and materials. For African Americans, that hidden treasure might represent any number of liberating cultural or financial potentialities waiting to be discovered, including the value of the Negro people and culture itself.

The Speeding Train

A Pictorial View of Idlewild, Michigan, The Exile, and *Two-Gun Man from Harlem* repeat specific themes and forms of transportation, high-tech modernity, civil masculinity, domestic stability, and the insistence of an urban relevant metropole. Representations of family and romance combine with concerns of property ownership and financial advancement. Certainly the growth and bounded crowding of black belts occurring in the early decades of the century created a desire for elbow room, freedom, and new options for success imagined in these motion pictures.

In these imaginative explorations of the West blacks adopted the rolling steam engine as an image of race, power, and national belonging. The speeding train in these films symbolizes black freedom as part and parcel of modernity and national progress. The train moves forward, and like the technology of film, carries black people into core national ideologies. The visual narratives of expansion replace a southern rural homeland with the urban center in a reworking of identity and ultimately a retelling of migration. In partaking of American progress blacks move not to the North from the rural South, but west from the city center. The speeding train becomes a symbolic hyperlink between a new expansionist American Negro at the urban center and the one at the redefined periphery. Both periphery and center become black, reducing the ideological distance between the two and in some instances collapsing them in an articulation of national belonging. Blackness also becomes centered rather than marginal in an ironic upended affirmation of imperial politics of identity. The films bear the hope of the train. A deep mirroring occurs here in the insistent reflection of subjectivities of space and form.

In these films Harlem as a metonym for black people and culture certainly took the range for a ride, reconfiguring the symbols of the West in a symbolic expression of African American experiences and hopes in the United States. Through idiosyncratic characteristics, such as representing black bodies, middle-class inclusion, the metanarrative of passing in *Exile*, and jazz and vaudevillian comedy in the "Harlem" series, African American entertainers and cultural producers placed their own stamp on the western form. In doing so they anticipated the future of the frontier as increasingly urbanized and prefigured the new frontier that was the internal conquest of technology and of the metropolis. Although the films were racially focused and culturally nationalist, they were also assimilationist in their reach for middle-class gentility and complicity in imperial discourses and perspectives. Thus despite the uniqueness of their appropriation of western representation, African Americans used the West as a space to imagine conservative goals of inclusion and equality within an existing national body. As a result African American representations of technology, the city, and civility imagine the West in a way that was *more* tame, *more* empty, *more* cultured, *more* regulating, *more* technological, *more* civilized, and *more* morally good in order to undermine stereotypes and to establish black fluency in national representations and agendas. Black primitivisms manifested a similar fluency in their performances of multiple overlapping national identities.

2

....

EPAULETS AND LEAF SKIRTS,

WARRIORS AND SUBVERSIVES

Exoticism in the Performance

of the Haitian Revolution

The arresting image of seven black men half-clad, adorned only in leaves around their heads, arms, and waists, staring past the camera, signals the exotic aesthetic of the WPA Federal Theater Project Negro Unit's production of *Macbeth* (see figure 6). In this stage play, wild sound effects, shrieks, and drums surrounded scenes of courtly decadence and glamour. Dance moves by an African choreographer and spells cast by a voodoo priest added intrigue to this theatrical production staged in Harlem in 1936. Two photographs of Rex Ingram as Henri Christophe, the leader of the rebellion against Napoleon's forces in the play *Haiti*, reflect images different from but as important as "savage" dancers. His patient, penetrating eyes and tasseled, heavy, expansive epaulets communicate a noble stature and steadiness (see figure 7). In contrast, a robust, shirtless, energetic warrior Christophe with a sword in one hand and a pistol in the other relates a different sort of virile power and violence (see figure 8). These publicity photos represent the contradictions in the plays *Macbeth* and *Haiti*. Images that might be considered racist and stereotypical when performed by other bodies combine with representations of pride and power. The enactment of wildness and control, anarchy and military discipline, savagery and nobility by African Americans displayed atavistic primitivism and high civilization in the service of domestic and transnational identities. The performances produced an aesthetic of the nation that both affirmed and rebelled against American identity while also abjecting blackness and claiming a black diasporic kinship.

Though different in overall presentation and plot, these two most

6. Actors in leaf costumes in *Macbeth*.

7–8. Rex Ingram as Henri Christophe in *Haiti*.
COURTESY OF THE LIBRARY OF CONGRESS, FEDERAL THEATER COLLECTION

publicly acclaimed plays performed by the Negro Units of the Federal Theater share important characteristics. Overwhelmingly popular, each played to more than 100,000 people, moved to a downtown venue to continued success, and experienced extended runs touring to other cities. Both treated the same historical subject matter of Haiti's revolutionary expulsion of the French at the turn of the eighteenth century. The suspense of both plots hinges upon imperial intrigue, the murder of rulers, and the violent ousting of usurpers. In fact the character of Macbeth in the Federal Theater production was very loosely conceived of as Henri Christophe, *Haiti*'s hero. Both plays offer a picture of black military victory and restored black rule.

Exoticism and violence link the distant location of Haiti, the exotic sets, primitive costuming, structured uniforms, revolutionary plots, and centrality of the black body in these plays to a virile, masculine black racial and political identity in America. Serving as a form of cultural imperialism, the exotic and primitive constructions in the performance of these plays juxtapose contradictory issues of power and subalternity, national identity and diasporic consciousness, disenfranchisement and radicalism, Americanness and blackness. The ways *Macbeth* and *Haiti* imagine and perform the island nation of Haiti reveal the complex nature of the relationship between separate black American national and racial identities. The deployment of exoticism and primitivism in the productions complicates and humanizes the nonwhite presence in colonial and postcolonial discourse by illustrating the capacity of African Americans to occupy a position of both colonial and postcolonial agency. Marta E. Savigliano suggests that "exoticism and auto-exoticism are interrelated outcomes of the colonial encounter, an encounter asymmetric in terms of power. And they contribute to the further establishment of imperialism. Perhaps exoticism is one of the most pervasive imperialist maneuvers."[1] The narrative of black national subjectivity that emerges in the production and analysis of these black plays demonstrates nonwhite people's engagement in several crucial projects to which they are often seen as marginal: American cultural production, the production of a national as well as racial American identity, and involvement in national negotiations of power and ideology on the level of culture.

Modernist uses of primitive and savage representations contribute to usurping cultural power through the process of othering. These representations build specifically on the backwardness of a designated other to assert the intellectual, technological, and cultural prowess of their performer. Thus primitivism and savagery serve specifically modern purposes in the establishment of the imperial gaze of an advanced culture. Marianna Torgovnick demonstrates the reflexive ways that primitivism constructs the invisibility and homogeneity of savage others and also implies a false and inconsistent insistence on love of the other, friendliness toward him or her, that suggests patriarchy more than equality. Torgovnick explains that the uses of the primitive are very much about desire, the changes wrought by modernity, and anxiety about modernity's "displacements and dislocations" wherein the primitivists "project feelings about the present and draw blueprints of the future."[2] In the case of *Haiti* and *Macbeth*, as in much imperial imagery, dark bodies serve as the ground upon which advanced Western civilization is cultivated and produced. Modernist representations often express nationhood and state power through imaginations of masculinity. Imperialism operates as a modern project in the delineation of boundaries of identity and nation. African American moderns performing these forms are not exempt from the power dynamics they imply simply because they were more often objects than subjects of representation. On the contrary, in the hands of black performers primitivism and exoticism remain powerful gestures of national and racial identities.

American Negroes' performance of these images was an enactment of consent to the terms of imperial projects of representation. This nationalist modernism became the grounds on which Negroes both manifested (acted out) and insisted upon (enacted) their inclusion in the nation. *Macbeth* and *Haiti* adopt high-modernist aesthetics and concerns in both form and narrative, allowing them to articulate a civilized American identity. Both plays exhibit a well-developed primitivism and savagery through the performance of native figures from West Indian islands. Yet there is a major contradiction in the use of these forms to actively other Africans, West Indians, and blackness and thus promote a modernist Western imperial masculine black American identity. The bare imperialism of primitive and savage performances — where blackness operates as shorthand for backwardness — breaks down as a result of the presence of a black performing subject.

Casts exceeding one hundred drawn primarily from relief rolls, themes of a crisis of power, the ultimate failure or removal of that power, and the makeup and response of the audience, all position these plays in the tradition of Depression-era activist representation. In this way *Macbeth* and *Haiti* are also consistent with the largely proletarian intentions of other Federal Theater plays. The convergence of modernist and proletarian traditions entrench black performers in a contemporary aesthetic. The themes reflected in these forms become the province of African American expressivity, demonstrating blacks' interpolation in ideological struggles of the moment. I do not claim that these plays self-consciously promoted this entire agenda, but their scenarios placed them at a crossroads of artistic and political movements that allowed the images and performances to resonate in these multiple ways.

Nationalistic Collusion and the Voodoo *Macbeth*

The voodoo *Macbeth* was one of the first plays performed by the Works Progress Administration's New York City Negro Unit of the Federal Theater Project. As few African Americans had technical or artistic experience in the theater, an overwhelming number of Negro Unit workers were nonprofessional. Difficulties casting the show seemed to confirm widespread assumptions that it was impossible for blacks to do Shakespeare. More than three hundred people auditioned. Most had little talent and no experience and were turned away. The play's assistant director described the attitudes of those auditioning as ranging from "deadly earnest" to taking the entire scheme as an elaborate joke. Even with the commitment to high quality on the part of white and black directors of the New York Federal Theater Unit, the idea of "doing Macbeth . . . became a matter of general controversy in Harlem. . . . The community was fascinated but wary: some thought this Shakespearean venture an unnecessary risk, others saw in it a white man's scheme deliberately hatched to degrade the Negro and bring the Theater Project into disrepute."[3] The appointment of a talented but young white man, who had only recently made a name for himself as a Shakespearean actor, as *Macbeth*'s director did not help things. Placing the twenty-year-old, radically minded Orson Welles in charge only increased suspicion. In Harlem blacks did not trust that a white director and producer would deign to work with black actors or treat black drama seriously. Ultimately more than 130 Harlemites were cast in the play, making it a broad-based community event. The huge turnout and the skepticism communicated by some of those auditioning indicate a community that was very aware of the production itself, the cultural environment it entered, and most of all of its possible impact.

Macbeth premiered in Harlem at the Lafayette Theater on 14 April 1936, in an environment thick with fear, controversy, and anticipation. Despite the controversy, indeed because of it, the show opened to an overflow house (see figures 9, 10, and 11). Photographs of large crowds and eager spectators only begin to signal the popularity of this show. On opening night the massed bands of a local benevolent society of Elks paraded in full regalia through the streets of Harlem, carrying two huge, crimson banners that read "Act One: Macbeth by William Shakespeare." Ten thousand spectators arrived at the theater hoping to procure seats that had been sold out five days in advance. This crowd was a startling increase on the more than three thousand viewers who had appeared two nights earlier to see the preview. Ticket scalpers sold seats to opening night several times over, capitalizing on the fervor.[4]

The first performance closed to numerous curtain calls. Black audience members showered bouquets on the principals and cheered for fifteen minutes after the curtain fell.[5] This production even brought the Federal Theater international acclaim, as foreign newspapers picked up the story of the Negro Shakespeare. A condescending quotation from a London journalist of an African American woman in the audience attests to how much people liked the show: "Everybody knew this 'Mr. Shakespeare had always intended his plays to be acted by Negroes,' according to one buxom black lady in a red and yellow dress who watched the show for the fifth time."[6] Despite their well-warranted fear and mistrust, the performing and viewing community enacted its own appropriation of Shakespeare, making it very much their own. Their support heightened the significance of the meanings produced by the play itself. Its images were not random, bizarre, or alienating, but meaningful, exciting, and highly attractive to the communities to which it played.

Ubiquitously referred to as "the voodoo *Macbeth*," the play pushed the modern form of primitivism to new levels by striving to achieve a total theatrical experience. The voodoo aesthetic that made the play black also served as shorthand for its primitivism. The term "voodoo" conflated blackness with a wild, mystical, and dangerous primitive contrasted against Western civilization. Representations in *Macbeth*

9. The crowd waits for the opening of *Macbeth*.

COURTESY OF THE LIBRARY OF CONGRESS, FEDERAL THEATER COLLECTION

10. Close-up of the crowd waiting for the opening of *Macbeth*.

COURTESY OF THE LIBRARY OF CONGRESS, FEDERAL THEATER COLLECTION

11. The audience at a performance of *Macbeth*.

bore little resemblance to actual Hoodoo or vaudun, a syncretic religious practice of spirituality derived from West Africa and combined with Christian symbolism. A fictitious voodoo drew authenticity from this material counterpart that was thought to wield mysterious powers. "Voodoo" became a way to name the exotic, and its concomitant aesthetics a way to perform it. *Macbeth*'s imperialism emerges in form, appearance, and performance. Its extreme aesthetics, exoticism and primitivism, expressionism, high modernism, and crises of masculinity and power repeat American anxieties about national identity and power during the modern period. It operated to empower blacks as national citizens in order to substitute a black or African American subjectivity for a white subjectivity in negotiations of American identity.

Producers originally conceived of the Negro Unit production as a loose allegorical depiction of the rise and fall of Haiti's first emperor, Henri Christophe.[7] Although lore maintains that the changes were the brainchild of Welles's wife, the production resonated strongly with black plays alluding to West Indian life performed contemporaneously in Harlem and the general trend to make traditional plays black by making them wild and primitive. Numerous recently published historical texts on Haiti established a vogue for things Haitian. Langston Hughes had produced a well-received play, *Drums of Haiti*, one year earlier, in 1935.[8] Many of the reviews of the "voodoo" *Macbeth* likened the show and particularly its main character to Eugene O'Neill's *Emperor Jones*, a play produced internationally throughout the 1920s and released in a film version in 1933. Jack Carter's Macbeth was "elegant and malevolent," "the Emperor Jones gone beautifully mad."[9] Consistent with these theatrical trends and exoticized blackness, *Macbeth's* witches became voodoo priestesses and the script was tailored to support a production characterized by action and suspense. The "voodoo" *Macbeth* was an action-packed, fast-paced spectacle in which the very human Macbeth was pitted against external evil forces that drove him to ruin.

The "voodoo" *Macbeth's* plot remained true to Shakespeare's, which dramatizes the murderous ambition of a noble who steals the throne and declares himself king, killing everyone who threatens his power. The play's action begins with Haiti (Scotland, in the original) at war against rebels. Victorious and still on the battlefield, Macbeth receives a prophesy from a trio of witches proclaiming that he will become a higher noble and later king. Macbeth and his wife plot to murder Duncan, the king, in order to actuate this prophesy. They stab him to death in his sleep, blaming the act on someone else. Once he is declared king, Macbeth finds it necessary to kill others to maintain the throne, including Banquo, his friend, and the children of Macduff, a noble loyal to Duncan's exiled descendents. He and Lady Macbeth go mad in their murderous guilt. Lady Macbeth commits suicide; Macbeth becomes dangerously paranoid and is visited by ghosts who foretell his downfall. These witches take on a greater role in the Federal Theater production. Macbeth is finally beheaded by Macduff, and in the final scene his speared head is presented at court. Order is restored as Malcolm, Duncan's son, is installed as king. This resolution more closely resembles later nineteenth-century developments in Haiti, when the revolutionary leader Henri Christophe commits suicide in the wake of an internal rebellion against him. The military and political intrigue in this tragedy proved fertile as an allegory of the Haitian expulsion of a corrupt colonial government. In the Federal Theater version voodoo conjure drives the evil developments. Since *Macbeth*'s plot might have been more apt for dramatization of later internal political intrigues, the revolutionary anticolonial themes and use of voodoo take on greater significance.

With cutting and line reassignments, Welles and John Houseman developed a bare and dramatic script, reducing verbal play and emphasizing the expressionistic environment. The set, noise, pace, and lighting of the show reflected the interiority of the characters in the tradition of expressionism, wherein outward display communicates emotion. These editing and staging techniques reflected a high-modern obsession with action and motion. Innovative uses of space, color, light, sound, and movement transported viewers to a strange world of technologically enhanced primitivism. The use of various light levels created movie-like dissolves and fades, bringing the industrial effect of cinematic technology into the theater.[10] Thunder and lightning, violently pounding drums, alternately melodious and suspenseful music, chants, and the screeches and cackling of the witches and their voodoo chorus pervaded and punctuated the show. Because vocal, music, and sound effects pushed forward each line, action, and transition, each character, including Lady Macbeth and even the wronged Macduff, seemed driven by a dark primitive force outside of themselves, complementing Macbeth's own puppet-like vulnerability to evil.

Beyond consciously breaking the "glib declamatory tradition" in which Shakespeare's lines had of late been performed, each actor manifested a singular rhythm consistent with his or her character. In sharp contrast to Shakespeare's creeping hags, the ever-present witches highlighted the individuality of each character's movement. Asadata Dafora, a choreographer from Sierra Leone, whose troupe also performed in *Macbeth*, choreographed chants and dances for the production.[11] The cast also included West Indians, creating within the production the conditions of transnational black contact for which Harlem was known. Under the sign of an American blackness the play served as its own version of an American melting plot. *African* music and moves in a black *American* show representing a distant tropical *West Indian* locale epitomized the heterogeneous mélange of all that was labeled "black" and "primitive" in modern society. The involvement of these actors and dancers showed blacks' desire for authenticity and budding diasporic connection among (rather than antipathy toward) black cultures with an avowedly African past.

The jungle set was "luxuriant, savage and ominous with shadows where the trees met in a great overhead arch of twisted trunks that suggested a gigantic living skeleton."[12] The leafy costumes of the voodoo celebrants rustled as they danced barefoot along the stage. The costuming naturalized their bodies, allowing them to blend into the dark, lush greenery of the jungle both visually and aurally. In contrast the set of Macbeth's castle was stark and angular, with a high walkway and a dark arched door that suggested the castle's deep interior. The physically alienating, modernistic set of multiple levels and depths permitted creative spatial relationships between the nobles, soldiers, armies, and witches, allowing one group after another to melt in and out of the play's action as if controlled by the space.[13]

Against this environment actors appeared statuesque in regalia based on uniforms of nineteenth-century Haiti, outfits that were themselves derived from the court attire of the imperial French. The same designs were used in uniforms worn by members of the Garvey movement, allowing the Federal Theater costumes to signify the black nationalist ethos of the United Negro Improvement Association (UNIA) and its mass support. The Garveyites "Back-to-Africa" movement sought to found a nation in Africa to which Negroes could emigrate. Black reaction to the Garvey movement was mixed. While many working-class black Americans supported Garvey, the elite criticized his efforts and ideas. Adherents wanted the freedom to colonize an independent black national home, while critics revealed their stake in American citizenship. The differing opinions about national affiliation and identity reflected in responses to this movement infused the ambivalent performances of national identity in *Macbeth* and *Haiti*. The use of French military attire to signify black racial nationalisms in Haiti, the UNIA, and the Federal Theater stage against and through white imperial nationalisms reflected a profound imperial circularity.

Martha Gellhorn, a white reporter for the mainstream press, was taken by the characters' rich and stately costumes. Her enthusiastic review describes a "hot richness" of "dominant shades of red, canary yellow, and emerald green, complemented by the shining boots of the men's costumes" and "salmon, pink and purple of the women's gowns."[14] Each of the nobles' costumes sported broad, elaborate epaulets and angular stripes that accented the stature of the actors (see figures 12 and 13). Hecate, the witch doctor played by Eric Burroughs, a Shakespearean

12. Macbeth seated
on the throne.

13. Lady Macbeth.

actor trained at the Royal Academy of Dramatic Arts, wore a full-length black cape and brandished a twelve-foot bullwhip that he cracked over the voodoo priestesses' heads like some demonic fiend. The priestesses wore floor-length draped gowns and head wraps. Both ends of this spectrum of militaristic and exotic attire physicalized a desire for power. Their presence together on stage dramatized parallels between traditional Western power, represented by Macbeth and the nobles, and primitivized native voodoo power.

The exotic effect was total, creating a "spectacle of thrills and sudden shocks" and depicting "a world dominated by evil." The atmosphere was "transparently illusionistic, a nightmare more than a reality" that transformed *Macbeth* into a "vehicle for expressive form," part of whose voodoo was the effect of the show on its audience.[15] These performative effects, the core of *Macbeth*'s modern aesthetics, mesmerized the audience, eliciting reviews that extolled the originality, sensuousness, excitement, and terror of the "voodoo" *Macbeth*.[16]

Macbeth's "wild," nontraditional, native forms of power, so insistently represented through costume and movement, ultimately act as a demonizing metaphor for traditional corruption. As evil as a murderous Macbeth might be, he is driven by dark and sinister forces, dramatized by light and sound. The play imagines an ambitious black ruler and intensifies his corruption through association with the uncontrolled and primitive. Traditional power becomes more insidious through contact with "blacker" forces. The primitive acts as an abstraction of and metaphor for uncontrolled power. This hyperracialized, blacker than black voodoo also represents an originating source of power, both as a culturally primitive other and as the deeper, naturalized version of Macbeth's twisted psyche. Primitivism in the performance demonizes and abstracts traditional structures of power (such as the aristocracy and the military, also represented by black people in this performance) and acts as an essentialized black interiority of an African American *Macbeth*. The overall effect is highly modern, as a single self-alienated man succumbs to an overwhelming world. An extended scene in which the voodoo priestesses and dancers slowly, steadily encircle and engulf Macbeth at center stage physicalizes this concept (see figure 14). The expressionistic investigation of the human condition broadly conceived radically revises the more traditionally Shakespearean exploration of Macbeth's own personal corrosive ambition. The high-modern technical precision of the

14. Macbeth is encircled by voodoo priestesses.

play's aesthetics enacts Macbeth's existential crisis and contrasts against the equally modernist primitivism that represents his baseness.

The voodoo *Macbeth* capitalizes on the traditional play's foregone universality and on *Emperor Jones*'s abstracted, primitive blackness to position a black Macbeth as a universal character. Shakespeare's Macbeth and O'Neill's Brutus Jones are universal characters struggling against transcendent internal and external conflicts of ambition, autonomy, and rule. The Federal Theater *Macbeth* appropriates the universality constructed through racism in *Jones* for a universalized black subjectivity. When this is combined with the appropriation of the historical event of Henri Christophe's revolution against the French and subsequent failed regime, the imaginative formation that was the voodoo *Macbeth* refers endlessly to crises in modern manhood, power, subjectivity, national identity, and self-rule. These concerns resonate throughout the plot, performance, historical context, modernism, and appropriative relationships.

Macbeth's aesthetics fit into the modernist forms and concerns of their time. The play is nostalgically expressionist and modernist while also being proletarian and activist in a manner that was characteristic of the Federal Project in general.[17] The play constructs an overwhelming natural environment that determines the narrative and character development.[18] The voodoo *Macbeth* displays extreme choices in sound, staging, and characterization which evidence modernist concerns of existential crisis that resonate strongly with postwar American fears about the status of human civilization. Modernist cultural productions represented a conscious break with previous forms of representation, narrative, tone, theme, and form. Each break contributed to the reimagination of human subjectivity, the ways in which thought operates, and the ways civilization plays itself out. For Negro subjects, black modernist form and expression constituted such a break and performed an empowered masculinity and an otherness that established nation.

Always at the center of expressionist interest, man as representative of humanity is perceived as capable of nobility and as a creature that strives for greatness. Early twentieth-century anxieties that fostered these artistic movements specifically concerned masculine identity and male-oriented power. Performed through modern discourses, representations of identity in *Haiti* and *Macbeth* are also obsessed with the male body and male forms of state power. The androcentricity of the cultural moment reproduces historical African American struggles with racial identity that mark the achievement of racial autonomy as synonymous with the achievement of racial manhood and with masculinized citizenship.[19] The Federal Theater plays that dramatized Haitian history used strong male bodies to construct notions of power and invariably focused on the trade of political power between men in the development of a nation.

In believing that man could reach a higher spiritual and moral plane, expressionists sought an understanding of man's noble spirit or soul and then sought to transform society to match this greatness, either through or within artistic expression. Expressionist drama manifested itself in two major forms; one focused on the negative aspects of the present, the forces that kept men from realizing their true greatness, and another looked forward to the transformation of society, to a time when harmony between man's environment and spirit could be achieved. "Expressionist drama, then, usually either aims at making the audience aware of the present's shortcomings, or suggests a program for accomplishing a more perfect future."[20] Later modernist traditions added a layer of a crisis over the split between this vision and desire and the seeming impossibility of its achievement. *Macbeth* exploited the expressionist tradition wherein outward display communicates emotion and worldview. The production served as a vehicle for the expression of human interiority and contemplation of the condition of humankind.

The voodoo *Macbeth* called all aspects of theatrical production—the music, sound, effects, set, costumes, lighting, physicality, and vocal rhythms—into service of a distorting worldview. The symbolically black voodoo aesthetic creates an environment that is beyond the control of human beings and that indeed controls them in the tradition of expressionist theater that exposes the "negative aspects of the present." Power is cast as a dark presence, an overwhelming evil that makes otherwise decent human beings murderous. It is disembodied through the play's aesthetics and overly embodied in the figures of witches and voodoo dancers. Male characters' interiority is manifest in Macbeth's imagining of Banquo's ghost, which appears as a one-story-tall mask filling the set's castle proscenium. The restoration of just rulers and moral right through the execution of Macbeth insinuates a purging of evil.

Performers enact the power to explore modern subjectivity and nationality through clearly and purposefully exoticizing an other. Simply setting the play in Haiti in order to support the use of a black cast removes the play from the familiar and domestic. The Haitian setting, however, justifies the production only as much as Haiti is already defined as different, foreign, and uncivilized. Black performers in the voodoo *Macbeth* participate in imperial projects through the appropriation of extranational cultural forms and the systematic othering of West Indians. Imperial representations denigrate developing cultures by divesting them of civilization, showing them as lacking culture, history, organization, and modesty and shrouding them in an aura of superstition. The exoticism occurring on stage allows the audience to disidentify with the staged action. Haiti becomes an otherworldly location in a reinforcement of national boundaries through the assertion of difference.

The exoticized, abjected, and abstracted foreign space also suggests a universal unrootedness in Macbeth's psyche. A distanced, primitive, exoticized Haiti becomes a nonspecific field for the exploration of universalized modern man. Through this in-your-face exoticism, the focus on self-alienated modern manhood also refers to symbolic crises of national identity, with Macbeth as a figure of American *black* manhood. Since imperial displacement always refers back to the constructing or performing identity, the fantastic construction of Haiti specifically mirrors American identities, in this case the establishment of Negro identities as American identities. This performative substitution of blackness for whiteness reconfigures Americanness as centrally black — a socially and racially resistant move that also assumes and reifies an American national character at the core of African American identity.

Thus highly modernistic versions of imperialist representation in this performance accomplish a kind of nationalist work, as the show establishes African American national identity by connecting it to American modernity. Constructing an extranational other occurs from an inherently nationalistic position. The othered identity doubles as as a field of exploration for a national self through the figure of the universal hero. The "not us" effect of othering aligns African American performers with a civilized, modern, Western identity consistent with their own national origin. Through modernist, expressionist, exotic, and primitive representations, all of which are imperial representations specifically concerning power and the exploration of the agency of the subject, the show becomes a forceful assertion of national inclusion for black Americans in its capacity as a performance of imperial national superiority.

EPAULETS AND LEAF SKIRTS

The alternately carefully clothed and disrobed, specifically Negro bodies of performers play a complex role in this production, justifying its setting, carrying off its action, producing the exotic aesthetic, appearing transparently exotic to some viewers, and performing a masked threat of rebellion. Descriptions that inventory and sexualize the players reveal the importance to viewers of virile male bodies performing this play. Reviewers referenced them as a way to communicate the success and quality of the show. They commented on the *"gleaming naked* witch doctor,"* on Jack Carter as a *"fine figure* of a Negro in *tight-fitting trousers* that do *justice to his anatomy,"* and on the fact that the actors' *"fine physiques* enabled them to wear their striking . . . costumes with uncommon distinction."[21] Martha Gellhorn's glowing review refers to a "frightened and driven and opulent people, with *shiny* chocolate skins."[22] The racism of the reviewers indicates the degree to which the show was not only exoticizing, but also further exoticized through the racist fantasies of white spectators.

The obsession with bodies and the embodiment of the players repeats imperialist discourses that reduce othered cultures to the limits of hyperphysicalized, sexualized, accessible, uncivilized bodies. The sensual enumeration of the players' bodies enacts further imperial displacement through their objectification. That is, these references are also racist in their insistence on the embodiment of blackness as spectacle rather than performance or play. White Americans objectified blacks even as blacks objectified a Haitian primitive in performance. The racism of the reception helps to demonstrate that the voodoo *Macbeth* was by no means transcendent with all of its technomodernist aesthetics and concerns. On the contrary, it was absolutely steeped in its moment, its details digging it deeper and deeper into national imperialist discourses.

The play and the audience's attention to an awe-inspiring, almost fearsome body and strength also indicated the provocative notion that these physically impressive men might actually possess the performative and political power they assume through their roles, effecting a terrific reality that linked fictions of theatrical performance to the fictions of performed identities. The voodoo *Macbeth*'s high modernism, though situating African American performers within a nationalist American aesthetic tradition, was also radically antiestablishment. The wildness demonstrates a serious lack of comfort with tradition and the status quo even as it establishes both. An objectifying exotic becomes transformed into a terrible and titillating threat as over-the-top aesthetics and savage dress, dancing and drums, spells and incantations become symbolic protest, a physically and emotionally overwhelming performance of existential, national, and racial *dissatisfaction*. Imperial representations enact a protest against social forces of evil. The racist form of exposed black bodies becomes a metaphor for political threat and a mechanism for the undoing of racist power as those bodies assume political power. For blacks, who applauded and repeatedly attended the show, this spectacle of black male bodies served as a demonstration of rebellious power and not necessarily (or only) sexual objectification. Power is also appropriated through images of virility, dignity, and nobility. In *Macbeth* (and *Haiti* as well) black performing bodies flout representations that have degraded and excluded them, express radical dissatisfaction with their place in society, accuse that society of being corrupt and morally destitute, and simultaneously demonstrate a desire to undo the paradigms they protest.

While the plot of *Macbeth* bears a less directly allegorical relationship to the plight of black Americans than does *Haiti*'s revolutionary plot, the themes of subversion, self-determination, and ambition speak to black Americans' desire to change the racial structure of the United States and lay claim to the throne of liberty and independence. Although one black commentator castigated *Macbeth* as "obviously missing fire" in its capacity as just "another warmed over white man's play with nothing in it relating to Negro Life," the community's embrace of the show undermines his estimation.[23] The journalist Roi Ottley of the *New York Amsterdam News*, reviewing the production during its Harlem run, applauded its move away from minstrel types and portrayal of the Negro as a "universal character." "We (blacks) attended the *Macbeth* showing, happy in the thought that we wouldn't again be reminded, with all its vicious implications, that we were niggers."[24] The voodoo *Macbeth* was a source of social (and financial) relief, of emotional release, and of pride. There was a sense of inclusion and boastfulness in what the voodoo *Macbeth* and *Haiti* demonstrated black people could do and, possibly, be.

Defeating the French, Ousting America

Tensions expressed in *Macbeth*'s and *Haiti*'s representations and anti-establishment plots echoed African American concerns about the American occupation of Haiti from 1915 to 1934. Although productions of both *Macbeth* and *Haiti* purport to allegorize an anticolonization effort that took place 130 years before, the more recent U.S. military occupation of Haiti presents a more vivid referent. In 1934 the United States returned sovereignty to Haiti. America's behavior over the course of the nineteen-year occupation had been characterized by racism and white supremacy. Haiti's civil strife, political disorganization, and poverty proved the inherent inferiority and savagery of the Haitian people to mainstream America. This essentialist evaluation of social ills was used to justify imperial efforts to civilize that nation in the first place.[25] U.S. Marines had set up a Jim Crow system, barring Haitians from access to facilities in their own country, murdered insurgents martyring a popular leader, and fired on protesters, to name a few more notorious developments. While some of the Haitian elite cooperated with the U.S. and supported the technological and infrastructural development the occupation brought, reactions to the occupation were mixed and became increasingly negative among Haitians and black Americans.

Early in the occupation African Americans supported the American involvement in Haiti and agreed with the goals of the occupation.[26] Evidence from black newspapers shows that black Americans considered Haiti politically reprobate, marred by elite corruption, and characterized by religious heresy. Consistent with the mainstream American discourse of imperialism, African Americans saw Haiti and Haitians as requiring the guidance and patronage of a more advanced, Christian society. After the First World War, however, black public opinion concerning the Haitian occupation became increasingly negative. African Americans became impatient with U.S. political references to the supposedly low mental age of Haitians as well as their "natural" tendency to revert to "savagery," the use of military force to support unpopular regimes, the violence of American soldiers, and the gross exploitation of Haitian labor, seeing these injustices as an extension of American racism. Physical abuse and blatant racism in Washington's policy toward Haiti and its citizens mimicked the more egregious racial policies in the United States.

Black Americans saw in these policies a reflection of their own conditions. They experienced a "resurgent black nationalism," a "decline of the accommodationist outlook," and a "greater prominence of civil rights organizations." Such changes in black self-assessment helped African Americans to view blacks in other parts of the world as kindred and subject to similar types of racist oppression. For many, Haiti became "part of a larger African world which must be redeemed from white control."[27] Though black political power in the U.S. was too weak to halt the occupation, black Americans exercised several methods of protest and intervention. They "wrote letters to the State department, to the black press, and to the President of the United States." They staged editorial campaigns in several black newspapers, attempted to use influence as Republican voters in election years to affect the Haiti situation, and agitated "for participation in policymaking" and research that affected Haiti. This participation occurred on the part of prominent "race leaders" and the black public alike. Black newspapers, including the *Crisis*, the *New York Age*, the *Amsterdam News*, the *Negro World*, and the *Messenger*, criticized American involvement throughout the 1920s.[28]

The American occupation was more powerfully vengeful than the colonial reign of the French politically, ideologically, and economically.[29] Consistent with traditions of protest, lower-class Haitians responded to the U.S. Marines' harsh and violent treatment with insurgent resistance. Revolts and demonstrations, however, were expertly and brutally put down, which further demoralized and abused the Haitian population.[30] African Americans had protested and witnessed protests against the American occupation of Haiti for nineteen years without much power to effect change. Thus in the 1930s the production and support of plays representing the Haitian Revolution of 1804 referenced this more recent triumph against U.S. imperial occupation. Federal Theater dramatizations of the Haitian Revolution continued the traditions of Haitian nationals in the U.S. in the 1920s who "produced theatricals to make the Afro-American community more aware of the Haitian culture" and political situation.[31] Across the Atlantic *Toussaint L'Ouverture*, a play by the Trinidadian writer C. L. R. James starring the American actor Paul Robeson, depicted the Haitian Revolution in terms of a global black radicalism. This play and James's *Black Jacobins* (1938) linked black revolutionary history in Haiti to black interventions in Abyssinia during the Italo-Ethiopian War (1935).[32]

Black representation of a 125-year-old anticolonial battle in the political context of the 1930s participated in Popular Front anti-authoritarianism and antifascism. Black appropriation of the Haitian Revolution to represent the 1935 de-occupation of Haiti makes the protest-oriented celebration of postcolonial freedom particularly opposed to *white* control. Jean Jacques Dessalines, a colleague of Henri Christophe who ruled southern Haiti after the Revolution, ripped the color white from the national flag to symbolize a new, independent republic and in 1804 ordered that whites be killed.[33] Many white Haitians fled to the United States, and Haitian military leaders became self-declared rulers.[34] The plays capitalized on this embedded antiwhite sentiment to signify within the white supremacist environment of the United States.

Temporal and spatial displacement in *Macbeth* and *Haiti* made time and place foreign and imagined, while history was appropriated and paralleled. Maintaining temporal distance also avoided the imperative for any distortion of the interior life of black people that aimed to make black American theater "accessible and palatable to whites and avoided the effect of alienating a white audience by presenting a black social paradigm it could not recognize."[35] This displacement allowed performers to confront "a complex of issues that no contemporary American location could contain."[36] Haiti and its history become a symbolic system to represent the local concerns of black Americans, who used Haiti to express nostalgia, recognition, displacement, and identification.

The portrayal of Caribbean themes and scenes in American theater was not a depoliticized expression or a simple extension of American Negro life. In the early twentieth century black ethnic groups, native African Americans, and black Caribbean immigrants did not conflate themselves into one racial category, and neither did American whites.[37] Therefore an articulation and negotiation of intraracial *difference* occurred across primitive representation. The relationship between black natives and ethnics in Harlem reflected cultural and religious differences and was sometimes strained. While Caribbean immigrants to the U.S. were unable to create their own neighborhoods the way white ethnics did, they often created their own churches and mutual aid societies. Many established professional careers that challenged the position of middle-class natives who had closed ranks against foreigners. W. A. Domingo claimed that prejudice against the foreign-born abounded where their number was greatest, as in New York's Harlem, but identified great "civility and intermixing" in younger generations who were "subject to the same environment and develop[ed] identity of speech and psychology."[38] At the same time that Caribbean nationals faced the same structural prejudice as blacks in the United States, some found that they might receive better treatment from whites as a result of being perceived as different from American blacks. Claude McKay, a prominent Harlem Renaissance writer, resolved to cultivate his Jamaican accent after receiving fair treatment from a judge in an incident of wrongful arrest.[39] He believed he owed the good outcome of his trial to the judge's consideration of his heritage.

Within the black population prior to the 1930s, a tension had been developing between the creation of a black global consciousness and a rampant nativism promoted by elite black leaders. One of the most marked examples of that tension and of differences between natives and immigrants was the native black community's reception of Marcus Garvey, the leader of the United Negro Improvement Association. During the middle to late 1920s Garvey garnered popular support for his internationally oriented black separatist organization and movement. UNIA organizations were established throughout the United States, and Garvey won the support of the masses as well as such prominent citizens as C. J. Walker, the first female African American millionaire and queen of an international cosmetics trade, and Henrietta Vinton Davis, a famous American elocutionist and actress. The black elite in general, however, were not so enamored of Garvey. He managed to find sharp critics in the Negro press and among race leaders such as W. E. B. Du Bois and James Weldon Johnson. Native black critics often cast Garvey as a rabble-rousing foreigner incapable of representing the interests of black Americans. Du Bois described him as a "little fat, black man, ugly, but with intelligent eyes," who was "seeking to oppose white supremacy and the white ideal by a crude and equally brutal black supremacy." According to Du Bois, Garvey's platform "did not represent the thinking of 'Intelligent American Negroes,' for the moving nucleus was black Jamaican peasants, 'mostly poor, ignorant and unlettered.'" Quite often critiques of Garvey problematized his nationality and thereby questioned his motives and credibility. Harlem slogans like that of the "Garvey Must Go" campaign and headlines in Negro papers about Garvey, such as "A Supreme Negro Jamaican Jackass," expressed the nativism inherent in the critique.[40]

The relationship among American blacks, West Indians, and the exotic primitivisms of *Macbeth* and *Haiti* appears even more complex when one recognizes the symbolic weight West Indian bids for freedom had historically for black Americans. The Haitian Revolution was crucial in African American imaginations of freedom, widely rumored as the inspiration for slave rebellions, including the Gabriel Prosser rebellion in 1800. The Harlem Renaissance writer Arna Bontemps had recently celebrated the Prosser rebellion in the novel *Black Thunder*, published in 1936.[41] Figures such as John W. Shaw, Toussaint L'Ouverture, and Marcus Garvey, all of West Indian descent, provided black "warrior heroes" to African Americans, imbuing the West Indies with a symbolic pride, power, and independence in the black American imagination.[42] The symbolic resonance of West Indian heroes coexisted with a profound social ambivalence and sense of national and cultural difference between West Indians and Americans. These tensions facilitated the nature of the performative appropriations seen on the stage.

Perhaps ironically, the production of the Federal Theater *Haiti* included an eye toward authentic detail. Haiti's aural history informed the play's musical director, Leonard De Paur. He based some of the score on Haitian folk music and for a ballroom scene wrote an original minuet based on music of the eighteenth century. During battle scenes a large choir sang songs Haitians would have been singing at the time. Two nights before the production of *Haiti* in New York the Federal Theater hosted "A Symposium on Haiti" chaired by Arthur P. Shomberg, a historian and archivist of black culture, at the Lafayette Theater. A distinguished panel of scholars and artists gave research-based presentations on Haitian history, current social conditions, songs of Haiti, the music of Haiti, and organizational support of Haiti and the play *Haiti*, among other subjects.[43] The symposium put the dramatic representations of the play into perspective. The presentation of the art and history of Haiti in a separate performative venue in connection with the play reflected on the play's theatrical construction of a material location, people, and past. The exoticism evident in the play existed alongside a sense of the humanity of the place and people the play represented.

The complicated relationship between Americans and West Indian immigrants and themes signals layered meanings in *Macbeth* and *Haiti*. The plays' primitivism and revolutionary ethos develop a representational tautology of identification, appropriation, and disidentification; denigration and admiration; abjection and reclamation as black America strove to resolve a tension between local resistance and global compromise; interpellation and exclusion; opposition and assimilation. The palimpsest of appropriated historical themes reflexively signifies expulsion, liberation, and autonomy, whereby African American desires for a future are mirrored in a Haitian past. The imperial nature of the representations locks the performances into cultural and theatrical expressions of power. Performances of power are instrumental in their ability to aggressively assert inclusion (as well as assume or display it) and in their manipulation by performers to insist upon the vitality of marginalized black identities. In performing an imperial exoticism and primitivism African American performers are caught in an unresolvable tension: the claiming of nation in and through the deployment of available imperial structures and the desire to claim international solidarities and disidentify with U.S. imperialism.

Haiti and the Possibility of Revolution

Haiti performs a muted version of formal characteristics of Macbeth, operating in an ideologically similar way to express imperial desire and othering. It goes a step further, however, in articulating an African American will to power by performing direct interracial conflict and violence. Haiti's action and characterizations are antislavery, anticolonial, pro-revolution, proletarian, and pro-black. African Americans clearly identified with the subjects and identities appropriated through a performance of the Haitian Revolution in this play. This identification elaborates the sense of diasporic transnationalism in Macbeth. The performance allowed American subjects to become the politically and culturally independent subjects represented by revolutionary Haitians and constituted a nascent form of black nationalism and diasporic consciousness through a celebration of Haiti's freedom.

Haiti's exoticism and primitivism appeared in its plot and action. Representations of masculinity, virility, and war in Haiti and Macbeth accomplished a similar function. Less concerned with modernist aesthetics, Haiti offered a display of primitive dress, shirtless men, spears, drums, and chants by a chorus of more than a hundred members who backed up the play's central action. Analysis of its performance indicates how exotic and primitive representation permitted African Americans to use these imperial representations to warp the hegemonic meanings of high modernism. *Haiti*'s action-packed, fast pace dramatized the heroic overthrow of a white regime by black revolutionaries.

Haiti's production details render this play a triumph in the interracial support of black freedom and antiracism in America. This accomplishment dates back to the earliest stages of production, with the development of the script. Written by a white southern journalist, William DuBois, the play is a fictional history of the Haitian expulsion of French imperialist forces in 1802.[44] Repeatedly rejected by the FTP Play Readers Bureau in its early form, *Haiti* was originally an antimiscegenation tale, whose main plot line was a romance between the white Odette and the black Christophe. The white director, Maurice Clark, was attracted to what he saw buried within the script: a "raw melodrama about Toussaint L'Ouverture and Christophe and the invasion by the forces of Napoleon to try to destroy the Haitian Republic, the first Negro Republic that ever existed." Recognizing that it "wasn't a good play" as it existed, Clark met with the playwright and convinced him to rework the story. Clark called DuBois "a southerner, a real southern Cracker," who was "very excited about the miscegenation theme." Clark managed to rewrite the play from "top to bottom," until the script told the story of "the victorious Haitian republic over the greatest army that had ever been in existence." Attesting to Clark's dedication to his subject, the black musical director Leonard de Paur recalled, "Maurice was a wonderful man. . . . He used to come and eat in my house and we used to have great philosophical discussions about these people. He was fascinated by these Haitians whom I had known all my life." Clark was "interested in overcoming race and race barriers" on more than an artistic level. Though he capitulated to DuBois's prohibition against blacks and whites touching on stage, he claimed ownership of the encore and placed "the whites among the blacks, holding hands, and that's how they took their bows."[45]

Although several reviewers called for the FTP to move *Haiti* to a downtown theater "where *Broadway* audiences could enjoy it" (emphasis added), with "Broadway" clearly a code word for white, records of group ticket sales indicate that plenty of whites traveled up to Harlem to take in the show.[46] These viewers, however, were not necessarily the middle-class Broadway-frequenting whites the mainstream press had in mind. While these plays enjoyed an incredibly broad mainstream appeal, interracial audiences who also maintained membership in leftist organizations purchased large quantities of tickets though group sales, substantiating the show's embedded radicalism.

Haiti attracted overwhelming support from political groups, including the Communist Party, the Socialist Party, the International Workers Organization, the Anti-Fascist Committee, International Labor Defense, and the Racial Unity League. Some groups made reservations as early as two months in advance for between twenty-five and eight hundred seats at a time. The names of some groups overtly suggest a concern with freedom and a sense of Negro history and pride, such as the Nat Turner Club, the Toussaint L'Ouverture Club, the Harriet Tubman Club, the Friends of Haitian People, the Negro People's Art Committee, and the Negro Culture Group. Reservations from union, labor, educational, and special interest organizations indicate religious, gender, age, occupational, national, racial, political, and professional diversity in *Haiti*'s audience. Records indicate sales to the Hebrew Teachers Bronx Local, the Habana Club, the United Laundry Workers, the Machine Operators, Group Welfare and Social Workers, the Medical Bureau, the Navajos Club, the Young Women's (and Men's) Christian Association, the Housewives League, the Friends of the Abe Lincoln Battalion, the Women's Guild of the First Baptist Church, Cheyne College, and Public School 89, among scores of others.[47] Fully developed cultural front politics of protest in this production attracted radical groups active around resistance and change. *Haiti* provided performers the opportunity to dramatize the political triumph of a common uneducated people effecting large-scale change and audience members the opportunity to empathize. With plots about the contest over power and the death of oppressors, *Haiti* and *Macbeth* permitted a formation between performers and audience around protest. The theater created a space of recognition for narratives of dissent as well as an environment where the more modernist elements of *Haiti* operated in the service of democratic, antiracist, Popular Front concerns.

From a poster advertisement for *Haiti* stares an intent black face crowned in military regalia, glowing with ominous determination in the color of blood. Palm trees rise from behind his adorned shoulders, indicating the tropical locale, and the text announces "A Drama of the Black Napoleon!!" The image suggests the figure of Henri Christophe, the former slave and military leader involved in the revolutionary defeat of Napoleon's colonial forces. The poster draws viewers into the play's dra-

15. The spy Jacques, Toussaint L'Ouverture, and Henri Christophe plot to overthrow the French in *Haiti*.

matic world even before they enter the theater. It illustrates the play's serious themes set against a primitive background which foreshadows Haitian independence.

The play's fictional depiction of Haiti's revolution conflates and confuses the role of key military leaders and politicians and condenses into one battle struggles that took place over several years. This increases the play's drama and underscores its allegorical rather than historical capacity. At the beginning of the play the military leaders Toussaint L'Ouverture (Louis Sharp) and Henri Christophe (Rex Ingram) vacate the castle on the Moreau Estate in the midst of tactical and ideological discussions, aware that a French delegation approaches (see figure 15).[48] They leave Jacques (Alvin Childress), a military officer, behind as a spy. In the wake of L'Ouverture's departure, the stage becomes the province of the French, who claim the vacated headquarters for themselves. White actors dominate the action as the suspense builds over the ever-present unseen Haitian reaction to French encroachment. The staging heightens the effect of insurgency. Through much of the play blacks only appear sneaking in and out of the set's layers. Rex Ingram, the famous black actor playing Christophe, makes frequent stealthy appearances on the set, tantalizing the audience with his bravado and reminding them of the Haitian will to freedom. Drums and chants from the faraway hills subtly increase in strength and volume. The signaling of a primitive threat through rhythm and chants mimics the use of sound in *The Emperor Jones* and *Macbeth*. Jacques discovers that the French intend to reclaim Haiti as a colony and reenslave black Haitians. A sympathetic relationship develops between Jacques and the play's heroine, Odette (Elena Karam), the French lady who remains unaware of her true identity as the mixed-race daughter of this servant and spy.

As the standoff between L'Ouverture's forces and the French drags on (for close to a year over the course of the play), the relationships among the French officers deteriorate. Through dramatic twists of plot, L'Ouverture is captured. Odette and Jacques arrive at a private understanding of their relationship just as Jacques is discovered and tortured. Rather than provide information about Christophe's revolutionary plans or be murdered by the French, Jacques take poison and commits suicide. Christophe sends troops against the beleaguered French, personally killing one officer by hanging him from a tree. In the final scene only Odette remains in the villa, standing near the body of her martyred father as Christophe's troops storm the headquarters from all directions amid musket firing, shouts, and the rising sound of the triumphant "Marseillaise." The revolutionaries have appropriated the French national anthem as their own. In this move they displace and appropriate a colonial legacy and embody it with a new black national identity. With the repetition of colonial forms the imperial past persists in the new culture. A jubilant crowd of men and women in various forms of native dress, bearing crude weapons and tattered Haitian flags, cheer the entrance of Christophe, who leaps over the balustrade at the top of the stage into the center of his celebrants. He makes sympathetic and understanding eye contact with Odette, resolving the show in a mixture of jubilation and pathos (see figure 16).

The play communicates clear support for the Haitian nationals. Antidiscrimination and pro-black, it condemns the racist imperialist attitudes of the French, signified by the negative construction of the primary French characters. Examples include the villainy of the war-

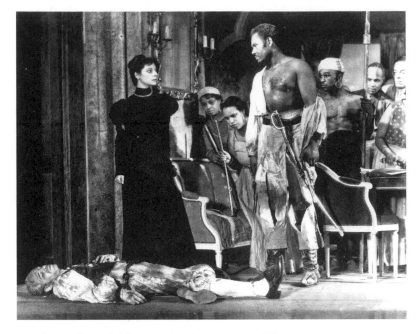

16. Christophe and Odette in the closing scene of *Haiti*.

COURTESY OF THE LIBRARY OF CONGRESS, FEDERAL THEATER COLLECTION

mongering colonels Boucher and Roche, the most racist representatives of the French side, and the self-centered condescension of Pauline
LeClerc, a white supremacist noble and sister of Napoleon Bonaparte.
Haiti performs shades of anticapitalist sentiment in its representation of
a repulsive French greed and materialism. The moral deterioration that
accompanies the race hatred and white supremacy of these characters is
signaled by their physical and mental decay: they become diseased and
insane. The primitivized natural forces of the island thin and weaken the
French soldiers, who seem naturally unable to withstand the Haitian environment. Thus the deterioration exists in the atmosphere and beyond
the control of individuals. As the play concludes, the major white characters Boucher, LeClerc, and Pauline, the most virulent racists, are killed
off, exiled, or lampooned as a result of their inner corruption. Their vulnerability undermines the notion of imperialists as naturally fit rulers.

Haiti's conformity to expressionist methods is constructed less in
form and aesthetics than *Macbeth*'s and exists in the correspondence
between the natural environment and character development as a func-

tion of the plot. The descent into a smoldering, disease-ridden summer and the concomitant deterioration of the Moreau villa parallel the revelation of French imperialist intentions. Similar natural developments correspond to General LeClerc's insanity and dementia. His corrupt behavior and visible deterioration take place in and on the body and reveal corrupt interior motives in personal and national interests. The nobility and greatness of the human soul are constructed through emblematic characterizations of the play's black heroes. This representation opposes mainstream attitudes that assumed whiteness as the racial subject of expressionism by communicating that the achievement of black racial freedom and self-determination constituted part of a program for "accomplishing a more perfect future."[49] This insistence on nobility of spirit was reflected in costuming and performed assertions of subjectivity and a revolutionary insistence on black dignity.

In contrast to portrayals of the white characters are the sympathetic renderings of the play's black heroes: Jacques, Odette, and Christophe. By communicating that Jacques was once beaten nearly to death by the slave master Moreau, the play creates sympathy for Jacques and indignity at injustice from its earliest moments. This narrative move and the actor's decision to play the role with a limp embody the horrible quality of the slave life that Haitians (and black Americans) have escaped. The Moreau Estate as the play's battleground and Jacques's persistent limp remind the audience what the revolutionaries resist (see figure 17). With his decision to stay on as a spy at the Moreau Estate, Jacques risks his life to see his long-lost daughter and to help the Haitian struggle against tyranny. Jacques emerges as an honest, dedicated, and loving father. His double loyalty to family and liberty eventuate his death. He sacrifices his freedom and his life in staying too long at the French headquarters to send Christophe a final battle message and taking too long to convince Odette to leave Haiti. As a servant and a spy, Jacques dramatizes a black performative strategy of shifting and masking identities in the attainment of freedom. His death communicates the high stakes of his identity play.

While reviewers heralded the performances of all of the black actors (the white actors received less acclaim), Alvin Childress received particular acclaim for his portrayal of Jacques. Leonard De Paur remembered Childress as "the linchpin of the whole damned thing. He was a brilliant actor. . . . Childress, for my money, was the man who along with

17. Jacques is humiliated by French officers in *Haiti*.

COURTESY OF THE LIBRARY OF CONGRESS, FEDERAL THEATER COLLECTION

Rex Ingram made that play."[50] Childress recalled with pride the standing ovation the "mostly Negro" audience gave him.[51] In a publicity photo Jacques's shackled hands and soft, pleading eyes beg attention and compassion from the viewer. His resilient, dignified humanity rejects pity (see figure 18). Although the image captures the love and pathos of a father estranged from his daughter, the emotions communicated in the direct gaze of the photograph are more personal than paternal, more universal than filial, and reach beyond the context and content of script and performance. Indeed the image is totally decontextualized since Jacques's character never actually assumes this pose in the play even after being tortured and dragged on stage in chains. Though he never pleads, it seems logical that the most emotionally torn, spiritually generous, martyred character issue the public plea enacted by this image.

The chains on Jacques's wrists, positioned just below his chin and forward in a position where he could not see them himself, speak a bondage that transcends both script and performance. The chains make direct referral to slavery and bondage. The direct gaze undoes historical anti-racist imagery by allowing the photographed black subject to stare back

CHAPTER TWO

18. Alvin Childress as Jacques in a publicity photo for *Haiti*.

and assert control over the viewers and, perhaps, over their response. In this gaze the reference to bondage, the call for help, and the interpellation of the viewer in the plight of the subject are dignified and immediate. The image, like the symbolic death of the character, demands that the audience recognize the humanity of the people and the experience represented and implores them to act on their empathy. The image trades on the liberal notion that empathy and understanding might impact the emotions, ideas, and behavior of the viewer. It also calls for dignity and justice for the contemporary sociopolitical plight of the Negro in the United States. This photograph denies stereotype and dismissal as a reaction to blacks' lack of freedom as it speaks a black racial subjectivity in a radically direct manner.

The play immediately establishes Odette, *Haiti*'s heroine, as its moral voice. Before French colonialist intentions become unequivocally clear, Odette pronounces her absolute sympathy for the black cause. She ardently defends their right to seize freedom and to overthrow tyranny, as the French did in their own revolution. Vocalizing the basic values of the American Declaration of Independence in a monologue, Odette becomes a timid ally of the Haitians and a forceful ally of the American audience. Her sympathies with the strong Haitian characters act as a conduit for the audience's sympathies. Her white and black parentage unites disparate racialized ideological perspectives around a single cause in a single body. Odette goes one step further than dominant American thought as she insists that justice is more important than race. She performs this imperative in her refusal to refer to Haitians as slaves, an opinion she voices to Jacques when he presents himself as a willing servant. Repeating DuBois's initial impulse, one of the FTP play readers' reports suggested that a romance be created between Christophe and Odette, the "Octoroon woman." The play refuses the possibility of such a romance, however, since Odette already has a white husband and a white lover. Leaving Odette in mourning with her lover and father dead, her husband killed by Christophe, and no more than a fraught platonic relationship with the black leader, the play does not deteriorate into sentimental romance.[52] In her decision to stay in Haiti, Odette becomes a race woman and a revolutionary rather than a wife. Her love of freedom ultimately seems a function of her hidden blackness, symbolically positioning an essentialized blackness as the bearer of freedom and justice rather than as a marker of degeneration and slavery. Her white appearance (the actress playing Odette was white) extratextually suggests that whites might also advocate freedom and justice as blacks' allies.

From the play's outset Christophe's dedication, energy, and loyalty to L'Ouverture position him as a worthy military hero. His bravery in infiltrating the French headquarters soon after the soldiers arrive cements this image. The play's excitement builds through Christophe's sneaking and leaping through the forbidden and dangerous territory of the Moreau Estate. Attesting to his heroism is his ability repeatedly to get away with killing white characters, to the great pleasure of the audience. Rex Ingram, the actor playing Christophe, received mixed reviews, however. Liked by many and credited with bringing violence and power to the role with his "commanding" presence and "savage majesty," Ingram was also widely accused of shouting his lines, overacting, and verging on farcical in his enthusiastic physicality.[53] Ingram's "antics," however, acted strategically within the production. His physicality signals a youthful, vigorous masculinity reminiscent of that epitomized by the mainstream actor Douglas Fairbanks between 1917 and 1928. This nostalgic performance of vigorous masculinity, much like the insistent tropes of modernism, capitalized on familiar historical images and performances to establish black inclusion and fluency in American symbols and culture. The star figure of Fairbanks established athletic masculinity as a particularly American expression of healthy patriarchy and national strength.[54] Drawing on this performative tradition, Ingram's energy makes him appealing and unthreatening in a way that circumvents minstrel stereotypes that often accomplished the same task. Ingram dons a U.S. nationalist physicality in embodying a national hero, collapsing discourses of black nationalism and Haitian independence with the movements of an American masculinity. Viewers physically and racially eroticized his Christophe, much as they did Jack Carter's Macbeth. He was described as "*massive* inside a gaudy uniform" as he brought victory "with all the *black force* of his *huge body*" (emphasis added).[55] The universalized hero was central in both plays as a figure of powerful, masculinized national identity. Further validating Ingram's portrayal of this dangerous and violent yet loveable soldier was his recent performance as "de Lawd" in the film *Green Pastures* (1936), one of Warner Brothers' biggest hits and one of the most successful Negro films of all time.[56] Ingram brought calm, depth, and power to a rather stereotypical characterization of "de Lawd" as a wise backwoods preacher. He garnered much attention for his ability to effectively shift between "triumphant anger" and soft "sympathy or remorse" as Christophe. He demonstrated a range as well as gentleness and sensitivity not credited to the actor to which he was most often compared, Paul Robeson.[57] Moviegoers' memory of his benevolent, silver-bearded God served to counterbalance the athletic violence of Christophe. Perhaps that widely distributed image helped to soften the otherwise shocking portrayal of the killing of a white man in *Haiti*, an action not present in the script, but carried out on stage.

Christophe's execution of his military foe mimics a lynching. This event demonstrates the radical reversal in racial power the insurrection accomplished. Within the context of the play and extratextually, this moment dramatizes revenge against the unchecked murder of blacks. Hanging Boucher with his own belt signifies the symbolic turning of a historically white means of racial oppression against white imperialists in Haiti's military, national, and racial revolution. The lynching of the white man enacts symbolic revenge on stage for the proliferating lynchings of blacks in the American South. Toussaint's pacifist power over LeClerc—he stops LeClerc's hostile advance with a mere glance—solidifies the breakdown of racial hierarchy. His summary assumption of dignity and noble self-possession finally undermines the onslaught of violence and weakens white aggression. These constructions speak through the structure of *Haiti* to African American struggles for freedom and justice and dramatize historic and potential means of resistance, including the possibility of violence and the insistence on humanity.

The self-sacrificing surrender of Toussaint L'Ouverture in the interest of preserving "his Haiti" adds yet another hero to the ideologically and emotionally winning set of protagonists. The play insists upon the humanity and moral fortitude of its black characters. These characters, especially Odette, are naturally honest, just, and freedom-loving. Their quest for independence is also natural and organic; they behave as if driven by an innate desire for freedom instead of an innate savagery. This sympathetic set of noble black characters allies the audience with the play's Haitian forces, inspiring full support of its Fourth-of-July-type Negro revolution against colonizing control.

The representations in *Haiti* enact a unique twist on expressionist environmental control and modernist forms of primitive, violent masculine identity. Primitivism and violence serve a protest narrative enacted by the expulsion of the French colonial force rather than a colonial narrative instrumental for oppressing natives. While organization and dignity unify the Haitian resistance, overcivility and corruption doom the oppressors, who are ill-suited to face the rousing energy of the primitive opponent. The beating drums, exposed chests, and bravado that suggest black primitivism also signify white doom. The primitive representations of blackness and Haiti serve revolutionary purposes, as a type of weapon to frighten and overwhelm the enemy, ultimately accomplishing their defeat. The expressionistic aspects of the play that render the interiority and actions of characters beyond their control position the developments in the play as almost inevitable, as society itself strives toward balance, justice, and nobility.

Though not nearly as artistically or socially controversial as *Macbeth*, *Haiti* was one of the few plays that came close to replicating *Macbeth*'s phenomenal popularity. Opening in Harlem on 2 March 1938 it ran until 5 November for 168 performances. In Harlem alone it played before more than seventy thousand people and after its New York run toured in Boston for one week.[58] The general praise characterized *Haiti* as "exciting," "a knock-out," "colorful," "full of movement, sound and fury and in all respects a lusty show," and as having "tremendous vitality and power."[59] Nearly all aspects of the production were acclaimed, including the acting, music, set, and sound. The *Brooklyn Eagle* called the show "beautifully staged" and noted the "fine scenery, enchanting costumes," and "cunning" lighting.[60] Even the *New York Times'* consistently racist reviewer, Brooks Atkinson, raved, "Anyone in quest of excitement is respectfully directed to the Lafayette Theater. . . . Nothing so good has exploded in the midst of Harlem since the racy nights of *Macbeth*."[61]

In spite of the participation of whites in its conception, production, and staging, the producers, actors, publicists, critics, and audience members understood *Haiti* to be a black show. It was performed by the Negro Unit; a photograph of the assembled cast shows only black faces; several reviewers commented on its "Negro theme"; Maurice Clark decided early that this was a story that needed to be told in Harlem. Press releases advertising the play even referred broadly to the "*Negro* struggle for self-determination," implying a struggle for black freedom generally rather than a specifically *Haitian* (or othered) fight for self-determination. As was the case with *Macbeth*, an overwhelming community response demonstrated black audiences' excitement. Their response to *Haiti*'s climactic battles against the French included cries of "Hit him again!," "Give him a lick for me!," and "Man, That's it! That's it!" A reviewer from the white paper the *New York Sun* noted that *Haiti* "had Harlem cheering at the close . . . like a college football crowd watching a long-legged halfback go to town."[62] When interviewed concerning his experience with the FTP, one black actor recalled,

> Uptown in Harlem there was no such thing as a wall [between actor and audience]. . . . Hot emotion—whether of grief or joy—flowed from the stage to the audience and back, in a never interrupted connection. And long before avant-garde groups were trying for audience participation, the Lafayette had it . . . It is a different style of theatre-going, a theatre content that serves different needs than "conventional."[63]

Audiences of Negro FTP plays readily vocalized identification with the content of the plays. The communicative style of theatergoing uptown was an elaboration of the active emotive communication that always occurs between an audience and a performance. In the scenario analyzed by the actor quoted above the symbiosis of live performance came alive as audience members' emotions "flowed" to the stage in a sort of reverse performance constituted by participation. This actor attributes this style to a "content" that served something different than "conventional" needs for entertainment, perhaps the needs of black people in America to see themselves represented fairly on stage and to imagine freedom in this mediated form of racial rebellion.

A white reviewer for the *Herald Tribune* commented that the "*smashing* climax, with Christophe coming down from the mountains to drive the French into the sea, took on *heightened intensity* before a predominantly Negro audience" (emphasis added).[64] The gaze of black audiences raised the stakes of the performance, creating an excitement that affected even this white reviewer. The overwhelming excitement of black audiences and the theater magic seemingly performed on whites who enjoyed the show surely had no small impact on the decision by Hallie Flanagan, director of the Federal Theater, that *Haiti* should not tour southern states.[65] The absorbing theatrical magic of black insurrection against white dominance would surely have had a decisively non-celebratory effect on southern audiences, whose Jim Crow social structure would be directly referenced by the play. This decision confirms *Haiti*'s inflammatory potential, which was generally understood as implicitly threatening to the racial status quo in the United States.

In these two plays embodiments of otherness facilitate levels of performance of identity beyond serving the formation of a nationalist identity.[66] In *Macbeth* and *Haiti* the performance of emotional and political struggles for freedom are displaced to a setting other than the United States in order to project notions of black subjectivity in a hostile American cultural environment. African Americans used the distant locale of Haiti as a performative opportunity to express elements of a specifically black subjectivity. The performances of *Haiti* and *Macbeth* accomplish the projection of black humanity through the reflection of conflict, love, loss, fear, hope, ambition, and sorrow. Other theatrical events from this period, including *Taboo* (1923), *Run, Little Chillun'* (1933), and *Black Empire* (1938), adopt similar techniques of displacement and masking that allow African Americans to lampoon stereotypes assigned them and, by extension, those who believe them. The existence of these other productions helps to demonstrate that none was the brainchild of an individual genius; rather all were part of a cultural formation in which performers and audiences signified black identity through African American expressive traditions of masking and by speaking through and against dominant cultural forms. For African Americans this geographical projection that occurs as part of a project of othering also derived from an emerging diasporic consciousness that was actively fostered during the 1920s and 1930s.[67] The appropriation in these plays performed a transnational connection — an identification across different experiences in the formation of a diasporic blackness. Diasporic identification permitted African Americans to recognize, if not celebrate, the culture of blacks in other countries through theatrical representation even as they appropriated it to reflect their own national identities. This simultaneous displacement and identification produced a means for black American performers to manifest aspects of an interior life and culture.

The achievement of an empowered selfhood through exotic and primitive representation enacts a deeply reflective and ironic cycle in which African American bodies establish black subjectivity through a frame that degrades abject blackness. At the same time, they critique the frame. The embodiment of primitivism refers endlessly (a) to itself as a cover, (b) to the interior life behind it, and (c) to the stereotypes and racism that make primitivism useful as a trope at all. Across representations in the same black play, the same dark body simultaneously referenced selfhood, masking, and otherness. The construction of black subjectivity becomes reflexive in a distorting manner. Even as the deployment of savage types constitutes a strategic reclamation of imperial forms, it also consents to them in ways that reinforce hierarchical relationships of power.

The revolutionary and subversive themes of these plays are particularly relevant to black cultural and ideological struggles against racism and oppression in the United States during this period. The plays explore personal and cultural aggression and sacrifice in the quest for autonomy. African Americans historically denied civil rights owned and asserted power in these plays. As a disenfranchised, disempowered, economically dislocated population, delimited and controlled by segregation, general prejudice, racial terrorism, and legal structural exclusion, African Americans had very limited means to productively express social dissatisfaction, that is, protest and achieve positive policy-based results, or enact national critiques. The same exoticism and displacement that allowed the formations of nation and national identity also facilitated the expression of radical protest in these plays. Elements of the plays' production and reception in addition to aspects of representation further contributed to themes of revolution and protest. The celebration of Haitian independence in the plays forged a transnational ethos of black freedom that transcended the boundaries of the U.S. nation that in one sense was so ardently claimed. The conditions of protest in and around the performances reflect the unique conditions of political expression and activism in the 1930s.

National Identity and Resistance

In the hands of black performers and couched within black performative traditions of masking, veiling, and signifying, exoticism and primitivism become no longer only imperial, but resistant as well. Primitivist aesthetic violence in *Haiti* and *Macbeth* supported the literal violence that accomplished the political subversion inherent in their plots. Blacks' use of violence as social, economic, or political protest in the United States was particularly taboo. Thus the masking and displacement of the plays' violence from the United States proved vital to the actual imagination of aesthetic and literal violence as a means of protest. In *Macbeth* hyperstylized and exoticized violence challenged the status quo. Each element of the production—its fierce lighting, scenery, sound, voices, and staging—underscored Macbeth's revolutionary schemes and his subsequent downfall. The narrative and physical violence in *Haiti* permit the audience to imagine their own racial revolution. The brave and elusive Christophe leads an army in a bloody military expulsion of white colonialists. Add to this the personal sacrifice embodied in Jacques's suicide, and the violence of *Haiti* is not only triumphantly revolutionary but poignantly tragic. The violence speaks both the joy and pain of acquiring a national racial alterity. The plays' special significance to other black artists is evident in the choice of other Federal Theater Negro Units to restage *Haiti* and *Macbeth* after the extended runs and tours of the original productions. Both reproductions, chosen by black artistic directors from the respective FTP Negro Units, had black directors.[68]

The potential of a symbolic and othered Haiti to awe and inspire Americans with its revolutionary power persists *despite* and *because of* its performance as exotic and primitive. The abjection of a violent and violently exotic Haiti removes any sense that this violence could actually exist in America. And yet the desire for power and autonomy gets performed freely and ecstatically on the American stage through a representation of Haitian racial and national otherness. Exoticism in *Macbeth* and *Haiti* allows blacks claiming an American identity through distancing and othering not merely to assert national belonging in America through these imperial representations, but to redefine the terms of that belonging through the very same process of exotic representation. Narratively these plays hypothesize the attainment of full citizenship for black actors and spectators in themes of political subversion in *Macbeth* and political overthrow in *Haiti*. The style of exotic and primitive performance in each bears out this cultural imagination in the enactment of inclusion and rage over its denial.

Black performers' deployment of primitive and modernist elements to achieve the overthrow of corrupt power resonates with the radical cultural politics of protest in the 1930s. The productions' interracial elements signal a goal of racial cooperation and understanding. The use of Haiti as a general symbol for black oppression and resistance indicates the development of a global sensibility toward racial oppression and unity against forms of white supremacy. The appropriations and displacement in the plays also developed the protest-based political orientation of the whites who were involved in their production and performance. The engagement with a domestic and transnational blackness permitted antiracist white artists like Maurice Clark and Orson Welles to protest American racism and global fascism.[69] Racially liberal Americans, including blacks, communists, and political radicals, linked Jim Crow and lynching to the global development of fascism. For Welles and other Popular Front artists antifascism and antiracism were part of the same project.[70] Denning explains that "for Welles racists were fascists," and he quotes one of Welles's speeches as an illustration: "I think that long after the last governments that dare to call themselves Fascists have been swept off the face of civilization, the word 'fascism' will live in our language as a word for race hate."[71] This stance rendered a race-stratified America vulnerable to the critiques leveled against fascist Germany and Italy. The positioning of American racism as a kind of fascism rendered black bodies and culture symbolically and strategically meaningful not just for antiracist artistic statements but for antifascist ones as well. Maurice Clark boldly reversed segregationist edicts in staging his curtain call with white and black actors holding hands, rebelling against the playwright and insisting upon triumphant interracial antiracism.

Haiti as a distant setting becomes a significant conduit for expressions of African American political and cultural sensibilities in addition to broader protest-oriented expressions. Further complicating black subjectivity in the production of these plays, it is possible to see Negroes as also engaging in antifascist discourse. A protest against the fascism of Jim Crow, lynching, and disenfranchisement occurred in the violent exoticization of Haiti and the aggrandized, incontestable power of voodoo evil. At the same time the use of Haiti and blackness to assert an indomitable evil becomes a racialized and aestheticized protest against global political fascism, represented most directly by Hitler and Mussolini. Welles's comment that the voodoo *Macbeth* imagined a mythical realm that could exist anywhere facilitated the possibility of allegorizing the action of the play to some other space, such as the United States. Even as the play's homogenizing and generalizing submits to imperialist representations by positioning the exotic location as nonspecific, it also opens up the possibility that the nonspecific locale could be "home." Thus the high-modern aesthetics enact protest even as they continually implicate their producers in traditions of imperialism. The use of black themes, a black cast, a black location, and black voodoo exoticism combined with high-modern aesthetics to unify *antiracist* and *antifascist* sentiment through the black body. By the 1930s Harlem had its largest

19. South Pacific warriors in full regalia.

black communist population ever. The Communist Party had initiated a nationwide antifascism campaign.[72] Robin Kelley's discussion of the African American involvement in the Spanish Civil War against Mussolini as a response to his invasion of Ethiopia in 1935 attests to the black communist antifascist sentiment.[73] African American performers embodied multiple American identities and desires at once as a result of their complicated position in American and global politics at this moment.

Oddly enough, the seven voodoo men on the brink of action in the cast photo of *Macbeth* remarkably resemble South Pacific warriors in full regalia captured in a travelogue, another mode of imperial envisioning, of Fiji filmed in 1925 (see figure 19).[74] This aesthetic appropriation of yet another colonized population positions black performance even deeper within a system of imperial citations and reflections. The primitive representations reference the self, the self as other, racial blackness, American national identity, transnational black identity, and also the power and exoticism of Fijian warriors captured in a travelogue that records and displays their native difference. Ceremonial warriors themselves, the voodoo men stand poised at a cross section of ideologies, their bodies

EPAULETS AND LEAF SKIRTS

reflecting layers of images, appropriations, and desires. They embody exotic and primitive forms as an imperial appropriation of island identities. African Americans' imperial performance manifests a national interpolation and insists upon black freedom and power. By representing both domestic *and* transnational freedoms in aestheticized, multiply masked, and direct ways, the players (producers and witnesses) appropriate these imperial tools as a stage for transnational looking, recognition, and diasporic identification. Like the collapsing of islands and embodiment in *Macbeth*'s mirroring of the Fijian war attire from an anthropological travel film, when African Americans set their sights on western Pacific islands instead of black Caribbean islands, primitivism collides with orientalism in the collapsing of imperial performances.

3

················

PRISMS OF IMPERIAL GAZE

Swinging the Negro *Mikado*

In 1938 the Chicago Federal Theater radically revamped a British classic in its landmark swing performance of the famous operetta *The Mikado*. In doing so the Chicago Negro Unit accomplished a first in its use of swing music, an all-Negro cast, and an exotic island setting. The original *Mikado, or the Town of Titipu*, written and composed by William S. Gilbert and Sir Arthur Sullivan in 1885, was produced in London at D'Oyly Carte's Savoy Opera House. Formative of complex cultural meanings in its own moment through its performance and representations, the swing appropriation of *The Mikado* reanimated many of the cultural significances of the original *Mikado* in a particularly American fashion. *The Swing Mikado* drew upon and complicated *The Mikado*'s embedded imperial and cultural history through details of production and staging. Tracing the imperial thread west from Britain across the Atlantic into an African American embodied imagination of the Pacific Islands shows how the black performance transformed *The Mikado* in America fifty years later. Joseph Roach theorizes performance, both staged and everyday, as being in a direct relationship with memory and surrogation. Though the meanings of performance are contingent and historical, inherently new in their status as a revival, they accomplish historical continuity by preserving other, older forms. Performance, such as that of *The Swing Mikado*, through ritual and historical inheritance, refers to, substitutes, and embodies something that has gone before.[1] Performance of *The Swing Mikado* in the United States occurred as a result of a transatlantic trade of cultural forms, meanings, and rituals whereby its performance continued, repeated, filled in, rebelled against, and changed meanings produced in older versions.

The Mikado, or the Town of Titipu is a canonical text. The highpoint of Gilbert and Sullivan's work together, it epitomizes their ironic humor about the configuration of British society and culture. Their artistic signature was to make the familiar strange, to turn the world upside down and flip it back again, in a style they called "topsy-turvy." A legal and romantic farce of sorts, *The Mikado* dramatizes a love affair between two already betrothed youth in a society where the penalty for flirting is decapitation. Central to the operetta and its success was its Japanese theme. It was set in an invented Japanese town, costumed in traditional Japanese clothes, and performed in makeup that supposedly reproduced the appearance of Japanese people.[2] While scholars have analyzed the play's aesthetics, social context, production history, gender and class structures, formal attributes, and canonicity, none has specifically understood these details as constitutive of the text's imperialism.[3] *The Mikado*'s imperial orientalism was constructed through its cultural appropriations of the Japanese, romantic subject matter, self-reflexivity, and striving for authenticity. *The Mikado* as well as the circumstances of its performance also reflected national and class identity and asserted British modernity. A postcolonial engagement with any of these issues in the original text and their critiques might fill volumes. However, this chapter identifies the imperial legacy and social continuities established by the operetta to show how African American performers were awash in imperial ideology. The imperialism in *The Mikado* remained remarkably intact in the performances of 1938 despite its ocean crossing and its aesthetic and racial transformation. Along with the opera's lines and lyrics, the Chicago Negro Unit reanimated the imperialism of the show *because* of these changes.

With the performance of *The Swing Mikado* in 1938, African Americans situated themselves as part and parcel of America's imperial origins and efforts. In *The Swing Mikado* blackness worked to facilitate an aggressively American appropriation of the operetta and, indirectly, to extend the imperial gaze across the Atlantic and into the Pacific and Southeast Asia. The Americans who performed *The Swing Mikado* inevitably engaged with the history of the show as well as its charged historical and canonical status, stepping into it like actors into costume, strutting and fretting their hour upon life's (cultural and historical) stage, signifying much.[4] The Negro performers added to and complicated the meanings of the show as they dragged its history onto the stage with them. The appropriation of Gilbert and Sullivan's hugely successful Japanese play positions *The Swing Mikado* to reflect on a British imperial past. The relationship of homage continues the opera's cultural arrogance in its dressing up as an unspecific South Sea island remarkably suggestive of stereotypes of Pacific locales that experienced American imperial intervention, such as the Philippines, Guam, and Samoa. An extraordinarily complicated performance, *The Swing Mikado* animates America's British cultural inheritance, resistance to that inheritance, (mis)understandings of racial identity, assertions of national identity, and imperial exoticization of a newly colonized population.[5]

The Federal Theater Negro Unit version of *The Mikado, or the Town of Titipu* in 1938 consented to mainstream American modes of imperialism as well as an element of protest through the enactment of forms that illustrate participation in the national body. The substance of the performance, the script, and the audience response, as well as some circumstances of production, reveal a certain complacent interpellation of African Americans within the imperialist society and nation of which they were part. This obtained even as little evidence exists of a specifically African American interest in a political and social imperial relationship to the identities performed in the production. The meanings embodied in *The Swing Mikado*'s imperial representation operate concurrently with a somewhat differently signifying historical experience of black internationalism. The history of African American ideas about Asia and the Asian Pacific islands conflicts to some degree with the power dynamics suggested by the performance, demonstrating African Americans' complicated relationship to instantiations of American power. African American performers embodied and committed to *The Swing Mikado*, and thus bodily and emotionally committed to its imperial representations, despite concurrent anti-imperialist sentiment in an African American social world.

The Imperial *Mikado*: The British and Orientalism

Traditional myth holds that the "miraculous" conception of the *Mikado* occurred in 1884, when a Japanese sword fell off a wall in W. S. Gilbert's study. The presence in this origination tale of the Japanese sword as decoration, its falling to the ground as a phallic metaphor of the decline of Japanese cultural power, and its capacity to *inspire* a comic opera encapsulate the relationship of orientalism in the production and performance of the show in 1885. The colonialist operations of orientalism outline the power dynamics in the *Mikado*'s representations. As Edward Said explains, "Orientalism is a style of thought based upon an ontological and epistemological distinction made between the 'Orient' and (most of the time) 'the Occident.'"[6] Orientalism does not require a real concern with Japan in order for representations of the Japanese to relate culturally to them as a performed other. Orientalist representation may well claim innocence of racism or imperial intent and thereby reify the representation as objectively real and its intent as mere interest rather than domination or erasure.[7]

The Mikado, as well as its cultural context and production details, enacts Said's notion that "orientalism responded more to the culture that produced it than to its putative object, which was also produced by the West."[8] The opera expresses a desire to know and access Japan and to flaunt that supposed knowledge in a way that is consistent with orientalism as a practice of looking, collecting, and creating knowledge.[9] This studying occurs without actually attaining knowledge in such a way as to produce respect or understanding, or even a recognition of the oriental other as subject rather than object. Indeed the *Mikado* imagines the Japanese as ultimately different and culturally inferior, "everything the West is not," as a means of carrying off its high comedy about British society.[10] That *The Mikado* was clearly about British society and culture only illustrates the way symbols of the Orient were easily appropriated to distance the Japanese and investigate Britishness.

The Japanese theme derived from both the ubiquity and history of Japanese imagery and culture in Britain at the time. E. P. Lawrence provides a brief history of Britain's "extraordinary rage for everything Japanese," including artifacts, museum collections of ceramics and paintings, and the study of art, literature, and folklore. The use of the Japanese theme in Gilbert's work specifically grew out of a popular sense of the Japanese as ridiculous that began in the 1870s.[11] By 1885 "such manifestations of Japanese culture as were available to the British were regarded by them as odd or ridiculous, a source of instant merriment."[12] Gilbert's own memoirs confirm his sense of the Japanese as "curious, odd, or ridiculous" and having "peculiar tastes, ideas, and customs" before significant contact with the West provided civilization.[13] The non-sense names used in the opera most clearly demonstrate a disdainful attitude toward the Japanese. Names like Ko-Ko, Pish-Tush, Yum-Yum, Nanki-Poo, and Peep-Bo, even the town of Titipu, infantilize the story and lampoon Japanese language, casting childish Japanese culture as lacking development and complexity.

Although Gilbert had first made reference to Japanese culture in an earlier play, the ethnographic exhibition of a Japanese town by Japanese workmen at Knightsbridge in 1884 fueled the fire of inspiration and mockery in the production of *The Mikado*.[14] Meticulously concerned with detail, Gilbert strove to achieve an impressive level of authenticity in an orientalist mode. The Japanese town in Knightsbridge provided a model for makeup, sets, and clothing, as well as behavior. "Geishas" from the Knightsbridge exhibition participated in rehearsals to tutor actors in proper demeanor, walking, and the spreading and snapping of fans in ways that would communicate specific emotions. An elaborate costume imported from Japan for the character Katisha was two hundred years old.[15] Scholars of *The Mikado* mention the building of the Japanese village in Knightsbridge by real Japanese laboring bodies in order to affirm its authenticity, the authenticity of the opera's representations, and perhaps the producers' and play's true interests in real Japaneseness, rather than an appropriative interest in racist representation. Scholars at all critical of the performance see only British fun at the expense of the Japanese without treating the significance of these appropriations as a trade of global power. Rony explains that the exhibition of only "authentic" people and customs from nonwhite nations at World's Fairs and museums confirmed hierarchical ideas about culture that cast non-Western societies as primitive, decorative, and prehistorical.[16] The straight-faced, meticulous performance added humor as well as interest through a visual and cultural thickness. Packing the play with authentic details manifested an appropriative British orientalism of knowing and constructing the East. For contemporary critics and Gilbert and Sullivan scholars, this authenticity improved, indeed made the opera. Rather than being innocent self-reflexive fun, however, Japanese style and aesthetic details stood in for a complex world of Japanese cultural values and social relationships that are made invisible and rendered irrelevant by the spectacular visibility of authentic detail.

The opera's self-reflexive treatment of British culture and society in its music, linguistic rhythms, plot, humor, and references bear out *The Mikado*'s orientalism whereby authentic detail still accomplishes erasure.[17] Critics agree that *The Mikado* does not represent or comment upon Japanese society as such. The opera opens with a proclamation of its falseness. A stage direction that precedes the opening lines in the script introduces the players "discovered standing and sitting in attitudes suggested by native drawings." Arranged thus a male chorus sings:

> If you want to know who we are,
>> We are gentlemen of Japan,
> On many a vase and jar, —
>> On many a screen and fan,
>>> We figure in lively paint:
>>> Our attitude's Queer and Quaint—
>>> You're wrong if you think it ain't.[18]

The stage directions and lyrics immediately make a joke of Japanese culture and British knowledge of it by citing the play's *re*production of artistic representations of the Japanese as evidence of authenticity. The play's characters "prove" they are Japanese by claiming to be true copies of imported inanimate objects—that is, fakes. Like the fan and the jar, the Japaneseness of the play is decorative, a cover of "queer" and "quaint" frivolity for the unfolding of the plot. The stress on the verse's final slang term, "ain't," establishes a British voice in its ironic rejection of audience doubt of Japaneseness and in the finality of its pronouncement of a false truth that sets the terms of the play.

David Cannadine calls the Savoy operas "a paean of praise to national pride and to the established order" in a context of international and domestic turmoil. In and of themselves the plays articulated Britain's "preeminence among civilized nations," a comment "not made ironically" in the operas or in criticism of them.[19] Any critical edge seems relegated to mere joke in *The Mikado*'s imagined world of quips and fakery. When *The Mikado*'s state administrator, Pooh-Bah, says that the particulars of a death decree were "merely corroborative detail intended to give verisimilitude to a bald and unconvincing narrative," he makes a metatheatrical comment referring to the completely insane and fantastical nature of *The Mikado* itself. Any real socially critical content thus remains rhetorically safe, ultimately confirming the British system through irony of its own irony.[20]

Compelling elements of production and context made *The Mikado* a particularly modern play. These details included an upscale setting, mass appeal, savvy use of advertisement and media outlets, meticulous planning and control of production, middle-class respectability, and respect of rank and hierarchy. Gilbert and Sullivan's Savoy operas, particularly their masterpiece, *The Mikado*, had a revolutionary effect on the development of theater in the nineteenth century, ushering in a new era for theater because of its modernity and middle-class appeal. D'Oyly Carte's Savoy Theater was the "most modern and glamorous theater in London" and the first to be outfitted with electric lighting. Carte engaged in extensive public relations, advertising his theater and promoting the Savoy-exclusive duo of Gilbert and Sullivan. The plays were planned down to the last detail on a model theater in Gilbert's home and executed in the Savoy with as much attention. Gilbert insisted that "his words and stage directions be followed to the letter. Ad lib, interpolations, and slapstick humor were absolutely forbidden and offenders were severely reprimanded."[21] Control, professionalization, moral rectitude, honorable associations, and clean humor brought respectability that succeeded in pulling estranged middle-class audiences back to the theater. The phenomenon that was the Savoy Theater began to cement the rise of the theater as an environment that coddled capitalism in its plays' appeal, content, and performance. The operas at the Savoy Theater were harbingers of a new age of middle-class, capitalist ascendancy and control, perfectly consistent with imperialist ideologies of expanding markets and British superiority.[22] This was true of *The Mikado* even though Japan was not a British colony. When the character Ko-Ko declares that "any little compliment like an abject grovel in a characteristic Japanese attitude would be esteemed a favor," *The Mikado* self-reflexively insults the Japanese to comment on British social structure in a manner that parodies and affirms British traditions of deference and ridicules a supposed Japanese obsequiousness — symbolically to Britain.

The Mikado's romance plot suggests a conservative understanding of power through its confirmation of a patriarchal order and the resolution of all conflicts in the bound hierarchical legal contract of marriage. The operation of romance as a trope of imperial desire and power brokering is well established.[23] In *The Mikado* the high jinks that develop in the humorous and complicated crossings of social position, law, and love serve to accomplish the romantic and civil union of the king's heir apparent,

Nanki-Poo (Britain or the U.S.) and his subject, Yum-Yum (any British or U.S. holding), in the preservation of the power structure. That the Savoy plays consistently unravel and then reestablish social order serves as a negotiation of anxiety about society and as a reassurance of its ultimate integrity and stability. Fear for the safety of the established order was the product of an overextended empire and the concomitant threat of loss of control and identity. The production of the operas, which were intensely controlled, copyrighted, and performed absolutely unchanged in Britain for a hundred years, reflects the desire for stability and consistency and the conservative maintenance of the original—perhaps an original and pure colonial metropole. Juxtapositions of soldiers representing the imperial military complex against virginal young maidens' domestic identities or, contrarily, of overdetermined, corpulent, aging women representing empire against honest, innocent young men standing in for a changing political order or perhaps the colonies, alternately "dismantled and reconstructed" the institutions and customs they invoked.[24] To some degree both cultural confirmation and critique existed in the show's formal details, revealing ambivalence about the history and future of Victorian society.

Gilbert and Sullivan's work is not only patriotic and supportive of the British system, but also, and more important, absolutely iconographic of British culture.[25] Their artistic longevity, lasting into the next century, and dispersal across oceans and borders suggest British culture's hegemony as well as its vulnerability to reimagination. Many of these conditions and characteristics were repeated in America in the 1930s. *The Swing Mikado* affirmed and celebrated the culture that produced it through embodiment by its marginal citizens.

Crossing the Atlantic

The performance history of *The Mikado* illustrates America's fast and eager transatlantic appropriation of Gilbert and Sullivan as well as the opera's popularity in the United States. In 1885 the Savoy Theater in Britain raced against the Standard Theater in the United States to open *The Mikado* in America. D'Oyly Carte, proprietor of the Savoy, scrambled to stop one Mr. Duff from premiering a pirated version at the Standard Theater in New York. When Carte sought an injunction against the stolen *Mikado*, a New York judge elevated the importance of the case when he pronounced, "No Englishman possesses any rights which a true-born American is bound to respect." These words echoed the race-based nativism of the Supreme Court's *Dred Scott* decision (1857), which destroyed slaves' legal and human rights and denied U.S. citizenship to any descendant of Africans. In the case of *The Mikado* copyright contest, the New York court invoked the language of white supremacy as a signal of national identity in articulating independence from British claims. British touring companies were sent across the United States while Americans continued to produce their own vernacular versions in a theatrical contest between colonizer and ex-colony.[26] Apparently the effect of this British imperial export was so great in America that "Mikado rooms became the rage in the smartest homes, to be filled with Japanese Knick-Knacks," marking a U.S. orientalism on the rise.[27]

Nineteenth-century African Americans also produced versions of the show. In 1886 a black minstrel troupe in Boston performed *The Black Mikado or the Town of Kan-Ka-Kee*.[28] Several years later a very different set of imperial circumstances, a celebration of the Japanese victory over Russia in 1904, initiated an interest in things Japanese among African Americans. A dark nation's defeat of a white nation in large-scale war seemed the harbinger of a new, more racially just world order. In the first few years of the twentieth century Japanese-themed church fundraisers, bazaars, socials, teas, drills, music, dancing, decorations, and costumes became very popular, replacing "Egyptian, Chinese, or Gypsy" themes.[29] Debates and events in churches and schools where teams called "the Japs" were pitted against "the Russians," as well as newspaper reports and individual accounts attributing the craze directly to international events, indicate a separate cultural formation creating an African American interest in *The Mikado*. This craze even spawned a very popular performance of *The Mikado* in 1905 to benefit the Indianapolis St. Philips Episcopal Mission building fund. The event was deemed "one of the most successful from the standpoint of merit and attendance ever given by the colored people of the city."[30] African American productions continued, as a publicity report for *The Swing Mikado* in 1938 noted that the principals, Yum-Yum and Nanki-Poo, had performed those roles a few years before with the Verdi Opera Company.[31] Many American appropriations of the opera had been performed, and yet no single show has received the broad scholarly note afforded the Chicago Negro Unit's production. Critics find the show surprising, but also a close reproduction of the spirit of Gilbert and Sullivan's own irreverence and distinctiveness. *The Swing Mikado*'s irreverence, originality, and success have drawn comment whether or not commentators have liked the production and, much like the original, without analysis of the specific racial component of its irreverence.

If "Negroizing" and exoticizing the opera were not enough of a departure, swinging it seemed to rip it from the provenance of the British. Swing music made *The Swing Mikado* quintessentially American, trading some of its celebrated reserve and subtlety for blatant spectacle. These two Americanizing aspects of production reinforced each other since swing music was indeed a black form that signaled American identity overseas.[32] The Federal Theater performance seemed to remove the show from the province of the British through its performance not only by Americans, but also by a subculture of Americans whose black racial identity supposedly removed them from mainstream culture. The opera became more distanced from the British by becoming more nationally and racially other. Indeed making the production black in itself created spectacle for avid Savoy traditionalists. Such critics approached the show skeptically and accused it of being a mere copy of the "voodoo" given to Shakespeare in the New York Negro Unit's *Macbeth* before it opened.[33] This complete stylistic co-optation and Americanization of the opera flouted the British tradition by asserting a unique, separate American identity. In a deeper sense, however, this very mode of performance repeated the spirit of Gilbert and Sullivan's *Mikado* in a powerful way.

When the Americans and then African Americans appropriate and reproduce this cultural product of their colonial forebears, they engage with their colonial past, perpetuate the colonial culture by reviving and resuscitating its cultural forms and ideologies, and are implicated in negotiations of power through culture. Performing the fifty-year-old piece produces a relationship of continuity, keeping the piece familiar and reproducing the imperial gaze and imperial forms instantiated with the play's first performance.[34] The memory of British influence, confident self-critique, and self-affirmation echo through the almost ritualistic repetition and reverence of the show.[35] Thus the Negro *Swing Mikado performs* the historical connection between British and American cultures and also a, perhaps oppressive, continuity in its perpetuation of the influence of the British imperial system.[36]

CHAPTER THREE

The Negro *Mikado*

The appropriation of *The Mikado* by the Chicago Federal Theater Negro Unit in 1938 was a sensation. A successful opening on 25 September followed extensive publicity in local newspapers.[37] "The audience at the Great Northern" responded "with thundering applause for every departure from the original."[38] The exoticism of the show's reimagined island aesthetic drew audiences for months and inspired a professional remake. The review in the *Chicago Defender*, "Mikado Rates as Season's Best," described "seven curtain calls," "spontaneous applause," and the audience's "sincere appreciation." The review celebrated the production team, crediting them with giving "sparkling life to a production already famous in music lore. One viewer, a professional violinist, said he could see it three times and still enjoy it."[39] Part of the appeal was offering something new, different, and surprising provided by the show's blackness, music, bodies, and comic forms. Every seat at Chicago's Great Northern Theater was sold out nearly every night for five months. The show played to more than 150,000 in Chicago, making it the most "successful production ever staged by the WPA Federal Theater Project."[40] An extended run in New York City played seven days a week to an additional "64,484 persons" between 1 March and 29 April 1939, in excess of 98 percent capacity.[41] Most performances sold overcapacity tickets to patrons willing to stand.

A distinguished guest list of famous and important figures graced the Chicago troupe's opening in New York. Among those in attendance were First Lady Eleanor Roosevelt, New York Mayor Fiorello LaGuardia, two heads of the WPA, the theater backer Lee Shubert, three New York City commissioners, the jazz singer Ella Fitzgerald, the band leader Benny Goodman, representatives from the D'Oyly Carte Company, and a host of other actors, performers, politicos, and community leaders.[42] The opening of *The Swing Mikado* in New York was a spectacle in itself. It brought WPA, musical, and theater brass, rocketing *The Swing Mikado* to the ranks of a Hollywood premier. It was a place to be seen and recognized, repeating the characteristics of modern mass culture like the Savoy shows in the 1880s. The conspicuous attendance of policymakers and culture makers marks this production as a defining event in American culture and lends official approval and consent to its representations already condoned by the state.

20. Promotional photo of the principals in *The Swing Mikado*.

The Swing Mikado appealed to a mixed-class crowd, with the price of admission beginning at $.55 and topping out at $1.10 ($.85 higher than the cost of most shows). In addition to reproducing the impact of bringing a middle class into the theater, this *Mikado* recuperated faith in the much maligned Federal Theater just as the original *Mikado* did for British theater. *The Swing Mikado* received credit for helping to challenge the "decrepit condition of the theater" in Chicago and to justify government involvement in theater.[43] Where direct federal involvement in the arts met intense skepticism, this performance proved the potential artistic strength of the Federal Theater by raising the poor condition of theater in America.

The show's director, Harry Minturn, described the setting that replaced the traditional Japanese village as an "imaginary coral island in the Pacific Ocean, with probably only one town on the island of Titipu." He added, "In producing, imagination should be used in accordance with the cast you have to work with."[44] Minturn said that the idea for the show did not come to him all at once. In fact an interview with Duncan Whiteside, the technical director for the Great Northern Theater under the FTP, reveals that the Negro version was originally rehearsed as a traditional *Mikado* under the direction of Kay Ewing.[45] During rehearsals the pianist, Sammy Davis Sr.,[46] began to swing some of the songs while "choristers tapped and trucked." From that moment on the "whole course of the show was changed. And it was redesigned and redirected and everything else." The bodies of the players, their performative talents, and the imperial imaginary produced the impetus for the aesthetics of the Federal Theater Negro show.[47]

Minturn summarized the musical changes as follows: "The opera was sung in its entirety as per the original score, but on three numbers, where there were encores only, a stop time and swing orchestration was made." Though use of swing was limited, "the entire tempo of the music was taken at a little faster pace than normal."[48] Choreographic choices also constituted the shows' swing changes. "A Wandering Minstrel" was put to stop-time and tap-danced while Nanki-Poo sang. In the second act the third verse of "The More Humane Mikado" was done in swing-time. " 'The Flowers that Bloom in the Spring' was sung 'straight' for the first two verses, then five encores were arranged for the principals and tap-dancing unit of twenty, utilizing the principals and four couples doing a shag." "Three Little Maids from School" was sung as the

Andrews Sisters might render it, in an upbeat three-part harmony. "My Object All Sublime" was performed as an up-to-date cakewalk. "Tit-Willow" wasn't sung at all but spoken with the music as an accompaniment to "Harlem Lament."[49] The performance became both swing operetta and danced musical spectacle. Afraid that traditionalists would detest the show, Minturn and others on the production team waited anxiously as the overture, first played traditionally, slowly transformed to swing. The "pounding feet" of audience members before the curtain even rose assured them that they had a "smash hit."[50]

A reporter for the *Daily Record* announced that the set and costume designers more than anyone else exploited "the possibilities of *The Mikado* in Swing" by adding "swing to the startling sets."[51] The revitalized stage environment provided a lush new setting that transported audiences to an alternate Titipu. Viewers conflated its softly interpolating exotic island appearance with an essential swing that suggested otherworldliness and blackness. The set and lighting design helped produce the island atmosphere. With "no semblance of the oriental features" remaining, the design provided a "background of ever moving, deep blue pacific waves, the mellow moon and those futuristic palm trees and exotic blossoms put the audience in the mood to fully appreciate the colorful, fantastic and undeniably becoming costumes that combine[d] Japanese, Malay and African ideas in the most artistic manner."[52] The set designer determined that the audience "were to see a different *Mikado*" and "transposed the play" to "a mythical Japanese Island possession, with a note of the South Seas."[53] The lighting was "eccentric." "In color, the lighting of *The Mikado* takes on the feeling of Joseph's coat, the basic colors being amber, blue, red and green." Soft, moveable gauze dropped from the ceiling caught the light, gave an airiness to the environment, and suggested an island vista in the background. "Six inch risers represent[ed] bright coral." "Hidden" among the coral were "rows of lights that changed colors according to the costume worn or mood." While the first act opened with "amber sun rays from floor and spots," the second act was visually cooler, with lights in deep blue projecting "clouds and waves at a sea shore." Trees and foliage made of "dyed cello glass" gave "all a transparency and illuminacy." In the second act the sea was "represented by a very flat stylized wave row" that permitted the "introduction of the Mikado and his party with grandeur in a 26-foot war canoe, brightly painted in Island design, bearing lights and streamers." Drama and technical modernism were built into the set as well as a change of location. "Instead of the usual mountain background which smokes slowly through the old production, there are three stylized volcanic cones which erupt with a great puff of smoke at the climax of the finale."

The costume designer for *The Mikado* tried to meet the need for "elegant, bizarre, and exotic clothes" suggested in the "requirements of various elements—African, Southern Pacific, Japanese. The only apparent handling of the problem seemed to be to abstract them, make them objects in themselves without implications of time or locale." The color scheme changed from scene to scene and act to act, building and becoming more rich and varied. With detailed attention to form, the outfits became more three-dimensional as the play wore on, to the extent of fastening rubber balls to some costumes.

The first act's environment emphasized newness and excitement. Bold bright lights and costumes in simple consistent colors introduced the new and strange place. Deep shades in the costumes tempered the hot lighting. The color scheme in the "first interlude was a brilliant red." The effect of the amber lights suggesting sun-rays and red costumes effected the "hot" feeling observers described. "As the action progressed blue elements were introduced in the costumes of the leading characters. The entrance of the women dressed in white and pale blue softened the rich and heavy effect of the strong reds and blues. The leading man was dressed in lavender, a synthesis of the other costumes," very likely so that he could be found on a stage crowded with fifty chorus members. The costumes made the look of the first act "sharp and cool in color and red, white and blue combination being rather pure." The color scheme of the opening numbers, besides suggesting heat, the outdoors, and red sassiness happened to be the patriotic colors of the American flag. The costumes' shapes in both acts were made to follow the colors. The clothes were "simple in form, following the lines of the human figure and relying on drapery for their elegance." "Stripes were painted on the first act clothes and maintained the two dimensional effect of the first act costumes." The two-dimensionality constituted a mild prelude to the second act.

The second act abandoned the sultry feel of the first for bold three-dimensionality that suggested a total experience. "In the second act the color became rich and shocking with a combination of yellows, pinks, purples and dark reds carefully avoided in the first act." "The shape of the costumes became elaborate and non-conforming. They attempted to achieve interest by their own extreme shapes."

The props used in the show—fishing poles, musical instruments, weapons, and combs and mirrors made of bamboo and wood— contributed to the exotic feel. Four kinds of feather fans appeared everywhere. Tom-toms, totem poles, leis called "Hawaiian garlands" by a reviewer for the *Chicago Daily News,* and lotus flowers completed the island feel. The choice of rude implements and tropical feathers and flowers as exotic dressing suggested the primitivism and savagery of the black, swing island.

The bodies of the actors themselves operated as part of the island aesthetic. Orientalist makeup was used to exoticize the actors' faces. Pooh-Bah's brows and eyes were extended with black liner, as were Yum-Yum's and Nanki-Poo's (see figure 21). The Mikado wore facepaint that darkened his skin as well as makeup that manipulated his features. Ko-Ko and Yum-Yum wore elaborate wigs, their hair standing straight up or woven into a coiled crown. The men's costumes resembled both loincloths and Indian saris, with careful draping around the waist and over the shoulder on some and skin showing through here and there. Male chorus members performed shirtless while women often sported bare shoulders and midriffs. One reviewer noted:

> You may recall that the Mikado opened with a male chorus. It still does. But these male choristers last night were as bare as a platitude, but for a single red sash with a knot falling to the knees. But the laugh was on you when you *peeped* furtively. The girls wore skirts, the girls wore bodices, the girls were tropic-clad only from shoulder to *wishbone*; and in several *ample* cases that was just as well [emphasis added].[54]

The bodies of the players as well as the setting and costumes drew comment in their capacity as exotic island spectacle. This reviewer's description of the costumes facilitated jokes about his desire to "peep" at male genitalia and see more of girls' "wishbones," except in the cases of women with more "ample" figures. Displaying the players' bodies in stereotypically foreign or premodern attire encouraged a lurid sensuality that completed the stock image of an exotic, savage other.

The show was visually rich and appealing and strange. The assortment of styles congealed in a stew of global appropriations and stereo-

130

21. Pooh-Bah in *The Swing Mikado*.

22. Flower-laden female dancers in *The Swing Mikado*.

COURTESY OF THE LIBRARY OF CONGRESS, FEDERAL THEATER COLLECTION

types. Photographs show a motley assortment of turbans and fans, dangling flowers, fringe, and round bouncy balls. Feathers rise three feet into the air out of the Mikado's black top hat. The makeup on Pooh-Bah, Pish Tush, and the Mikado lift their eyebrows and extend their eyes in a strange suggestion of the yellowface makeup used in the original *Mikado*. The makeup on the Mikado resembles blackface in the minstrel tradition. Promotional advertisements feature an ensemble photograph, with Katisha and the Mikado cakewalking center stage among a swaying chorus as wild background. Cartoon drawings of graceful long-limbed minstrel figures with exaggerated lips and limbs decorate the edges. The visual and stylistic effect was one of extreme exoticism introduced at every turn.

The exotic effect created a sense of Gilbert and Sullivan in the modern moment. The poet Dorothy Parker asserted, "Gilbert and Sullivan are not being treated disdainfully. . . . They are being fulfilled."[55] C. J. Bulliet of the *Chicago Daily News* said the show was "as logical as automobile following the ox-cart. They both go on wheels and they both get there." Bulliet ultimately asserted the "naturalness" of *The Swing Mikado*, affirming its temporal and technical relevance.[56] Its modernity was as logical as the advent of the automobile and its reflection of advanced civilization as quotidian as the obsolescence of the ox-cart. Viewers implicitly linked a celebrated Western modernity with representations of the primitive, black movement, and swing.

The blackness of the show was absolutely central to viewers' understanding of its success. The *Daily Northwestern* ran a review that proclaimed, "New version of 'Mikado' has *Harlem-Congo* swing!" The writer described a "South Sea Island with overtones of Japan, the Congo and Harlem."[57] Harlem acted as a metonym for black America and was used to describe the characteristics brought by Negroes as well as the exotic aesthetic to this version of *The Mikado*. The race of the actors was the organizing principle of an overwhelming number of reviews. Many commentators considered not just how good the show was, but how good it was in the hands of black performers.

The cast received general kudos even by newspaper reviewers who disliked the show.[58] Ko-Ko, Nanki-Poo, and the chorus were particularly lauded. Filling the role of Ko-Ko was Herman Greene, the son of a vaudeville comedian who started his stage career at the age of eight in Birmingham, Alabama, and performed in theater for twenty years. The audience and journalists appreciated the consistent humor Greene brought to Ko-Ko. Ko-Ko performed in vaudeville style was effective, funny, and a significant revision of the cringing that usually characterized the part. A review in the *New York Sun* noted that Greene brought "immense and engaging jocularity" to the part, while the other actors' work had "a marked tendency to congeal into dignity," negatively comparing the classic performance to the minstrel tradition.[59] Accolades abounded for Maurice Cooper as Nanki-Poo, a professional concert tenor, alumnus of the Chicago Musical College, and winner of a talent contest sponsored by the National Broadcasting Company, RKO, and the *Chicago Daily News*.[60] "If Maurice Cooper's Valentino aspect and caramel tenor (he can sing a ravishing pianissimo without opening his mouth) isn't the best Nanki-Poo our stage has seen, then the audience is wrong and so am I," wrote one representative reviewer.[61] Other observers commented on Cooper's physical beauty as well as his voice, calling him more attractive than most of the women on the stage. The chorus won unilateral praise as the "star" of the show.[62] "It wasn't the maids themselves, nor the songs (as such), but the fast and manead-like [*sic*] chorus, who do things that neither Gilbert, nor Sullivan, nor yet D'Oyly Carte ever dreamed of."[63] For many, the success of the cast produced pleasure with their ability to significantly remake Gilbert and Sullivan in this swing appropriation.

The shameless borrowing from and mixing of cultural styles that forged the opera's difference gave substance to a kind of voyeurism and international appropriation that was virtually postmodern. The production elements threw together styles in a way made possible only by the development of a globalizing world. The appropriation and performance of these aesthetics, made imaginable and possible by the presence of a black cast, constructed an imperial relationship to the performed identities through the (cultural) production of otherness. African Americans seemed to possess hyperperformative bodies able to carry multiple cultural and national meanings on the stage and, for the audience, to act as a repository of ultimate otherness. Black racial identity and black performance permitted a highly constructed yet totally un-self-critical and sometimes jubilant imagination of the other—in this case an other so far-flung as to be unrecognizable. The performers became signifiers of almost unlimited racial and national identities.

Yet the total embodiment of the images by black subjects requires that these performances be thought of in some other way besides through a framework of stereotype and domestic white racism. Both white and black producers shaped and enjoyed the performance. The black cast's commitment to rehearse for ten months and their refusal to defect to Broadway attests to their sense of ownership of the show. General enjoyment among white and black audiences indicates broad support. Reviews in black newspapers demonstrate popular African American support of the production. The *Chicago Defender* and *New York Amsterdam News* printed considerable promotional pieces hyping the premier of the operetta in those cities. Maurice Cooper's interview with the *New York Amsterdam News* is revealing: "The Federal Theater is tearing down the antiquated idea that the Negro in theater is a buffoon. He has been given a chance to display his ability as a serious artist."[64] Cooper defends the adherence to classic form and relatively conservative use of swing music in the Federal Theater productions (the show "swung" in only three of about twenty numbers) and draws attention to the "folks" who went to see the production ten or twelve times. The *As-*

sociated Negro Press, Chicago Defender, and *Pittsburgh Courier* published favorable reviews that lauded the skill and grace of the performers and unanimously congratulated the show. The *Chicago Defender's* glowing review celebrated every aspect of this "supreme achievement." Using the opportunity of the review to defend the race, the *Defender's* Nahum Brascher wrote:

> One of the true inspirations to me is in my knowledge of the fine ambitions of so many of the men and women, trained in the best schools and colleges of the country, and fitted for the very work they are so efficiently doing, but present national economic conditions had to open this new "Door of Opportunity" for them. These people are not amateurs, novices. They rise to the occasion because they love their work, and because they have the vision of a new day for demonstrating to the world their ability to bring entertainment and appreciation to the American public.[65]

The black press does not mention the exoticism of the show at all. Thus it seems unreasonable and inaccurate to understand the performance only as a series of images assigned to black bodies by a white superstructure, production team, or (multiracial) audience raised on racist images. The black press treated the show as a black cultural triumph iconic of national dignity.

The exoticism pervasive in the design and appearance of the production locates *The Swing Mikado* within imperial discourses in a manner similar to the Japanization in the original show. Exoticism proffers a kind of homogeneity in its wildness that removes specific identity from the exoticized objects such that they barely exist. Thus *The Swing Mikado* can claim to have no material referent. The idea that the South Sea island lacks a location or referent adds a certain universality and irresponsibility to the images that purport an innocence consistent with America's view of itself as an nonimperial nation and of its power as innocent. Rather than subjugate or exploit, American imperialism sought to uplift, modernize, democratize, and, often, Christianize (non)imperial subjects. Histories of violent representation and of American international occupations belie this ideology. Although the exoticism of the show lacks the detail of the orientalism in the British version, the mixture of elements African and Japanese in a tropical setting greatly resembles the "dark" (nonwhite) native cultures on Pacific and Southeast Asian islands. American protectorates in the South Seas—Guam, Samoa, Hawaii, and the Philippines—made convenient and particularly vulnerable referents for this kind of representation. Of course not claiming to represent any real South Sea island, *The Swing Mikado* could use a hybrid racial and cultural aesthetic in an imperial, self-reflexive capacity. The assertion of native wildness and savagery enacted a relationship of superiority and autonomy that very closely resembled the British lampooning of the "ridiculous" Japanese. The American lampooning seems even more directly imperial, however, since the United States actually did maintain a relationship of colonialism, and not just one of condescension, with Pacific Islanders.

Although the changes in appearance were significant, the production team strayed very little in the dramatic structure, dialogue, or even scoring from the original script, seeming to want to demonstrate an ability to both change and properly manifest a classic British play. Echoing Gilbert and Sullivan's performative conservatism, producers used "an exact reprint of the original, as written by Gilbert and Sullivan . . . with one exception (of the harp part specially arranged for this production) and several additions (of introductions, interludes, and a finale)."[66] Producers swung only three numbers. "Outside of these [the] score was sung perfectly legitimate and straight."[67] The exotic primitive aesthetic and swing intensity, therefore, were not allowed to interfere with the script, allowing the show to signify in two cultural languages: modern Negro swing and Victorian comic opera.

A script from a *Swing Mikado* performance indicates only minor changes of very few terms. The concept of swing in some cases helped to transform the language along with movement in the opera. "We are Gentlemen of Japan," became "We are High-steppers from afar."[68] "High-steppers" was borrowed black idiom for a good dancer. "Japanese Marionette" became a "dancing marionette." When Pooh-Bah lists his administrative positions for the Mikado in act two, "Groom of the Second Floor Front" became "Groom of the back stairs," a play on the word "groom" as not a political position but as menial labor and a cutting joke about work available for blacks in service. When Nanki-Poo has escaped after his false execution, he has gone off to "Greystone Park" instead of "Knightsbridge." The song "Tit-willow" in *The Swing Mikado* is about a "tomcat" crying in a tree, not a "tom-tit" (a bird). In Katisha's response the word "hen" is changed to "pussycat." The substitution of "high-steppers" and "cat" trades contemporary jive slang attributed to Harlem for original wording to update lyrics, provide relevance and humor, and "blacken" the language of the play.

Interestingly enough there is no evidence that the word "nigger" was changed. It appears twice in the script, in the lyrics "nigger serenader" in Ko-Ko's "I've Got a Little List" and "Is blacked like a nigger / With the permanent walnut juice" in the Mikado's song "My Objects All Sublime." These references appear as part of the list of those the Lord High Executioner and Mikado could do without were he to actually punish or execute anyone. The "nigger serenader, and the others of his race / . . . they'll none of them be missed," as well as the walnut-juice fellow, refer to American blackface performers common in nineteenth-century Britain.[69] The persistence of this term in the script invites speculation. In the songs the minstrels are punished as cultural offenders. It may be that the term remained because the sentiment toward blackface performance expressed in the songs was echoed by performers who were otherwise willing to change and update ill-fitting terms. Perhaps the point was that the Negro performers were neither minstrels nor "n——s." Perhaps the term remains as testament to the pervasive racism accepted in American society.

The upholding of elements of the traditional performance of *The Mikado* seemed to surprise and either disappoint or please reviewers, depending on their attachment to Gilbert and Sullivan Britishness or swung Americanness. Many reviewers and observers commented on whether the swing violated the show and noted the treatment of the original text and music, commonly referred to as the "straight" *Mikado*. The idea that the original style of *The Mikado* was somehow "straight" indicates the level of difference the swing element added to the show. On the contrary, the tongue-in-cheek, self-jibing, Japanized version had proudly been considered "topsy-turvy," over the top, and not "straight" at all. Since the script remained the same, so too did the topsy-turvy nature of love, law, and power in *The Swing Mikado*, only overlaid with "gay abandon" and "weird gyrations."[70] The opposition between a "swung" and a "straight" *Mikado* implies an inherent lack of legitimacy in *The Swing Mikado* when compared to the *real Mikado*. And yet from reviews and audience responses, it is clear that this swing of the opera's form lends legitimacy to the *American* performance of *The Mikado* that a "straight" performance could not manage.

As with the "voodoo" *Macbeth*, the cast's ability to carry off the original work provided a basis for the appreciation of the changes and even, in some cases, an assertion that the show was *so good* that the changes may not have been necessary. One observer noted, "None of it needs what swing it has to reach across the footlights as a crackling show, nor does it need the occasional rewriting of a lyric. . . . When *unadulterated* Gilbert and Sullivan meets this gifted Negro Cast, something *universal* happens by way of entertainment" (emphasis added).[71] Maintaining the original aspects of the canonical *Mikado* linked African American performers to the *universal*, where "universal" means "unadulterated" British, white, and orientalist performance. Such reviews posit the high quality of the show despite the sense that *The Swing Mikado* violated the immortal, universal worth.

On the other hand, many more observers wanted more swinging and less Gilbert and Sullivan, seeming to bask in the revisionist "gay abandon" that Americanist swing and the Negro cast brought to the performance. "So long as the thing were done it had better be done more thoroughly," one writer suggested. It "suddenly explode[s] into modern rhythm after toying with the limpid coolness of Sullivan's music . . . [then] slump[s] back into the orthodox score for an hour or more."[72] Another writer insulted Gilbert and Sullivan in expressing his desire to see more swing: "Director Harry Minturn has stuck too close [to] the Gilbert and Sullivan version. . . . The audience came to *beat a tattoo* with their hands and feet and only had the opportunity on three occasions. . . . Not only the audience resented the use of the original script as a ball and chain. . . . The *boys and girls* in the cast showed their sentiment plainly in their reaction to the chance to let loose with tap dancing, swinging tunes, and specialty numbers."[73] The "high-swinging" finale number, "The Flowers That Bloom in the Spring," consistently played multiple encores.

Rena Fraden argues that while swing music and dancing confirmed what audiences knew and expected, that blacks performers could sing and dance, the conservatism of the production allowed actors to portray nontraditional parts successfully. Their ability to entertain in an amalgamated form of swing spectacle, comic opera, and multiple cultural identities pushed the boundaries of what was expected of black performance. The originality and uniqueness of the show permitted a "theatrical and professional liberation" for black performers to forge a character and stage identity, feel success, and make a living through art.[74] Since the performative excess was dependent upon black bodies' ability to swing and take swing excitement to the furthest degree in the production of pleasure, the performative excess itself constitutes a high-modern embodiment of a social desire to assert inclusion and to achieve performative power. This liberation for the actors also served a nationalizing purpose for the show.

Meaning Made American

A publicity report announced, "Gilbert and Sullivan's tuneful fantasies have become a symbol of a very English Englishman's ironic humor. But not until the all-Race version of their most popular work is heard will Chicago theatre-goers realize how American their operas can be."[75] The Federal Theater administration and Harry Minturn agreed that the show was *all-American*, though they asserted this by saying that *The Swing Mikado* was not "specifically Negro" in an attempt to publicize its national "universality."[76] *Time* called it "the finest musical in America." A version of the show even went to the World's Fair in New York, a venue for the demonstration of the newest and brightest examples of Western culture.[77] The black performance was claimed as a national symbol and held up as such for the world. In both its public approval and aesthetic details blackness operated as a symbolic structure for representing nation, included and instrumental even as it persisted as an abject other within the same structure of meaning.

In the hands of blacks in America the swing version of *The Mikado* was an imitation and also a significant remaking. This restaging created new meanings even as it revived old ones and made them relevant to a new context. For the most part the swing version continued primary meanings in *The Mikado* through its assertion of national identity, consent to imperialism, and social critique embedded in a resonance of formal characteristics. On the surface the black cast and jungle island swing spat in the face of tradition, yet these aspects also rendered the show a harbinger of quintessential Americanness, echoing *The Mikado*'s nationalist capacities. Making the show black was practically enough to make it American all by itself. Fraden observes that "black entertainers and blackface performance mark the national American difference."[78] The *Mikado* script itself contains references to America by twice mentioning blackface performers, making constructions of race endemic to conceptions of American identity. The Federal Theater's crafting of a Negro *Mikado* and the show's ensuing popularity among diverse audiences marked an insistent Americanizing of the production in a form of national appropriation.

A major element of *The Mikado*'s renewal lay in speeding up certain numbers and singing them in swing. Swing music and swing dancing came to represent American culture in the 1930s.[79] Ideas about swing were charged with questions of morality, propriety, racial identity, national definition, political patriotism, and more. Like ragtime, jazz and swing became national and international markers of American identity and culture. Ragtime, jazz, and swing, as forms of music, dance, and expression, were foundationally African American expressions. America's relationship with swing was ambivalent but irrepressible as jazz music and its concomitant black culture became central to American identity. The artistic modernity of swing was inherently bound up in expressions of American blackness. Together Negro exoticism and swing doubly positions blackness as a carrier of an American modern sensibility. Both permitted the Federal Theater to mark *The Swing Mikado* with a particularly American stamp. Through swing the opera conformed, in its new setting, to the function of the original play that reified national identity. As many critics have argued that only the British could have forged the quintessential, original *Mikado*, only the Americans, with their black cultural history and body of black performers, could have offered a swing version like that of the Chicago Negro Unit. The great irony of a black musical and visual aesthetic performed by blacks symbolizing American identity is of course the marginal status of African Americans in the nation. The conjunction of conservative narrative, aesthetic excess, and swing exuberance performed by Negro bodies in this Federal Theater play facilitated the appropriation of popular swing music and dancing in the service of American national identity and, given the exotic representations accompanying this national celebration, American imperialism.

Swing dancing as an embodied manifestation of musical and social trends packs the political and cultural meanings of swing with highly personal and symbolic stakes. The dancing is popular, public (performed in public dance halls both segregated and not), appropriated, and personal. The frenzied movements shocked and excited onlookers as trembling hands, fast graceful turns and lifts, angled legs, and kicking feet spoke of a society with loose and changing boundaries, moving forward at an unstoppable pace.[80] Like the music, the movement could not be pinned down or defined. And yet the dance would end, the body would tire, the wild pace of sound and music would wear down, bringing the uncontrolled movement, form, and sound under the utter dominance of silence and stillness, a duality inherent in representations of modernity.[81] Modernist representation embraced the landscapes of change in the industrializing world and often offered tropes of stillness and control in tandem with uncontrolled and uncontrollable forces, as in the voodoo *Macbeth*. A photograph from *The Swing Mikado*'s opening performance in New York shows a young white couple dancing in the aisle while viewers in a crowded theater split their attention between the spontaneous audience participants and the dancers on stage (see figure 23).[82] The image emblematizes the relationships of appropriation as well as the social and individual investment in swing that facilitated the understanding of swing as universal.

The moves articulated youth, freedom, power, and abandon that provided a respite from Depression-era poverty and symbolized national hope. In its perpetual newness and its association with youth and energy, swing was mythically American, unquestionably modern, and foundationally black. The development of swing as a national symbol was an appropriation of a black cultural form whereby African American identity was objectified and erased to promote general (white) Americanness. In *The Swing Mikado* blacks reappropriated swing music to establish American national identity in the British opera. Consequently African Americans performed their own racial identity as quintessentially American in an expression of black agency. Swing and its blackness associated *The Mikado* with American national trends and identity. Symbolically this positioned blackness as central to American national identity. The cultural obsession with a performative assertion of a distinctive national identity resonated with British desires to accomplish the same. In its exuberant insistence upon American singularity the performance served as an appropriation of the kind of national and cultural power the British wielded.

The Swing Mikado asserted American particularity and ascendance through specific changes to a British canonical text: complex substitution and primitivist blackness. As a performance of iconographic British culture, *The Swing Mikado* engaged with a British cultural heritage and

23. "Jitterbugs" in the aisle of *The Swing Mikado*.
COURTESY OF THE LIBRARY OF CONGRESS, FEDERAL THEATER COLLECTION

with America's imperial past. As American blacks donned the cloak of the leading imperial nation they entered into conversation with the past two centuries through performance. Enacting *The Mikado* paid homage to the colonial forbearer as a sort of recognition of influence, a direct engagement with a culture that had a formative influence on American national identity. In appropriating a past, the performance asserted the changes achieved by the ascendant present from an inherently retrospective point of view. The *Swing* production team's updating and racial Americanization of the opera manifested this historical and symbolic relationship theatrically. As America replaced its colonial *pater*, the aesthetic and music modernized and reasserted cultural chic. The ubiquitous "savagery" signified an uncivilized, premodern past, the position relegated to the old British version. But then of course it was the system of global imperialism, emblematized by the British Empire, that helped to produce notions of the black savage as an instantiation of a living past in the first place.[83]

The *Swing Mikado* gestures toward multiple performative pasts. Since the Carte Company maintained a strict hold over the performances in Britain, the pirating of *The Mikado* by the Standard Theater in 1885 created an American tradition of irreverent appropriation that was upheld by U.S. courts. The impertinence existed in the perceived *illegality* and the cheek of mimicry, since the American performances mirrored the British production. *The Swing Mikado* continues both a history of American appropriation that ignored Savoy copyright and traditions of American performance of British-style orientalism. *The Swing Mikado* also fits into a history of *African American* performative agency that sometimes relocated and sometimes simply reproduced the show. In a productively reflective manner, the performative irreverence of tradition, form, and origins in the exoticization of *The Swing Mikado* also continues the comedic tradition of the original *Mikado*'s novel dress and topsy-turvy jokes. Savoy scholars consider the Negro *Mikado* a notably extreme remaking because of its exoticism, blackness, and swing. For them the success of these versions, however, indicates Gilbert and Sullivan's longevity and susceptibility to modernization.[84] *The Swing Mikado* formed a part of the discourse of national and imperial identities, both rebelling against and repeating an expansionist British imperial past.

The *Mikado* became *African* American through an uncanny resonance between Gilbert's comedic methods and African American cultural styles of performance. *The Swing Mikado*'s resonance with African American comedic forms facilitated black performers' ability to claim the show. Gilbert and Sullivan's work in the nineteenth century traveled the line between parody and satire, mimicking, and mocking, as did *The Swing Mikado*.[85] Carolyn Williams identifies Gilbert and Sullivan's characteristic pastiche of styles and "parodies of style in recombinant mixtures of disparate generic take-offs, juxtaposed and jostling against one another." Black vaudevillians and writers constructed shows that mixed parody, burlesque, and musical entertainment in a similar manner.[86] African Americans' theatrical and performative stylizing borrowed and re-created forms to forge original material that would compete with and invigorate mainstream theater and please black audiences.[87] When Ko-Ko ceases to be cringing and pathetically foolish, as he is in traditional versions, and becomes Herman Greene's bumbling and deluded vaudevillian jester, the role slips seamlessly into a tradition of black performance that plays upon and ridicules racial stereotypes of the self-important fool.[88] It seems the joke was on Gilbert and Sullivan, as "neither they, nor yet America" could have imagined such a fit. While the repetition of performative styles confirms a Gilbert and Sullivan tradition, the context of black performance and culture simultaneously enacts a near complete removal and reclaiming of the play through recontextualizing its expressive forms as black forms.

In *The Mikado* the Japanese aesthetic became a mask that referred to itself as temporary and false. This aspect of the performance resonates with *The Swing Mikado*'s exotic setting and also with the notion of the performance of racial identity in America as a mask. Blacks perform exotic identity in the opera as a mask that refers to the exotic as temporary and false. For black Americans, performing parody, satire, and a masking of identity carried high stakes in the use and exposure of racial performance as a cover. As blacks masked and reflected Britishness, Asianness, and other racial and national identities on their own bodies, they rendered blackness a foundational symbolic structure for the signification of Americanness.

Racial representation in *The Mikado* went a step further than exoticizing black and South Sea Islander identity with wild performance and odd settings and props. Black actors wore a version of yellowface to suggest stereotyped notions of Asian influence.[89] Even though producers proclaimed the South Seas as a referent and even though colonial images of South Sea inhabitants provided a template for the aesthetic abstraction, the play participates in a minstrel orientalism consistent with traditional performance. *The Swing Mikado* gains performative authenticity for its imperialism by incorporating these referents into its orientalist history. The persistence of yellowface also insists upon the stereotypical misunderstanding of South Sea Islanders as mysteriously Asian brown-skinned people. Black performance in yellowface borrows from the orientalizing cultural power of the traditional British performance. The spectacle of blacks in yellowface trades on the darker skin color of black performers to symbolically invoke an othered Sea Island identity. Racial blackness adds authenticity to this imperial performance as brown skin and yellowface become symbolic signifiers of a national other. Black American yellowface helps to establish an American imperial relationship to the South Seas by assigning it an oriental identity and thus appropriates a similar historical British relationship of power between colonizer and colonized through representation.

Black performers in blackface referenced white supremacist constructions of blackness and whiteness in blackface performance, most often in ways that revealed the instrumentality of the mask. Often this doubling critiqued racism.[90] Black performers in full brown- and yellow-face visually echoed the establishment of supremacist racial structures. At the same time, the possibility of critiquing supremacist representations lingered in the fact that black people had so much experience knowing that facepaint distorts. Their irony upon irony held out the possibility of redoubling criticism of racism, but instead seemed to remove it. The mask permitted a performance of *blackness* as such by providing blacks with a constructing power of the gaze present in blackface performance.

Equally bizarre is the portrayal of the Mikado by what seems to be the only white person in the production, Edward Fraction, a detail completely ignored by critics (see figure 24). Fraction regularly played white characters in Negro Unit plays. One such role was the corrupt real estate agent in *Mississippi Rainbow*, the only white character in a play about a black family. The Mikado wears dark face makeup and his features are exaggerated with orientalist black liner. Though he may not have been racially white, he is the sole player whose entire face is darkened.[91] Against the spectrum of brown faces of the all-Negro cast, whose faces were not darkened, Fraction's blacking up and the use of blackface in general signify (his) whiteness.[92] This signifier of whiteness occupies the most powerful role in the structure of the play.

Fraction's full-face makeup further carries a triple function signifying black, Asian, and brown identities of color. First, Fraction is darkened to fit in with his black American cast. Here the blackface ironically attempts to cover whiteness rather than accentuate it. Second, the yellowface accents riff on the orientalist Japanese-ism of the British that along with the makeup on the black actors incorporates aspects of that orientalism into an American tradition. Third, together both constitute Fraction's brownface through which he performs an Islander other. The multiple meanings of this darkening dramatize the layers of racial performance occurring in *The Swing Mikado*.

Negative cultural references to Japan technically are more directly racist in an African American performance of *The Mikado* since they are forced to reference Japan proper and not British or American culture. The condescending relationship is direct and no longer laboriously self-reflective. The word "Japan," though it could easily be substituted with

24. The Mikado in blackface with Katisha in *The Swing Mikado*.

"the land" or "the island" in a rhyme scheme, often was not. When the British Ko-Ko requests "an abject grovel in characteristic Japanese attitude," the joke makes fun of a Japanese cultural characteristic and also derives humor from a recognition that the Japanese would never say this, so that it also satirizes British understanding of Japanese culture in a double entendre. Japanese culture was copied and borrowed in detail to make fun of British fascination with Japan and to pull off the elaborate (ultimately condescending) joke of the British pretending to be Japanese. It is an arrogant joke regardless of the fact that on some level the joke is on the British. *The Swing Mikado*'s island aesthetic removes any irony from the use of the words "Japan" and "Japanese" in all remaining jibes that worked with the hyper-Japanization of the original.[93] Other jokers refer to girls' "artless Japanese way" and their coming of age at fifty. Some lines repeat or make up Japanese words in *The Swing Mikado* performance, retaining the ridicule of Japanese language. These references to Japan—positive, negative, and neutral—in the script preserve an echo of a Japanese presence in this representational melee.

The script of *The Swing Mikado* announces itself as a fake copy or imagined creation of its culture. The swung version refers to "the high-steppers of afar" instead of "gentlemen of Japan," appearing on "vase and jar, screen and *star*," instead of "fan." The displaced references to Japan and an island aesthetic do not operate, however, in quite the same ironic way in American culture with African American performers as Japanese references did in the thickly orientalist performance of the British. To be similarly ironic, the representations might make fun of the dominant culture's (U.S.) interest in the exotic, the culture of exoticism, or interest in the exoticized culture in question. But there is no solid referent, so each of these models fails to make the jokes in the text ironic or even sensible. The jokes become slurs on the Japanese, where "Japan" is not changed and where the exotic culture suggested by the setting and bizarre aesthetics fails to substitute as its own slurred referent. Part of the difference here resides in the different ways orientalism and exoticism operate in culture. Orientalism cultivates knowledge in order to produce identities and power relationships. The original *Mikado*'s careful re-creation of the Japanese performs the Occident's production of itself by imagining an Orient. But the exotic distorts and abstracts, eschewing specifics and producing a reflexive identity through *lack* of substance in the other, not *fullness* of substance in the other. Only the produced self obtains any sort of fullness in this practice of exoticization. The possibility for irony and self-critique is low in a modernist expression of exoticism that emphasizes homogenization and generalized abstraction of others over specifics in representation.[94] The Federal Theater performers carried the show's significations westward. It is difficult to determine whether they served as stepping stones, emissaries, or craftsmen of an imperial culture on the move. In any case they performed the role of conduit for cultural change and developing American sensibilities of cultural selfhood and cultural power. Cast support of the production gestures toward blacks' performative consent to the imperial implications of *The Swing Mikado*'s exoticism.

While it is almost never possible to confirm the existence or level of performers' commitment to the ways representations operated in culture, historical evidence does demonstrate the performers' commitment to *The Swing Mikado* and their performance of it. During the show's Chicago run, a controversy developed over whether *The Swing Mikado* would be sold to a private producer. Attempts by the regional and state director of the Federal Theater Project, John McGee, to effect the private production of the show without the knowledge of the local theater or the show's participants precipitated his dismissal.[95] Before being fired McGee tricked the principals and a few chorus members into signing exploitive contracts for his private venture that made the principals seem disloyal. Performers left out of the private option accused those who signed contracts of being selfish in thinking about themselves and not the (more important) whole. It was clear that after ten months of rehearsal, without the principals *The Swing Mikado* would close with an unlikely reopening, leaving all without work. During an administrative summit between the actors and staff both sides expressed loyalty to each other and to the show. Though deep misunderstanding threatened to divide the cast, the actors were enthusiastic and insistent about continuing the Federal Theater production. Herman Greene, one of the principals likely to have signed a contract, declared that he was "100% behind Minturn and the show."[96] In a demonstration of devotion and faith in the success of the show and the good intentions of the Federal Theater administration, the entire cast stayed on with the Chicago production in the face of at least three simultaneous ventures to option the uncopyrighted show. The continuation of the show demonstrates a sense of fidelity, dedication to craft, value of invested time and the success of the work, and embodied commitment to continue the show's imperialist representations.

Michael Todd, however, a private producer who spent considerable time in the audience, was thrown out of the backstage wings several times as he copied the show for his own commercial production. The Todd production demonstrates the indomitable popularity of the show, but more important, it illustrates the ways the cultural possibilities for Negro adaptation fueled concepts of American modernity, further positioning black bodies and cultural production as symbolic of a sense of American identity. The competition between the shows to get to New York resembled the Savoy-Standard race in 1885. Todd's *"Hot"* *Mikado* opened in April, during *The Swing Mikado*'s second month in New York.[97] Later, when the original *Swing Mikado* was finally optioned commercially, it opened with the original cast on 1 May 1939 directly across from *The Hot Mikado* on Forty-fourth Street in New York before touring the U.S.[98] *The Swing Mikado* and *The Hot Mikado* played opposite each other for six weeks, the entire run of the *Hot Mikado* production only matching the commercial *Swing Mikado*'s New York tenure. While on Broadway soloists and chorus members of *The Swing Mikado* participated in *The Magic Key* radio program on NBC's Blue Network. Cast members performed three songs live, allowing the FTP show to cross media from stage performance to modern mass-mediated performance.[99] *The Swing Mikado*'s musical and dramatic faithfulness to the original became even more obvious when a pirated version made its appearance on Broadway. *The Hot Mikado* did not relocate *The Mikado* from Japan, but modernized, jazzed up, and swung it without reservation. The cast of this show was not classically trained, but was significantly more famous than the Chicago set. Bill "Bojangles" Robinson played the Mikado and "tapped the second act into oblivion" along with dancing Lindy-hoppers borrowed from New York's Savoy Ballroom.[100] In appearance and rhythm *The Hot Mikado* reeked modernity, making use of the latest fashions in clothing, designs and prints, aesthetics, and performative styles. It helped prove the commercial viability of black theater and the popularity of black performers and provided what mainstream theater often offered: a choice of Gilbert and Sullivan productions.[101]

Less exoticizing than highly modern, wild, and randomly oriental, this remaking demonstrates another possibility for modernization and

149

Negroization inspired by Americanization and a black cast. For its slick modernity, *The Hot Mikado* played in the Hall of Music at the New York World's Fair, a venue for the demonstration of the newest and brightest examples of Western culture.[102] By comparison, the Federal Theater goal not to change the play too much evidences the strong sense of conservatism brought on by the question of what the federal bureaucratic structure deemed appropriate for black theater and its general audiences. The brand of exoticization demonstrated in *The Swing Mikado* becomes a mainstreamed, almost mundane tool for abstracting black and othered identities, as it appears almost conservative when compared to the more modernist and extreme *Hot Mikado*. The process of using blackness as a template for abstraction indicates a cultural comfort and arrogance with exoticism akin to the British impulse to make *The Mikado* Japanese in the first place.

Invading the Pacific: Embodying Imperialism

The relationship between representations of otherness in *The Swing Mikado* and the imperial perspective and behavior of African Americans as national citizens is complicated and in some ways contradictory. The language of the play and its aesthetics link African Americans to discourses of American international power. The imperial meanings of the show's form articulated African American national inclusion, cultural fluency, and interpolation in hegemonic discourses of American identity. The American attitude toward empire and its justification eschewed specifics and verisimilitude, producing interest within the performance through its claim to represent nothing true or material. An exoticizing of representations of Gilbert and Sullivan concepts of the oriental occurs here, filtered through an American racism that conflated othered identities and purposefully distorted the object.

The Swing Mikado's construction of a tropical island is far-flung and ambiguous, exhibiting an assumption of an alternate sensibility through the complete imaginative construction of a fictive other. The constructed imaginary other supposedly does not exist at all. However, the elements and appearance of *The Swing Mikado*, produced in this same fully imagined manner, uncannily suggest a figment of American imperial victimization in the Pacific. *The Swing Mikado* adopts characteristics of imperialism that abstract the identity of the performed other, enacting an American sensibility that insisted on the lack of culture in imperial lands.[103] Fanon writes, "Colonial domination, because it is total and tends to over-simplify, very soon manages to disrupt in spectacular fashion the cultural life of a conquered people. This cultural obliteration is made possible by the negation of national reality."[104] *The Swing Mikado* symbolically obliterates its referents through their putative nonexistence. The discourse of paternalism constructed disorganization and infantile dependence in the colonized society, sustained by an abstraction and exoticism that insisted on the othered culture as empty and in need of civilization. The vulnerability to imperialism existing in the lack of culture tautologically signifies a need for the Western imperial presence.[105]

The Swing Mikado's strange South Seas costumes and sets, swing dances, and exposed bodies came together to produce an unspecific, loosely imagined island. These representations abandoned the notion of a meticulously copied and reproduced other. The broad cultural abstraction of the sea off the coast of the U.S. mainland and the island holdings there mystify, conflate, and fictionalize the identity of whoever might exist over the coastal edge. A black island might be somewhat West Indian, a South Sea island might be South American; throw it further east (though geographically west), closer to the original Japanese aesthetic, and an exotic oriental influence reappears. The performance evoked a plethora of national and ethnic descriptors referencing native people layered upon the American label "Negro." In reviews, press releases, observations, and colloquialisms these included "Africa," "Congo," "Harlem," "Malaysia," "Samoa," "Hawaii," "Ethiopia," "Banda," "Bali," "Celebes," "coolie," "Japan," "Pacific," "tropic," "native," "Covarrubias," and "Zamboango." The aesthetics rejected classification in a manner that also blithely rejected responsibility for the cultures distorted by the show. The arrogance of "unspecificity" mirrors the colonial impulse to settle, civilize, and erase the "savage" and "ridiculous" cultures of imperial holdings as abstract and unimportant, if not nonexistent. The representations in the performance mixed stereotypes heaped upon the tropical or South Sea islands in a manner reminiscent of American colonial holdings such as the Philippines, Guam, Samoa, or Puerto Rico, though they still failed to invoke a specific colonial location. Michael Salman critiques claims to "inadvertent" imperialism characterized by benevolence and innocence that have supported and justified American colonial and imperial ventures since the turn of the century.[106] The same inadvertence of American empire suffuses these imperial representations. The operation of power resides in the exotic abstraction that suggests but fails to specify a referent that does not ultimately matter.

The Philippines in particular were considered the Pacific frontier of American manifest destiny, the next western post for expansion and the development of American empire.[107] Americans understood the inhabitants of these Southeast Asian islands as alternately Asian, black, or native islander, and assigned the stereotypes of each at different moments. The borrowing and conflation of racist terms in the description of colonial subjects suffused the articulation of empire. The archipelago was often understood as an oriental nation with "dark" natives and a multiracial past. Official understandings of the people incorporated notions of oriental duplicity, native childliness, feminization, and savage jungle lawlessness and lack of civilization.[108] While conjuring up a Japanese island holding, the production of *The Swing Mikado* looked more like travel, census, and ethnographic photographs and stereotypes of a U.S. island holding in the Pacific.[109] By 1938 the U.S. had officially held and occupied the Philippines for nearly forty years. The intended American purchase and eventual conquest of that island facilitated the trade of images of people that did not fit into an American racial structure despite efforts to quantify difference and designate racial and cultural identity.[110] Early twentieth-century Americans saw a vaguely hybrid savage oriental culture in the Philippines, one incorporating shades of "brown, black, and yellow," physical descriptions reproduced exactly in descriptions of *The Swing Mikado*.[111] Notions of the "White Man's Burden" as a justification for U.S. imperialism blended and elided racial and national differences linking American blacks, Filipinos, "Porto Ricans," Haitians, and Cubans as racial and cultural inferiors in need of uplift by Western whites. At the turn of the century these nations and cultures were conflated in the U.S. imperial imagination in terms of their place in a racial hierarchy of civilization. Although each posed different policy issues based on their location, history, and resources, they were all inferior and incapable of self-government. Their aesthetic conflation in *The Swing Mikado* echoes these colonial cultural politics.[112] Nerissa S. Balce charges the brutal racialized physical violence against California's Filipino immigrant workers in the 1930s to this same conflation, a matrix that connected racial stereotypes, the violence of lynching, and the language of empire in the conceptualization of Filipinos with turn-of-the-century stereotypes of blackness.[113]

The U.S. had acquired Puerto Rico, Samoa, Guam, Hawaii, and the Philippines by war and treaty. The Senate ratified a treaty to pay Spain $20 million for the Philippines in 1898. A treaty between the U.S. and Spain signed in Paris on 10 December 1898 assigned independence to Cuba and made Guam, Puerto Rico, and the Philippines U.S. possessions. Ratification of the treaty coincided with Filipino rebellions against the U.S. military. American soldiers called Islanders "niggers" and "injuns" and were given free rein to kill and burn indiscriminately.[114] In this way the U.S. maintained a traditional colony on the Philippines and other South Sea islands.

In appropriating a South Sea referent, *The Swing Mikado* also dons a U.S. colonial model. The social structure within *The Mikado* reproduces an imperial system. In the song "My Objects All Sublime," the Mikado declares his rule over his subjects "morally correct." He rules in a "fatherly kind of way" over "each tribe and sect." His nature is "love and light," and he pronounces himself a "humane philanthropist." All this before he elucidates the way he'll "make the punishment fit the crime" of various cultural offenses that reads like a sequel to Ko-Ko's arbitrary and vengeful "I've Got a Little List." The Mikado's parental self-assessment asserts benevolent control with dire consequences for violations. In a very matter-of-fact way, he decrees a punishment for Ko-Ko of "something lingering with boiling oil in it" or "melted lead." In a similar fashion the self-declared benevolence of American imperial rule belied harsh methods such as conscript labor and anti-disease campaigns that included burning villages and carrying out a war of domination.[115] Themes of discipline and reformation in U.S. colonial rule in the Philippines resonate with themes of romance, discipline, and death in *The Mikado*.[116] The topsy-turvy system in the opera requires utter obedience under threat of death. The humor of the play derives from characters' attempts to conform to the disciplinary structure of the imperial system that legislates death for flirting and requires periodic executions. Securing a proper romantic union saves characters from death sentences for violating colonial rules. A happy feminized submission within marriage mirrors subjects' submission to the state through marriage. In an Americanist valorization of heterosexual romance as a narrative of domestic stability, capitulation to dominant power structures in marriage provides the discipline and reform necessary for conformity to colonial strictures. *The Mikado* symbolically replicates the colonial system, with the Mikado as an American colonist of abject citizens.

During the 1930s the character of the U.S.-Filipino imperial relationship changed to one of cultural imperialism and run-of-the mill American racism. After the First World War and during the Depression era belligerence subsided, and a cultural rather than purely military U.S. imperialism seemed to develop. Protected colonial elites prospered and absorbed American music, education, and language, and an impoverished populace became producers of agricultural exports.[117] During the 1920s English replaced Tagalog in a new American-style Filipino educational system "as the principal medium of instruction as part of a general dissemination of American values and culture."[118] Language change initiated a lasting fundamental shift in the character of a Filipino future and national identity, entangling the nation with its American colonizer. The 1920s brought Filipino immigrants to American cities for higher education and large numbers to California's farming industries.[119] In the 1930s the economic strain of the Depression exacerbated racial tensions between white American and Filipino laborers in California, initiating a xenophobic backlash that demonized Filipino men as hypersexualized and drove them from communities.

African Americans and Filipinos very likely came into contact serving in the U.S. Navy prior to and during the Second World War since Filipinos, as U.S. nationals, could enlist. Both groups were limited in the roles they could play in the military and in the war effort, though Filipinos faced far fewer restrictions early on; their participation ranged from firemen and machinists to mess attendants. After the war both groups performed menial labor until 1922, when African Americans were officially excluded from participation in the navy and Filipino enlistments swelled by comparison. The Tydings-McDuffie Independence Act initiating Filipino independence was declared in 1934 as a means of halting Filipino immigration to the United States and, consequentially, participation in the U.S. military.[120] On 15 November 1935 the Roosevelt administration established the Philippines as a commonwealth in a step toward full independence within ten years. It is possible that, as in the case of Haiti, black embodiment of an exoticized Philippines also constituted an embedded commemoration of this move toward its postcolonial independence from the United States.

In their flailing inadvertence, the imperial representations in *The Swing Mikado* also exoticized the African Americans performing and perpetuating constructions of imperial identity. At least in the eyes of some viewers, the opera's exoticization had an internal referent: black identity. On the level of representation African Americans, though performing these images and embodiments of island others, were also victims of the exoticization that positioned the abstracted islander as national other. African American racial identity becomes a tool for the purveyance of imperial ideology through which performers gain inclusion, recognition, popularity, love, respect, and jobs. All at once the performers of an instrumental symbolic, an abstraction contingent upon racial blackness, become victims of those same representations. Stereotypes of black bodies, black racial identity, and social exclusion inspired and permitted the images traded and embodied in *The Swing Mikado*. The representations worked because of their resonance with dominant primitivist ideologies and because of the outside position of blacks that facilitated their imagination.

Positive reviews of *The Swing Mikado* were double-edged, as reviewers called upon racist language to praise the racial transformations of the show. An exuberant supporter called the opera "a rhythmic walk melodiously cadenced to rich *black, coffee,* and *caramel colored voices,* but brilliantly Savoy in spite of some *gala quirk* of *racial inflection,* some tropical costume invasions of a *surprised Japan.*" Later the same writer reported of this "first-rate use of [the] crack Negro Unit" that "the show itself is so endlessly alive, so completely resilient that it fairly dances to the tune of *dusky skins, white teeth,* and a *fringe of jungle décor*" (emphasis added).[121] Reviews included the terms "grinning," "joyous," and "cannibal" to describe "Negroes" who "mugged" in a "general madness" of "tom-tom abandon," "stamping out the hot rhythms with an animal frenzy." In his reversal of the paper's assessment on 26 September, C. J. Bulliet's "positive" review for the *Chicago Daily News* mimicked the excitement of a radio announcement:

> Did you know that Sir Arthur Sullivan's melody, "Flowers that Bloom in the Spring," is so *primitive* in its elements that it can be *reduced* to a *jungle beating* of tom-toms? Or that "Three Little Maids from School Are We" is so *pagan,* despite its surface innocence, that it calls for a dozen encores when a *little brown girl* in the chorus *winds it up* with climatic movement

of a *Mata-Hari dance*? Or that the song about letting "Punishment Fit the Crime" can be gradually speeded up so that, toward the finish, it is a *perfect orgy of bacchanalian dancing*? If not, you haven't seen the All-Negro version of "The Mikado" being presented by the Federal Theater at the Great Northern. . . . New customers are flocking in and old ones are returning again and again, I know one woman who has seen the show eight times and she's *intelligent* (emphasis added).[122]

Bulliet said of the chorus, "*Hordes* and *hordes* of black and brown and yellow girls and boys weave the intricate, mad patterns. . . . The humor is the *grotesquery* that is found in African sculpture. You feel the *voodoo gods* presiding under an *African moon.*" This commentary transforms from reluctance to conversion, convincing others of the musical's merit in strong eager language. While the excitement in the description is vivid, the language of the review is disturbing in its exoticization of swing, the players, the play, and the cultures it references. The writer's "discovery" gives rise to a graphic inventorying of the skin tones of the women and an overt sexualizing of the dancing and dancers. His "hordes" repeats the fearsome stereotypes of threatening, overpopulated Asian nations. The overstatement of the "humor" provides an opportunity to liken black performance to "grotesque" African sculpture, further exoticizing the players and the cultures he assumes they represent. The invocation of voodoo gods, primitive jungle tom-toms, Mata Hari, and an African moon further exoticizes an already exotic performance through capitulation to ready stereotypes.

African Americans are seen as embodying their own otherness in the Negro performance. Simultaneously, however, their very capacity as performers undermines the status of blackness or black performers as the object of the performance. Black players also operate as subject (as well as primitive object) in this performance. In their attitude and appearance the performers seem to bask in the sheer transgression of their theatrical embodiments. Photographs of the scene that includes "The Flowers That Bloom in the Spring" printed in an article entitled "Mikado in Swing: A Classic Gets Its Pace Lifted" show smiling half-dressed dancers absorbed in joyful, exuberant swing moves (see figures 25 and 26).[123] The enjoyment on the faces of the performers caught in the midst of a song appears genuine. As the performers joked and played up the minstrel exoticism permitted by the show, they provided an experience that seemed pleasurable to themselves. The pleasure in the exuberance and excess makes a statement about black racial identity in the United States. An expression of desire for a performative unboundedness resided in the excesses of *The Swing Mikado* as well as in the precise reproduction of parts of the original *Mikado*. The show became an embodied lexicon of mimesis, creativity, skill, and originality.

In their role as subject, as performers of exotic tropes and appropriators of difference, they reify their own empowered identity as performers of otherness and crafters of meaning. They also reject an objectified position by demonstrating the performativity, the falseness of savage tropes by invoking an altogether different othered identity as the object of the performance. Black savagery is the seriously played joke as a savage difference assigned to black people is ridiculed and rejected. In the space of exotic excess, African Americans "become" American as they explode the terms of their own marginalization to signify an other. Embodiment of a symbolic exoticized blackness becomes an abjecting signifier of difference, instrumental and hypersymbolic in carrying the objectification of blackness beyond black bodies to colonized ones.

The Swing Mikado's exoticism reinforced American imperial identity by appropriating, abstracting, and abjecting the identity of Islanders. Its images reproduced racism while positioning blackness as central to American identity. The island was hot, distant, and wild, establishing, drawing upon, and rearticulating difference. Though the performance clearly drew from an abstract (lack of) knowledge about Asia and the Pacific, the cultural power assumed through appropriating aesthetics of difference to create the identity of the island dramatized a sense of American dominance over the locales and bodies suggested. The inheritance of British imperial stature resonates through the performance.

African American international history with the groups imagined suggests a power dynamic different from an unabated imperialism, however. What happens historically on the level of performance, where African Americans' swung performance constructs American imperial identities, coexists with African American critiques of an American imperial relationship with Asian nations and South Sea islands. African American performing bodies suggest an imperial identity in seeming contradiction to a political history that was also *anti*-imperialist. Because the performers in this production are African American and thus invoke specific African American discourses of internationalism, brotherhood

25. A dance scene in *The Swing Mikado*.

26. Three men of the chorus swing to "The Wandering Minstrels" in
The Swing Mikado.

for people of color, and freedom, there is more here than the mundane conclusion that African Americans operated in culture as Americans and within dominant American discourses. Communities of African Americans had been intimately involved in movements promoting diasporic consciousness and unity for the previous two decades. Black internationalists supported anticolonial resistance and freedom movements of nonwhite populations around the world.[124] Ubiquitous African American performances of exoticism and primitivism seem to fly in the face of these broad-based and culturally powerful movements. The recognition of global racial inequity on the level of international relations encouraged African Americans to identify with, respect, and support "colored" nations as they saw their domestic plight repeated on a global scale through American imperialism.

In the case of the Philippines, as was true early on in the case of Haiti, some African American sentiment saw civilizing, missionary, and economic opportunities for American blacks in initial American imperial ventures in smaller countries in the Western hemisphere and in Africa. Not only could black Americans participate in these ventures, but the colonized natives were also believed to benefit from the encounter with less racist colored Americans. From early on, however, critics strongly voiced their opposition to African American participation in the U.S.-Filipino war and U.S. colonization.[125] As early as 1899 a leader in the African Methodist Episcopal Church condemned "the enlistment of colored soldiers to embark for warfare against Filipinos," stating that such efforts "should be met with universal protests from Afro-American citizens everywhere" since black soldiers would find it difficult to "fight against foreign members of [their] own racial household."[126] Many African Americans respected the Filipino resistance against American forces. Internationalist sentiment was carried into the twentieth century in the pan-African and Garvey movements and the pages of African American newspapers that covered international developments from a racial angle.[127] Notions of racial brotherhood among the oppressed colored peoples of the world dominated African American public discussion of international politics into the 1930s.[128]

Ironically this diasporic internationalist impulse showed a strong imperial trend through black valorization of Japan that began in the early twentieth century, with Japan's defeat of Russia in 1905. African Americans developed a sympathy with Japan that persisted into the

1940s. Black sentiment idealized Japan with their support of native rule in Africa in Ethiopia's contest against Italian colonialism (1935–36). Racially nationalist black messianic organizations that positioned Japan as savior and emancipator of the American Negro cropped up in Chicago and other American cities. Filipinos were at times prominent in the leadership of such organizations. The 1930s also saw, in some quarters, the development of a fictive Asiatic identity by members of small mass-based, black organizations such as the Moorish Science Temple of America and the Nation of Islam / Allah Temple of Islam.[129] Japan served as a model of antiwhite power into the early stages of the Second World War. As the only nonwhite imperial power, Japan was perceived as an example that contradicted global imperial discourses of race that assigned "darker races" a status subordinate to white imperial races. Many African Americans supported the Japanese invasion of China; some writers even characterized the resistant China as an "Uncle Tom" for its search for help from white nations in an effort to impede the development of a unified, autonomous "Asia for the Asiatics."[130] This sentiment grew in power and became increasingly controversial throughout the 1930s, when "many government officials came to view the rising campaign of African American protest as a sign of disloyalty and sedition threatening to domestic security."[131] Among others, W. E. B. Du Bois articulated overwhelming support of Japanese imperial efforts, believing that in the ravenous dividing of the world according to color, Japan was the best agent to preserve Asia from European and American domination.[132] This sentiment was in itself highly imaginary since African Americans in general had little direct contact with Japanese. It was also powerfully instrumental in its capacity to foster a critique of racist American policies internationally and domestically. The idea of a potential world leader against white oppression encouraged global thinking and a sense of internationalism that insisted upon race as a major determining factor in global politics. African American internationalism found echoes in the international solidarity encouraged by Popular Front culture. Many workers left communist organizations, however, to join groups supporting Japan and began to critique "black Reds" as "traitors to African American liberation."[133] However, it was only the black left that leveled a critique of Japan's fascist policies, represented perhaps by Langston Hughes's deportation from Japan in 1933 for openly criticizing its policies as antidemocratic.

Given the complexity of the role of Japan in black political thought, it makes a certain cultural sense that the African American performance of *The Swing Mikado* in 1938 failed to directly lampoon the Japanese. The play of Asian aesthetics in the tropical relocation of *The Swing Mikado* signifies multiply. In black hands, or rather on black bodies, the echo of Japan in the conjuring of a tropical island could thus be highly revolutionary as a statement against American racism and yet also radically conservative in its overlay of Japanese imperialism and belligerence upon blacks' sense of colored brotherhood in the embodiment of colonized Islanders.[134] It is possible to consider the performance triply imperialist in its enactment of British, American, and ostensibly Japanese gestures toward empire. The appropriative miming is a mix of antinationalist antiracism and anti-Western pro-fascism combined with hypernationalist pro-coloredism. Neither the meanings of the performances and their historical resonances nor the language in which one might discuss them invite clarity. The appropriations, mirroring, mimicking, and positivist enactments reflect multiple, deep, repetitive, and counterposing identities and political desires.

Looking to the East for racial vindication and establishing a sense of international racial brotherhood coexisted with the social logic of African American imperial representations of the South Seas. The performances operated on a national level, indicating simultaneous imperial and anti-imperial sensibilities in the African American experience. *The Swing Mikado*'s abstraction from Japan to some savage island seemed to be about making the show "Negro," but instead made it a display of American Empire. Despite burgeoning international activity, however, there was little in *The Swing Mikado* to suggest resistance or irony in its performances of otherness. A critique of racial representation perhaps undermined a Negro exotic but did not resist the notion of a Pacific primitive.

African American performers attracted spectators into the theater to sit at their feet and participate in the fantastical enactment of black culture pretending to be, actually enacting and so being, something other than itself. The experience of *The Swing Mikado*'s performance provided an active presence for the performers and the audience in its live production and at the same time provided a sense of freedom and escape in its exuberant, fantastical fictional representation. To the extent that performance summons an imagined community into being through the performance itself and a material community into being through the meeting of performer and audience, *The Swing Mikado* brought multiple communities of understanding and identity into being at once.[135]

The Swing Mikado operates in several capacities: to assert relationship to and freedom from the British; to establish an American identity; to assert and continue the imperial aesthetic though exotic performance; to place African American identity in relation to American identity; to invoke the relationship between African Americans and America's imperial holdings; to toy with the meanings of blackness in American culture; and to reveal the packed and sometimes contradictory cultural implications of performed identity, as in the case of African Americans who performed an exotic South Sea island but were supportive of anti-imperial efforts in the U.S., of Filipino resistance, and of the rise of Japanese imperial power. Imperial representation as suggestive of power gets appropriated and used in ways that become more complicated in the hands of African Americans as a group with an ambivalent relationship to national identities.

African Americans were both product and producer of imperial culture in the performance of *The Swing Mikado*. This *Mikado* absorbs America's racist fascination with otherness, brings it home by making it Negro, pushes it away again by setting it on an Afro-Polynesian Caribbean jungle island, and ultimately assents to and confirms American imperial power in a manner totally unexpected by the audience—making the performance no longer a mere echo of the efforts of America's colonial fatherland but a representation of its own imperial identity. It was not respectable, clean fun or brand-new modern electricity that brought masses of people and an illustrious audience to the theater, as was the case at D'Oyly Carte's Savoy, but rather the revival of a ripped-off classic set to modern swing in a wild raucous spectacle. The middle-class prim propriety of Victorian England had been replaced by the loose primitive symbolics of American modernity. Rather than have their own mores served to them line upon line, cleverly twisted, this crowd was treated to a view of multiple others. The sense of self they experienced was an outward gaze of imperial culture refracted through a prism of a uniquely American Negro exotic swing. An English past was properly revered and spanked. An American imperial past and neocolonial present were embodied and celebrated. Imperialism as a signal of American national identity emerged as culturally integrated and nostalgically reified on the bodies of black citizens. Simultaneously an aesthetically and politically embattled cross-oceanic looking emerged for colored peoples whose postcolonial status remained to be seen. As an imperial tool, ethnography enabled colonial as well as diasporic looking in Katherine Dunham's performance of filmmaking and concert dance elaborating cross-oceanic transnational connections in black performative expression.

4

....

LENS/BODY

Anthropology's Methodologies and Spaces
of Reflection in Dunham's Diaspora

Katherine Dunham's ethnographic research and performance in the
1930s create a methodological and geographical pathway for understanding black American relationships with otherness and diaspora.
American bodies dancing a meticulously researched market scene native to the island of Martinique in modernist forms on a Chicago stage
for a WPA Federal Theater ballet demonstrate the ascendance of anthropological discourse in African American performance. The representation of extranational black cultures in black American performance
activated a transnational relationship of looking, appropriation, and
representation that both reproduced hierarchical structures of power
along the lines of nation and culture and dismantled them in a demonstrated desire for recognition—a cultural re-production and reflection
across transnational boundaries between black populations. Perspectives, methodologies, and representations emblematic of ethnographic
anthropology become the grounds for the imagination and enactment
of black diaspora in African American performance. The worlds imagined by anthropological black performance in the U.S. often presented a
fictionalized, abstracted, and simplified black culture. The performances
and scenarios also demonstrated, however, an investment in social and
aesthetic authenticity in representations' form and narrative detail, as
well as in the history and substance of black cultures in the Western
hemisphere.

Called the "handmaiden of imperialism," the science of anthropology defined those racially and culturally different from the white
West as inferior to justify securing economic, military, and political

power around the world. The process of collection and investigation, of research and description secured studied populations in a hierarchical relationship below civilization. The racialized native body remains more physically real than other bodies, proving its own difference and the superiority of a civilized identity. This automatically manifest primitivism obtains even, and especially, in live performance and seems to be the case whether the body is an ethnographic object or fictitious and imagined.[1] The process of researching and representing culture through black American ethnographic practice both challenged and succumbed to hierarchy and racism in methodology and representation by exposing and reproducing a black racial otherness.[2]

The matrix of ethnographic anthropology, film, and performance reveals the linkage between performance and a sense of access to real "primitive and savage" culture, whether noble or degenerate. African American performances marked by intellectual developments in anthropology in the 1930s moved away from purely savage and fantastical representation, even as they negotiated the political chauvinism in cultural appropriation and inherent in anthropological practice. Compared to the primitive and savage screen and stage productions of the period, including those discussed earlier in this book, Katherine Dunham's ethnographic films and ballet *L'Ag'Ya* actually show the complex process through which ethnographic perspective influenced black performance and identity. As a result, black representations of otherness became less exotic and less objectifying as it continued to perform primitivism and negotiate ideas about national and racial identity and power. In my discussion of *Macbeth* in chapter 3, for instance, this drive for an ethnographic authenticity manifests itself in the hire of real-life witch doctors and Asadata Dafora Horton's African dance troupe from Sierra Leone. *Macbeth* purported to include authentic spells and chants. Horton's authentic African dancing bodies and choreography did triple duty: adding to the important exotic feel of the show; providing authentic thick detail of original, black, African culture; and creating a diasporic experience and connection with African Americans on an American stage in an American show.

The research films of the anthropologist and performer Katherine Dunham provide a performative template for the ways this ethnographic representation enlivened filmic and staged performances. Films of dances in the West Indies demonstrate the slippages between ethnography, performance, and genres of stage and popular film. In these films staged dances act as the site of contact between anthropologist and native. Dunham's concert ballet *L'Ag'Ya* deploys ethnographic information as a reassertion of black history and a theorizing of black identity as diasporic through choreography, imagery, narrative, form, and its performance context. The presence of ethnographic representation and performance in anthropological film and dance choreography raises questions of power, hybridity, diaspora, and the crossings of black and Western subjectivities. This chapter engages the ways modern identity, national belonging, and diaspora were imagined through anthropological discourses that were imperial at their core. Dunham's research and creativity reflected black anthropology's complicated history. An understanding of this history clarifies the operation of an imperial ethnography, and its relationship to primitivism and diaspora, in her work.

Anthropology's Black Transformations

The written ethnography of one of Franz Boas's most famous students, Zora Neale Hurston, demonstrates the propensity for black anthropologists to shift between traditional disciplinary modes of seeing native others and an African Americanist ethnographic subjectivity.[3] In *Tell My Horse* (1938), Hurston shows herself capable of a U.S. national arrogance in her use of the U.S. as a model by which Haitian society is judged.[4] She characterizes the fifteen-year occupation in purely positive terms, insinuating its civilizing effect on the island, its government, and its people. Hurston even uses the liberated status of American women as a standard against which to measure the violent disenfranchisement and restriction of West Indian women, particularly in their relationship to men. Not only does her patriotic nationalism for a (fictitious) U.S. egalitarian notion of uplift and opportunity dominate sections of *Tell My Horse*, but Hurston also asserts a commitment to a more generally Western-style modernization and imperial uplift by her own actions. When visiting the Jamaican maroon community of Accompong, she helps the community to build a stove. It is her concern for the back-breaking work of cooking endured by the women of the community that inspires her experiment in leading the construction of this industrial improvement. Despite her intersubjective empathy, Hurston's interference amounts to the kind of maternalistic imperialism endemic to U.S.

international outlooks. At the same time she sees herself as and attempts to behave as one of the people.[5] She engages in a participatory ethnography whereby she interacts with native Islanders as equals, mentors, and friends.

Hurston's ethnographic engagement with a U.S. domestic folk positioned black rural poor and working-class people as other to a burgeoning urban black modernity. Her filmic envisioning of herself before the camera with her folk subjects, however, structured that viewing relationship as reflexive, facilitating both a distancing and a collapsing of folk and urbanite, researcher and object of study, subject and other. Her American anthropological positionality supported clearly imperial perspectives in both theory and action in her meanderings on Haiti. Her thoroughly civilizing stance on the U.S. occupation of Haiti and her construction of modern conveniences in mountain communities during her fieldwork, however, seem overcome by her deep immersion in the lives of Haitian people and spiritual ideologies. Hurston's traditional and intersubjective performance of international relations and transnational and transcultural black selfhoods in ethnography bear out the very contradictions of black imperialist looking. Hurston was a recorder and a writer, an ethnographer, novelist, playwright, performer, and trickster in her own right. Her stretching of the boundaries of ethnographic anthropology into creative, layered performance earned her the title of foremother of black performance studies.[6] The spirit of her efforts and contradictions resonate in less baldly imperialistic ways in Katherine Dunham's research and dance practices.

Black anthropologists and artists inherited a double-edged legacy when, in the 1920s and 1930s, they took up the racialized tools of ethnography, a legacy that marked cultural production in direct and indirect ways. Disciplinary recuperation of anthropology's history as an instrument of racism and white supremacy has garnered much discussion and intellectual energy.[7] Reflecting the ethos of African American predecessors — Frederick Douglass's critique of ethnology in 1859 and Du Bois's appellation of black people as the "football of anthropology" in 1939 — William S. Willis still decried anthropology's history as an imperialist tool in the service of maintaining the dominance and supremacy of the white race as late as 1979.[8] The science of anthropology developed during the early nineteenth century along with complicated justifications for the economic and political subjugation of many of the world's smaller, poorer, generally nonwhite nations by bigger, whiter, and more power-ful ones.[9] As an empirical science of human development, anthropology proved preexisting, culturally determined ideologies, including the in-trinsic biological inferiority of darker races and the existence of sav-age and primitive societies that lacked culture and intelligence and thus were unfit to participate in advanced civilization or properly administer their own resources.[10] Throughout this history black racial identity and black people defined anthropological paradigms.[11] Thus leading black intellectuals' and artists' adoption of anthropology as professional and artistic practice was ironic and bold. The potential they saw in anthro-pology's methods to reveal the substance of black life attracted them.

The qualitative changes to biological, evolutionary perspective and methodology instituted by the white scholar Franz Boas and the black scholar W. E. B. Du Bois in the early twentieth century directly chal-lenged biological and Darwinian understandings of culture and laid the groundwork for black cultural appropriation of anthropological modes of research for representation. Called the "father of American anthro-pology," Boas defined the field in 1887, disarticulating race and evolu-tion and emphasizing culture as a driving concept and ethnography as practice. His contributions had become entrenched in the U.S. by the 1930s. The Du Boisian intellectual model critiqued scientific and popu-lar racism through rigorous research, conceived of research as a form of activism, emphasized historical and comparative methods, viewed racism as a central problem in the contemporary world, stressed the intersection between race and class on both national and international levels, and synthesized and reconciled divergent theoretical strategies.[12] Their transformation of anthropology into a discipline and its removal from the province of museums and governments offered the possi-bility of humanizing the populations studied, positioning them as sub-ject rather than object through ethnography's extended, firsthand study of culture represented in detailed and objective thick description. The reflections of anthropological methodology in black performance mir-rored Boas's values and strategies.

Yet even as Boas's criticisms attacked traditional anthropology's "clas-sificatory and typological assumptions," his ethnographic school man-aged to reproduce some of scientific anthropology's pervasive struc-tures of racism and objectifying perspectives.[13] A global racialized power dynamic positioned colored societies to be researched in order to illuminate universal truths about more advanced Western white societies. In 1939 Boas observed, "Conditions of life fundamentally different from our own can help to obtain a freer view of our own lives and of our own life problems."[14] Ethnographic anthropology required an other to permit the disciplinary "freeing," that self-liberatory effect for the ethnographer in the pursuit of cultural knowledge, and its empirical difference, to uplift his or her own (consequently native) advanced society—a form of primitivism. Willis observes that even Boasian cultural relativism in anthropology distances an other since the *idea* of culture as a tool alienated and classified a naturalized notion of difference.[15]

Elaborating such critiques, Mina Davis Caulfield identifies anthropology as "foundationally rooted in and sustained by systems of imperialism and their effects."[16] Although the idea of the dark-skinned savage at the bottom of the evolutionary structure went out of style in anthropology, along with biologism and scientific racism, the designation of darker-complexioned primitive cultures outside of (or within) white Western civilization as objects of study reified the hierarchical relationship between white Western science and dark savage culture. The potential for exoticism and a relationship of hierarchy in the very pursuit of anthropological knowledge existed in the studied search for an ostensible location of organic, pure cultural manifestation. Boasian reimaginings of white supremacist Darwinism did not disentangle anthropology from the structures of power inherent in imperial perspectives. A shift from booty colonialism to imperialism, whereby power relations required willing workers, weak governments, and buyers, coincided with a transition from scientific racism to cultural relativism. Changes in anthropological perspective to examine a humanized object other paralleled imperial practices and conditions.

As object, subject, methodological template, and practitioner of anthropological inquiry, American Negroes walked a tightrope of signification and identity in deploying the technical and intellectual tools of anthropology.[17] Struggling with an imperial racist methodological and ideological paradigm, black anthropologists and practitioners forged strategies of "ethnographic subjectivity" and "vindicationism" based on a Boasian framework of culture. Ethnographic subjectivity assumed a "framework that was contextual, literal, creatively symbolic, and participatory," permitting black anthropologists to understand their relationship with their subjects in a more malleable way.[18] This methodology rejected the objectivity that anthropology espoused at the time, allowing black anthropologists to form new discourses of race and culture and new methodologies for studying and understanding them.[19] Assuming the separation of race and culture in a Boasian framework, the practice of black anthropology developed vindicationism to counter cultural and biological arguments used to prove the inferiority of the darker races and change hierarchical, discriminatory views of race.[20] Yet these unique and ultimately transformative perspectives still occurred under the permissive structure of Western colonialism's imperial shift.

Given the practical history of an embedded assumption of cultural and racial superiority in anthropology, it is not surprising that notions of exoticism and primitivism might still materialize in black representations marked by anthropological discourse and, likewise, a concomitant power of the gaze of those doing the representing. Thus the structure of othering persisted in liberal, humanizing efforts, both black and white, to research and collect cultural information about different(iated) peoples.[21] Black anthropology layered antiracist vindicationism, participatory methodology, and international diaspora over relationships of power and chauvinism upon which the field was premised and practiced.

Hymes describes "scientific colonialism" as a relationship whereby the "center of gravity for acquisition of knowledge about a people is located elsewhere."[22] The existence of the West Indies as harbinger of a more pure cultural and racial past for African Americans repeated these structures of power. In examining cultures and identities in the West Indies, black anthropologists were involved in projects based in historical systems of diaspora, but that also animated contemporary cultural and political hierarchies. Such work produced intercultural trade through its own documentation, reproduction, publication, and, most important for this discussion, aestheticization and performance of native black cultures in an American cultural context. African Americans became part of a system of studying and codifying other peoples, even as that process often self-consciously reflected specifically black American identities. This process repeats, however ironically, ethnographic structures of othering so clearly objectifying when white, civilized researchers lock black primitives in a relationship of savagery that illuminates origin, lost or repressed interiority, and past. The notion that the self could be located in the more historical, more racially undiluted culture inherently adopts a degree of the chauvinistic perspective that defined anthropological practice in its earliest stages. While vindicationist anthropological methods and theories could be adopted to study and at times appreciate diverse black cultures, they also prepared the conditions for enacting processes of othering, appropriation, and mimicry through participation in the ethnographic apprehension of knowledge, difference, humanization, racial equity, and selfhood.

Performative representations in the 1930s presaged the articulation of a politicized goal of global connection through diaspora defined by St. Clair Drake. In the 1950s Drake defined black diaspora as yet another perspective in which anthropological practice countered racism.[23] In the 1930s the process of ethnographic subjectivity and the invention and activation of diaspora began to militate against the dominance of the pervasive determining structure in anthropology. The details of the cultural performances I analyze indicate some ways black cultural producers bridged conflicts of cultural perspective inherent in meetings across the distance produced by anthropological practice and within diaspora across national boundaries. The tradition of African American anthropology was to transform anthropological discourses into a conduit for African American and, more generally, black liberation against and through its appropriation of discourses of power.

Dunham and "the Primitive"

In its relationship to structures and concepts of ethnographic inquiry, Katherine Dunham's work and its meanings both eschewed and depended upon primitivism. Even as Dunham's performance of *L'Ag'Ya* in 1938 epitomized the expression of a new black subjectivity that valued diaspora, her anthropological and dance practices relied upon a clear conception of a black primitive. Neither her research nor her performances exploited diasporic cultures by mining them for something like exotic spectacle. The structures within which she worked, however, and the language used to describe that work reveal the complicated politics of race, culture, and power during the time that she made her own interventions in black cultural development and understanding. Dunham's work is characterized by an infiltration and assumption of dominant, mainstream power dynamics in the identification of and investment in the primitive. The search for one's own history elsewhere, the appropriation of the cultural material of that history, and the capacity of that history to serve as a recovery of something lost and a location of authenticity reproduces imperial relationships between cultures.[24]

Anthropological notions of the primitive were a pivotal part of Dunham's oeuvre. She explained, "Haiti presented a particularly fertile field for the study of primitive dance. . . . It had not been greatly industrialized and in isolated sections of the island original African forms and rituals were presented almost intact."[25] Concepts present in her identification of the West Indies as a site for locating purer, black forms and other statements and explanations from the period veritably define the notion of the primitive as preindustrial, isolated, original, simple, authentic, and basic.[26] Though ultimately she sought idealistically to access and represent universal human emotion in indigenous dance, Dunham's description of that work (and possibly the very goal itself) repeated the problematical ideas that the culture studied was ahistorical and simple. It would seem that the diversity and complexities of the social significance of movement might reveal complicated societies to observers, yet the anthropological and intellectual rubric of the period that designated a society as preindustrial and premodern (or outside of the modern) cast the rituals and movements of diasporic dance as primitive.

Nevertheless, Dunham's abstract theories of complicated, nonessential culture seemed to leave room for the belief that basic and primitive culture could be found in West Indian Negro dances that were closer to the dance forms of Africa. With reference to the possibility of understanding diasporic culture as an opportunity to "restore lost traditions" to "[her] de-racinated people in the United States" with "dance forms which are truly Negro," Dunham constructs a desire to connect American blacks to their "roots" through dance.[27] In this combination of beliefs, she gestures toward an ahistoricity of the black cultures outside of the U.S. that seem to have maintained a closer relationship to past cultural practice and memory. This view of the dances as *not* or *less* de-racinated, uprooted, perhaps removed from the assonant "race" by time, history, and the implied modernity of the West and as maintaining a purer Negro identity despite their own colonial distance from Africa positions them as a specter of an American Negro past. This relatively hierarchical perspective obtains even as Dunham intended to infuse a black American culture, heretofore overly subject to assimilation and exposed to diluting influences, with these more pure, original, authen-

173
....

tic forms. Her black nationalist position to restore and regenerate by creating connections to Africa celebrated Africa, invested in American blackness, while also reproducing imperial structures of anthropological inquiry. Transnational differences and geographical shifts in black cultures fade as a linear past in the articulation of a homogenized Western blackness is manifested in dance. The practice of anthropology in this instance animated these cultures with a history of origins even as that history was also its present. The perspective held that contemporary cultural manifestations could be mined for their manifestation of a black *American* past.

Invested in separating Dunham from the racist politics of primitivism, her biographer Joyce Aschenbrenner sees the concept of the primitive as outside of Dunham's own practice. In an apparent attempt to reconcile the irony of the terminology and perspective with the goals and content of Dunham's artistry, Aschenbrenner explains away the use of the term by attending to the way it was "applied" to Dunham's work in reviews and to the way its use went out of style in anthropological discourse. Aschenbrenner shows how Dunham's understanding of the meaning of "primitive" over the decades was influenced by an understanding of race as affected by culture and by a conception of African societies as highly developed civilizations. Aschenbrenner states, "It is obvious that rather than pursuing the primitive 'exotic,' she was searching for that which was shared by all peoples."[28] Dunham describes this pursuit of a shared humanity as a basic attribute of all artistic endeavors. She did not, however, stop using the terms "primitive" and "exotic" to describe native dance and culture; they continued to signify something she thought was meaningful and necessary in her research and technique. The terms appear in Dunham's writing throughout her life and in descriptions of the technique that incorporated West Indian movement.[29] In her conception of her anthropological work during the 1930s, and the cultural performance and choreography that emerged from it, contemporary evolutionary views on the material existence of primitive culture and movement persisted as an element of description and practice. This was even as Dunham eschewed connotation of the primitive as "loose," "inferior," or "simple."[30] Dunham herself seemed caught in a bind of language, ideology, and race that limited her ability to shatter objectifying structures of understanding culture.

The operation of imperial perspectives in Dunham's work achieved surplus meanings that were contradictory to typical effects of superiority and subjugation. Though permitted by a politics of domination and cultural hierarchy signaled by the persistence of primitivism as a defining concept, this gaze and deployment of power operated to explore and establish unity and understanding instead of domination. Dunham's research experience as well as the cultural products that were her dances illustrated her drive for understanding over domination. In a poignant moment when she used dance as an expression of her own cultural heritage, Dunham convinced political powers in Jamaica to allow her to pursue her search for native movement. During one of her research trips she was nearly denied the opportunity to travel to mountains in search of the maroon communities and cultural materials she sought. To obtain the moral backing of urban society and political leaders to conduct native research, Dunham herself danced "a concert for them and included only numbers which were traditional ballet or aesthetic interpretation." The performance consisted only of traditional European and modern dances: "They loved it, and I was given a free hand thereafter to search out my 'primitives.'"[31] Permission to access primitive dance firsthand was secured through a concert that was traditionally Western and divested of black forms. In Dunham's telling, it was her performance of high art that secured "moral backing." Perhaps this signaled African American removal from African forms, proximity to whiteness, and lack of blackness that deserved amelioration. In this gesture of national and cultural submission, Dunham displays her own performing body. On some level performance may have acted as evidence of her perceived lack in a black American cultural heritage and as a display of the classical artistry she brought to her practice. Her choice not to perform a cakewalk, Charleston, Lindy hop, or other black urban dance form suggests her own performative strategy in achieving her goal. In the theater of looking constructed in this transnational event Dunham's anthropological gaze is sublimated, while the black national gaze of her West Indian subjects ascends. Her request reversed the relationship of power such that she became the human subject submitted to their gaze for observation. Positions of looking are exchanged and perceptions of culture refracted through dance. The feminization of the object of the colonial gaze and the masculinization of the gazer are multiply reflected through enactment, refusal, subversion, and reversal in this (post)colonial exchange. In the symbolic activism of Dunham's dancing body, performance superseded argumentation. Dunham participated in a meta-ethnographic conversation that posited her as a *participant* in ethnographic exchange as observer and observed. Her performing body, imbued with its European history, becomes a conduit for access to black cultural forms. Ironically Dunham enacts a profound agency in acquiescing to a certain kind of objectification and surveillance in her representation of what amounts to a cultural lack. Her performance insinuated that black American dance performance lacked a rhythmic cultural heritage. At the same time her virtuosity in European forms validated her sincere interest in dance. Here Dunham's research deployed the kind of African American ethnographic subjectivity that allowed her to view herself, as well as modern society, as subject to the gaze of her purported subjects. This is a clear example of a postmodern participatory form of ethnography that opens up a "performance of possibilities," wherein the ethnographer opens herself to being seen, evaluated, affected, and changed. The mirroring of pasts and presents, power relationships, race, access, and knowledge in this moment reverberates endlessly.

Acting as more than mere observer, Dunham also becomes judge and ultimately creative re-presenter.[32] Her training and choreographing served to reimagine the history and culture of black Americans. The stages of looking at and reforming the dance cultures of black West Indians reproduce the visual echoes of darkening mirrors as embodied reflections of culture and identity are seen, captured, reproduced, and seen again; the dances were sought, located, reviewed, staged, collected, studied, rigorously reproduced (performed *again* with great difference), structured and narrativized through choreography, and performed.[33]

Ethnography, Film, and Embodied Theories of Transnationalism

Proverbially before her time, Dunham straddled early and late twentieth-century methodological modes. She embodied a shift in critical consciousness as well as racial and national consciousness. The last decades of the century developed a postmodern anthropology that was participatory, intersubjective, antiracist, and anti-imperial. Its methodologies insisted upon an awareness of the invisibility of much of culture, that what is seen is metonymic and not metaphorical of cultural systems. A postmodern anthropology questions the authority of the observer and attempts to engage the fact that power articulates itself in ethnographic relationships.[34] Dunham's work positions ethnography itself as performance, recognizing studied cultures and her own activity as continually in process. Fifty years before he described it, Dunham animated Dwight Conquergood's claim that *"homo performans,* humanity as performer, rather than author, of her own identity, is always historically situated, culturally mediated, and intersubjectively constituted. Furthermore, *homo performans* socially constructs the very world that undergirds her enactments. Self and society are mutually implicated in and enabled by a continuous process of reconstitution."[35] Dunham's scholarly and artistic practice ultimately performed a theory of transnational identity and communication in research and dance in a manner that both asserted and dismantled ethnography's imperial structures. With Dunham the "colonial gaze," black performing body, and ethnographic display merge uncomfortably in one body, her own, and in one body of work. This merging ultimately collapses distances between primitive and civilized, savage and modern, center and periphery, self and other through the reenactment of the categories themselves on the black body for multiple audiences.

Dunham completed her master's training in anthropology with Robert Redfield at the University of Chicago, one of the hotbeds of the new anthropology. She was supported and trained in fieldwork by Melville Herskovits and came in contact with Margaret Mead and Ruth Benedict in her studies.[36] Fellowships she received for fieldwork in Haiti, Jamaica, and Martinique provided the basis for publications, choreography and performance, teaching, social activism, and a lifetime of intercontinental diasporic and pan-Africanist activity.[37] She managed to build connections through an enactment of Western privilege—the privilege of advanced education in American anthropology and its concomitant funding and mentoring opportunities, of transnational movement, cross-cultural viewing, resuscitation and exposure of history, the assumption and development of an audience for her scholarly and creative work. Her imperial privilege, as it were, as an American subject ironically disrupted the imperial effect of the cultural erasure of colonized peoples through participatory ethnography and dialogical performance.[38] Her practice in all its capacities fostered a kind of *recognition* that was self-reflexive and self-subversive in its cross-cultural interactions.

As an anthropologist Dunham embodied a transnational practice in her travels to specifically black nations to conduct research. Her transnational movement combined with the budding black anthropological philosophy of ethnographic subjectivity that postulated participation and identification with the object of research to forge a theory of black transnational connection. Dunham's research and subsequent choreography was possible through a performative recognition of transnational otherness within black diaspora as a version of the self. That is, beyond the first level of transnational movement and boundary negotiation, Dunham's choreography and dance enact a further embodied contemplation and activation of the possibilities of transnational contact.

Films from Dunham's research, dance methodology, and concert performance form a pathway through which to trace the impact and consequences of transnational contact and interpretation. Adherence to disciplinary methodologies can be seen in the crucibles of form (film, choreography, performance) through which Dunham's creative work came into being. She used film as a research tool in much the same way the founders of the field had. Methodological consistency can be observed, for instance, between Herskovits's research films from West Africa and Jamaica and Dunham's from the West Indies. Extant films from Herskovits's research provide a textual and methodological context for Dunham's own strategies of research and recording.[39] The films themselves indicate that Dunham used the medium as a research tool to achieve a unique end. Her work slides between the ethnographic and the artistic, as even her research materials have an artistic cast.

The combination of film and anthropology united empowered ways of seeing. The use of film in anthropology initially sought the achievement of "greater scientific objectivity and neutrality — and it was argued that the cinematographe would surely assist in the cause."[40] In her pioneering analysis of ethnographic film, Fatima Rony suggests that film became central to the execution of ethnography as a means of visualizing the truth of the cultural other and as an expression of the imperial power of the ethnographer. She explains, "In such diverse genres as colonial propaganda film, Tarzan movies, and scientific films seen as positivist recordings, ethnographic cinema is often harnessed to ideologies of nationalism and imperialism; it has been an instrument of surveillance as well as entertainment, linked like the written ethnographies of cultural anthropology to a discourse of power, knowledge, and pleasure."[41] Since ethnographic film drew upon and visualized the evolutionary investment in an ahistorical other, aspects of this perspective suffuse the adoption of an ethnographic viewpoint in filmmaking. The research films as document become voluble texts in and of themselves, rendering research methodology a form of representation. As a standard practice of investigating the native other, ethnographic filming also captures relationships of viewing power, that is, the positioning of the observer and the relationship of observation, in the structure of the film and its content. What is captured is not only the actual bodies of the objects of research, but also the perspective and presence of the researcher. The films are testaments to a historical moment in the lives of researcher and subject and of the politics of investigation that construct both.

Herskovits's Africa films record tribal ceremonies and rituals and display them (described with intertitles) as if they were captured in the regular cycle of quotidian and ceremonial tribal life.[42] His Jamaica films show everyday experiences, recording footage of a road to a market, a market, and groups of men and women at work in fields. The films give the impression of capturing life in progress: the workers working, the dancers moving within the context of an ongoing event, the people performing for themselves and not for the interloping oddity, the camera. The looks of shyness, curiosity (both demure and open), eagerness, and puzzlement bear out the impression of the camera as novelty, itself a furtive looker upon the scene, though a spectator with a sustained gaze. A long segment in one of the Jamaica films shows a woman on the road to the market who walks out of the frame and back in three times, engaging others in conversation and managing to remain in front of the camera, looking at and past it curiously. In footage of dances filmed along the Guinea coast, audience members peek at the camera and look away; some stand passively before it, and one man faces it aggressively, closely approaching the lens.[43] Traces of strangeness support an ethnographic objectivity, as if the camera and ethnographer do not interfere but only observe what transpires, including the subjects' natural curiosity and uneven self-consciousness before the nonparticipatory lens. Whether or not this was the case in the ethnographic exchange, the camera's view constructs a disinterested objectivity, ironically in the very same moments that the natives looking back resist the camera's objectification. This alienated relationship to the camera also nativizes the research subjects by articulating both their distance from technology and the seemingly bounded observable nature of their cultural practices. Rony makes clear that these films operate as cinema with specific conventions, as an institutional matrix, and as technology.[44] Although they purport to relay cultural information through direct representation, the films construct narratives of indigenous people, most often as "trapped in some deep frozen past, inarticulate, not yet evolved, seen as primitive, and yes, Savage."[45] As a mode of cinema, ethnographic film has structured the native by allowing him or her to reveal his or her own primitive nature.

Ethnographic films from Dunham's fieldwork repeat and change the relationship established by the ethnographic camera in anthropological research. In Dunham's films a stationary camera records clips of activity in the natives' locale, producing the collecting function of the camera and its nativizing gaze. Continuity of the structural relationship of othering existed in the collecting function of the camera to view, record, and remove the information to another context for contemplation and interpretation. Anthropological interest in dance sprouted from a notion of dance as primitive and arose in the study of black cultures through a similar assumption of primitive culture.[46] Anthropology imagined dance as one of the most basic expressions of human emotion and communal behavior. The anthropological basis of Dunham's foray into the study and collection of dance as a form of indigenous expressive culture grew out of and contributed to a view of dance as primitive. She said, "My desire was to see first-hand the primitive dance in its everyday relationship to the people; and anthropology which leads one to origins and the simple basic fundamentals of art which is made complex and esoteric by civilization, was the answer."[47] Thus the operation of the filmic impulse in Dunham's work was embedded within disciplinary concerns and perspectives.

Dunham made films of dances in Haiti, Martinique, Trinidad, and Jamaica. In contrast to Herskovits's films, Dunham's research subjects often seem to maintain a position at center stage within the shifting frame. The lens does not purport to establish objectivity through stationary impartiality. As if aware of its boundaries, the subjects very rarely disrupt the frame, even in sweeping movements and gestures, and never express a vulnerable or defiant relationship to the camera; in fact they do not seem to look at it directly or take notice. Spectators in the films focus on the dancers and not the camera. When dancing subjects look toward the camera, they often look beyond it, engaging the presence beyond it.[48] Dunham's films evidence a shift in the way the practice of ethnographic filmmaking itself signifies. She wanted to make her subjects feel comfortable, to minimize the intrusion, and to be welcomed even as she "pointed something" at the people she hoped would share their ceremonies with her.[49] The subjects' secure relationship to the camera and performative display of social and ceremonial dances reveal the ways ethnographic subjectivity as practice provides the conditions for recognition through and around the camera as a mediating entity.[50] The films themselves attest to the relationship of acceptance, or hospitality, between subject and researcher. The recording camera, the ethnographic exchange between researched and researcher, and the condition of intentional mutual performing — of dancing and of collecting — produce a deep reverberation of images and identity production. Dunham's films enact the possible distancing objectification wherein an outsider examines another culture, but she also bridges that gap and achieves a critical *recognition* (to see and have that vision resonate; to recuperate through active envisioning) of other and self-in-other through the camera.

The films often display actual performances, unlike Herskovits's films, which present themselves as capturing cultural practice in motion with the compliance, but not necessarily the performative complicity, of the dancers. In Dunham's films the research subjects do not just agree to be seen; they participate in the staging of the dances. In a film of an urban social dance, a woman pretends to dance with a partner, her arms propped up in air to demonstrate the female part in a dance for two.[51] Dances in a film that lacks the usual drummer and ring of spectators from Jamaica and Martinique are very clearly staged. The single couple make jokes in movement, converse, and glance at the camera, including whoever is beyond it (presumably Dunham) in the laughter as they make sexually suggestive moves.[52] Sometimes it appears as if they are responding to comments from the filmmaker. They look beyond the camera, speak or nod (the films are silent), and continue dancing. They display participation and pleasure in being seen.[53] In theater methexis is "group sharing."[54] The audience creates and improvises the action of the ritual. As Dunham takes part she activates a relationship of methexis between herself and the performers, her performance of ethnography, and the production and capturing of danced performance.

Dunham's footage does not merely capture performative ritual as a form of revealing cultural material, but captures *stagings* of performative material both within and isolated from their social context by the dancers and the ethnographer. The more carefully staged films demonstrate the relationship of consent and participation she achieved as well as the highly developed relationship between researcher and subject. Dunham demonstrates a form of ethnographic subjectivity in the staging and recording of these films. She engages the participatory methodology pioneered to structure black ethnographic relationships to black people within the United States. Her intersubjective methodology constructs her own participatory nativity and simultaneously activates blackness as sameness despite national, cultural, and linguistic differences. Her work seems to split open binaries of research and identity, not by asserting or denying her own cultural position but by negotiating a hybrid space of cultural interaction, overlap, and inclusion.[55] Cross-cultural recognition is actuated and made visible through and across the camera apparatus and in the projected images on the screen. The participatory exchange through filmmaking humanizes the subjects even as the collecting function and removal of the film sustain a more traditional power structure. Dunham's radical giving-back in ethnographic practice encompasses more than a simple representational fairness; it is an attempt to restructure the ethnographic gaze and shape of the practice of study in an example of postmodern performative ethnography.

Dunham's films served as the groundwork for the creation of ballets in a process of transnational appropriation and embodied translation. Her research films were also used in academic presentations to scholars and anthropologists and as a teaching tool for dance training at her school in St. Louis.[56] For scientific inquiry the films served as evidence of another culture and, for art, as a template for the embodiment of West Indian movement in dance. D. Soyini Madison explains that for performers enacting cultural difference as art, "the transportation (between self and other) is mentally and more viscerally intense than traveling to the world of others; it is making those worlds your 'homeplace.' The virtuosic performer is not only *engaged*, but she strives to *become*. For the performer, this is not only an endeavor to *live in* an individual consciousness shaped by a world, but to *live in* that *social world* as well." Madison sees the performative process of taking on and taking in a character as a process of intersubjective trade between self and subject or other.[57] The performer enlivens, not an object in and through her body, but a human

182

participant, the social context, and "visceral ethos" of that world. The performer's body itself becomes a metaphor for political connection and social transformation, especially as it also takes on and performs its own social context and concerns.

The process of the translation of Dunham's filmic material from ethnographic data into dance *methodology* is evidenced in technique films that demonstrate the rigorous nature of the Dunham technique for training dancers.[58] A cultural shift occurs in the process of choreography when collected moves become subject to the formal structures of narrative Western concert performance. Dunham trained professional dancers to reproduce, fictionalize, and perform the moves collected in the films as translation, interpretation, and a mode of appropriation. The choreographic process constituted a recuperation of history and transmission of this reinterpreted past, and thus reenvisioned present, to an American public. Her performative practice mirrored another black culture on the body as a reimagination of black American cultural identity connected to other black cultures and global histories. The intersubjective connection became an opportunity for the reinterpretation and perhaps remaking of American (black) identities.

Eventually Dunham's training methodologies were codified for transmission to dancers over generations. Films of students practicing the Dunham technique shed light on the mediation of dance forms that occurred between the moment of collection and the moment of performance on the stage in the 1930s. While Dunham's early performances were simplistically understood as merely copying or re-presenting found narratives and found materials, the intermediate step of technique disrupts this narrative of a mere geographical shift, of pure appropriation from the field to the stage. The application of technique thus disrupts the idea that the native in the ethnography reveals the truth of her own culture, her own inferiority; there is no native here. The movement changes significantly from its form in situ in the research films to the concert stage. Technique films show the meticulous training of movement within each part of the body: the hand, foot, neck, shoulder, spine, et cetera. Movements are slow and rigorously controlled, requiring great strength and skill. Each movement is minutely articulated in each part of the body and smoothed into more complicated progressions and dances. Dancers bent at the hips articulate each element of the Dunham contractions, rolling their back through the tailbone, pelvis, spine, and neck, lifting to their toes, engaging the balls of the feet and heels, with uniform precision. The precision of the Dunham method enacts a disciplining and technology of the body consistent with modernist concerns. Dancers maintain perfect form and motion as this simple step is incorporated into slightly different, faster, and more complicated series of movements in a dance such as "Yonvalou," an undulating wave or snakelike dance honoring the serpent-god Dambala and his wife, the goddess of the ocean.[59] One can see the maintenance of form and tension in each part of the body as isolations sweep into larger gestures. The isolation and emphasis of the location of specific movement in specific parts of the body and the emphasis in the concert pieces of the body itself change the social, festival, and functional uses of native dance significantly. Modern dance techniques reform research materials into artistic production of kinetic narrative. Concert films of L'Ag'Ya demonstrate an articulation of movement clearly based upon but not the same as movement collected as research. L'Ag'Ya manifests Dunham's desire to discipline, train, and professionalize Negro dance forms into a more "dignified art," a tradition in dance, and a technique that would be universally important.[60]

Both her dance methodology and the narrative content of her ballets foregrounded transnational black cultural practices in a remaking of black racial and national identities in the U.S. Moving the research material from its status as ethnographic data to the concert stage reclaimed a historical and lateral sisterhood of black cultures in different nations even as Dunham's concert removed the dances from their initial context, performer, and audience. In Dunham's work the body takes the place of the page, transferring and transforming knowledge and theorizing meaning. In her dance ethnography she not only exposed the hybridity of black cultures in the Americas, but also identified and produced idiosyncratically black Western forms.

Dunham's combination of research, dance, and choreography on stage for the Federal Theater in L'Ag'Ya provided a performative example of a burgeoning ethnographic and diasporic discourse in African American identity. Artistically she united concepts of dance as an object of anthropological study, as a nonlinguistic form of psychosocial communication, and as performance.[61] Culturally she united ideas of lived culture, artistic expression, and planned public artifice. Dunham produced American and African American culture in artistic endeavors through a mingling of selfhood and otherness in black identities. In her struggles to separate artistic fictionalization from social authentic representations of folk culture, she demonstrated a sense of the implications of appropriation and identity in her work and the complicated consequences of ethnographic methodology. Her vigilance constituted a refusal to confuse symbolic structures of cultures and their lived experience with imaginative symbolic structures of art. This practice divorced much of the abstraction in artistic production from the subject represented and appropriated. For Dunham, the effect of diaspora on art produced a revitalized African American culture in the United States. Her appropriation of dance moves was a form of inspiration and was handled in a manner that respected the appropriated cultures rather than denigrating or annihilating them. In the process of creating these performative materials, she placed black American identity as the center of gravity illuminated by cultural information, however vital, from the periphery, even as the artwork operated to restructure hierarchical patterns of transnational black relationships in which they were embedded.

L'Ag'Ya: Dancing Culture and Diaspora

Dunham's approach was ethnographic and research-oriented, but also stylized, fictionalized, and artistic. In her first full ballet, L'Ag'Ya, introduced at the Chicago Federal Theater in 1938, she used her ethnographic work to bring black anthropological concerns to the American concert stage. As an artist Dunham benefited from domestic training in black vernacular dance in the basements and living rooms of Chicago's Bronzeville and in modern dance and ballet with the recognized modernists Vera Mirova and Olga Speranzeva.[62] After completing her fieldwork she gave up the strictly academic pursuit of anthropology to pursue a career in professional dance and performance.[63] Her signature shows include L'Ag'Ya, Tropics and Le Hot Jazz (1940), Broadway's Cabin in the Sky (1940), and Tropical Revue (1943).[64] Her repertoire has survived decades of performance in South America, Africa, and Europe. The mark of distinction in Dunham's technique was her incorporation of what she called the primitive dances, styles, and rhythms of diasporic cultures into her choreography.

L'Ag'Ya was the final segment of the Chicago Federal Theater's Ballet Fedré (1938). Dunham's contribution, the thirty-two-minute folk romance *L'Ag'Ya*, was the last in a program of five modern pieces and was the only segment choreographed and danced by African Americans. Other dances in *Ballet Fedré* were done in "a wholly modern vein" as opposed to Dunham's "folk dances," which carried the evening's "first honors." Ironically, however, the piece considered most modern, "Midsummer Triptych," "mimed a country celebration of country folk."[65] Thus the folk and the modern collapsed in the definition of American dance form. As the modern was constructed by notions of the primitive, the relationship between the folk as derived from the primitive and the modern is circular. Dunham's work embodied a black modernism through its basis in anthropology as a scientific discourse and its performative form. As in the voodoo *Macbeth*, *L'Ag'Ya*'s modernism negotiated the terms of national belonging and domestic inclusion. *L'Ag'Ya* performed African American appropriations of transnational hybridities, black diasporic recognition, and the humanity and particularity of black cultures that embodied a black nationalism.

L'Ag'Ya's story is a simple tale of love, jealousy, mischief, and tragic competition between suitors. The rather classic plot is layered upon narratives of cultural appropriation and hybridity expressed in movement. Loulouse and Alcide fall in love in the first act, set in a market and on a fishing dock around noonday (see figure 27). Julot, interested in Loulouse, attempts to attract her attention and displace Alcide. Unsuccessful, Julot purchases a powerful love charm, the *cambois*, from the king of the zombies in act two. The charm allows him to bewitch Loulouse into a ritual stripping until Alcide manages to break free and save her. In the third act, set at a holiday dance, the two battle, dancing the fighting dance, *ag'ya*, until Julot triumphs and kills Alcide.[66] *L'Ag'Ya* had a cast of thirty dancers.[67] Henry Pitts played Alcide and Woody Wilson, Julot; Dunham starred as Loulouse.[68] The love and competition between the lead characters dramatize a shifting morality tale of encounters between cultures. Say, for instance, the heroine represents an idealized black modern culture as an object of desire. Her suitors, depending on one's point of view, could alternately represent "authentic, root" or "outside, imperial" cultures come to claim her.

The representation of cultural and national otherness in this performance showed a concern with the significance of transnational connection and the detail of black life, unlike similar, significantly more exotic representations that appropriated an island environment. At every level

27. *L'Ag'Ya*, Act I.

COURTESY OF THE LIBRARY OF CONGRESS, FEDERAL THEATER COLLECTION

of performance in *L'Ag'Ya*, the ballet mirrors and trades racial and national power and resistance through kinesthetic and visual appropriations of movement. *L'Ag'Ya* speaks relationships between black American performance and multiple dance forms, including Western and indigenous West Indian forms; between imperial and colonized cultures; between ethnographer and subject; between performer and audience.

The title of the ballet is the name of a Martinican fighting dance that resembled African forms of wrestling, the French savaté, and the Brazilian capoeira.[69] Likewise, the performance mixed European, African, American, African American, and West Indian elements. The ballet incorporated at least five dances collected during Dunham's research in the Caribbean: a Martinican creole mazurka, beguine, myal, majumba, and ag'ya. The language of movement and mise-en-scène in which the tale unfolds creates the ballet's cultural and narrative complexity. Through multilayered meanings of movement, history, and plot, the dance narrative expands to include a story of identity and culture as well as tragic romance and gorgeous movement. The creative mixture

LENS/BODY

of origins and movement, both geographical and cultural, emphasizes black diversity and black transnational connection. In the ag'ya black American dancers perform Martinican identity in moves derived multi-nationally in a Federal Theater state-sponsored ballet. With its hybridity of form *L'Ag'Ya* theorizes and constructs African American identity as historically, culturally, and performatively transoceanic and creole.

The dances from Europe, Africa, and the Americas weave a narra-tive of the trade of culture into the rich fabric of *L'Ag'Ya*. Creolization

of movement in the ballet becomes an embodied representation of cul-tural hybridity and postcoloniality in black culture. Black dance is placed in conversation with a colonial past even as it appropriates and changes its forms. Hybridity of culture is both demonstrated and appropriated by African American performers on an American stage dancing pieces from locations within the transatlantic slave trade. Dunham's singular traveling, dancing body collecting and transporting cultural material produces and affirms concepts of hybridity and exchange, motion and unity expressed in the idea of diaspora. Through the collective mirror-ings of all of her roles, Dunham embodied multiple cultural styles and positions, enacting the hybridity of a colonial past, diasporic contact and desire, and hierarchical power structures.

Exchanges of power occur in dance through movement and the gaze. Various symbolic identities position themselves in and through move-ment and its performance for an audience.[70] Marta Savigliano says, "It actually takes three to Tango." She explains that while it takes "two parties to generate otherness, two places to produce the exotic, two people to dance," it takes a third party to enact the gaze that transforms the ritual of dance into spectacle.[71] *L'Ag'Ya*'s dancers were both viewers and performers of native movement, dancers and third party appropria-tors of other forms and othered performing bodies. While some ele-ments of *L'Ag'Ya* insist upon idiosyncratic, unapologetic normalcy in black life, other elements display as performance and dramatize as nar-rative exotic and erotic forms. The performance and its context act as reflections of cultural positionality and trade. Tango produces and rep-licates multiple relationships of power between the dancers, between the dancers and the audience, and between the dancers and broader cultural forces. Likewise, *L'Ag'Ya*'s fisherman and sellers, zombies and charm seekers, competing suitors and lovers participate along with the audience in deeply reflective exchanges of identity, gaze, and power.

Multiple gazes of unequal power are invoked in the ballet. These are visible in the conditions of production, the show itself, and the responses to it. Its federal sponsorship supplied a governmental gaze both *of* the performance and *in* it. Like other Federal Theater work it was approved by the government and thus reflected its federal sponsorship. Both black and white reviewers extolled *L'Ag'Ya*'s West Indian elements, casting them as "authentic primitive" and "abject other." *L'Ag'Ya* stood out for many reviewers as the best piece in the *Ballet Fedré*'s interracial program. The black actor Maurice Cooper, who played Nanki-Poo in the Chicago Federal Theater Negro Unit's *Swing Mikado*, explained that the "Negro ballet . . . brought down the house every time it went on. . . . It was presented in conjunction with two white ballets and was by far the best of the trio."[72] Blacks read a straightforward Negro authenticity of black dance in no palpable recognition of difference between national black cultures, only in recognition of black difference from and superiority to white dance. Some comments in the mainstream press collapsed the artistry of the ballet with a nativized authentic truth attributed to the black body. For white reviewers *L'Ag'Ya*'s unspecified "folk subject" and "preservation" of the Negro dancers' "native grace" made it stand out against the white ballets.[73] The dancers were their subject. Yet in one insistent exoticizing of the show, the white reviewer Claudia Cassidy did actually distance ethnographic material from the American bodies in performance: "The evening ends in a splash of dusky rhythm with *L'Ag'Ya*, Miss Dunham's setting of a Martinique legend crammed with the mysticism of voodoo, zombie and the serpentine writhings of Negroes who *dance like natives though five weeks ago they were tap dancers.*"[74] Praise for *L'Ag'Ya*'s "lack of affectation" and authentic American tap dancing juxtaposed to its "native writings" exoticized primitive movement as distinguished from the dancers' real selves.[75]

Multiple viewing publics enacted diverse gazes in relating to the performance. Though the ballet's value and power was universally recognized, the evaluations invoked multiple interpretations of Negro identity as a baseline for criticism. That is, the gazes locate the dancers, the context, and the movements as a part of the structure of recognition. These positionings become the basis for evaluating the show and measuring its success. The performance manifested simplistic primitivism and humanized cultural expression for different viewers at different times. For African American performers as gazers (at West Indian cul-

189

tures) and gazed upon (by American publics), national identity signifies in different ways all at once. L'Ag'Ya maintained the simultaneous capacity to reflect authentic primitive identity, exotic native identity, and humanized folk culture.

Moves that were repeated and modified in all three acts assert the interdependence of the three modes of living they reflect: work life, the sacred, and holidays. The movements express continuity and integration between the mundane, fearsome, and formal. Repetition of moves throughout L'Ag'Ya provides a narrative circularity that communicates a consistency and integrity of culture in its grounding in and return to familiar gestures. This circularity allows the ballet to depart from an overarching Western linearity of the narrative.

Threads of meaning looped in repetition in the structure of L'Ag'Ya undermine the traditional effects of exoticism in performance. Representations that seem strange and exotic are rooted in normalized actions and interactions. The ritualistic and erotic suffuse the mundane and quotidian and vice versa through movement and its repetition. This is contrary to typically exotic representation, which posits the strange, extreme, and unfamiliar as abstracted other and not as integrated self. The ballet begins with an illustration of black cultural universality in the market act's normalized behaviors and ends with creative assertions of a black cultural distinctiveness in the holiday quadrille and war dance battle. Neither of these bracketing moments is exoticized. The most alien and culturally particularistic moments, in the jungle voodoo scene of act two, are couched between representations of more common and familiar occurrences in everyday life, the market and holidays. The aesthetic order of L'Ag'Ya dramatizes a core cultural identity that is hard to access and protected.

Vévé Clark shows that three primary moves recur and become characters in the piece: (a) a low position, (b) a lifted position, and (c) a hip roll. The low, grounded movement, second position plié (a), signals meeting, trading, and competition. This motion communicates everyday interaction of the living, zombie motions of the dead, and combative belligerence between the suitors. The opposite, a lifted, aloof position (b), indicates the reverse of these more common or base interactions, signaling the dramatic or out of the ordinary. It occurs in the lovers' trysts, in zombie intimidation, and in the organized festival celebration of the people. The third move, a hip roll (c), becomes a gesture of both work and eroticism in each of the acts. Each movement appears within the specific context of each of the three acts: at everyday market and labor in act one, at a native vaudun ceremony in the woods in act two, and at a holiday festival in act three. The moves communicate specific relationships between individuals, groups, and experiences that thicken the dramatic narrative. Gestures repeated and recontextualized throughout the ballet transform the dance narrative into a complex, internally reflexive system of cultural meaning. The circular internal references of the dance create a mode of storytelling that fits within a tradition of African folk styles.[76]

Through internal self-referentiality, the movement tells a story of cultural cohesion in a culturally specific representation of black village life. The emphasis on African ways of knowing and the integrity of black life renders the African American choreography anticolonial in its embedded rejection of Western narrative structure and lifestyles and its focus on internal meaning. The ballet affirms black life in its setting and subject, and despite its specificity approaches the universal. Various forms of group life develop the universal story of passion and romance. Each act occurs on an occasion of an easily recognizable communal gathering. Minimal sets emphasize the action of the people. Dunham calls on community experience in a tapestry of dance to emphasize the steady importance and cultural centrality of community experience, labor, and leisure, to black identity.[77]

Dunham's choreography posited everyday scenes of black life, group activity, and personal relationships as fit subjects for the concert stage. She insisted that black subjects were worthy of high art. The ballet portrays black communal moments as beautiful and diverse through its compelling and shifting rhythms. The sense of community infuses various experiential and geographical spaces: the seaside market, the jungle ritual, and the town festival. L'Ag'Ya's geographical and ritual diversity samples moments in lived experience in an adroitly ethnographic manner. The performed subjects of her ballet—the players, their characters, the cultures, and lived spaces—emerge both humanized and fictionalized, both authentic and imagined through creative and ethnographic dance. The value of black life and the hybridizing impact of the practice of diaspora develop a *diasporic* black nationalist ethos consistent with nationalizing traditions in modern dance.[78]

The central placement of the voodoo act in the ballet demonstrates

28. *L'Ag'Ya*, Act II.

the value and importance of black cultural traditions. Act two begins as Julot, the rejected suitor, backs fearfully into a jungle clearing filled with zombies. Demonstrating a physical opposite to the first act as well as a moral inversion, the evil zombie king sits rocking in a chair on a raised platform presiding over and above the action. A reviewer for the *Chicago Daily Times* described his performance "alone" as "worth the price of admission."[79] Male and female zombies dressed in black voile angle about on stilts, while others newly risen from the dead lay attached to the ground, lifting their bodies periodically and falling, as if sinking into an unseen depth, but a depth of death instead of the seaside scene's depth of water and life. The set is black with a jungle scrim and green lighting, creating a feeling of the macabre (see figure 28). Similar to the haunting environment of *Macbeth*, the theater "filled with the sound of animal cries and frightening noises intermittently joined by the cascading cackles of the Zombie King himself."[80] The beginning of the zombie dance is driven by the hypnotic rhythms of multiple drums. Zombies hop from one foot to the other to eerie effect, elbows even with their shoulders and dropped hands quivering. With these moves the dancers blend South American and West Indian traditions, re-creating the secret

CHAPTER FOUR

myal dance of the maroon people in Jamaica collected by Dunham and a habañera from Cuba.[81] The stiff grace of these puppet-like motions generates a mixed ethos as the myal steps communicate defiance and the sinister habañera a sense of seduction. An entranced Julot crouches, terrified, in a corner. His terror indicates that the vaudun experience is particularistic and fearsome even to some island natives.[82] Everything in the act exudes revulsion and seduction, distancing and drawing in. Dominating the act from its subtle beginning through the weird, trance-like dance, the zombie king presides over the act's closing, when the zombies strangle each other and collapse to the ground dead.[83] The king's raised position asserts the ascendance of native power through the living figure of the zombie king himself.

L'Ag'Ya's costuming in this act indicates the ambivalence between humanizing black island life and projecting generalized primitivist difference. The zombie king wears a headdress of long feathers, a tattered, stringy cloak draped over dark clothing, and an African-looking mask.[84] Head wraps, large hoop earrings, and feathers insist upon an embodied difference of island culture. Dunham's husband, John Pratt, designed these voodoo costumes, which, like his costumes in *The Swing Mikado*, combine structured form with island elements. Pratt's randomly exoticized costuming promoted an anticolonial sensibility through a focus on black experience and native forms and an exotic sensibility through the zombie king's tribal outfit. The tribal representation is consistent with trends in the Federal Theater and the 1930s to exoticize black cultures in an attempt to access and perform the primitive. The mask and tribal appearance, however, also mark the show's search for an African past through a performance of an imagined voodoo aesthetic in a Caribbean island locale. The performance appropriates African and island power for American and diasporic black identities. In the same gestures the zombie king also enacts an othered exoticism in his macabre display of alien island difference.[85]

Although cultural and ritualistic difference combined with unrealistic native costuming get performed here, the performance of the island other, as such, significantly manifests an investment in *avoiding* wild exoticization, extreme abstraction, abjection, and racism typically evident in traditionally exotic performance. The ballet recuperates voodoo by imbuing it with productive power. Voodoo produces cultural continuity, supernatural myth, and tragic romance. Voodoo performance becomes structurally significant in its shaping of narrative. The performative environment establishes the power of the cambois, the enchanted object, in determining characters' futures. The instrumental use of the drum in driving the narrative distinguishes this performance from others, where drumming served a purely exoticizing function. The direction "hypnotic rhythms of the drums" indicates the beginning of specific dances that bear functional meaning in the story. Rhythmic sound is used to mount tension and produce drama in specific ways that signal meaning rather than mere foreshadowing or entertainment for the audience. Drumming, while still positioned as terrifying in this act, is contextualized and particularistic, not random as in the voodoo *Macbeth*, *Haiti*, or *The Swing Mikado*.

The order of the acts displays *L'Ag'Ya*'s transformation of the effect of the exotic in black performance. The use of the exotic shifts from an active othering to an active identification by privileging and protecting the most exotically performed and culturally unique scenario. For some audiences seeing a show performed by blacks in costumes representing the islands was exotic enough. In the world of *L'Ag'Ya*, however, the island aesthetic is normalized, and its exotic appears at the center. Vaudun as a dark, secret element in black culture is indeed exoticized and portrayed as difficult to access and potentially dangerous when tapped. Rather than being abstracted, however, this most culturally alien and most intensely exotic of acts is claimed and protected in a performance of vaudun culture through the structure of this piece. Voodoo display is rather typically rendered. It is abstracted as different and fearsome in the black and green colors, stilts, trembling, and suggestion of death. This voodoo fearsomeness, however, is posited as performatively and culturally relevant and powerful in black culture, in part through this difference and fearsomeness and especially in its precipitation of the ballet's resolution, the tragic end of the love triangle. The events of this act determine the outcome of the ballet. The terrible effects of the cambois obtained in the jungle figuratively dramatize a deep, untamable power in black culture.

The ballet embeds voodoo at its core, in a scenario that is the most African, performatively exotic, and foreign to American culture though unique to black cultures. As an organized religious practice, vaudun is portrayed as important to everyday culture even in its physical and aesthetic distance from it. As the centerpiece, the zombie act positions difference in cultural identity as central to expressions of black life and dance. The terror and strangeness of the jungle world come between and appropriate the motion of the two, less otherworldly acts, the final act being a mix of the normalcy of the first and the magic of the second. The repetition of moves from the zombie dance in the market scene and in the ag'ya illustrates the influence or integration of elements of vaudun culture in the everyday. Julot's simultaneous desire and terror in the zombie scene reflect a relationship of desire for and antipathy toward difference in transnational black culture. Exoticized voodoo performance and vaudun practice dramatized simultaneously in the structures of the ballet reveal similarly ambivalent relationships between black American cultural identities and other(ed) black identities.

Act three takes place the very next day, at carnival, a communal day when villagers are free from the strictures of colonial rule and mandated labor. Townspeople dance a creole mazurka, a version of a Polish mazurka brought to the colonies by the French, followed by an African beguine.[86] In a tango of colonial reflection and exchange, both are dances of fertility or mate selection; the dances reflect each other geographically and culturally. The mazurka is stately and lifted. Dressed in costumes of their eighteenth-century French colonizer, the villagers appropriate the look and behavior of their former owners in performing this dance. The drum changes, transforming the feel and tempo of the dance to the erotic smooth bumps and intimate grinds of the Martinican beguine. The beguine following the mazurka reverses the tradition in French dance halls to play the beguine first and then cool the dancers in a more distant and formal mazurka. Thematically Dunham's choreography not only reverses physically conservative French tradition, but also the developmental history of the dances. Dunham explained that "the beguine is a dance of fecundity, as is the ancient form of the mazurka."[87] The African-rooted beguine grows out of and replaces the mazurka on the concert stage. All at once the beguine culturally preexists, repeats, and replaces the meanings of fertility and the performance of the European mazurka. The beguine, thought to prefigure the European mazurka's performance of fertility rites, is also a manifestation of an ancient African dance creolized in West Indian island culture. Clark explains that this order permits the villagers to metaphorically "strip the forms of their former owners."[88] This choreography performs the power of precolonial (African) and postcolonial (West Indian) cultures in relationship to colonial cultural forms in their claiming, transformation, and replacement of them.

The postcolonial stripping becomes rhythmically literal as Loulouse begins to remove her clothes. During the height of eroticism in the beguine, Julot appears with the love charm, the cambois, sending the stage into a hush. Despite his fear in the jungle, he adopts the role of the zombie king, enacting absolute evil control over the people in the village. The power of the charm brings everyone under its spell. Two villagers hold a bewitched Alcide while Julot brings Loulouse center stage, causing her to dance the majumba, "a Brazilian sacred dance of possession controlled by the charm and drum."[89] The hybrid dance forms and historical references are infused with native culture: a native song to Yemanja, the goddess of fertility and of the ocean, rises as accompaniment, with background drums gathering strength. Relatively innocent themes of love and desire revealed in the music and dancing turn violent and frightening under Julot's power. Just before Loulouse reaches her last petticoat and Julot, circling her in a threatening fighting pose, prepares to embrace her, Alcide breaks free from the charm in rescue. A reviewer declared in 1938, "The real strength of the action lies in the long sustained dance in which Woodie Wilson, aided by a Zombie charm, forces Miss Dunham (an exquisite figure) to yield him her clothing item by item until Henry Pitts, her rightful swain, suicidally intervenes."[90] The reviewer corporealized and sensationalized Loulouse's erotic disrobing by replacing the characters' names with the dancers,' conflating the imaginative action with the dancers' own agency. After the spell is broken "the villagers call for ag'ya, the drum takes up the rhythm," and the two men rock back and forth in fighting poses.[91]

Professional artistic concerns and cross-cultural interpretation in movement can be seen in films of Dunham's stage ballet L'Ag'Ya made in 1947 in comparison with her research films of the ritual. Dunham describes the ag'ya as a fighting dance from Martinique that locals would perform on Sundays to enjoy the competition and entertainment. The ritual was a great attraction, and people would place wagers on the dancers. The locals called the participants "fighters"; Dunham called them "dancers." In fieldwork films, sporting men spar in light-colored shirts, long pants, and hats, keeping the rhythm of the drummer, while gentlemen, similarly clad or in suits and jackets, watch.[92] The fighters step around each other a good deal, waiting for the opportunity to strike. Dunham explained that "some kinds of motion are pure dance and some kinds of motion are lethal."[93] In some practices of the ag'ya in Martinique, actual fighting would occur, with bets placed on who would "stain the torso of his opponent in the most blood" or "break the leg of his opponents in one of those amazing quick throws."[94] Preparing for months, Dunham, in a gender reversal, taught this men's dance to her company until their mastery garnered reactions from the audience comparable to those from an audience at a boxing or wrestling match. In this case Dunham even undermined embodied manifestations of gen-
der identity in her culture-shifting dance practice.

This titular dance is used on stage as the climax of the ballet, a high-stakes fight in which the hero dies. The most dramatic moves from the ag'ya are choreographed into a fast-paced, high-energy battle, eliminating much of the strategic standing around in the field version.[95] Modernist art making should not imply that the artistic material in cultural production always further abstracts native material, rendering social moves as art. The ag'ya is already dramatized fighting. In competition practitioners (fighters) act out a battle in which no one is meant to be seriously harmed. On stage the ag'ya seems to lose a level of performativity and artifice rather than gaining more. The concert performance dramatizes real violence, and a character is dead at the end of the act. The ballet uses the dance to reference a lethal fight as opposed to referencing a dance that constructed or imagined a battle to the death. In this instance of figurative and kinetic transformation of research materials, their use becomes a mode of appropriation for local (American) artistic and narrative goals. The dances of Martinique help to produce exciting black American art.

Julot kills Alcide and flees the village. Left alone on stage with her dead lover, Loulouse mourns Alcide. She closes the ballet in a lifted, soaring arabesque in relevé over his body as the lights return to the everyday blue of the first act.[96] Interestingly, as tragedy the plot of L'Ag'Ya resists a satisfying romantic coupling of the hero and heroine. Rather than consummating their love in a neat domestic marriage that insists upon the stability of nation, the ballet separates the lovers through death, leaving the woman to suffer and search for peace. The lighting suggests that this peace will be found in the everyday operation of black life. In plot structure the ballet allegorizes a continuing search for black nationhood, communicating separation and loss through its tragic resolution and the fate of its heroine. In form, however, *L'Ag'Ya* recognizes the national hybridity of culture while subtly undermining hierarchies of culture and nation that rank white forms and identities above black ones.

In direct conversation with the effects of European domination gestures in *L'Ag'Ya* thematically articulate blackness as a counterdiscourse and perform postcolonial desires for liberation. The inclusion of colonial culture in the ballet demonstrates a black cultural hybridity that claims European influences. Manthia Diawara describes blackness as a way of being human in the West or in areas of Western domination whereby colonized "people whose destinies have been linked to the advancement of the West" have therefore learned the "techniques of modernity" in order to articulate identity in, through, and against it: "Blackness insists on a discourse of difference which enables it to combat 'the image of the black as an aberration of Whiteness,' and, by undermining white privilege over aesthetics, economics, and law, to posit relativistic aesthetics and the aesthetics of relativity."[97] *L'Ag'Ya* embodies this relativity as it insistently escapes and undoes the dominance of colonial forms and a colonial gaze. Colonial clothing and movements, however, consistently get undone and reversed even as they infuse other elements in the show. Set in eighteenth-century French colonial Martinique, the ballet occurs only in moments when the characters operate freely from colonial supervision. The anachronistic setting adds a note of racial resistance in the staging of black autonomy and the absence of a white presence. In some performances the powerful zombie king wears tattered remainders of formal colonial attire. His costuming both appropriates and rejects colonial power as represented in his deteriorating vestments. European dance structure gets symbolically stripped through movement and literally stripped through removal of traditional European clothing in act three.[98] Choreography in *L'Ag'Ya* recognizes European context and modernity as determining forces in black identities and also dismantles their centrality.

Recognition and Diaspora

Black American dancers appropriated and embodied multiple forms, acknowledging black performative traditions. As a performance of the culturally and choreographically hybrid ballet in the United States, *L'Ag'Ya* demonstrates black cultural hybridity and asserts the relevance of that hybridity as a condition of everyday black life as well as an interpretive and artistic tool.[99] The genealogy of this performance shows a clear appropriation and manifestation of West Indian forms and articulates those forms as part of a *black* past. The hybrid and syncretic culture of movement *L'Ag'Ya* recognizes is American, West Indian, and African. Dunham's appropriations of movement *embody* a transnational identity for African Americans that asserts race-based collectivity and cultural vibrancy. A long-standing trade of culture and power pervades the history of black culture told in the performance of colonial, community, and zombie representations. Seen this way, *L'Ag'Ya* is a historical and cultural commentary on black diasporic identity. Black American identity is almost sublimated as transoceanic remainders and transformations receive primary choreographic and narrative attention. The ritualistic preparation through rehearsal and performance of this multilayered narrative of identity embodies a concern for diasporic experiences and representation.

The community sensibility evident in *L'Ag'Ya*'s scenes and creolized movement is echoed in the international and diasporic perspective of its performance. *L'Ag'Ya* establishes diaspora through the conditions of its production and its content. The ballet results from, activates, and celebrates black diasporic culture. Dunham's creative use of movement, trade of cultural meanings in choreography, ethnographic and artistic blend, and use of ethnographic material in choreography resulting from the appropriation of hybrid forms of African, European, American, African American, and West Indian cultures facilitate the proliferation of those forms as a future of black cultures.

Both her dance methodology and the narrative content of her ballets foregrounded transnational black cultural practices toward a remaking of black racial and national identities. The move of the research material from its status as ethnographic data to the concert stage enacted a reclamation of a historical and lateral sisterhood of black cultures in different nations even as Dunham's concert ethnography (the scholarly product that renders the studied culture to an audience) removed the dances from their initial context, performer, and audience. In her dance ethnography Dunham managed not only to expose the hybridity of black cultures in the Americas, but also to identify and produce idiosyncratically black Western forms. Like the small gestures of the body sweeping into larger gestures of movement, the small gestures of Dunham's research swept into hypotheses of black cultural hybridity, black particularity within a dominating culture, transformation of black cultures into cultures of modernism, and assertion of a common blackness across transnational borders.

Dunham's work evidenced and posited diasporic hybridity. Her choreography demonstrated her sense of value in re-creating these cultural connections, a value that became a central characteristic of her life and work. Performance constructed a two-way mirror wherein oceanic crossing facilitated reflections of identity. The images closed in on each other, forming a unity of diasporic negritude and blurring boundaries of authenticity, origins, and difference. Researchers and artists sought, found, and created prisms of self. The subjectivity insisted upon when imagining diaspora was grounded in black racial identity by representing other black people; it was historical, activating a discourse of origins and development over time; it was cultural in a seeking of and attraction to everyday and ritual practices, whether in common or different; and it was global in an imaginative and physical crossing, in Dunham's case, between West Africa, the West Indies, North America, and South America. This diasporic definition and crossing operated within an imperial structure of space and international relationships even as the concept of diaspora forged something new within those boundaries. Dunham's transnational oeuvre might serve productively as a template for understanding the figuration of diaspora through sisterhood in popular ethnographic film.

5

....

ETHNOGRAPHIC REFRACTION

Exoticism and Diasporic Sisterhood in

The Devil's Daughter

Produced for black audiences, the film *The Devil's Daughter* (1939) features techniques of ethnographic anthropology in its visual and narrative making of meaning.[1] In the film, performance culture reflects and reshapes anthropological perspectives in a complex feminized negotiation of black national identities. The anthropological perspectives of cultural relativism and thick description of ethnographic information laid the foundation for closer knowledge of typically othered forms of performance, identity, and culture in the 1930s, when African Americans began to use them to represent black cultures. This fictional film reinforces the influence of ethnography as an emerging mode of representing and negotiating black identity. In it, the deployment of ethnographic technique secures a Western perspective while also offering utopias of diaspora provided by that very structure of closeness supposedly achieved through ethnographic knowledge. In fact the closeness of knowledge is realized in the film's structuring of the sisterly relationship as a figuration of black diaspora. Ironically the truth-claims of ethnographic representation verify these diasporic utopias as real.

The ethnographic approach to culture and the visual methodology of ethnographic film influenced the imaginative treatment of people and culture in representation through content, perspective, and form in a range of artistic representations of black culture and diaspora, ranging from Katherine Dunham's scholarly demonstrations and concert dance to commercial film. This popular film draws on the characteristics of ethnographic research films that deploy images to produce an authentic tone and content and also structures viewing relationships and metanarratives of identity and power through the visual referencing of ethnographic relationships of viewing and research. Likewise the replication of the ethnographic eye in commercial film positioned ethnographic images to produce and verify imaginative material. In this chapter I examine the black imperial gaze, film technology, ethnography, and gender in the apprehension of transnational black citizenship. Central to this discussion are the multiple forms of black performance that appear, including native dance, vernacular games, comedy and joking, and religious ceremony and ritual within the context of African Americans negotiating diasporic black connections in film.

Performance culture in *The Devil's Daughter* manifests and manipulates ethnographic images and methodologies of viewing that traditionally distanced others and signaled national difference and division. Structural and aesthetic fictionalization of ethnographic detail became a representational strategy for depicting a black American identity that was invested in transnational kinship. This film, set amid images of native people and lands, demonstrates the influence of this discourse in its story of half-sisters, Isabelle and Sylvia, who compete over the inheritance of their deceased father's island plantation. The resolution hinges upon each sister's relationship to native culture even as their American urban heritage impinges on their access to property and domestic happiness. African American participation in anthropological discourse capitalized upon knowledge and truth in an apprehension of a black other. *The Devil's Daughter* engages in D. Soyini Madison's *performance of possibilities* that "collectively articulate[s] a common affective vision of a shared political future, based on a politics of practice — what people do, what they invest in, where they belong."[2] The performances in the film — its status as a cultural text, its production, and its internal performances and meanings — center "on the principles of transformation and transgression, dialogue and interrogation, as well as acceptance and imagination to build worlds that are possible."[3] The performed possibility of a shared future incorporated blacks from different nations into a transnational family despite problematic modes of representation and manifestations of international inequality.

The use of film in anthropological study constituted a process of collecting and documenting that produced authority and knowledge through visual representation. This owed to the fact that visual material was presumed to transmit "the real." Ethnographic representation in popular film grows out of this scientific method of viewing culture and of positioning and embodying race. Appropriation of this mode of viewing in an American film about extranational black life secured the truthfulness of the representations the camera collected. The process of *collecting* and *representing*, under the added rubric of a *scientific* outside gaze, triples the operation of an empowered view that presumes to assign authenticity to the collected subject. In reproducing the structures and images of ethnographic sight, black performers in popular film both produce their own empowered position and complicate it. Ethnographic representation becomes not only an aesthetic of othering, but through that othering also becomes an aesthetic of diaspora as a matrix of ethnographic images and dramatic narrative recuperates the envisioned other. The images and narratives include reconciled sisterhood, failed voodoo exoticization, inheritance of property, and romantic marriage. The position of cultural power inherent in this representational structure reified national difference between American blacks and the subjects they performed, but the form and its implications also permitted the appropriation of the film for antiracist expression that sought to bridge and recuperate difference. Ethnographic representation secured visual and representational authority in a manner consistent with the form's imperial history, but also allowed for the humanizing of native material through its transmission in a fictional narrative that imagined a transnational black sisterhood. Ethnographic use of film became a permissive structure that underpinned new understandings of blackness. Thus an empowered eye, an empowered discourse, and an empowered creative positionality deployed as performance envision black people as members of a transnational community characterized by surmountable cultural differences.

The fictional representations of *The Devil's Daughter* traffic in the production of realness and truth to carry its larger diasporic claims. The viewing structure here relied on the perspectives of ethnographic subjectivity to alleviate the othering impact of blacks studying blackness. The film abandoned exotic distancing in representation by using a truth-producing medium to contextualize cultural behavior and humanize native subjects. Realness and authenticity become part of the process of developing diaspora imagined by this entertainment film. Artifice and the real, native and urbane, civilized and primitive, center and periphery collapse in the undoing of binary reflections of difference. Consequently

ETHNOGRAPHIC REFRACTION

all of the black identities in this "all-colored film" could be understood as authentic representations of blackness.[4]

Of course, the transmission of the real is problematic if the discursive subject is positioned by the form as always and only primitive.[5] As an expressive tool, the ethnographic eye distanced and objectified its subject by purporting to reveal an unmitigated truth of an entire culture.[6] Typically this imperializing gesture insists upon simplicity and primitivism. In *The Devil's Daughter*, however, Negro American performance complicates even this relationship through specific narrative choices that insist upon the validity and modernity of the non-American black cultures in contradistinction to sometimes farcical representations of an American backwardness. *Daughter's* juxtapositions of performative forms and narrative plotlines disrupt and complicate the nativizing function of the ethnographic eye.

Daughter's vision of Jamaica's people and landscape and its fictional characters humanize black subjects and negotiate complicated racial identity in several ways. First, the film manages overwhelmingly to avoid stereotypical images, even as it presents images that have been typically performed through ethnographic and primitivist perspectives. Second, in various visual and narrative ways *Daughter* insists upon the modernism of native space. Third, ethnographic images of dancing and vaudun ritual (a religious practice) perform and recuperate primitivism through ethnography and through voodoo exoticism through pretense. The performance of both primitivism and exoticism as pretense refuses to essentialize and other native difference and contributes to the film's construction of the integrity of nation, representation, and diaspora. *Daughter* undermines the tradition of randomly exotic and wild othering of non-U.S. cultures. Fourth, national identity is rescripted in a family drama that posits a blood connection between American and West Indian black nations imag(in)ing harmony between chosen and abandoned siblings.

Ethnographic Authenticity

The process of verification and truth established by ethnographic vision supports the other claims accomplished in the film. *Daughter's* initial images and two classically ethnographic scenes that have nothing to do with the film's plot, a native dance and a cockfight, provide a heuristic for the film's themes. Ethnographic images in the film perform double duty, both establishing and undermining primitivism in the representation of the island. On the one hand, the use of ethnographic film subjects and techniques insists upon a racialized primitivism of the subject on screen. On the other hand, the appropriated project of ethnography provides a concern with cultural accuracy and detail that deploys the rhythmic practices and rituals that begin and end the film as a humanizing frame.

Filmed entirely in Jamaica the film provides visual access to native difference in a manner consistent with ethnographic collection. The ethnographic gaze reveals itself in the film's opening sequence, where panoramic views of the native landscape are first accompanied by faint drumming and voices, then interspersed with fuzzy shots of people. The initial lingering distant aerial shot of the island conforms to an imperial impulse to absorb and control. The encompassing view of mountains, a city, and a long coastline supports the assumption of alterity evident in ethnographic representation. The panoramic shots of ocean, beach, mountain, and city scored to drums and singing immediately signal a geographic, spatial, rhythmic, and aural context outside of the United States. A group of people walk unobtrusively among silhouetted trees blending into beachside greenery. These introductory images bleed into shots of a native dance that confirms spatial and cultural distance. This dance scene repeats the look and structure of danced steps and rituals recorded in ethnographic films, resulting in a visual link between this fictional representation and ethnographic ones that show natives walking past the camera or performing their culture before it. Its presentation of native performance serves as one end of performative brackets that enclose the action of the film between danced and vocal performances of a cultural identity that is black and not American. A lighthearted beat changes three times as a prelude to the indigenous dance that dramatizes a romance.

The disembodied drums and voices materialize as the walkers enter a courtyard in a line. Men wear crisp slacks, though tattered in some cases, and light-colored shirts with hats; women wear long dresses or blouses and skirts. The women balance large, empty baskets on their heads throughout the dance. The line of dancers circles a guitarist and three drummers, who appear to have been playing the music heard so far. Thus the film cuts into a found performance already under way. The musicians are in the center but mostly unseen as the lead dancers stand in center front and the troupe, the Lynsted Market Dancers, performs steps around them in a circle.[7] About six couples keep step to calypso-sounding beats in pairs behind the musicians. Their moves are simple and spontaneous within an informal structure. Choreography consists of light circular hip movements, bodily swaying, and feet tapping in easy rhythmic pattern. The moves are repetitious, like the repeated chorus that the group sings over and over again. Lyrics in the short romance scene repeat the line "Sweet Charlie, Sweet Charlie." In the foreground a mini-drama ensues, wherein a man dancing next to a young woman on a mule is tempted away by another woman who seems to have a prior claim. These two dance together in the center of a semicircle of dancing couples. The camera pans the group as it did the shoreline, resting briefly on the leisurely, improvisational swaying and shaking of each couple. As part of the film's first images the dance plays a significant framing function in its absolute unrelatedness to the plot. The loosely choreographed steps and vocals authenticate cultural context and a truth-oriented ethnographic perspective.

The constructed unstaged appearance of ethnographic film recurs here. Like dancers recorded in anthropological films, these talented nonprofessionals stage an event the camera purports to *observe* rather than to construct, almost as if the dance would or could have been happening even if the camera was not there. On some level the scenes in ethnographic films appear to be naturally occurring, though participants' stealthy glances toward the camera belie this pretense. While the people in the "Sweet Charlie" dance sequence cooperate with the presentation of their performance as a seamless found phenomenon, the mule on which one of the female leads rides disrupts it by wandering away, forcing the male lead to pull him back to maintain the frame and keep the story moving. With its controlled repetition of the ethnographic view, the film announces its authenticity along with its participation in discourses of power inherent in an ethnographic gaze in film. With a more liberal impulse to display the authentic, the dance scene also posits the cultural integrity of the indigenous performance and of the film itself.

To solidify the ethnographic viewpoint, the iconic dance scene bleeds into even more classically anthropological images of a cockfight. The cockfight also suggests a primitive society. Anthropologists have identified the cockfight as an important ritual entertainment, the dynamics of which have been used upon occasion to make generalizations about social relationships and gender structure.[8] An unseen narrator, not heard before and never heard again, asks, "What's this, a cockfight?," guiding the viewer and disrupting native culture as found phenomenon even as it tries to establish such. The narrative voice that announces the scene introduces a presumably uninitiated audience to the event. The camera obscura approach that would normally posit the natural, found occurrence of the cockfight reveals itself as an empowered perspective that transmits native reality. The narrative voice invites the viewer to enjoy the spectacle along with the people who are already there. It creates an educational aspect and encourages viewerly participation rather than distanced observation. An audience of about twenty men and women stand around a pen, cheering on a fight between a white rooster and a black one. The camera approaches through an opening in the low wooden gate enclosing the event. The roosters squawk, jab, and flutter. They circle each other in a kind of natural dance while the spectators root for a winner. Close-ups of the viewers display youngsters in crisply pressed clothes engrossed in the excitement of the game and happily participating in the fun. Further disrupting the found, natural positioning of the cockfight, Percy Jackson gives the cue to end it. When he says "Well all right, well all right," two people immediately pick up the roosters and the cheering subsides to segue into the narrative portion of the film. The previously boisterous group is silent and the cockfight remains unfinished.

The cockfight has multiple symbolic functions in this film. It can be seen as a representational and interpretive tool for understanding the primary relationship performed in the film. Signifying in many interpretive languages, the cockfight serves as a visual, anthropological, gendered metaphor for conflict between the sisters. Visually the fight symbolizes the battle between the sisters and creates an aura of conflict that increases suspense. As an instance of anthropological display, the cockfight links the film's plot structure to a native drama. As a cultural metaphor, the cockfight maintains the cultural specificity of the fictional narrative by using indigenous practices to figure imagined relationships. The cockfight also naturalizes the sisters' conflict by analogizing the women to the battling birds. This metaphor reveals the very conundrum of how this anthropological approach can humanize a typically exoticized population by providing ethnographic detail and also problematically objectify it by representing the women as animals.

The cockfight as a cultural symbol usually enables an analysis of competition between men or masculinized forces in society. Its use to figure a relationship between women is a cross-gendered reference to Isabelle's and Sylvia's struggle for power and position. This transgression of the gender code to frame a conflict between women in masculine terms also provides a structure by which Isabelle and Sylvia also symbolize the more lofty ideas of nation and race.[9] The unfinished cockfight leaves no champion. It also prevents the film from having to show one of the roosters gouged and killed by the other, an event that might undo the careful avoidance of exotic, primitive, and luridly spectacular images. Since, in a sense, both women win in the end, the unfinished cockfight, with both competitors alive and thriving at the end, becomes a model for Isabelle's and Sylvia's conflict. The interruption of the cockfight facilitates the introduction of the movie's plot but also foreshadows a (stereotypically) female-gendered conclusion of cooperation and coexistence.

These ethnographic images operate as documentary specificity and as ethnographic detail.[10] The dance and cockfight were not inserted from separate ethnographic footage, as happened in other films from the period, such as *King Kong* (1933) and *Sanders of the River* (1935), but were made for this movie. In this way they are specific to this film and do not randomly homogenize black native scenes. Not directly related to the plot structure, however, these scenes specify a *native* cultural context. In their narratalogical superfluousness (they neither further nor elaborate the story) the images act apart from and outside of the plot. The scenes contextualize *Daughter*'s fictional characters as really there, as part of the native scene. The dance and cockfight are not necessary to specify a *Jamaican* context, just an island one. They establish nativeness as opposed to Jamaicanness and in this way are not specific at all. Rather the ethnographic images are positioned to purvey hyperfictional truths—extraneous to the plot of the film yet about the film. They display the film's concern for authenticity and verify its truth-claims. These scenes produce the native by providing particularities of natural environment, sound, movement and rhythmic structure, ritual, entertainment, and performing native bodies. The performing bodies also serve as "authenticating evidence of cultural difference" that constructs an altern gaze.[11] These scenes invite a mental tourism central to the film's ultimate assertion of transnational connections.

Iconic Spaces and Bodies

Throughout the film an ethnographic perspective surveys the cultural and environmental detail while a complexity of human interaction dominates representation. Images in the background of the film's action show a geographic and social diversity on the island. Two reviewers described the film as part "travelogue" to account for these ethnographic moments.[12] The reviewer for the *Motion Picture Herald* enumerates the local sites featured, "the Myrtlebank Hotel; The Glass Bucket — one of the leading night clubs; Spanish town; banana loading docks and plantations; open air markets." Isabelle's haunts include a lovely, secluded garden near the mansion. She and Ramsey, her overseer, hold a conversation walking up a long flight of stone steps surrounded by wilderness. The forest contrasts with the opening scenes of the beach and the open yard, where the dance occurs. Elvira, a plantation servant, lives in a small cottage on a hill and is shown walking with Percy, Sylvia's manservant, through endless rows of tall banana trees on the plantation. Sylvia's mansion has an elaborate sunny porch fronted by birds of paradise that contrasts with Ramsey's simple patio. A scene takes place at the docks, where railroad tracks provide the foreground to a vista of waves rolling against a beach. Sylvia and John Lowden, the sisters' love interest, take car rides on meandering paved roads shared by local cyclists, and golfers in the background. The film samples activities, spaces, and everyday life in a way that demonstrates the geographic and social complexity of the island and banishes the exotic as a dominant mode of representation. The island is depicted in a manner that seems to obliterate the possibility of an entirely primitive culture even as ethnographic perspective drives its vision.

A panoramic view of the spectrum of black life occurs as the story unfolds. *The Devil's Daughter* takes place within a context free of white people. There are no white actors or extras. The intraracial relationships represented are varied and complex since only blacks inhabit the various economic, national, and social identities. Diverse characters provide opportunities for harmonious meetings of different experiences, classes, and identities. Rich meet poor, workers meet overseers, landowners meet laborers and people in service, Jamaicans meet Americans, all of whom are black. The treatment of black relationships expresses a workable economic, social, and national diversity. The care shown in the representation of economic strata and the complex relationships between them contributes to the human complexity in this not so "burning tropical drama."[13] *The Devil's Daughter* thus maintains a consistent presentation of social detail after the anthropological dance scene and cockfight establish its ethnographic nativism. Multiple relationships between black people in the film achieve a nuanced communication across difference, the exploration of interactions between differently empowered individuals, and the assertion of diaspora.

The Devil's Daughter shows an awareness of the potential for a primitivist understanding of island culture embedded in its representational structure and challenges these assumptions with the first dialogue. The film begins to grapple with the problem of primitive othering in its treatment of the relationship between black national identities in a performance of dress, national origin, and language in the acting out of a game. When the native cockfight is interrupted, it is with a stereotypically urban, American pastime: craps. The relationship between Harlem and island cultures is evident in a short comedic interaction between Percy and an island man. Percy Jackson is a stock character from black American vaudeville; he tells jokes, is naïve, rolls his eyes, and performs Amos-and-Andy vocal antics. He appears during the cockfight, flirting with Elvira, who rides in on a mule like the character in the dance prologue and wears a striped outfit and hoop earrings that signify her native island identity. Her attire contrasts against Percy's sharp Harlem clothes. His crap game grift is a city slicker's attempt to get over on island natives, using what he assumes is an impenetrable urban jive. Percy draws an islander into "a new game direct from Harlem called Put and Take," saying, "You keep puttin' and I keep takin.'" He bets the Empire State Building and Radio City Music Hall against the locals' roosters. Of course Percy figures he can win the birds without risk, with the people around him being none the wiser. He issues verbal challenges (also known as trash-talking) and rubs the dice on the other man's head as he throws his two winning rolls. The man who humored Percy in the bet is not willing to be cheated, however.

Man: Wait a minute brother, I don't want to get you out of your delir-
ium, but I lived in Harlem and Sugar Hill for twenty-five years. Don't
pull none of that jive on me.

Percy: So you is a hep cat. You has got yo' boots on. Why don't somebody
tell me these things. Feet, get ready to do the duty, cause y'all has got
some new territory to cover.

The man has been wise to the grift the whole time. Percy is chased
away by five men in addition to the one he tried to cheat. His assumption of island innocence and ignorance to sophisticated Harlem ways is
challenged by the Islander's unexpected experience. The interaction de-
stroys the idea that Percy can make assumptions about his environment
or that the people around him are inherently vulnerable and stupid.
The boundaries between Harlem culture and identity and that of the
island are fluid instead of rigid. Through Percy's game, the film challenges notions that the island operates as a space of isolation and difference. Instead transatlantic crossing and international experience assert
composite identities and undermine island stereotype. Just as Percy's
feet "got new territory to cover," so too does the film and its viewers in
understanding the intercultural exchange it illustrates.

As a figure of stock Harlem identity, Percy represents the challenge
of cultural integration and the persistence of difference. John Lowden
says of him, "He doesn't get acclimated very easily; he still has Harlem
written all over him." The question becomes whether Percy can adapt
to the island. When Elvira directs Percy, whom she affectionately calls
"Harlem Boy," out of the jungle, where he was chased by his supersti-
tious fear of spirits and "dead people," she does not show him a path
but a hop-step that he then repeats behind her. Isabelle pretends to cast
a spell, convincing Percy that his soul will be protected from spirits by
being transferred into a little pig, which he then struggles to protect
from being eaten. Percy's sharp clothes, speech, humor, superstition,
and gullibility make him the vulnerable outsider positioning Harlem as
other in the island context. He escapes at one point to an impressive,
leafy cotton tree with a trunk large enough to swallow him. The image of
Percy inside the cotton tree encapsulates one of the film's major themes:
absorption into island space. Commenting on the tree's overwhelming
size, he declares, "I'm glad I ain't no cotton-picker!" Percy's slang response shows the actual difficulty of this integration, however, in his

pun on "cotton-picking" that is a derogatory epithet based on the stereo-typical occupation of rural blacks in the U.S. The developing romantic relationship between Percy and Elvira incorporates him, though it does not change him. He is included even if he cannot be assimilated.

Percy's minstrel joke acts as a humorous means to posit Harlem as a placeholder of American racial and performative identity. Through Percy, Harlem is pitted directly against island culture. As an emblematic black American homeland, Harlem figures prominently as a signifier of difference and a point over and through which commonality and harmony must be achieved. Percy also becomes a means of trouncing the figure of Harlem as an ascendant, dominant black identity. Several aspects of his character undermine the performative power of the national racial identity he embodies. As a supporting buffoon character who is also a servant, he lacks significant social (or narrative) influence on the interactions in the film. His status as a male signifier of national identity ironically marginalizes him within the film's female logic of national identity. His superstition separates him from the studied rationality evidenced by all of the other characters. The fake vaudun hoodwink accomplished by Elvira and Isabelle on Percy assesses his Harlem sophistication at naught. Percy deflates an empowered American nationalism. In his impending marriage to Elvira, as in the sibling relationship between Isabelle and Sylvia, the transoceanic intraracial relationship is figured as an intimate partnership. The purely Harlem Percy and the purely island Elvira represent a subplot of the creation of diasporic union and coexistence, where American identity in the figure of the male partner does not dominate. While Sylvia's and Isabelle's parentage represents a hybridity that already exists, Percy's and Elvira's marriage symbolizes unity across difference.

In addition to Rony's observation that "the viewer is presented with an array of subsistence activities, kinship, religion, myth, ceremonial ritual, music and dance, and—in what may be taken as the genre's defining trope—some form of animal sacrifice," this film presents technology in the form of cars, phones, and planes, as well as social competition, trade, and economics.[14] Moreover the specter of animal sacrifice is undermined in the joke of Percy's "hoodoo"-ed pig. After Sylvia pretends to transfer Percy's soul to the little pig, it gets cooked for Ramsey's dinner in a "soulful dish right from Harlem." Unraveling an investment in the stereotypes of animal fetishism in obeah and of the ethnographic portrayal of ritual sacrifice, Percy insists that his "ain't no ordinary pig." Rony states that "in the popular imagination an 'ethnographic film' . . . purports to portray whole cultures within the space of an hour or two. Like a classic ethnography which encapsulates a culture in one volume, an 'ethnographic film' becomes a metonym for an entire culture."[15] In *The Devil's Daughter*, on the contrary, the viewer gets the sense of seeing a panorama of the culture and its possibilities. Natives are neither noble nor wild, but civilized and subsumed in organized culture.

An impression of cultural complexity also occurs when the camera pans over the horse races and shows groups of people involved in a variety of social activities. Even the horse race itself is a system too complex to fully understand in the time devoted to it, much less an entire culture. The fairground sits among hills and mountains with clouds rising gently off the ridges. This complex event, however, with its well-dressed race-goers, fit horses, and traditionally attired riders and trainers, serves as a display of organized social structure. The outfits and reserved spectacle reference a colonial past.[16] The industrial and conventional technology on the island as well as its social organization and peaceful class differentiation posit a civilized, modernized native society. The undermining of primitivism and unilateral nativizing that typically others black populations and the attempt to represent a complex social world undo strict assertions of cultural, national, or racial power and emphasize the emergence of diaspora through representation and performance.

The ethnographic interest in showing the texture of the life of a people in a specific place and context is complicated by the constructing power of the gaze assumed by American filmmakers stepping in to document and represent another culture. Sylvia's character manifests the way *Daughter*'s conditions of production bear out the film's American dominance of form and gaze. *The Devil's Daughter* was the first American black feature filmed on location in Kingston, Jamaica.[17] American production provides an extranational, intraracial gaze in the treatment of an island subject. The production relationship of traveling is echoed within the film text in one sister's movement from Harlem to Jamaica. She moves from the United States into what is for her a different and alienating environment. The island seems new and different to her even though it is a part of her past that she feels should be familiar. Her American status affects her standing in the film's negotiations of identity. She is a privileged, empowered outsider seeking access and acceptance. The exterior American gaze of the film seeks a similar mediated cultural access. The operation of power that exists in staging, collecting, recording, structuring, and viewing is intensified by the national difference between the American production mechanism and the island subject. Even though the camera expresses a desire to record a naturally occurring event, the natural and the event are both staged and, for the most part, produced.

International power dynamics remain at play extratextually in the fact that all of the lead and supporting actors are American. Thus whether the characters they portray are Jamaican, Haitian, or American, American stars dominate the story and the screen. The background figures, such as dancers and workers, are played by Jamaican locals.[18] These extras are figures without a voice in the film narrative. There are voluble exceptions to this generality: the man who plays dice with Percy and the Jamaican dance troupe that performs in the "Sweet Charlie" scene. In both instances the casting and the story support a Jamaican or island agency. The extras neither act nor draw attention to themselves by being uncomfortable before the camera. Their participation is minimal and naturalized in its marginality. Like the dance scene and cockfight, use of locals as background figures provides authenticity and nativizes the action. While use of local extras contributes to a professional hierarchy in production, it also provides labor and representation for Jamaicans.[19] *The Devil's Daughter* lacks the reciprocity of representation and production present in Dunham's ethnographic filmmaking, but in its effort to cast and employ Islanders this fictional film performs a material inclusion of Jamaica's native population. Behind the scenes the production and design teams, however, were also American. In one very obvious moment, Jack Carter as the overseer Phillip Ramsey fakes a Jamaican accent. This unsustained effort demonstrates a desire to portray an authentic Jamaican despite casting choices. The minor effort and its failure emblematize the embattled categories of authenticity and nation, reciprocity and hierarchy in this film. *The Devil's Daughter* was clearly an American movie set in Jamaica establishing an American perspective in its making of identity. The notable lack of an explicit British colonial presence in this Jamaica emphasizes the effort to construct an all-Negro environment peopled by West Indian and American blacks.

CHAPTER FIVE

Transnational Sisterhood

Before the audience meets either sister, Sylvia's manservant, Percy (Hamtree Harrington), and Isabelle's assistant, Elvira (Willa Mae Lane), explain the film's central conflict over the plantation. These two supporting characters not only serve as the narrative chorus, but also enact a resolution that mirrors the ideological positions of the film. They inform us of the sisters' past, a history that in its spatial implications allegorizes international identities and power relationships between a youthful, empowered, black U.S. and an older, petulant black West Indies. Since younger sister Sylvia's (Ida James) arrival from New York, the native, older Isabelle (Nina Mae McKinney) has taken to hiding in the jungle, refusing to see or communicate with her estranged sibling. Sylvia, having gone as a child to live with their father in New York to receive the "education," "culture," and "opportunity" he wanted for both of them, has been favored as heir to the entire plantation. Sylvia has returned to claim her property and position. In light of her urban American past, a return to the island seems perplexing to a very innocent Sylvia, who expresses a great deal of discomfort. Alone Isabelle has managed and maintained the plantation in her father's and sister's absence. Through her capable administration of the plantation she has gained local power, the respect of a childhood friend and love interest, and the admiration and obedience of her workers, and she wants to keep it all. Isabelle understands her disinheritance as punishment for her refusal to quit her native home for Harlem, the urban black metropole. Harlem becomes shorthand for a dominant notion of blackness and a marker of struggle over identity and power in the film. Enraged over her loss and the filial betrayal consequent to her disinheritance, Isabelle determines to get the plantation back by using island voodoo to scare her sister into relinquishing it. Isabelle sees Sylvia as an interloper and resents the legitimization of her choice to become American inherent in her receipt of the property. Further complicating the national allegory is a second object of desire, the rich West Indian mutual love interest, John Lowden (Emmett Wallace), who owns the neighboring plantation. Isabelle envies her childhood friend John's romantic designs on Sylvia. The women negotiate ownership not only of valuable property, but of romantic claims to the male body—both of which stand in for the possibility of national and international island domination. Positioned to lose her property, her beau, and any matrimonial stake to his plantation, a resistant Isabelle goes down fighting. Her ambition contrasts with Sylvia's simple desire to stay on the island, share the plantation, and befriend her sister. With the help of her overseer, Phillip Ramsey (Jack Carter of *Macbeth* fame), and workers, Isabelle slowly unnerves and then terrifies her sister. Her efforts culminate in a fake obeah ceremony at Witch's Blade designed to drive Sylvia from the island forever. Sylvia gives up the plantation to maintain peace and marries their mutual love interest, thus capitulating to native autonomy but maintaining a claim to the island nation through romantic coupling.

Through the film's images and plot, a theory of diasporic interaction and cultural trade develops based upon a model of family. The nations are represented historically in the reversal of age in the sister's inheriting status. The younger sister (and the more recent black population) is willed the inheritance. Sylvia's nonnative difference becomes her central challenge on the island. Sylvia was born on the island, then raised and educated in Harlem. Isabelle, who shares Sylvia's father but has a Haitian mother, stayed behind in Jamaica, remaining close to its culture and people. When Sylvia, who for all intents and purposes has stolen the birthright, comes benevolently to town, the sisters are at odds about their places in the family and social order. They compete over property, standing, and men. In the strangest of displays of ambivalence, the Jamaican Haitian sister trades on her mother's identity to *pretend* to be a priestess of vaudun. Isabelle drugs her American sibling, carries her to the woods, and pretends to cast a spell over her in hopes of tricking her into relinquishing her place. As the underdog, Isabelle draws upon the native power of collective support and vaudun pretense to oust her legally empowered younger sister. Forgiving Isabelle for her drugging and the voodoo, the American sister gives up everything *except* their mutual love interest, the rich owner of a neighboring plantation.

The central tale of *The Devil's Daughter* unfolds through representations of womanhood. Significantly, sisterhood, not brotherhood, serves as the figure of diasporic unity. Women's bodies act as signifiers of race and nation. The radical differences of gender characterization in each sister's personality, demeanor, and intentions set up an opportunity to establish peace between opposing perspectives and positions. Sylvia is a slight, soft-spoken, vulnerable, but determined girl who will share with her sister but not leave the island. Isabelle, even more determined and called "uncannily smart" and "proud as a peacock," is composed and commanding. Sisterhood is posited as the antithesis of competition and the reason for unification. Sylvia, John Lowden, and Phillip Ramsey, observers and participants in the situation, repeatedly cry "But you're/they're/we're *sisters!*" as an opposing argument to Isabelle's plans. Since they are sisters they should get along without conflict and work out their differences in the interest of family love. Yet the film makes clear that this connection is not automatic; each sister must *choose* to rebuild and maintain the sisterly bond.

Transnationalism is not authenticated in a male body or recuperation of manhood, but in sisterly cooperation. The driving conflict between the sisters over property and kinship allegorizes national and diasporic relationships, especially in the array of national origins and affiliations represented in the characters. While geographical affiliation provides a basis for national symbolism, parentage further nuances each woman's status as a national icon. The sisters are each already hybrid in their national identities through a combination of national geographical affiliation and parentage. One might easily assume from the representation of the women's lives that the father was American, but the film does not actually identify his national origin (just as it leaves its own Jamaica unnamed within the film text, both universalizing and homogenizing gestures that operate in opposite ways). His fatherhood consists of a strong desire for and location in Harlem as home. None of these parents has survived, barring the possibility for the representation of pure national identities in the family. The parents' legacy is national hybridity and international movement. The unknown origin of the absent father makes the maternal line central in the story and refuses to identify a dominating narrative of paternal origins. The echo of U.S. affiliation through his Harlem origins left in his absence, however, casts the nature of his daughters' diaspora, at least in part, in African Americanist terms. The father-land is not Africa or the Atlantic or an American South, but a modernist Harlem. That the island mothers are also gone leaves the negotiation of family ties and property to the nationally hybrid generations of women left in their wake. This model of sisterly conflict and reunification restages black identities as a product of national indeterminacy and diasporic unity. The use of women and sisters as arbiters of national identity circumvents classic paradigms of belligerence and competition that might obtain through more masculine representations.

Sylvia's American identity is located in a black urban Harlem and combined with an island origin through her having been born on the island to a Jamaican mother. The conditions of her inheritance signify the dominance of her American identity. In Sylvia's mission and travels, she embodies a benevolent Americanism, vested with ability and choice to bestow wealth and position upon her sister, despite her predominantly outsider status. Sylvia is nicer, well-intentioned, and generous, while Isabelle, though having a just complaint, is childish and selfish, a not so unfamiliar representation of the relationship between colonizer and native. Sylvia's American enculturation makes her uncomfortable on the island. She feels afraid, "strange and creepy," and wonders why she cannot fit in anymore. In her struggles to understand her discomfort, she wishes she were back in Harlem. The narrative insistently figures her migration to the island as a return, perhaps to blackness, family, and home, as well as to a lost past and future. As a black American Sylvia displays a conflicted sense of belonging as she searches for her true inheritance. Her legal and national dominance is undermined by her fear and sense of alienation on the island that serves as a lost home. Despite this fear, she feels inclined to become reintegrated into this space. Her empowered position is destabilized by her loyalty to her family and homeland.

Isabelle's character manifests a combination of Harlem paternity, island spatial location and personal investment, and Haitian maternity as identifiers. Isabelle grew up on the island and is familiar with its ways. Fully integrated into island culture, she trades on the identity of her Haitian mother to pass as an obeah priestess. She insists upon her dignity by refusing to accept charity or acknowledge Sylvia's presence, despite her position as a native dispossessed. She refuses to share the property, but wants it all to herself so she can become a "great lady," running the "most successful plantation on the island." Complementing Sylvia's ambivalence, Isabelle's response rejects a model of American hegemony by rejecting benevolence. Isabelle maintains the support of native plantation hands who recognize her as the rightful owner and resent Sylvia's encroachment. Armed with local support and her staunch determination, Isabelle is positioned to stage her ousting of Sylvia. Symbolically black, indigenous island voodoo culture operates as resistance and as a means by which to reclaim autonomy and position. Isabelle is an American expression of island identity, and as such the film expresses a strong investment in maintaining the agency of other in the construction of her character. When discovered in her ruse Isabelle immediately confesses to wrongdoing in order to protect her people, and for this even seems willing to give up her fight.

The sisters and nations operate as equals engaged in filial conflict. Sisterhood triumphs, as both sacrifice some of their desires and compromise. Having always wanted to share goods and power, Sylvia generously gives over the entire plantation to Isabelle. Not left empty-handed, however, she procures her own wealth and position through marriage to Isabelle's love interest, John Lowden. The American symbol maintains a rich inheritance and the moral high ground. Isabelle's story does not end in marriage, but in the ownership and management of a successful plantation. Within the gendered logic of the film, it is important that this female symbol of native autonomy remain outside the patriarchal confines of heterosexual marriage. In the final shot Isabelle stands in the center of two embracing couples (Sylvia and Lowden and Elvira and Percy), remaining fully integrated in the social system. Her character maintains the equality and integrity of the national diasporic identities she signifies. The preservation of family love, however, facilitates happy endings for both. The film hereby offers a moral. Through cooperative sacrifice the women achieve a mutuality satisfactory to both that also permits them to commune together. In the last line of the film Sylvia declares that she and her husband will dine on roast pig at her sister's plantation, summing up the realignment of national identification and hierarchy. In this feminized formation of diaspora black women act as symbolic representatives and arbiters of nation. Representing diaspora through sisterhood hypothesizes a safe and nonviolent transformation of black identities separated by tempestuous national histories.[20] The sisters' economic and romantic resolutions permit allegories of both unification and autonomy in the resolution of international and intraracial conflict in the film.

Fake Real Exoticism

Although its advertising promised exotic spectacle, the film failed to deliver, in fact undermining the representational validity of exoticism and challenging the existence of exotic culture. The film offers conflict, drama, and voyeuristic travel, but for the most part abandons representational expectations of blacks as randomly wild and violent. *The Devil's Daughter* contains all of the elements typically combined to perform exoticized identities and other exoticized culture: a distant tropical island, black performers, national others, drums, and ritual magic. Advertisements for the film hype its exotic potential. The title suggests hell, sin, and evil in the form of a woman. A promotional poster shows a collage of images, including a man in a safari hat with his fist raised threateningly at a voodoo priest (figure 29).[21] Both men stand over the body of a woman (Sylvia) wearing a swimsuit lying on an alter, and the film star Nina Mae McKinney looks on threateningly, holding a staff. McKinney appears again, this time smiling prettily for the camera, wearing a swimsuit and reclining invitingly. Complementing her genuinely sweet appearance are devil's horns drawn in above her head. Jeering over her left shoulder is a drawing of a devil. In the poster the women wear less than they ever do in the film, where they are always clothed in dresses. Also pictured is a silly-looking man carrying a small pig. Palm fronds suggest a dense tropical background. "See the Sensational **Blood Dance!**," the poster announces in the bottom left corner. In the top left is the description "*Sister against Sister* in a **Burning Drama** of **Love** and **Hate** in the **Tropics**." Multiple significations of blood become an exotic metonym for familial relationship and tropical evil. The poster's center carries the title in bold red letters and announces an "All-Star Colored Cast." Exotic images are used to package and sell the film, promising as much exoticism in the film itself. The packaging offers hot, terrifying action in an extrafilmic insistence upon the exotic nature of the people, place, and subject depicted. The film, however, disappoints such expectations. Offering exotic spectacle already undermined by the plot and property squabbles, the film falls short of its promise.

Part of the humanizing effect of the film is the way it undermines the exoticism possible in the voodoo plot. Although the film's promotional material and title refer to an exotic and mystical evil, the film itself overtly and laboriously downplays exoticism. The film refers to traditional practices of an island religion with the more culturally accurate term "obeah" instead of "voodoo." This terminology contributes to the film's ethnographic accuracy and its efforts to take native culture seriously. The representation of obeah as fake, however, was instrumental in getting the film past the Jamaican Board of Film Censors. The board approved the film for "showing up the wickedness and stupidity of Poco-

220

29. *The Devil's Daughter* movie poster.

mania and other Pagan rites."[22] In the end the "hoodoo" or obeah works, however, producing its intended outcome.

The narrative insists that the chants, spells, dances, and drumming enacted by native black bodies are fake and strictly "performative." The first representation of a belief in and practice of voodoo is yoked to humor. Elvira has convinced Percy, "a civilized Harlem citizen," that the only way to avoid the "duppies" (spirits of dead people) out to steal his soul is to let Isabelle cast a spell on him. Isabelle and Elvira conspire to fool a gullible Percy into believing that his soul has been transferred into meal and then to the pig that eats the meal. Knowing glances and winks between Elvira and Isabelle confirm this use of obeah as a joke on Percy and as a performance intended to scare Sylvia's household with the mysterious forces on the island. Percy's attempts to keep his soul from becoming soul food produce the film's humor, and his belief in the exotic performance becomes the film's comic narrative. The underlying humor undercuts the cruelty of Isabelle's plot since the audience sees its falseness.

The elaborate ceremony that Isabelle executes to scare Sylvia away is as false as the Percy hoodoo. The hexed pig incident provides evidence of the pretense of the obeah ceremony in an insistence that no true violence will take place. The exotic practice is not real, but performance. Thus the performance is not exoticizing because it is not real. Isabelle's aggressive behavior will not harm Sylvia. She merely intends to "put that sweet society sister of [hers] into an obeah psychofright scene that'll make her so scared she'll leave this island and never come back!" The implication, however, is that even fake obeah, the spectacle of the exotic, is effectively "psycho-frightening" and repellant. Drums that pound rhythmically in the hills unnerve the unwitting Sylvia, who finds them eerie and menacing, though they only serve to call the plantation hands to a rehearsal in the jungle. In order to make the act effective Isabelle administers powerful native herbs mixed in wine offered under the guise of the "family manners" taught them by their father. Sylvia is placed in a "semi-trance; she'll know everything going on but will be powerless to move or speak." Even though the film denies its ability to show real obeah, it relies on mystical stereotypes of the island to imply the existence of trance-inducing native flora (which in the film actually subdue Sylvia).

Isabelle offers her mother's Haitian identity as evidence that she is capable of practicing obeah. She cannot, however. Correctly, John protests, insisting that having a Haitian mother does not "make her a witch doctor," that is, produce knowledge of obeah or the ability to practice it. Isabelle's cohorts, Elvira and Ramsey, also know she cannot perform obeah. Ramsey asks, "How are you going to pull off this obeah thing when you know you can't do anything like that?" Isabelle's retention of her plantation, however, rests in her sister's vulnerability to the lie. Despite her own admission that she cannot perform obeah, Isabelle, seemingly knowledgeable about everyone's actions and motives, continues to orchestrate the hints of obeah practice, the drumming, and the aura of superstition designed to make her sister believe that she can.

The film's climax is a fake voodoo ceremony performed with utter sincerity. The ceremony is not performed in a manner that lampoons the practice, though everyone who has been rehearsing knows it is not meant to work. In a secluded clearing in the hills called the Witch's Blade, Isabelle and about twenty men and women from her plantation dance, sing, and wail around a paralyzed Sylvia. In the center are unidentifiable ceremonial objects on a blanket. They are blocked from view for the most part by the dancers. Constant drumming repeats and manipulates rhythms heard in the background of earlier scenes. Two men appear dressed in white robes and headdresses and perform spinning moves, jumping into the air and shrilly yelling. One of them stands behind Sylvia and pronounces, "Brothers and sisters, we meet here today for blood! blood! blood!" In between each shout of "Blood!" the celebrants bow and wail, waving their arms. The group dances around in a circle and in place. At one point they surround a woman dressed in a grass skirt and halter and a man in a loincloth. Isabelle wears ceremonial jewelry; the dancers and other participants carry spears, staffs, and poles topped with a wooden triangle. They kneel and bow in a circle and in a formation of two parallel lines facing Isabelle. The ceremony has three phases, during which Isabelle moves to the center, stretches out her arms, and chants in a church-like cadence with religious formalism, incantations that repeat sinister ritual language invoking evil spirits and personal power:

> Oh Great One, come forth from the secret places of the jungle so that I
> may be armed by the mighty force of thy mystic power. . . . Come forth
> omnipotent one . . . and dwell in the heart of these our people gathered

ETHNOGRAPHIC REFRACTION

here to pay thee homage, . . . so that I, thy handmaiden and priestess of the secret circle, may be given the key to unlock the gateway through which death comes as I call.

(participants hop in a circle and howl)

Loose the destroying power of thy will and let this woman . . . become an instrument of thy vengeance. Let her sight become dim so that her soul might be enclosed forever in the darkness of the black pit.

(participants kneel, shake, and bow)

Let her beauty become disfigured. Let the roundness of her limbs become flat and the strength of her young body become palsied and old. Let the icy touch of thy fingers, O Great One, . . . dissolve the living flesh from her bones . . . transform her into the ghastly image of death. Death! Death!

Her stance and spell are similar to the pose she took in transferring Percy's soul to the pig. Each stanza is punctuated by rhythmic steps and hops, dancing, wailing, chanting, and the shaking and waving of hands. Exotic dance, music, singing, religion, and extreme and unusually exotic language conjuring up the devil are performed in this scene. The performance is serious; it contains no Percy-esque winks and glances, no sly insinuations that it is a ruse. The victim of the fake ceremony will believe it to be real. In this way the audience can also experience it as real, an ethnographic moment, even though viewers know the spectacle is a performance.[23] One must question whether *rehearsal* of vaudun practice performed as a *fake* performance to be rendered sincerely can be voided of whatever sacred powers it holds. In fact it seems that the magic transforms Isabelle, the performer, rather than her sister, the object of the ceremony.

When John interrupts the ceremony to save a shrieking Sylvia, Isabelle has him seized by two of her men. She offers to stop only if John will ensure that Sylvia leave and give up the plantation. He knows the ceremony is a fake and refuses. Isabelle proceeds with the ceremony and her chilling incantations. He finally gives in to her demands if only to preserve Sylvia from being scared to death. Isabelle succumbs to overwhelming guilt and admits that it is all a fake. She confesses, "Oh, she's all right. I only did this for her own benefit to scare her so she'd return to New York and never come back. She's only drugged. She'll be all right in a few moments." When Elvira appears and informs Isabelle that the police may be on their way, Isabelle claps twice and quickly sends everyone home. She reminds them if questioned to say that they "were only having a little pocomania" and not performing real vaudun. Her intranational island dominance remains intact.

The film incorporates the historical detail that obeah and ceremonial drumming had been outlawed in Jamaica, providing a narrative reason for the obeah being fake. Though the film provides an excuse for fake voodoo, the ideological purpose of undermining the power of exoticism as a form of representation stands. In the film the participants are conscious of their own performance as such. They have rehearsed and practiced for the show. The island culture supposedly cannot be exoticized through a performance of voodoo since the obeah that occurs is already performance. Although a thing is false or a copy it still performs cultural effects.[24] Exoticism in *The Devil's Daughter* indeed exoticizes. Even though the performance is a fake within a fake, the film maintains authentic cultural difference in the dancing native bodies performing their version of the authentic "blood dance."[25] The buildup and execution of the voodoo scene here provides the titillation of popular exotic performance despite the film's insistence upon its constructedness and performativity. A tension exists in the film's denial of and capitulation to structures of othering. The ceremony even works within the context of the film as Sylvia finally gives up her claim to the family plantation.

This fakeness suggests a metacommentary within the film about the representation of voodoo in American culture more generally.[26] Since the movie is already performance on film, the pretense of obeah in the story becomes a metatheatrical comment on the metaphorical nature and performativity of exotic voodoo. The film and its characters use black performance of the exotic instrumentally within and beyond the film's performances. The exotic becomes doubly faked and powerfully denaturalized even as it operates to signal native difference and agency. Representation of a *black exotic* is only false and performative and is revealed as instrumental in its entertainment and ideological functions.

The insistence that Isabelle cannot perform obeah by sole virtue of her Haitian blood indicates that the practice requires training and knowledge. The existence and power of obeah are never denied, making it a kind of cultural fact. Belief in a real vaudun potential that can be copied or faked drives the power of exotic voodoo performance in the film. The film does not deny the existence and potential power of obeah as a form of culture and worship, but rather establishes it through an insistence that the fake does not approximate the cultural reality. The potentially denigrating and abjecting power dynamics replete in exoticism are rejected in the film by the insistence upon exotic voodoo as performance and upon obeah as sacred practice. Exotic performance of sacred practice operates as a means to accomplish Isabelle's justifiable goals of retaining personal power. Isabelle obtains parity with Sylvia through the performance of native power. As a means of achieving power and recognition, the performance of exoticism operates metaphorically to assert the validity of non-American national identities in the black diaspora and the transformative power of performance itself.

Authentic Diaspora

Ethnographic content and modes of collection found repetition in artistic form in a manner that challenged the traditional meanings of both. The African American anthropological methodology of ethnographic subjectivity evidenced in *The Devil's Daughter* and the construction of its characters posited participation and strove for belonging in the society depicted, even as the film expressed the difficulties of material integration into island life. An in situ or performing other looking back challenges the politics of objectification at play in ethnographic film. This reflective looking back occurs in the production and content of this film through a rescripting of the typically alienating ethnographic structure that portrays black identities. The film indeed posits a racialized native subject. The heroines and heroes, however, derive power and comfort from and seek integration into that native home.

The imperialist implications of viewing and representing populations through an ethnographic lens did not merely evaporate because African Americans were involved in filmmaking or because a black perspective was performed. Instead anthropological methodologies and perspectives became complex signs in black expressive culture and performance. The specific interventions employed to undo the assumptions of an ethnographic gaze show artists in dialogue with these overarching structures of representation. The use of ethnographic detail became a means by which to manifest a drive for racial and cultural authenticity and diasporic connection. This drive sometimes led to historical and cultural accuracy in representation despite the persistence of its hierarchizing structures. In the desire to find subjective authenticity in an other, however, persists the rubric of unequal power. An identity is imagined, formulated, and donned in an expression of individual identity and inheritance from a palate of romanticized choices. The sense of lack and, subsequently, of becoming through colonial contact performs an imperial relationship. Yet a significant change occurs in the practice of othering in the performances described. The politics of othering become about bringing an other closer to a notion of self rather than abjecting it. Performers deployed a participatory model to frame other as self and self as other. Rather than becoming more rigid the boundaries between such identities became increasingly fluid, even within a structure, such as ethnography, that sought to aggressively maintain aspects of difference. Seeking an authentic racial self, black American performers found national identity in diaspora. African American identity developed a dimension of global citizenship, and racial belonging became transnational. In a form of counterdiasporic symbolics, the advent of the Second World War instituted a push for black national inclusion in representation that appropriated black performance for domestic claims.

6

....

NO STORM IN THE WEATHER

Domestic Bliss and African American Performance

In the opening scene of Twentieth Century Fox's film *Stormy Weather* (1943), an invitation arrives at the picket-fenced, rural ranch home of Bill Williamson. A bash is being thrown to celebrate his performance career. Surrounded by bubbly, impeccably dressed six-year-olds, Williamson narrates a journey through his past and black performance that begins with his return in 1918 from combat in France. Celebratory images of participation in the two world wars bracket the film. At the beginning, heroes return from overseas, and at the film's conclusion Cab Calloway presents his uniformed son and his own touring band as his contributions to the new war effort. Scenes of successful, dedicated, intergenerational black participation, images of victory, a romance plot, the promise of domestic bliss, and popular exoticism firmly situate black Americans within a stable American framework. Imperial images of the folk and black primitivism contribute to the film's Americanism and are also central to the construction of particularly black imaginations of black belonging. In this film performing black bodies, as physical and collective bodies typically infused with notions of resistance, assert black inclusion in the body politic through investment in discourses of Americanism.

Black performance in *Stormy Weather* speaks powerfully to black Americans' domestic identities before the Second World War—their sense of themselves as American citizens and the complicated terms of that citizenship. Belonging is articulated even to the elision of important international connections and experiences suggested very early in the film. Emphasis on domestic identity positioned the film production and content as part of a larger United States's war effort. Even beyond the trappings of Hollywood, however, embedded in *Stormy Weather* is a narrative of black identity dramatized in the performative terms with which African Americans negotiated black national identities throughout the period. To the extent that black identities remained in conflict, the war was an exclamation point of Americanness in the midst of these embodied conversations, these struggles of identity around questions of nation addressed on the level of performance in black culture. At its appearance in 1943, the film served as a capstone to such discourses as black performances of modernity and primitivism. In this film these potentially countercultural performances merged with specifically mainstream appropriations of black performance and displays of black national inclusion. In the case of *Stormy Weather* expressions of margin and center coexist in the same performances in the same text. Cultural appropriations occur in both directions at the same time, darkening the mirrors of national identity and race such that the differences between complicities and resistances are barely discernable.

Ironically the more mainstream values reflected in the film mirrored existing black investments in modernity that envisioned blacks' humanity in the face of historical and representational indignities. In this film a broader national imperative merges with and uses black scenarios of identity. Mainstream representation appropriates black modes of self-expression and performative resistance in an embrace of black people and blackness that insists upon inclusion. A close analysis of the film's performances and performance styles demonstrates a deeper, embedded investment in black modernity and success that is simultaneous and contributive to, but different from, a discourse of national belonging. Though the film asserts belonging as a national value, it manages to do so in a manner that also articulates black uniqueness and integrity in inherently African American cultural terms. For instance, while the film presents minstrelsy, tap, and primitivism in a spectacular, almost voyeuristic manner, the terms of performance within the film complicate these black performances with their own narrative of black identity. The performance styles from the interwar period are a modernist finale to black cultural performance in the early twentieth century. Mainstream national imperatives external to the film itself meet traditionally black modes of expressing black consciousness in a seemingly unified narrative. As the film displays a positive representation of famous blacks as a gesture of inclusion, black performance within the film elaborates a more complicated version of black national desire. *Stormy Weather* forcefully demonstrates both black American nationalism and black American racial singularity, a form of *black* nationalism. African Americans ironically articulated inclusion through a powerful, consistent sensibility of their marginality within the nation and its discourses of race and culture.

The film looks like a simple cabaret picture that allows viewers to enjoy the exquisite performative stylings of all of the early twentieth century's biggest Negro stars: Lena Horne, Katherine Dunham, Bill "Bojangles" Robinson, Cab Calloway, Fats Waller, Ada Brown, and the Nicholas Brothers (see figure 30).[1] Classic songs are rendered in black contexts and performance styles. Its visual, rhythmic, and aural pleasures reach beyond entertainment, however, to portray a mainstreamed, nationally invested African American populace in a moment of global strife and racial turmoil. The insistence on black humanity in performance that has often operated as a form of resistance and national critique collapses with an insistence on black national inclusion and representativeness. Black artists perform images of international travel, U.S. victory, and othering representations to mediate domestic racism and establish their own domestic inclusion, racial integrity, and national belonging.

Stormy Weather is a celebrative tour of black performance cultures of all kinds and classes, especially traditional forms with which Americans would have been very familiar, such as blackface minstrelsy, tap dance, and jazz. It juxtaposes forms that had significantly different meanings in black culture. The film reclaims certain black aesthetic practices in order to imbue them with an aura of integrity and modernity. In organized and spontaneous performances it inventories styles from north and south, from the urban and the rural, and from upper- and lower-class entertainments. In performance black life gets encoded by architectural and social spaces of labor, leisure, and love. The multiple contexts of black performance — the parade, dance hall, front porch, ferry deck, speakeasy, and concert hall — provide a journey through the rich variety of black life. The sampling of performance types and venues becomes a vital sweeping gesture of inclusion that draws blacks from all walks of life into this domestic celebration. My analysis attends to the ways these repeated combinations of traditional and contemporary performance styles made meaning and probes the cultural consequences

30. *Stormy Weather* movie poster.

of these combinations. Central to this discussion is the African American treatment of performances of southern nostalgia, primitivism, and modernism in this vehicle for national inclusion. The way these representations come together catapults African Americans into modern citizenship by insisting upon rural plantation life and primitive blackness as *past* and reformulating blackness in terms of a high-modern present. Nonetheless all performance spaces and performative modes in this film were celebrated—some are posited as more relevant to black identity than others—but the sounds and images are rendered familiar, safe, and claimed as "all American!" *Stormy Weather*'s high production values give black performers and performance their aesthetic due, at last respecting black artistic contributions to American culture.

Form and Fiction in *Stormy Weather*

Musical and romance genres promote the triumph of romance over social strife as a seamless adventure into an ideal world where justice and happiness prevail. This musical is no different. Horne shines gloriously as a model of professional success. Robinson is finally masculinized as her, albeit unlikely, love interest, revising his film history as Shirley Temple's desexed sidekick. The names of famous performers and musicians were matched with their faces and made accessible on the silver screen for a nationwide public. A romance story ensues between the two main characters as they develop their careers between the armistice and going "over there." In the first scene Bill Williamson (Bill Robinson) meets Selina Rogers (Lena Horne), the younger sister of his deceased war buddy. Their "stormy" romance begins with instant attraction despite the clear interest of the attractive, supportive, and famous bandleader, Chick Bailey (Babe Wallace), who also loves Selina. We meet the historical figure Jim Europe (Ernest Whitman) in the club as he directs the orchestra and greets Bill and his friend, Gabe (Dooley Wilson). The integration of real and fictitious names and characters establishes an explicit desire to integrate the film narrative with real life, as if dramatizing a tangential journey in black reality instead of the constructed reality of performance and film. The device constructs truth around the bodies of the star players.

When it has received scholarly attention this film has been dismissed as merely a series of vaudeville vignettes. Donald Bogle aptly classifies

Stormy Weather in "the entertainer" tradition of the 1940s, when blacks emerged from the dominant stupid or comrade servant roles of Hollywood in the 1930s only to be limited by a new manifestation of the objectifying stereotype of blacks as entertainers.[2] Thomas Cripps concurred with many contemporary reviewers in observing that "only the superior music saved the actors' limited range, awkward cutting around its two putative stars, an inchworm pace, and a story so devoid of heavies as to lack dramatic conflict. . . . Besides as did each all-black musical, it risked portraying African America as a happy place with happy problems."[3] Bogle often extols, however, a transcendent characteristic of black performance within Hollywood films, noting "that audiences could have cared less" about Bojangles's poor line delivery in comparison with his dancing or about a weak story line compared with the Nicholas Brothers' spiraling "beyond and around the movie, framing [it] with fierce energy."[4] Acting as much more than respite from ubiquitous stereotype, however, these very transcendent performances were the primary spaces of cultural content where black performers made meaning within often problematic representational structures. Important here are the ways *Stormy Weather* as a performance makes meaning and the ways representations internal to the film express cultural imperatives of blackness.

While the film has problems in both its dramatic and visual development, such inconsistencies highlight the importance of the parallel narrative of performances internal to the film as constituting their own system of meaning. The plot and filmmaking do little to cover the romantic miscasting of a twenty-something Lena Horne against a sixty-five-year-old Bill Robinson. There is no narrative justification for the two falling in love. They are rarely framed intimately and their minimal interaction renders the basic plotline unbelievable. A nonexistent eyeline match between them during Horne's singing of "Stormy Weather," the key scene where their love is supposedly reconnected, makes the film's romantic resolution hard to understand. The film never quite justifies Williamson's status as an entertainment icon, even though its raison d'être is a gala celebration of "the magnificent contribution of the colored race to the entertainment of the world." The event specially honored Williamson, much as the film was intended to honor Robinson. The success of Selina's career is more strongly developed, demonstrating the extratextual weight of Robinson in the weaker role of Bill

Williamson. The poor technical and plot development of romance weakens claims toward domestic unification. The doubling of fictitious and biographical celebration puts the film as much in service of its black actors' success as its characters.'

Though it is technically a musical, *Stormy Weather*'s songs develop differently than in traditional musicals. For the most part they are not a break from a prose reality that communicates a character's emotional state and forwards the plot. Only two numbers awkwardly use this generic device, the "Stormy Weather" number and the finale that confusingly resolves a stage romance that never really occurred. Otherwise the film's internal performances are neither narrative nor episodes of emotional development, but staged episodes in a variety show stream of numbers. In this way the film awkwardly performs a mix of genres — a cabaret format and a musical narrative — in its attempt to bring a black romance to Hollywood film. For this reason it is difficult to know when we are merely being entertained as opposed to when we are getting more narrative development of Bill's and Selina's romance. Thus the narrative itself breaks down in the wake of the film's generic schizophrenia. The entertainment value resides in each performance number, highlighting a famous name or style. It is the content and arrangement of these performative vignettes that subtly constitute the cultural meaning in this film. The film evidences traditional Americanism with intrinsically mainstream and African American methods of representation: romance, domesticity, war patriotism, primitivism, the folk, and middle-class sensibilities.

Representing War and Nation

Polarized reviews of the film in the press indicate the conflicted social politics *Stormy Weather* articulated. The politicized environment made the film controversial as a historical event. *Stormy Weather* was caught in the changing values for artistic and social representation of blacks in Hollywood. Thomas Cripps details a complex process of wartime government, leftist, and Negro organizational pressure in Hollywood that had filmmakers aiming to achieve the goals black independents strove for in the late 1920s and 1930s. These efforts butted against embedded Jim Crow practices, studio egos, and racism in changing the usage and portrayal of blacks in film.[5] Representation of blacks as educated or the recognition of racial discrimination was good; zoot suits, "clowning," and persistent stereotypes were "obscene." At times white liberal papers blasted a film's stereotypes and segregation, while black trade papers, promoting the creation of jobs for black actors, heralded the same films as examples of new roles and the upcoming "sepia star."[6] Walter White and the NAACP bemoaned *Stormy Weather*'s focus on entertainment and the Jim Crowing of representation in an all-black film.[7] A black paper extolled the lack of "bandannas," since no one actually played a mammy, though Ada Brown dresses up as one for a show number, thereby allow-ing performance to address stereotype. In *Commonweal* white leftists panned its stereotypes, calling the film "flawed."[8] In contrast, the Office of War Information, invested in positive portrayals of black support, welcomed the film's patriotism.

The film's earliest images include actual footage of uniformed black soldiers parading up Fifth Avenue in New York City. Two of the film's main characters are cut in, beating a drum that announces "Jim Europe's 15th infantry." These were soldiers famous for their music and combat experience in yet another layer of American national identity imbricated in black performance. When the famous jazz band leader's 369th Negro Regiment "Hell Fighters" Band arrived in France on New Year's Day 1918, it was the first African American combat unit to set foot on French soil. The soldiers reported being proud to be the first African Americans in the trenches. In addition to fighting on the Western Front, Jim Europe's band entertained troops and citizens to great enthusiasm in every city they visited in Britain, Italy, and France. Noble Sissle said at the time that the "Jazz germ" had hit France, and it spread everywhere the 369th went. The band introduced the Old World to black culture as the hippest American culture. Images of their work in Europe were dis-tributed in the United States.[9] Their representation in *Stormy Weather* immediately signals a positive black relationship with the First World War. It calls up a collective memory of patriotism along with national and race pride. This permitted the U.S. in 1943 to do what Europe had done in 1918: embrace blackness as American. *Stormy Weather* positions its tour through black culture between the wars, drafting it all in the service of a national exceptionalism and embedding black patriotism within a narrative of nationalism.

During the first half of the twentieth century African Americans had an ambivalent relationship with American participation in the two world wars that defined the period. Produced around the start of the Second World War, *Stormy Weather* covers the entire interwar period. The film's representation of black experience in America elides and distorts significant cultural developments of this period. Their experience of major domestic and international events positioned blacks as significantly less invested in the nation than the film purports. They were treated poorly during and upon their return from the First World War. The NAACP sponsored a united front campaign despite segregated military units, substandard housing and supplies, and black relegation to menial labor, along with stateside lynching, segregation, disenfranchisement, and limited access to jobs and education. Despite black support and participation in the First World War there were no tangible changes in the conditions of black American life. Uniformed soldiers met with violence in the streets. The Red Summer of 1919, in which multiple American cities erupted in prolonged deadly racial violence, signaled the country's response to blacks' postwar expectations of equitable treatment and their agitation for black freedom. The positioning of Jim Europe's world-famous infantry among initial images of wartime celebration in this film links American blacks and U.S. war participation in a manner that aggressively overcomes this rift and initiates a process of cultural forgetting around issues of war and social injustice in the United States.

As an illustration of black inclusion in the nation, race-based systemic social problems become personal or irrelevant. The *very* segregated nature of this "all-Negro" film seems to belie the validity of any claim to true national inclusion. Bill throws up his hands in protest against and resignation to his frustrating postwar poverty, stating, "I wish someone would give me a gig." His joblessness seems not systematic, but personal. This personalization ignores the systemic betrayal of black veterans and absolves the nation of its responsibility to them, resulting in an erasure of their alienation from the nation. Donald Bogle observes that early twentieth-century black-cast films fell short in examining black American life because they were unable to portray interracial strife or the profound impact of American racism. In *Stormy Weather*, however, the villain-free "all-star, all-Negro" cast is instrumental. Specifically excluding white bodies, and thereby eliding white racism, the film develops a discourse of patriotism and nationalism for the segregated black communities at which the film was targeted.

The violent aftermath of the First World War and continued injus-

236

tice in the U.S., made blacks ambivalent at best about the Second War World. This was in part a result of the failure of the Senate to pass anti-lynching and civil rights legislation during the interwar period.[10] Many blacks thought of the war as a white man's war. They perceived the Nazis as similar to the Klan and could not see going to war to fight them when nothing was being done about racial terrorism at home. At the same time, however, African Americans had a long tradition of fervently proving and celebrating their patriotism and Americanness. President Roosevelt had offered some economic and labor support to blacks during the Depression. Eleanor Roosevelt publicly championed black rights throughout the 1930s. Thus the presidency had fairly strong black support, especially from the middle-class elite and those who were considered race leaders and could deliver a Democratic black vote in cities. This significant trust was instrumental in 1941 in stopping A. Phillip Randolph's March on Washington of blacks and the poor against labor conditions and segregation and discrimination in the U.S. military and war industries. The march would have been a major show of national division and dissatisfaction, and it would have been an interracial demonstration, giving strength to the protest while also aggravating deep structural racial tensions. Racial unity in national critique proved an undesired outcome. African American dissent was considered a threat to internal intelligence and national security, a domestic powder keg waiting to explode. The terms of Randolph's calling off the march included Roosevelt's taking some steps to equalize black status in the military. Gestures and desires on both sides demonstrated not only a stake in the nation, but hope for a better future.

Black national inclusion as part of the war effort extended to Hollywood lots and screens. In February 1943 the *New York Times* announced, "Two major studios, Metro Goldwyn Mayer and Twentieth Century Fox, in producing movies with all-Negro casts, are following the desires of Washington at this time."[11] Popular war pictures of the period, including *Bataan* (1942), *Stage Door Canteen* (1943), *Crash Dive* (1943), and *Sahara* (1943), often featured a black cast member. He was usually sweeping a ship's deck or singing a Negro spiritual, but his presence among caricatures of a spectrum of ethnicities signaled the positive diversity of America. These black figures were humanized with families back home, jobs, and their own desires.

Stormy Weather was an expansion of an ethos of representative inclusion sponsored by the government in the face of the war. Officials in the Office of War Information reviewed scripts and screened films with a specific eye toward their portrayal of blacks.[12] This monitoring occurred to manage the movies' impact not on the United States, "but rather their impact as eventual exports to allies, usage as armed forces fare, and even for showing to lands regained from the enemy."[13] Social and ideological changes in the 1930s supported new racial politics. For instance, pressure by black civic leaders and performers, general liberalism in a critical press, and the NAACP created more, if not better, black representation in films. Audiences and organizations eagerly anticipated *Stormy Weather* as the realization of studio promises to the NAACP in 1942 to "regard the Negro as an integral part of American life" and broaden Negro employment and representation in films.[14] In some ways this race film constituted propaganda that contributed to attempts by the Office of War Information to alleviate racial tension through ideology. *Stormy Weather* was instrumental in producing black patriotism with its insistence on black belonging and success. During production the principals would broadcast over short wave "the choice bits they had just performed to the boys overseas."[15] Ironically the film was released "just as riots broke out in Harlem and Detroit and the 'zoot suit' riots hit Los Angeles."[16] The riots heralded continued entrenched racial problems in the United States. Popular despite mixed reviews, *Stormy Weather* toured army camps and was shown internationally.[17] Its broad distribution at military bases with Negro and white soldiers solidified Lena Horne's stardom. Although the film makes no mention of the "Double V" campaign for "Victory at Home, Victory Abroad" in 1942, promoting an end to racism in the United States as part of the war effort, the film itself arguably responded to the call by offering blacks labor opportunities and representational inclusion. Mirroring its benefit finale, the film itself bolstered the war effort.

Performing National Belonging

Stormy Weather was the only Twentieth Century Fox film for which risers were constructed to seat the scores of people who came to watch the production as if it were a live show. The layered filmic, live, and cinema audiences complicate the racial and national gaze while also further blurring the relationship between the stars and the characters. The participation of black stars and the overwhelming acceptance of the film by contemporary audiences indicates that black performers, black critics, and the black viewing public anticipated and welcomed this kind of inclusive representation in hopes of and indeed as confirmation of material improvement of the conditions of blacks in America. Selina's and Bill's success shadowed Horne's and Robinson's. The fictional characters projected the possibility, and the stars the actuality, of black success. Selina's and Bill's impending marriage and middle-class resolution seemed to seal domestic belonging. The film text promoted inclusion and patriotism, first by simply representing blacks on screen, second by a positive portrayal that used as little negative stereotyping as the times allow, and third by imagining black success. The celebration the picture enacted resulted from mere representation itself. This was even as some of the performances boldly identified and served as a corrective to long-held racisms that undermined the notions of celebration, inclusion, and opportunity.

Although a race film, *Stormy Weather* was positioned for interracial appeal in its production by a major studio. The stars united the nation with their ability to draw both black and white audiences. Bill Robinson, Lena Horne, Cab Calloway, and Dooley Wilson, of *Casablanca* (1942) fame, were artists with mass allure. This crossover appeal united traditionally separate audiences in their acceptance of the film and its performers. Horne's crossover stardom served as an important vehicle for the greater claims of the film. Her interracial appeal formed a national audience that served as a ground against which to proclaim the message of nationalist black American domesticity. Richard Dyer argues that, from the beginning of her career, Horne's physical appearance and performance styles offered a liminal understanding of race. Her inscrutably Negro body invited the gaze of black and white audiences to her shifting performances of raced styles of singing. Her performance style throughout *Stormy Weather* resembles what Dyer calls her mainstream voice, which showed not her mastery of the sexy blues tradition, but an upbeat, crooner tradition characterized by white soloists.[18] As a signifier of both blackness and whiteness, her star image became a space of racial negotiation and cultural integration through performance. Her crossover cachet in the role of the film's heroine challenged racial division by insisting on a combination of forms and performance across racial categories.

As Horne's stardom and style suggest black acceptance and integration through racial performance, the symbolic suggestion of racial belonging in transition also occurs through Selina's role in *Stormy Weather*'s romance plot. Selina prioritizes her international career over marriage and the home that Bill hopes to provide her. She has goals and travel for her career that keep her from submitting to the domestic stasis of marriage and children. Her world has become so empty, the weather so "stormy" without that life, however, that she croons, "Can't go on, every thing I had is gone. . . . Since my man and I ain't together, keeps rainin' all the time." For "love love love love" she finally gives in. Selina expresses her new desire by wishing that she had a son to send to war. Her submission to domestic discipline comes in an expression of war patriotism. Her romantic resolution signals the transformation of an uncommitted population to domestic compliance and happy unification—blackness secured within a domestic context of marriage and nation. In this moment the film narrative and the content of the musical club numbers collide, with the songs substituting for dramatic development. In a rousing stage finale, the film foreshadows the two moving into Bill's home and suggest they'll bear a gaggle of zoot-suited sons. Selina's costume change from a virginal white frock of a southern belle to a black close-cut sequined gown of a sophisticated married woman signals her domestic transformation.

The ultimate goal of marriage and the ownership of a suburban single-family home as the underlying domestic plot dramatizes Negro investment in the American dream and its successful attainment. The film displays a casual black investment in the capitalist promise of heterosexual marriage, property ownership, and upward mobility. The successful working woman becomes domesticated by choice, perhaps foreshadowing a message to all women to abandon the workplace when the war is over. Love, home, and marriage are signs of national belonging. Prior to Selina's consummation of a heterosexual, suburban ideal of the nuclear family in this story of romance and personal success, "Uncle Bill" had become the bachelor patriarch of his own porch, sharing stories and lessons with children from the neighborhood. Not yet a father and not yet located within his own domestic space, Bill represents incomplete domesticity. The porch acts as a liminal space, a stop on the way to the domestic, where the trappings of middle-class mainstream existence seem to be in place in his life and that of the race. As such the porch suggests a transitional attainment of domestic or national belonging as well. It is interesting that except for the partial living-room set of Horne's "Stormy Weather" number about romantic longing and stymied domesticity, there are no interior home scenes in the film. Perhaps in 1943, in a mainstream American narrative of domestic inclusion, black people get only as far as the front porch.

Black Modernism as Racial Inclusion

Stormy Weather's articulation of citizenship involves a subtle performative critique of traditional stereotypes in black performance, primitivism, and plantation nostalgia. Performatively the film dismantles the significance of these as indicators of black identity, supplanting them with showcases of black performative modernism. Black humanity is constructed through a modernity that trumps traditional forms. In this manner black performance directly challenges stereotypes and antiblack racism, part of the basis of second-class national citizenship. In one of the earliest dance numbers, a chorus line of attractive, light-skinned young women file onto the stage. They wear petals around their heads, turning their faces into lovely flowers. As they prance in coordinated movements, filling the dance floor, they simultaneously turn their backs to the audience and camera. At the center of the flower on the backs of their heads are minstrel faces that are periodically and flirtatiously exposed. The static minstrel smiles provide a stark contrast to the colorist casting of cream-faced chorus girls. The monochromatic chorus is a symbolic counterpoint to distorted representations of the past. The minstrel faces nod to and dismiss a performative tradition and ugly stereotype that now serve as a point of opposition and irony to the shining faces of the chorus line.

A similar rescripting of racist representation to create a modern identity occurs in the performative style, language, and plot of *Stormy Weather*'s blackface scene. "Bum Garage," seen first in *Shuffle Along* (1921), was performed by Flournoy Miller and Johnny Lee, who replaced the late Aubrey Lyles. Blacks had appropriated blackface performance for their own purposes since the turn of the century. One point of these re-visionings of the blackened face was to denounce its status as a symbol of racist folk Americanness.[19] "Bum Garage" mixes minstrel notions of the folk with the trials of black urbanism. Black performers in blackface use a style that traditionally ridiculed rural lack of sophistication to comically bemoan the failures of modern technology. A car that billows steam serves as the set of the number and falls apart loudly as the scene progresses. Interestingly, the failing automobile also signals a critique of modernity's reliability, elevating the importance of black social connections and communication, the true stuff of the performance. In contrast to visual blackfaced folk stereotype and a sonic dialect mask, the repartee between the performers evidences extreme verbal sophistication. The performers don't sing, dance, or clown, but carry on a lengthy conversation that is grammatically correct but syntactically idiosyncratic. Barely a subject or object is spoken, yet the conversation is absolutely, and almost transparently, comprehensible through verbal rhythm, facial expression, and tone. The number reveals the complexity of the process of translation by which closed communities can be selectively exposed to outsiders. The logic of the conversation relies on shared contacts, urban geography, and unspoken experience embedded in the interaction. The audience must assume the powerfully articulated yet unspoken familiarity between the characters. Their verbal exchange is highly stylized and delivered in a vaudevillian minstrel voice that belies its complexity yet at the same time heightens it through contrast. The verbal style carries over both from and into their "offstage" (in the film) lives as they discuss narrative issues in the same syntax as they speak when in character on stage.[20] The mode of modernist articulation accompanies their application of blackface. The facial masking reveals the masked nature of the verbal styling and toys with the blurred line between the "real" and the performative within the film.

Stormy Weather complicates black primitivism in two numbers, "Tom Toms" and "Diga Diga Doo," by changing it from a symbol of black inferiority to a display of a savvy black modernism. Siglinde Lemke explains, "Several key expressions of modernism assumed their shape only through the incorporation of black forms. 'The other' . . . has been an integral part of modernism from its origins."[21] As the embodiment of its opposite, the primitive delineated the modern. In Western primitivism all things black, African, and Negro represented that lost self of modern white Western civilization. In *Stormy Weather* blacks perform a black modernism that stands in contradistinction to various primitive forms that they also embody. In doing so they manifest and define the quintessential primitivist modernism of the era. They simultaneously confound it by refusing to be simply the object of modern discourse, demonstrating their own modernity, and elaborating modernist forms.

A black primitivism that reflects an uncivilized Africa is ridiculed and overshadowed in the "slow beating of the tom-toms" and is trumped by Bojangles's performance of tap. In this scene the folksy form of tap dancing illustrated in an earlier soft-shoe performance experiences a modernist reversal as a counterpoint to primitivism. Bill and Chick are competing for the same girl, and the animosity between them is demonstrated by Chick's assignment of Bill to a chorus role as an African who pounds his drum while perched in a tree. Bill grumbles as he places a wig on his head (see figure 31). Resembling a hat more than a wig, the primitive costume lampoons African hair in a nativist gesture. The moment seems meant to be humorous in its irony, but works only if the stereotype references uncivilized Africans instead of black Americans.

The on-screen audience is unresponsive to Chick's deeply felt bass ode to primitivism, "the slow beating of the tom-tom stirrrs your bloood." His costume plays on explorer duds seen in movies and travel films. Enormous drums fill the stage, stolidly beaten by performers in primitive attire and hideous wigs depicting African hair. The number is a sung version of Langston Hughes's poem "Danse Africaine" (1922).[22] The poem romanticizes the internal rhythm of an African drum resonating with the sound of one's heartbeat and driving a beautiful dancer spinning around a fire. The poem signifies a time when a black aesthetic claimed primitive images in an expression of racial particularity and exploration of a lost past. As a so-called blues poem, "Danse Africaine" in *Stormy Weather* honored an idiosyncratically African American musical and literary tradition and one of America's celebrated black poets. The inclusion of this poem signals an ambivalence about the primitivism of the scene's costumes and set. Hughes's poem reflects in its lyricism a certain sincerity about Africanist inspiration in black American culture that contrasts with the film's use of it. Hughes's poem might be understood as an attempt to celebrate an Africanist aesthetic or as a capitulation to the primitivist demands of publishing and patronage. In either case "Tom-Toms" plays to and undermines the weight of a sincerely or ironically offered primitivism in black culture. Chick's performance and the primitivism of the number stir no one. The supposedly primitive tom-tom beating of the drum in this painfully boring rendition elicits no response from the audience. In the midst of this perfor-

31. Lena Horne and Bill Robinson in costumes from "Diga Doo" and "Tom Toms."

mance Bojangles begins an impromptu tap act that brings the number to life. He hops from drum to drum, replacing the beating of the tom-toms with a rapid, syncopated new rhythm. The (clearly rehearsed) improvisation delights the audience and cast, much to Chick's consternation. This negotiation of primitivism resolves male conflict in the film by affording Bill more performative power than Chick—a power that turns physical as Bill punches Chick backstage. The contest for culture contributes to the overarching domestic romance narrative of assimilation. Performatively "Tom Toms" dramatizes a cultural history and future of black performance and modernity. The high-modern style of primitivism that so diligently required black bodies as symbols and participants is comically trounced, stomped into shame in the wake of an American form performed by the king of tap himself. It is not the folk, soft-shoe, working-class pastime Bill displays on a ferryboat, but a modernist African American concert style that replaces a hackneyed, objectifying insistence that black culture is in fact primitive. The second of three tap numbers, "Tom Toms" links expressions of black modernity to black vernacular forms, thus disarticulating to some degree black modernisms from black primitivism.

At the same time that primitivism is superseded by alternate forms of modern black performance, primitivism's racist undertones emerge in the number "Diga Diga-Doo." "Diga Diga-Doo" and "Tom-Toms" articulate both modern fluency in and a rejection of modernism's racist implications. Energetic and wild, with a large chorus of beautiful young women dressed as sexy zebras wearing headdresses of long feathers, "Diga-Doo" is the most primitive display in *Stormy Weather*. Horne presents a tame counterpoint, singing in the midst of all the movement. The number creates a decidedly alienated relationship to Africa (or South America) through exotic sexualization and animal objectification. The pure showmanship of the number is highlighted in wilder solos of the darker skinned, darker dressed dancers who play the savages in "Diga Diga-Doo." Choreographed by Katherine Dunham, the movement of these principals incorporates modernist steps of performative club dancing and very likely moves collected during Dunham's Caribbean research, evident in the flexed feet, low center of gravity, shimmies, and frenetic imbalanced grace. The impressive choreography in "Diga Diga-Doo" contrasts with the primitive set and costuming. Ironically the combination of modern dance, primitivism, and the intimation of native performance conceptually links this duet most closely to Dunham's actual ethnographic and choreographic practice that ultimately sought to trace and produce transnational connections between black populations. The inclusion of both "Diga-Doo" and "Tom Toms" displays an ambivalence of representation: the persistence of primitivism in black performance and its rejection.

Signature modernist performances by Cab Calloway, the Nicholas Brothers, and Katherine Dunham further overshadow primitivism and folk stereotypes. A conversation in jive between Dooley Wilson and Mr. Hi De Ho himself indicate that a conscious uber-modernist form was seeded within black culture at the basic level of colloquial language. When Calloway says of Bill, "Hey, this cat ain't hep to the jive," in spite of himself Bill responds to parting exclamations of "Righteous!" and "Solid!" with "Crazy." Sharp angles of bodies and instruments doubled by their enormous shadows constitute the modernist aesthetic of Calloway and his band's jazz performances of "Gichi Joe," "My, My Ain't That Something," and "That Man Is Dynamite." The gravity-defying acrobatics of the tuxedoed Nicholas Brothers redefine movement and rhythm as they tap in high style across an oversized split white staircase (see figure 32). The set serves as a sparse playground of perpendiculars and arcs for the dancers' synchronized embodiment of extreme angles and diagonals. This performative capstone elaborates a final chapter in a danced tap narrative of black modernity begun in Robinson's numbers.

On and off stage in the film Cab Calloway wears generously cut zoot suits, with their baggy tapered pants, broad shoulder pads, and long jackets. His sharply angular shape is architectural, setting off the high energy of rhythm in music and his movement in a display of black modernism. The zoot style was hipster culture's opposition to wartime politics and mainstream values.[23] The extensive use of fabric defied wartime rations, and the body image and lifestyle associated with zoot rejected "both black petit bourgeois respectability and American patriotism."[24] But when Calloway visits the front porch and personally invites Bill to the benefit celebrating Negro contributions to the U.S., his cool style becomes part of a middle-class patriotic ethos in the film narrative. Two short scenes later a zoot-suited Calloway presents his army-uniformed son as the next generation's soldier. Zoot as a symbol of a modern dissenting body is emptied of its oppositional weight and refigured as a bearer of national loyalty. The embodiment of zoot in *Stormy Weather*

32. The Nicholas Brothers tap-dancing in *Stormy Weather*.

exemplifies the appropriation of resistant black performative forms to reflect a narrative of patriotism and national belonging.

Dancing the Modern

The titular dance by Katherine Dunham most powerfully demonstrates the significance of black modernism to this film and its articulation of racial integrity and American national identity. A formal placard on the club table introduces "Katherine Dunham and Her Dancers" as Selina begins singing "Stormy Weather."[25] Several verses into this long seven-minute piece, Selina runs upstage to shut a window through which we see an urban street under an elevated train. The location could be any urban black ghetto from the period. This geographical abstraction is part of the modernism of the piece. Selina closes the window and peers through a reflection of herself in the glass into another world. In this unreliable mirror she sees an imperfect, redoubled image of Katherine Dunham as Selina acting out the emotional texture of the scene in dance. Beyond the window is a creative space of abstraction and imagination, of change. The reflected and transmuted self ultimately returns through the window, becoming Selina once again as she makes a decision that will alter the course of her life. Darkening reflections in the window inspire personal and cultural reckoning.

Entering the urban world through that window, the camera focuses on Dunham, miserable and put out by the rain falling around her—a "pitterin' patterin'" of the rain drops echoing Selina's heartbeat and her tears. Dunham, this window world's lonely Selina, declines company as men and women pair off to find comfort out of the storm. Their costumes are the snappiest of contemporary street clothes, short dresses and zoot suits; the imprint of windowpanes on the sleeves, shoulders, and skirts indicates their abstract existence and embodies the mirror. The aesthetic of this world is markedly different from the rest of the film, as is its rhythm; with each character and couple displaying a singular way of moving through the street, the ensemble's stretched and intentional movement suggests a different concept of time. Life and movement become both communal and idiosyncratic. Moving off on her own Dunham becomes the principal of an even more removed, abstract performance of the storm itself. The setting and costumes change as the audience is transported into the storm. The wind blows through

33. "Storm Scene" in *Stormy Weather*.
COURTESY OF THE ACADEMY OF MOTION PICTURE ARTS AND SCIENCES

the all-encompassing environment of the clouds. Delicate ribbons of fabric stream from the dancers' costumes as if they embody the wind itself even as they dance through it. Dunham and her dancers display bent knees and moderate limb extensions, emphasizing both the fragility and solidity of the body (see figure 33). The hip movements are grounded and heavy, while the torso and shoulders suggest an airy weightlessness. Consistently upright posture and graceful choreography offer shades of classical balletic movements of the feet and hands. The focus is clearly on the representation of emotion and on the human form as opposed to any linear narrative. The smooth and languid motion transitions into distinctly more sensual, though painfully subtle, undulations of the pelvis and hips, consistent with modern and vernacular black and diasporic dance forms. The suggestion of feminine sensuality and heterosexual eroticism never, however, becomes explicit. Shades of Dunham's ethnographic collection of indigenous black dance forms suffuse these movements. Like the abstraction in costumes, narrative, and time, this choreography departs from any other moments or representations in the film.[26]

Dunham's choreography contains many subtle, tight movements within larger gestures and collective kinetic statements. Choreographic arcs are intensified with shoulder, hip, and hand movements that could be analogized to punctuation in a sentence or paragraph. Her dances contain layers of emotion, simultaneous tensions, gesturing in multiple directions enacted individually and collectively by a chorus of bodies. In this number a mainstreamed version of the blues, a musical and vocal style that gestures toward a working-class rural past, is accompanied by a danced performance of memory and reimagination of the future. The street scene references club dancing of the 1920s while Dunham's modern improvisation on a theme prefigures the development of black concert dance. Smooth encompassing modern movement performs a sublime freedom that is hoped for even as the movement is weighted, counterbalanced by small, tense, restricted movements of the hips, torso, and shoulders.[27]

The number experiences seven layers of bracketing as a deep core moment within the film; to get to it we travel through increasingly black spaces: the film scenario, a Negro club, the jazz stage, a black home — and its living-room window, a Negro ghetto, and up into the storm clouds of a black existential heaven by way of stormy emotions. The bracketing distances the dance from primitive numbers that precede it and also from the film itself. The nonrepresentational flowing costumes emphasize human form in the developing tradition of modern dance, demonstrating a cosmopolitan black participation in the newest aesthetics. The dance's position within the film is absolutely impossible, of course — not just from a metaphorical point of view, but from a staging perspective. Even though we know that the dancers are not really in the clouds, the number as presented also could not take place in the film's reality on a club stage, but only in the imagination.

This singular break with realism actually constitutes one of the film's most honest moments. This embedded, core dance number intimates a state of sublime hope in the midst of many kinds of rain and storm. The placement and organization of the dance; the understated undulations of the torso, shoulders, and hips; and the dancers' averted gaze in the storm cloud communicate a tense, contained state of unsettledness and struggle. The rain and storm represent not only Selina's heartaches and newfound desire to connect with her suitor, but the Dunham dancers' clear and deliberate discontent with the dreary conditions of urban life that shuttles them all into the abstract minimalist blues performance in the clouds. The film's title, chosen for the song's popularity, carries racial significance, though like this dance its resonance is deeply embedded within the film's representations. The unequal conditions in the U.S. that required such racial propaganda in the first place constitute the racial storm. Understanding black experience in America as stormy, however, opposes the film's overarching goal of racial success. Thus the reference gets buried at the core of the gilded social experience reflected in the film. In Selina's decision to marry Bill, the film suggests that, like her blues, any such storm of racial inequality is over.

The "Stormy Weather" number performs several connections and inclusions through the stages of its bracketing. It performs a deep black inclusion in a high-modern aesthetic and through this high art displays national and Western artistic relevance. It connects black physical and choreographic modernity to the vernacular form of jazz dance performed in numbers that precede and follow this one. The exaggerated, angular movements of couples walking in the rain dramatizes the modernism of jazz dancing. Through an association with jazz movement and images in the narrative context of the street scene and the rest of *Stormy Weather*, modern dance expresses a grounding in community rather than difference from it. In the abstracted dark and rainy streetscape misery finds solace in company, emphasizing the role of community in the process of coping. Modernist abstraction facilitates the expression of communal sensibilities and allows for the mediation of the aloneness of the Dunham/Selina character. The alleviation of this discomfiture occurs in the soft smooth movements of Dunham's modern dance in the clouds. Though its goal was to communicate emotion through movement and elevate dance to art, modern dance here serves the same emotional and social function as the blues being sung by Horne in a slightly different rhythm from the music of the dance. The high-art status of modern dance is linked to the traditionally low-art form of sung blues through the echoes of Horne's melodious voice. A spectrum of domestic African American forms, the blues, jazz, urban ghettos, and movement become connected to American modernism. Simultaneously modern forms are performed as embedded, as core within black culture—and black modern forms, seeded deeply within a black expressive consciousness, perform a gorgeous existential reckoning, ascending to the heights of heaven in a sublime negotiation of despair.

Rejecting Internationalism

The "Stormy Weather" dance number gestures toward the film's general sublimation of African American international ties and investments in service of domestic ones. This performance de-emphasizes the history of Dunham's signature international, intraracial research. Likewise this performative narrative of Americanization and national inclusion de-emphasizes the impact of transnational experience on black domestic life. *Stormy Weather* is unique in its acknowledgment of international travel as a component of black life. In the lives of celebrities, travel and transnational interaction had become commonplace; famous artists were icons of success, celebrity, of racial breakthrough for the black public. Their international ties and world fame were part of this symbolic status. The historical impact of fair treatment and of physical and personal freedom in other nations contributed to black artists' activism against segregation in the United States and thus their status as race leaders. In this sense travel and celebrity helped radicalize black entertainers with regard to issues of racial injustice. Dunham and Horne were among many stars whose travel overseas reduced their tolerance for American racism; both protested and refused to perform before segregated houses, whether military, international, or domestic.[28] But the thin veiling of celebrity personas in the film exploits international experience as a marker of black fame in order to diminish it. The travel that bolstered celebrity status in real life became immaterial in the lives of their fictional characters. The film presents international experiences as tangential and insignificant, erasing the politicizing effects of black internationalism.

In *Stormy Weather* Bill and company return from a tour of duty "over there" wanting neither to go back nor to compare the structure of life in the U.S. to freedoms experienced abroad. Selina returns from her own extended European tour ready to settle down in the little white house the audience has seen since the film's earliest frames. The film's domestic framing with images of the white, single-family home closely parallels the film's framing between World Wars, constantly offering domestic bliss as counterpoint and solution to international movement. Instead of identifying a black global perspective and its enormous impact on African American domestic life and ideology, *Stormy Weather* passes over these experiences as practically inconsequential in the development of national identity. Thus the film's dismissal of the impact of black experience outside of the United States becomes a crucial conduit for the film's insistence upon a secure black national belonging within the United States. Part of the fiction of the film is its erasure of the substance of black international experience even as it passes this fiction off as history through its parade of stars that play themselves. Perhaps this uncomfortable collapsing of domestic—that is, national and marital—experience (international experience, fictive characters with their real-life counterparts) provides logic for Bill and Selina never actually getting married in the film, on or off the club stage. Given that the love story operates as a metonym for the inclusion of blacks in American society and cultural discourses of nation, this lack of narrative confluence makes sense on a material level: black people and culture were *not* seamlessly integrated into the nation despite hopeful metaphors of heteronormative romance, domesticity, and ardent displays of war participation and patriotism.

This film repeatedly suggests and suppresses moments of black international travel and experience as well as extranational perspective in a process of international forgetting. At separate moments the heroes and supporting characters travel or return from abroad. This serves as an important part of the narrative without impacting it. The aesthetic of the Haitian Revolution that was so popular in black performance of the 1930s and repeated in the aesthetic of the Garvey movement is noticeably absent in *Stormy Weather*'s performative sampling. To tour early twentieth-century black American cultures without a hint of the French colonial aesthetic that had come to represent black nationalist movements seems a glaring omission. The film ignores this suggestion of diaspora through its historical exclusion of the major black international movement contemporary to its periodization. By eliding international experience, *Stormy Weather* consequently de-emphasizes an African American connection to either Africa or the West Indies as an alternate locus of national identification. Contributing to the narrative of domestic inclusion, primitive performance distances extranational blackness. Contrary to the insistence upon domestic authenticity, the costuming in the primitive performance scenes makes no pretence to a faithful representation of extranational black populations. The embedded transnational activity and perspective are defused politically in a manner that serves to focus the film's transnational energy on domestic celebration.

With alienating stereotypes largely dismantled and an active civilized modernism installed, African Americans are a national treasure and resource rather than a national problem. The interracial celebration of black talent performs national unity in place of racial division. Calloway's finale is a war benefit to send off soldiers to fight in the Second World War, one of whom is his only son. The film ends with an intergenerational trade of national loyalty. Black dedication and sacrifice for the war effort becomes a vehicle for the embrace of black people signified by the film. The visual pleasure of the film, the familiarity of its cast and forms, and its celebration of black performance history all converge to lull the viewer into an easy patriotism. Contrary to the suggestion in its name, *Stormy Weather* imagines calm in the midst of international and domestic storms of race and war.

Performative Reappropriations

Stormy Weather dramatizes the ironies and contradictions of identity and performance in black imperial representations of nation. In fact its mainstream message of inclusion appropriates black performative codes of inclusion, nearly collapsing super- and subcultural expressions. Black performers' complex discourse of complicit and dissenting identities developed throughout the era is embedded in a *segregated* mainstream spectacle of black national *inclusion*. The spectacle was celebrated by some as such and critiqued by others for its clear shortcomings in its confrontation of racism, and thus its shortcomings as a national assertion of black belonging. Black performative resistance to mainstream forces permeates this wholesale appropriation of black performance styles in the service of a national discourse of inclusion — performative forms of black modernity, rejection of the primitive and the folk, and simultaneous appropriations and manifestations of mainstream devaluations of blackness of primitivism and minstrelsy. Blacks become included in *Stormy Weather* and simultaneously manage to dramatize their own subjectivity through the powerful cultural mode of performance. The film is a mainstream appropriation of the black performative insurgency embedded in blacks' insistence upon their own humanity. The appropriation seems to accomplish what the performances sought — only at the cost of valued transnational connection and a critical relationship toward the state. As an example of the mainstream appropriating resistance already borne within itself, *Stormy Weather* endlessly reflects tensions of complicity and resistance, autonomy and inclusion. The appropriations and redeployments of meaning, the reverberation and resonance of images signal the complex figuring of identity and nation in black performance.

EPILOGUE

> As the margins resisted and decentered the center, they also
> transformed themselves. Unable to sustain a seamless, autonomous
> selfhood of Otherness, some margins embarked on internal critiques
> of their own homogenization. The center/margin dichotomy
> was undermined and spaces opened up between center and
> margins. . . . Some margins moved into the center. Some margins
> began to communicate with each other, without the center as
> interlocutor between them.
> — Smadar Lavie and Ted Swedenburg, introduction to
> *Displacement, Diaspora, and Geographies of Identity*

James Baldwin attended his first play, the voodoo *Macbeth*, at age thir-
teen, taken by a white mentor who introduced him to revolutionary
ideas through theater and film. Of witnessing the play's powerful spectacle, Baldwin averred that it drove his conversion to the church and
the ministry. For him the "terror and exhilaration" of "seeing living
black actors on a living stage," playing *Macbeth*'s "majesty and torment,"
"blood and crime," proved "we are all each other's flesh and blood."
Baldwin found that theater and church alike were venues for sustain-
ing life and faith. The encounter was spiritual. He felt himself aware
and a part of an audience on the verge of an adventure promised by the
contingent, mortal "ribbon of light" at the base of the curtain. Light
that like flashing projected images illuminated the connections between
black people and places across thin boundaries of curtain and screen
and border. Baldwin's response communicates the power of black per-

formances in this moment. He uses *Macbeth* to distinguish a complementary mutuality between theater and film. In theater the "flesh and blood" of the audience is challenged by the "flesh and blood" of the players. The theater insists upon the liveness and activity of players and audience. Baldwin was drawn in by the vibrant performance and awed by the duality of the players' stage lives layered upon everyday existence. He was exhorted by the prophetic rhythms of living flesh actually becoming the powerful and transnational possibilities played. Subsequent critics have insisted that cinema provided the same opportunity in a different manner for blacks in the city. To the cinema Baldwin ascribes the ability to "corroborate one's fantasies," to tell lies in the "language of our dreams."[1] Imaginations of selfhood and of power across forms link modern theater and film in black cultural life. The structure and content of stage and screen performances served as far more than entertainment for black people; they moved the populace with the hypotheses of the terrible and wondrous character of being black. They called overlapping communities into being and forced an awareness of the collective nature of experience.

As such, images and news of the performances addressed in this book were the subject of public discourse and the stuff of social networks, at the same time in the same spaces. On 1 October 1938 the *Chicago Defender* published promotional articles on *The Swing Mikado* and a "new movie, a western drama!" in production with Herbert Jeffries and Mantan Moorland on the same page.[2] Zora Neale Hurston reviewed Katherine Dunham's written ethnography, *Journey to Accompong*, based on her first research trip to the West Indies, a trip that also served as the basis for Dunham's early choreography.[3] John Pratt, a white designer and Katherine Dunham's husband, designed costumes for both *The Swing Mikado* and *L'Ag'Ya*. Later in her life Dunham purchased the Haitian estate of Napoleon's niece, the character represented as Pauline LeClerc in the play *Haiti*.[4] On her Haitian estate Dunham's presence filled a geographic space historically occupied by an imperialist noble specifically implicated in artistic productions about black freedom. The critic Robert B. Stepto cast the Idlewild resort of the 1930s as an idyllic space of childhood on the cusp of urbanization in his memoir *Blue as the Lake*.[5] The writer and political activist Richard Wright served briefly as a publicist for the Negro Federal Theater in Chicago and critiqued its lack of radicalism in his autobiography, *American Hunger*.[6] The players wanted shows to make the public love them, while Wright envisioned plays with clear political content and direct social relevance. The actor Jack Carter appeared on stage as a young vibrant antihero in *Macbeth* and on screen as a villain in *The Devil's Daughter*. The composer Leonard De Paur wrote and arranged music for the voodoo *Macbeth* and *Haiti*, and Canada Lee, a former boxer, acted in both. Designers, music directors, dancers, actors, extras, and writers shared work across multiple forms and performances. The collaborations evidence the historical formation of players, performers, cultural producers, and audience members articulated by these performances and the issues they invoked during the early part of the twentieth century. Symbolic resonances of racial and imperial exchange resound, their reverberation impure, at once historical, textual, political, and ideological. A discourse of national desire in black public culture was manifested in a community of artists and audiences that made and watched various modes of imperial representation. Though constantly maneuvering around the dominance of the center, African Americans acknowledged and engaged margins and peripheries to refract relationships of power.

The consequences of black manifestations of imperial discourses are uneven, inconclusive, and sometimes contradictory, but they are neither disingenuous nor compensatory. The identities took many forms: sometimes assertive, sometimes resistant, sometimes habitual and chronic, like breathing or a bad cough. For African Americans, racial, national, and nationalist (black, diasporic, American) identities were suspended in mutual contradiction. A clear sense of black Americans' investments in black, U.S., and transnational identities remains elusive as complicities collide with antipathies in performances of otherness. Black stage and screen performances constitute expressions of local resistance yet global compromise, local compromise, and global aspiration in a calibration of usable national identities. The clear boundaries of a cultural center and periphery become subject to the circular envisioning of the darkening mirror of black performance as black people struggled over their sense of global place and significance. Studies of identity and culture in diasporic and transnational, hemispheric and translocal frames on American and global stages continue to reveal such contradictions on the part of many black national and ethnic identities.

The child's "I" of the prologue might repeat ethnocentric nationalism in the recursive gaze of the singular subject. There is only the self

in the mirrored room. As a symbol of black Western national identification and the hope of diaspora formation, "she" repudiates objectivity as
an epistemological position and contemplates the problem of a proliferating self in African Americans' early twentieth-century extranational
consciousness. The "I" acknowledges that knowledge making originates
in specific positionalities and that radical recognition across national
and cultural differences takes conscious effort and a looking characterized by intention. The bounded child strives for relief and escape from
the dizzying recursivity of the self as point of reference. The outward
looking and acting of the performers, producers, and audiences in this
study reveal the struggle over the constitution of a national, transnational, perhaps, transsubjective "I"—and "we"—in the performance of
blackness. A black transsubjective "I" or "we" seems to fulfill the possibilities of diaspora or disruptive self-lessness for which this book hopes.
And yet the reflective model of transnational black selfhood persists,
often calling for a radical empathy and conflation of identities to promote humanitarian recognition and intervention. Bridging difference
constantly negotiates the intervening self. Transsubjective and translocal studies of diaspora from various positionalities hypothesized by
the child's "I," however, promise to illuminate transnational collisions
and interactions around and across postcolonial margins and centers.

....

NOTES

PROLOGUE

1. Gilroy, *The Black Atlantic.*

2. Conquergood, "Performance Studies," 145–56. Work by Jacques Lacan and Frantz Fanon also reverberate in this conception of black visioning and re-visioning, imaging and imagining transnational identities and reflections of blackness. See Lacan, "The Mirror Stage"; Fanon, *The Wretched of the Earth.*

3. "Tain" is a noun used here to extend the metaphor of illusion. It refers to the thin tinfoil that renders glass a mirror.

4. African American performativity signifies a break from aesthetics as a description of high culture or a determining set of terms or standards of one staid cultural mode of representation. For further explanation of mimesis and aesthetics, see Auerbach, *Mimesis.*

5. For more on postcoloniality, mimicry, and the politics of representation, see Bhabha, *Location of Culture.*

6. I thank Michael Witmore for helping me flesh out these connections.

7. For a discussion of theater space and the possibilities of transformation, see Dolan, "Geographies of Learning," 417–41.

INTRODUCTION

1. There are numerous investigations into the historical, political, and cultural milieu of this time. See Kornweibel, *"Seeing Red"*; Robinson, *Black Marxism*; Robinson, *Black Movements in America*; Denning, *The Cultural Front.*

2. For more on the efficacy of performance, see Madison, "Performance, Personal Narratives, and the Politics of Possibility" 278.

3. H. Baker, *Modernism and the Harlem Renaissance,* 6.

4. For more on the capacity of U.S. blacks to be positioned in alliance with notions of Western power and perspectives with regard to Africa, see Appiah, *In My Father's House*. Particularly useful for this study are sections on Alexander Crummell, Edward Wilmot Blyden, and W. E. B. Du Bois, figures from the nineteenth century and early twentieth.

5. For constructed notions of Africa in the Western imagination, see Garvey, "Africa for the Africans (1923)"; Garvey, "The Future as I See It (1923)"; Mudimbe, *The Invention of Africa*.

6. Conquergood explains the capacity of performance research to reveal cultural relationships in "Performance Studies," 145–56.

7. Anderson, *Imagined Communities*, 3.

8. Roach, *Cities of the Dead*, 13–16.

9. Diawara, "Cultural Studies / Black Studies," 209.

10. David Krasner notes that "social action came to be linked with expressivity," resulting in "the formation of a communicative infrastructure within the black community, with black performers playing a significant role in structuring black identity" (afterword, 348).

11. Rampersad, "Langston Hughes," 52. For more on black modernism, see H. Baker, *Modernism and the Harlem Renaissance*.

12. Krasner, "Black Salome," 192–211.

13. For further commentary on some of the impacts of modernity and modernism, see Habermas, "Modernity — An Incomplete Project," 3–16; Krasner, "Black Salome," 192–211; H. Baker, *Modernism and the Harlem Renaissance*; Gilroy, *The Black Atlantic*.

14. *The Emperor Jones*, directed by Dudley Murphy (1933; Image Entertainment, DVD, 2003); *Jericho* (released in America as *Dark Sands*), directed by Thornton Freeland (Buckingham Film Productions, 1937).

15. For more on Paul Robeson, see J. C. Stewart, "Paul Robeson and the Problem of Modernism," 90–101; Dyer, "Crossing Over," 64–136; Debo, "Interracial Modernism in Avant-Garde Film," 371–83; Dorinson and Pencak, *Paul Robeson*; Robeson Jr., *The Undiscovered Paul Robeson*. For more on Josephine Baker, see Jules-Rosette, *Baker in Art and Life*; Henderson, "Josephine Baker and La Revue Negre," 107–33; Martin, "'Remembering the Jungle,'" 310–25; Colin, *Josephine Baker*; Rose, *Jazz Cleopatra*; Coffman, "Uncanny Performances in Colonial Narratives," 379–94; Nenno, "Femininity, the Primitive, and Modern Urban Space" 145–61.

16. Lemke, *Primitivist Modernism*, 5–9. African Americans participated in the development of modernity through industrial invention as well as cultural representation. Blacks are credited with inventing the railway signal apparatus, hydraulic jack, postal meter, typewriter, and shopping cart. Great Lakes Patent and Trademark Center, accessed 2000, http://www.detroit.lib.mi.us (site discontinued).

17. Robeson, "Primitives," 111.

18. Robeson, "Primitives," 111.

19. Robeson, "Primitives," 112. For more on Robeson's standpoint on race, see Robeson, "Paul Robeson on Negro Race," 98–100.

20. Keyssar, *The Curtain and the* Veil, 67–74.

21. For an exploration of signifying and black aesthetics in literature, see Gates, *The Signifying Monkey*, 44–126.

22. Du Bois, *The Souls of Black Folk*, 5; Dunbar, "We Wear the Mask," *Lyrics of a Lowly Life*, 167; Hurston, *Mules and Men*, 2–3.

23. For challenges to the development of a "black stage reality," see Sanders, *The Development of Black Theater*, 5.

24. Gilroy, "'. . . to be real,'" 16.

25. Diawara, "Black Spectatorship," 211–20. For more on black moviegoing, see Everett, *Returning the Gaze*; J. Stewart, *Migrating to the Movies*.

26. For a discussion of the way bodily actions in performance convey meaning, see Desmond, "Invoking 'the Native,'" 83–109. See also Butler, *Bodies That Matter*, for further investigation of the performative nature of the body as it relates to gender.

27. Elam, "The Black Performer and the Performance of Blackness," 288–305.

28. In order to assume whiteness and Americanness, white minstrels and their audiences assigned all of the negative qualities attributed to being poor, working, ethnic, or immigrant to a performed, embodied blackness and gained alterity by assuming cultural and racial whiteness. See Roediger, *The Wages of Whiteness*. Scholars of nineteenth-century cultural processes have outlined this phenomenon well. See also Rogin, *Blackface, White Noise*. Although studies of the previous century provide some of the clearest models of colonization within and through culture, scholars like Torgovnick in *Gone Primitive* and McClintock in her final chapter, "No Longer a Future in Heaven," in *Imperial Leather* demonstrate that this process is clearly at work in the twentieth century. See also Lowe, *Critical Terrains*.

29. Bean, "Black Minstrelsy and Double Inversion circa 1890," 171–91.

30. Chude-Sokei, *The Last "Darky,"* 1–81.

31. The "not me" concept is developed in Bhabha's discussion of stereotype and abject in *Location of Culture*. In a parallel exploration of othering and abjection in performance studies, Schechner deals with the relationship of "not me" in *Performance Theory*.

32. Style operates as a marker of racial performance in White and White, *Stylin.'* Complex layers of embodied, staged, and social performances take on national, global, gender, and racial significance in Roach, *Cities of the Dead*.

33. For an excellent study of black transnational and anticolonial activism, see Von Eschen, *Race against Empire*.

34. Von Eschen, *Race against Empire*, 7–21.

35. Gallicchio, *African American Encounter with Japan and China*, 21–24; Plummer, *Rising Wind*, 68–71, 42–44; Scott, *Sons of Sheba's Race*, 106–62.

36. Kelley, *Race Rebels*, 123–24; Plummer, *Rising Wind*, 61–65.

37. Allen, "When Japan Was 'Champion of the Darker Races,'" 23–46; Gallicchio, *African American Encounter with Japan and China*, 6–57.

38. Gallicchio, *African American Encounter with Japan and China*, 74, 104; R. Kearney, *African American Views of the Japanese*, 87–91.

39. Kapur, *Raising Up a Prophet*, 48–49, 87–93.

40. Naison, *Communists in Harlem during the Depression*, 3–94, 169–226; Kelley, *Race Rebels*, 103–22.

41. For a discussion of diaspora as it pertains to this period, see Edwards, *The Practice of Diaspora*. For more on the nature of diaspora as it relates to masculinity, see Stephens, *Black Empire*. With reference to an earlier period, see also Brooks, *Bodies in Dissent*.

42. Gallicchio, *African American Encounter with Japan and China*, 71–72, 74; R. Kearney, *African American Views of the Japanese*, 59, 74.

43. Plummer, *Rising Wind*, 67.

44. McKay, *Harlem*, 96–204.

45. Kaplan, "Black and Blue on San Juan Hill," 230. Materially, however, the imperial war did not favor blacks' inclusion in an American political or symbolic structure, as the relationship between Roosevelt and the troops and the way Roosevelt represented them were virulently racist. Lawrence Little explores black participation in and relationship to American imperialism in *Disciples of Liberty*, 94–101.

46. Little, *Disciples of Liberty*, xvi, 81, 84–85, 106–9. For further discussion of black exceptionalism and intraracial hierarchies, see Gaines, *Uplifting the Race*.

47. Little, *Disciples of Liberty*, 110–46; Plummer, *Rising Wind*, 9–36.

48. Von Eschen discusses radical and international political involvement in *Race against Empire*. See Sitkoff, *A New Deal for Blacks*, for discussion of domestic political action. On black communism, see Naison, *Communists in Harlem during the Depression*; Kornweibel, *"Seeing Red."* On radical movements, see Robinson, *Black Marxism*; Kelley, *Freedom Dreams*.

49. Edwards, *The Practice of Diaspora*, 47. Edwards cites Paul Gilroy's discussion in "'. . . to be real'" (36–37) of a musical counterculture of modernity that produces the possibility of the transfiguration of the racial subject.

50. North, *The Dialect of Modernism*; Lemke, *Primitivist Modernism*.

51. For more on the interrelation between African American cultural expression and developments in technology and American identity, see Dinerstein, *Swinging the Machine*. See also Stowe, *Swing Changes*, for a discussion of the way African American music and dance influenced American culture and identity formation.

52. Locke, "The New Negro," *The New Negro*; Huggins, *Harlem Renaissance*.

See also Du Bois, "Criteria of Negro Art"; Schuyler, "The Negro-Art Hokum"; Hughes, "The Negro Artist and the Racial Mountain."

53. Denning, *The Cultural Front*, xvi–xx.

54. Fraden, *Blueprints for a Black Federal Theater*, xv.

55. See Schwartz, *Voices from the Federal Theatre*, xi–xxii; Witham, *The Federal Theatre Project*, 1. For more on the Federal Theater, see Kazacoff, *Dangerous Theatre*; Brown, *Liberty Deferred*.

56. Mathews, *The Federal Theater*.

57. A trio of black administrators — Carlton Moss, Augustus Smith, and Harry Edward — took over leadership of the New York Negro Theater in 1937. Initially leadership by a white man was understood to be fiscally practical given discrimination and segregation in federal administration.

58. Fraden, *Blueprints for a Black Federal Theater*, 4.

59. One actress auditioning for a part in *Haiti* volunteered that she was a bit nervous about working with blacks because they "smelled differently" to her. She was not cast in the production. Fraden, *Blueprints for a Black Federal Theater*, 27.

60. Cripps, *Slow Fade to Black*, 153.

61. Cripps, *Slow Fade to Black*; Bogle, *Toms, Coons, Mulattoes, Mammies, and Bucks*, 35–100.

62. Reid, *Redefining Black Film*, 16–18.

63. Cripps, *Slow Fade to Black*, 203–35.

64. See J. Stewart, "Negroes Laughing at Themselves?," 650–77.

65. Everett, *Returning the Gaze*, 191, 268–69.

66. For more on the Hays Commission and their role in regulating subject matter on film, see Cook, *A History of Narrative Film*. On the construction of race by the Federal Government in WPA federal arts programs, see Sklaroff, "Ambivalent Inclusion."

1. "HARLEM RIDES THE RANGE"

1. H. N. Smith, *Virgin Land*. See also Fenin and Everson, *The Western*.

2. Analyses of the West assert its assumed whiteness. See H. N. Smith, *Virgin Land*; Tompkins, *West of Everything*; Kaplan, "Manifest Domesticity," 581–606.

3. H. N. Smith, *Virgin Land*; Tompkins, *West of Everything*; Kaplan, "Romancing the Empire." Lee Mitchell identifies constructions of the West as a reaction to the impact of modern industrialized culture and urbanization and also links the nostalgic idealization of open space evident in westerns with the cultural impact of American landscape painting of the nineteenth-century (*Westerns*, 26, 29–93). The notion of open, unclaimed idyllic wilderness entrenched in American visual and cultural history laid the foundation for how such space was seen, imagined, and represented. For visual imaginings of empire, see also Miller, *Empire of the Eye*.

4. See Slotkin, *Gunfighter Nation*.

5. Lee Mitchell identifies westerns in part by their engagement with specific problems of progress, honor, law or justice, violence, and manhood (*Westerns*, 3). Though these films do not all approach these problems in the same way that generic westerns do, these problems motivate representation in each film. The black films discussed in this chapter manage these themes in idiosyncratic ways, sometimes through direct representation and sometimes through their constructed absence. Mitchell further observes that the western itself "has so little to do with an actual West that it might be better thought of as its own epitaph, written by an exuberant East encroaching on possibilities already foreclosed because represented in terms of a West that no longer exists, never did, never could" (6). Black Americans' carefully imagined West bears this out poignantly.

6. *A Pictorial View of Idlewild, Michigan* (Chicago Daily News, 1927); *The Exile*, directed by Oscar Micheaux and Leonard Harper (Micheaux Pictures Corp., 1931); *Two-Gun Man from Harlem*, directed by Richard C. Kahn (Merit Pictures Inc., 1938).

7. William Cronon argues for this conception of the Midwest in *Nature's Metropolis*.

8. David Rothel explains how technology in traditional westerns represented a "modern" West, "where cars, radios, machine guns, and airplanes were a part of everyday life for almost everyone." But only the bad guys used these devices and usually as a means to accomplish evil ends (*The Singing Cowboys*, 25). See also J. Stewart, *Migrating to the Movies*, for relationships between blacks, film, and urban modernity.

9. Tichi, *Shifting Gears*, 17–40.

10. See Allmendinger, *Imagining the African American West*. Allmendinger also points out that the term "West" and its relation to the prevailing American frontier myth functioned for black Americans much like it did for whites, resulting in the romanticization, and sometimes failure, of expansionist movements.

11. Tom Gunning analyzes an early cinematic experience in which the visual impact of the train on the screen frightened viewers and compelled them to run from the theater ("Aesthetics of Astonishment," 114–33). Whether this reaction was genuine or a performance of consent to the pretense of the film's reality, the image of the oncoming train as the pivotal stimulus in the scenario links this image, modernity, industrialization, motion, and technology to the drama of cinematic experience as a symbol of the age. The repetition of this image in all of the films I analyze demonstrates the filmmakers' obsession with technological savvy, motion between East and West, the train as a literal and symbolic national glue that brought distant spaces within reach, and the brute force and power of the fastest, strongest means of transportation and trade available.

12. See Goodyear, "Constructing a National Landscape." Goodyear charts how photography served as a vehicle through which the Midwest became imag-

ined as a vacation site. *Pictorial View* follows the tradition set by stereographs and advertisements that documented and sold the natural visual beauty of midwestern space as national space to urban Americans.

13. Tom Gunning describes modernity as a change of experience "dependent on the change in production marked by the Industrial Revolution. . . . It was also, however, equally characterized by the transformation in daily life wrought by the growth of capitalism and advances in technology; the growth of urban traffic, the distribution of mass-produced goods, and successive new technologies of transportation and communication" ("Tracing the Individual Body," 15). As the antithesis to the ascendance of technological change, modernism held within it a search for organicity and authenticity. The beauty of the uncivilized primitive inherent in primitivist modernism is an example of this.

14. My extensive survey of travel films from the 1920s and 1930s housed in the Library of Congress Motion Pictures Collection shows that other travel films include transportation without the obsessive repetition of cars and trains as leitmotifs that structure the narrative.

15. In Stepto's *Blue as the Lake*, Idlewild operates temporally as a space of childhood in this "personal geography," an autobiographical memoir explored through geographical space. Stepto's autobiographical structure indicates the lasting impact of ideologies of regeneration and identity formation in the wilderness. A pastoral Idlewild becomes the site for mapping a personal journey from a childhood past to maturation and sophistication. The earliest stages of personal development are protected in Idlewild's idyllic black wilderness. In *Blue as the Lake* Idlewild also operates spatially as a release from racial exclusion and attack. The road to Idlewild was laced with racial landmines of segregation, exclusion, and insult. As a result of past discrimination and abuse on the road, Stepto's father carefully planned their road trips to avoid staying in white-owned hotels and using white-owned facilities. Arriving at Idlewild resolved these dangers. Stepto's family's connection to the area was personal, intergenerational, and economic. His parents and grandparents owned Idlewild property (*Blue as the Lake*, 3–35).

16. During the 1920s caravanning in automobiles, as opposed to riding the train, indicated a freedom from schedules and the ability to enjoy nature directly at one's leisure. Though an expression of modernity, the caravan as a community experience signals a positive and intentional relationship to nature. For more on the human place in the wilderness, see Cronon, *Uncommon Ground*.

17. Canning, "'The Most American Thing in America,'" 91–93. The Chautauqua was a performance that united a *white* American populace around a homogeneous manifestation of British Protestantism, smoothing ethnic difference into a normalized Americanness. This history further adds to the irony and significance of black appropriations of the name and performance form in *Pictorial View*.

18. Both are featured in Reed, *The Chicago* NAACP.

19. Chesnutt's literary stature is uncontested; see Heermance, *Charles W. Chesnutt*. For criticism of Chesnutt's work, see McElrath, *Critical Essays*.

20. In the *Conjure Woman* tales, Chesnutt reclaimed "Negro dialect" slung by white writers, humanized the stock figure of (post)slavery's "uncle," and removed the symbol from white control.

21. In 1925 Micheaux used popular culture to bring Chesnutt's work to a new generation by turning the novel referenced in *Pictorial View*'s intertitle, *A House behind the Cedars* (1899), into a silent film that broke attendance records. Interestingly, Micheaux's *House behind the Cedars* (Micheaux Film, 1925) was also concerned with self-improvement, self-sufficiency, and middle-class gentility. The film was released in 1925, just two years before *Pictorial View*. Attendance at this film broke all records at the Roosevelt Theater in New York City. See Sampson, *Blacks in Black and White*, 16.

22. Walker and Wilson, *Black Eden*, 70–71, 231.

23. See Katz, *The Black West*. Katz describes the African American presence in the settlement and formation of the West from colonization through U.S. international expansion during the nineteenth century using photographs, court records, letters, and newspapers. For more on blacks' movement into the West, see Painter, *Exodusters*.

24. In the case of *Dred Scott v. Sanford* (1857) the U.S. Supreme Court established the right of slavery to expand into the territories and denied the right of black people to hold U.S. citizenship.

25. Katz, *The Black West*, 83–106.

26. Katz, *The Black West*, 35–79.

27. Katz, *The Black West*, 167–265, 289.

28. Katz, *The Black West*, 301–5.

29. Katz, *The Black West*, 196.

30. See Gaines, *Uplifting the Race*, 11, 28, 96–98, 108–18.

31. See Katz, *The Black West*. *The Symbol of the Unconquered*, directed by Oscar Micheaux (Micheaux Film Corp., 1920), is an exception. In this film a black homesteader battles the Ku Klux Klan to retain ownership of oil-rich land. In *The Realization of a Negro's Ambition*, directed by Harry A. Grant (Lincoln Motion Picture Company, 1916), the hero, a black family man, endures racism and gains the right to prospect oil by saving a white oil man's daughter.

32. See Bederman, *Manliness and Civilization*; Cohen, *Making a New Deal*.

33. Stedman suggests that in films produced during the early twentieth century Native American "vanishing" occurred not only through death, but also through the obsolescence of Native culture resulting from assimilation and deterioration. Stedman also notes that just as sound was being introduced to motion pictures, Native American articulation became characterized by the "Friday-Tonto school of speech"—that is, silence (*Shadow of the Indian*, 173–80).

34. In order to afford the expense of producing sound film, the Micheaux Film Corporation became an interracial combination of the sort that produced almost all-Negro sound films from the period. Estimated to cost $4,500, the film was produced and distributed by Alfred Schliffman for $15,000 (*Variety*, 27 May 1931). See also Reid, *Redefining Black Film*, 18; Everett, *Returning the Gaze*, 187–89.

35. See Micheaux, *The Conquest*.

36. Micheaux, *The Homesteader*. For more on Micheaux and the frontier see Brown, "Black Patriarch on the Prairie."

37. Review of *The Exile*, directed by Oscar Micheaux, *Baltimore Afro-American*, 14 March 1931, quoted in Sampson, *Blacks in Black and White*, 371.

38. In *Toms, Coons, Mulattoes, Mammies, and Bucks* Bogle asserts that these stock scenes were included in black films primarily to please white audiences enthralled by night club performances and interested in revues. The review from the *Baltimore Afro-American*, however, pays as much attention, if not more, to the revue numbers as to the movie plot and characters, indicating that the performance material also appealed to black audiences. Some black films from the period consist of little more than a series of performance numbers. Examples include *Low-Down: A Bird's Eye View of Harlem* (Vitaphone/Warner Brothers, 1929); *The Darktown Revue*, directed by Oscar Micheaux (Micheaux Film Corp., 1931); and *The Duke Is Tops*, directed by William L. Nolte and Ralph Cooper (Million Dollar Productions, 1938; later released as *Bronze Venus*, 1943).

39. Although African American desires to preserve gentility in the wilderness appear in *The Exile*, the development of Jean's masculinity in the West follows Kaplan's nationalization thesis in "Romancing the Empire." Jean achieves an invincibility in the West that follows mainstream representations of western men and masculinity.

40. See Bederman, *Manliness and Civilization*. Also see Studlar, *This Mad Masquerade*, 10–89.

41. Drake and Cayton, *Black Metropolis*, 58–85. Drake discusses the immigration of 50,000 blacks from predominantly southern rural areas into Chicago. See also Goodwin, *Black Migration*; Grossman, *Land of Hope*; A. Harrison, *Black Exodus*; Lemann, *The Promised Land*; Marks, *Farewell*. The Great Migration is one of the few group experiences that might be described as universal for African Americans either personally or by association. Nearly all major cities in the country, both northern and southern, experienced enormous influxes of black migrants during the early decades of the twentieth century. Regarding specific cities, see D. Baldwin, *Chicago's New Negroes*; Gottlieb, *Making Their Own Way*; Phillips, *Alabama North*.

42. Because of its representation of interracial romance, the film was temporarily banned in New York City in 1932 (Sampson, *Blacks in Black and White*, 18). A review in *Variety*, "The Exile, Negro Talker," 27 May 1931, reports Harlem audiences laughing at the love scenes.

43. *Midnight Ramble: The Story of the Black Film Industry*, directed by Bestor Cram and Pearl Bowser (WGBH Television, 1994).

44. Bogle, *Toms, Coons, Mulattoes, Mammies, and Bucks*. Most critics of Micheaux's casting of fair-skinned actors, especially women, rightly draw attention to the fact that this choice seems to value whiteness and reinforce inequalities and color prejudices in black communities. I want to offer that this problematic aspect of production and representation has another impact related to concerns about black equality in America. I analyze the filmic impact of this choice as it interacts with penchants for narratives of upward mobility and the insistence upon the blackness of these apparently white characters.

45. This assumption of equality capitulates to white supremacist notions of identity where whiteness is normalized. Discourses of racial equality, however, also adopted this unfortunate quality due to the structures of racial understanding and social organization during the period that argued that blacks were equal to whites (instead of the reverse, for instance).

46. Although Micheaux attempts to push the limits of racial identity with his use of light-skinned actors, his use of dark-skinned actors is still stereotypical. His villains all have darker skin than his heroes.

47. See Gunning, "Tracing the Individual Body."

48. Just as early film studies of the body sought to understand and control movement, display identity, and collect and preserve information, so too does the camerawork in these films with regard to nature and people. See L. Williams, *Hard Core*, 34–57.

49. African American historical figures like Deadwood Dick (a.k.a. Nat Love, a braggart of a wild man who actually wrote an autobiography), Bill Pickett (called the "greatest cowboy," who performed in rodeos and pioneered bulldogging), Cherokee Bill (fabled to be the worst man in the West), Bass Reeves (a famous lawman), Edwin McCabe (established multiple towns in Oklahoma), Sutton E. Griggs (a black nationalist writer from Texas who wrote Afrocentric tales and novels), and the Seminole Negro scouts and other black military troops in the West are passed over as subject matter. For more on black western icons, see Katz, *Black People Who Made the Old West*.

50. Bogle, *Toms, Coons, Mulattoes, Mammies, and Bucks*, 108. Tex Ritter and Gene Autry were white singing cowboys whose serial B westerns dominated the industry during the 1930s. Autry starred in fifty features between 1934 and 1942 (Rothel, *The Singing Cowboys*, 25). In *The Exile* Peter Stansfield's assessment of singing cowboy pictures shows their construction of a type of masculinity that is more consistent with what I have described. Loy asserts that B westerns, such as the singing cowboy series, had a tendency to affirm community rather than unilaterally celebrate individualism (*Westerns and American Culture*, 136–39). African American production of generic westerns capitalized on some characteristics

of this subgenre with which certain thematic elements resonated with African American values.

51. See Rothel, *The Singing Cowboys*.

52. *Midnight Ramble: The Story of the Black Film Industry*, directed by Bestor Cram and Pearl Bowser (WGBH Television, 1994). Herbert Jeffrey used the name Herb Jeffries as a singer.

53. The B westerns from the late 1930s were not the first westerns made by black filmmakers. Several black westerns were produced more than fifteen years earlier, in the early 1920s. For the most part the black westerns of the 1930s did not draw upon stories from blacks' past in the West, nor did they feature working cowboys the way films of the 1920s did.

54. Descriptions of *Harlem on the Prairie* exist. This film stars Herbert Jeffrey and Spencer Williams, as did the next three. The hero is named Jeff Kincaid rather than Bob Blake. In this slightly different plot, Kincaid saves an endangered gold fortune for the daughter of a murdered outlaw gone straight. See Sampson, *Blacks in Black and White*, 219. The gold, of course, represents wealth, value, and moral fiber; the "Harlem" of the title seems to stand in for blackness, migration, and corruption.

55. *Two-Gun* combines genres, blending the B western with the elements of the city gangster film from the same period that adapted its mythic material to the concerns and imagery of the New Deal and the Depression, namely urban corruption and the end of prohibition. See Slotkin, *Gunfighter Nation*, 265.

2. EPAULETS AND LEAF SKIRTS

1. Savigliano, "Fragments for a Story of Tango Bodies," 215.

2. Torgovnick, *Gone Primitive*, 244–45.

3. Houseman, *Run-Through*, 185.

4. Houseman, *Run-Through*, 198.

5. Houseman, *Run-Through*, 200.

6. Mathews, *The Federal Theater*, 76.

7. Houseman, *Run-Through*, 192.

8. Hughes's *Drums* saw two subsequent incarnations, as *Emperor of Haiti* in 1938 and the opera *Troubled Island* in 1949. See Keyssar, *The Curtain and the Veil*, 67–79. Contemporary plays that employed a similar primitivist aesthetic include *Taboo* (1923), *Emperor Jones* (1921–33), *Run Lil' Chillun* (1933), *Haiti* (1936), *Black Empire* (1938), and *Swing Mikado* (1938). For historical studies, see Vandercook, *Black Majesty*; Seabrook, *The Magic Island*.

9. Houseman, *Run-Through*, 194; Burns Mantle, "WPA Macbeth in Fancy Dress," *New York Daily News*, 15 April 1936. The comparison forges some of the ways *Macbeth* worked to universalize black manhood and produce an imperial

perspective. If Eugene O'Neill was influenced by Shakespeare, then the Federal Theater *Macbeth* was certainly influenced by productions of *The Emperor Jones*. They reflexively enact an expressionistic manifestation of an ambitious, self-alienated man in existential crisis. While both figures are sympathetic, a significant shift occurs in the conceptualization of the black hero. Carter's Macbeth does away with the buffoonish qualities of the gambling, uneducated Brutus Jones. Both performances imagine a West Indian setting. In *Jones* an American character invades and colonizes a West Indian island. In the voodoo *Macbeth* the colonization is imaginative, through a displacement of (black) American concerns about racial autonomy and desires for power. Both plays focus on a crisis in power.

10. France, "The 'Voodoo' Macbeth of Orson Welles," 67.

11. Perpener, *African American Concert Dance*, 114–21. He was also known as Asadata Dafora Horton.

12. Houseman, *Run-Through*, 199.

13. Susan McCloskey thoroughly compares Shakespeare's *Macbeth* and Welles's adaptation in McCloskey, "Shakespeare, Orson Welles, and the 'Voodoo' *Macbeth*." Although the Federal Theater collections were not available in 1985, when McCloskey published her article, her uncanny descriptions have been valuable in my own understanding and imagination of the production. The Negro Unit production of *Macbeth* seems to have served as a visual and atmospheric template for the iconically high-modern film version of *Macbeth* Welles produced in 1948. In this sense blackness provided an opportunity to experiment in forms of American modernism for one of America's noted modernists.

14. Martha Gellhorn, quoted in Houseman, *Run-Through*, 201.

15. France, "The 'Voodoo' Macbeth," 67.

16. Houseman, *Run-Through*, 200–201.

17. See Flanagan, *Arena*, for a description of plays performed by the Federal Theater. See also Mathews, *The Federal Theater*, and Melosh, *Engendering Culture*, for analyses of protest and proletarian politics in Federal Theater plays.

18. Expressionism emerged in 1910 as a modernist reaction to realist theater. Though it ended as a conscious movement in 1925, its premises continued to influence American theater. According to Brockett, "Truth for the Expressionist . . . is to be sought in the personal vision of life. Unlike the Realist who seeks truth in the observation of external facts, the Expressionist seeks truth within the human mind" (*The Theater*, 298). For the expressionist, nature is ascribed with human characteristics and is portrayed in such a way as to suggest human feelings, ideas, or perceptions. In expressionist productions the forces of narrative and the mise-en-scène combined to express the interiority of human characters and the human condition.

19. Historically, racial manhood and national citizenship have been linked in discourses of African American inclusion in the national body, just as male

identities have been central to articulations of national identity in mainstream formulations. See Horton and Horton, "Violence, Protest, and Identity," 80–97; Bederman, *Manliness and Civilization*.

20. Brockett, *The Theater*, 299.

21. Brooks Atkinson, "Macbeth or Harlem Boy Goes Wrong," *New York Times*, 15 April 1936; John Mason Brown, *New York Post*, 15 April 1936 quoted in Adubato, "A History of the WPA's Negro Theater Project in New York City," 85.

22. Houseman, *Run-Through*, 201.

23. Lew Amster, *Sunday Worker*, 5 July 1936, quoted in Adubato, "A History of the WPA's Negro Theater Project in New York City," SCAGMU, 74; see also 76, and the same source generally for further investigation of community reaction to the WPA Federal Theater Project Negro Unit's *Macbeth*.

24. Roi Ottley, *Amsterdam News*, 18 April 1936. Negro Press Clippings, Press Releases of the Department of Information, RG69, NA.

25. For further investigation of the historical, cultural, and psychological effects of the occupation of Haiti by the United States, see Schmidt, *The United States' Occupation of Haiti, 1915–1934*. See also Weinstein and Segal, *Haiti*; Shannon and Prince-Mars, *The Haitian Elite*; Farmer, *The Uses of Haiti*; Plummer, *Haiti and the United States*; Renda, *Taking Haiti*.

26. Blassingame, "The Press and American Intervention in Haiti and the Dominican Republic, 1904–1920," 27–43.

27. Plummer, "Afro-American Response to the Occupation of Haiti," 328.

28. Plummer, "Afro-American Response to the Occupation of Haiti," 314.

29. Schmidt, *The United States' Occupation of Haiti, 1915–1934*, 6 10; Plummer, "Afro-American Response to the Occupation of Haiti," 316–18.

30. Schmidt, *The United States' Occupation of Haiti, 1915–1934*, 64–81, 189–206.

31. Plummer, "Afro-American Response to the Occupation of Haiti," 326.

32. *Toussaint L'Ouverture* premiered in 1936 at London's Westminster Theater starring the socialist actor Paul Robeson. See James, *Black Jacobins*; Paul Robeson, "Intervening in Abyssinia," *New Leader*, 4 October 1935.

33. Weinstein and Segal, *Haiti*, 18–19.

34. The politics and events of both the Haitian Revolution and the American occupation of Haiti are internationally and internally complex. Please see referenced texts for comprehensive discussion of these events.

35. Keyssar, *The Curtain and the Veil*. In her discussion of Langston Hughes's play *Emperor of Haiti* (1935), Keyssar argues that Hughes uses the dramatic trope of a century of historical distance to express a nationally, nonspecific *black* "inner life once removed" (50, 73). See also Leslie Sanders's discussion of "black stage reality" in *The Development of Black Theater*.

36. Keyssar, *The Curtain and the Veil*, 74.

37. Irma Watkins-Owens considers the views of black Caribbean immigrants on race in *Blood Relations*. In African America national and geographic identities

are complex and shifting. Non–U.S. citizens could become submerged and assimilated in a single generation. The musical director of *Haiti*, for instance, claims a historical familial or social connection to Haiti without identifying himself as Haitian. Where the productions I discuss are produced in the U.S., the American creative and symbolic context through which they are produced and their execution by what appear to be American performers on work relief qualifies them as American performances. The personal identities of the participants, black and white, however, may incorporate multiple identities, ethnic, national, racial, geographical, and classed.

38. Domingo, "Gift of the Black Tropics," 349. Domingo provides a sociological account of black immigrant populations, particularly British West Indians, in New York during the 1920s. He intimates that the forces of assimilation in African America and of homogenization by the mainstream can be such that international distinctions become muted and overcome by racial distinctions in relatively few generations.

39. Watkins-Owens, *Blood Relations*, 5.

40. Watkins-Owens, *Blood Relations*, 119–120.

41. Bontemps, *Black Thunder*.

42. Craig, *Black Drama of the Federal Theater Era*, 146. Loften Mitchell concurs, asserting that West Indian leaders and artists revitalized black Americans' interest in Africa, which provided them with a renewed sense of self (*Black Drama*, 24).

43. *Haiti*, Playbills File, FTCLC.

44. This is not the same DuBois as the famed African American philosopher, writer, and sociologist, W. E. B. Du Bois. William DuBois was a white newspaper reporter from the South.

45. O'Conner and Brown, *Free, Adult, Uncensored*, 119.

46. Bond, *The Negro and Drama*, 171.

47. Record of group sales for *Haiti*, FTCLC.

48. Later during the show's run the boxer Canada Lee replaced Ingram as Christophe.

49. Brockett, *The Theater*, 299.

50. O'Conner and Brown, *Free, Adult, Uncensored*, 118.

51. Gill, *White Greasepaint on Black Performers*, 99.

52. Interracial sex does exist in the play, however, in the active participation of Jacques, a plantation servant who had an affair with the married mistress of the manor, Lady Napoleon's niece, no less, to produce Odette.

53. *Haiti*, play production file, FTCLC.

54. For a discussion of the performance of masculinity in film, see Studlar, *This Mad Masquerade*, 10–89. With reference to an earlier period, see Kaplan, "Romancing the Empire," for more on depictions of masculinity in literature.

274

55. Brooks Atkinson, "The Play," *New York Times*, 3 March 1938.

56. Bogle, *Toms, Coons, Mulattoes, Mammies, and Bucks*, 67.

57. Bogle, *Toms, Coons, Mulattoes, Mammies, and Bucks*, 70.

58. O'Conner and Brown, *Free, Adult, Uncensored*, 117–18.

59. Promotional advertisement in the *New York Post*, FTCLC.

60. Arthur Pollack, "The Theater," *Brooklyn Eagle*, 3 March 1938.

61. Published reviews file, *Haiti*, FTCLC.

62. Herrick Brown, *New York Sun*, 3 March 1938 quoted in Adubato, "A History of the WPA's Negro Theater Project in New York City," 188–89.

63. "Letter to the author from FTP actor Kevin O'Morrison, 2/25/80," quoted in Gill, *White Greasepaint on Black Performers*, 4.

64. Howard Barnes, *Herald Tribune*, 3 March 1938 quoted in Adubato, "A History of the WPA's Negro Theater Project in New York City," 181–83.

65. Ross, "Black Drama in the Federal Theater, 1935–1939," 167.

66. Among others, the following texts provide examples of the operation of othering and the uses of race in culture for processes of national identity formation: Roediger, *The Wages of Whiteness*; Saxton, *The Rise and Fall of the White Republic*; McClintock, *Imperial Leather*; Lott, *Love and Theft*; Bhabha, *Location of Culture*; Said, *Orientalism*; Goldberg, *The Racial State*; Lowe, *Immigrant Acts*.

67. Von Eschen, *Race against Empire*, analyzes African American efforts in anticolonialism and development of diasporic consciousness and activism.

68. Production records, FTCLC.

69. By the 1930s whites and blacks agitated against what was considered fascist American racism in a number of different political and social forums. Sitkoff in *A New Deal for Blacks* and Denning in *The Cultural Front* show how collaboration and mutual support occurred in the creation of social cooperation and cultural meaning in the 1930s.

70. Denning, *The Cultural Front*, 395. In addition to Welles's film of a Scottish *Macbeth* (1948), many of his subsequent plays drew on methods and themes of aesthetic political protest he established in the voodoo *Macbeth*'s experimentations in blackness.

71. Denning, *The Cultural Front*, 376, 380.

72. For an exploration of domestic political action against fascism, see Naison, *Communists in Harlem during the Depression*, 126. See also Robinson, *Black Marxism*.

73. Kelley, *Race Rebels*, 123–58.

74. Unidentified Harry Wright No. 4: Fiji (1925), Harry Wright Collection, MPLC. See discussions of travel films in chapter 2 and anthropological films in chapters 5 and 6 of this study.

1. Joseph Roach examines the way every performance exists with relation to the past in *Cities of the Dead*, 1–7.

2. For discussions of yellowface in film, see Marchetti, *Romance and the "Yellow Peril"*; Oehling, "The Yellow Menace."

3. Comprehensive engagement with *The Mikado*'s performances, textual meanings, and critical history exceeds the scope of this chapter, which is concerned with its imperialist assumptions and legacy.

4. As opposed to Macbeth's words: "Life's but a walking shadow, a poor player / That struts and frets his hour upon the stage / And then is heard no more. It is a tale / Told by an idiot, full of sound and fury, / Signifying nothing." *Macbeth*, Act 5, scene 5, lines 26–28.

5. The affirmation of American national identity that resulted from the opening of the swing *Mikados* came at a time when Japan was attempting to expand its naval and imperial power in the East. These plays reflect anxiety toward Japanese imperialism and can be seen to "demonstrate how distinct racial categories were deployed against one another within white fantasies of difference in an attempt to shore up the racial and geopolitical boundaries of the American nation-state" (Steen, "Racing American Modernity," 169; see also 167–87).

6. Said, *Orientalism*, 2–3.

7. Said calls orientalism "a *distribution* of geopolitical awareness [of a Western articulated and imagined Orient] into aesthetic, scholarly, economic, sociological, historical, and philological texts; an *elaboration* not only of a basic geographical distinction (the world is made up of two unequal halves, Orient and Occident) but also a whole series of 'interests' which, by such means as scholarly discovery, philological reconstruction, psychological analysis, landscape and sociological description, it not only creates but also maintains; it *is*, rather than expresses, a certain will or desire to understand, in some cases control, manipulate, even to incorporate, what is a manifestly different (or alternative and novel) world; it is, above all, a discourse that is by no means in direct, corresponding relationship with political power in the raw, but rather is produced and exists in an uneven exchange with various kinds of power, shaped to a degree by the exchange with power political (as with a colonial or imperial establishment), power intellectual (as with reigning sciences like comparative linguistics or anatomy, or any of the modern policy sciences), power cultural (as with orthodoxies and canons of taste, texts, and values), power moral (as with ideas about what 'we' do and what 'they' cannot do or understand as 'we' do). . . . Orientalism is— and does not simply represent—a considerable dimension of modern political-intellectual culture, and as such has less to do with the Orient than it does with 'our' world" (*Orientalism*, 12).

8. Said, *Orientalism*, 22.

9. Said, *Orientalism*, 73.

10. Said, *Orientalism*, 39.

11. Lawrence, "The Banned Mikado," 160–69.

12. Lawrence, "The Banned Mikado," 160, 162.

13. Lawrence, "The Banned Mikado," 160–62.

14. Baily, *The Gilbert and Sullivan Book*, 268–69. Gilbert referenced Japan in his play *Patience* (1881) to mock aesthetes who "adopted certain features of Japanese art as among the shibboleths of their movement" (Lawrence, "The Banned Mikado," 161, 163).

15. Baily, *The Gilbert and Sullivan Book*, 265–66, 269.

16. Lawrence, "The Banned Mikado," 152, 161, 169; Rony, *The Third Eye*, 36–40.

17. Lawrence, "The Banned Mikado," 165; Baily, *The Gilbert and Sullivan Book*, 268–69. Paul Revitt asserts that the plays suggest a political, economic, and social comfort, serving as a "mirror in which the Englishman can privately behold himself and chuckle" ("Gilbert and Sullivan," 19). A controversy in 1907 over whether the play should be banned during a Japanese diplomatic visit created a general stink in Britain. When Japanese representatives actually saw the play they saw "nothing in it relating to Japan" and thus nothing that the Japanese might find offensive, except perhaps that the British might think them silly and sensitive enough to take offense (34). Japan had actually entertained a troupe of Americans performing the play under the title "Three Little Maids" in 1887 (Lawrence, "The Banned Mikado," 156, 158).

18. Gilbert, *The Mikado*, 3.

19. Cannadine, "Gilbert and Sullivan," 19–20. This is the argument made by Cannadine, Lawrence, Revitt, and Baily. The distinctive Britishness and affirmation of British culture is also made in Geoffrey Smith's chapter on *The Mikado* in *The Savoy Operas*.

20. Cannadine, "Gilbert and Sullivan," 19. For further investigation of the historical, cultural, and political influences on Gilbert's operas, see Sproul, "Modus Operandi," 2.

21. Cannadine, "Gilbert and Sullivan," 16.

22. Cannadine, "Gilbert and Sullivan," 20–23.

23. Munich's "'Capture the Heart of a Queen,'" 23–44, and "Queen Victoria," 265–81, both make this argument about Gilbert and Sullivan's work.

24. C. Williams, "Parody, Pastiche, and the Play of Genres," 2. Williams discusses the ways a pastiche of genres (inherently dependent upon and irreverent of its pieces) served as a means by which meaning was made in the Gilbert and Sullivan comic operas. Very often, she argues, appropriations of various genres in the context of certain social themes create an oblique critique of social forms through a mixing of entrenched meanings. For additional discussion of specific genres as they apply to performance, see Drewal, *Yoruba Ritual*, 3–5; Hutcheon, *A Theory of Parody*.

277

NOTES TO CHAPTER THREE

25. Cannadine, Revitt, Lawrence, Baily, and Smith, among others, characterize Gilbert and Sullivan's operas as emblematic of the best of British culture. Gould's article, "The True Embodiment of Everything That's Excellent," defends his lifelong love of Gilbert and Sullivan by arguing that the operas are major art, universal and timeless.

26. Baily, *The Gilbert and Sullivan Book*, 281–84. Baily and Smith demonstrate the popularity of Gilbert and Sullivan in America, mentioning performances by the D'Oyly Carte Company and by Americans during the twentieth century. See Baily, *The Gilbert and Sullivan Book*, 5–10, 445–47; G. Smith *The Savoy Operas*, 154.

27. G. Smith, *The Savoy Operas*, 153. Yoshihara's dissertation on U.S. orientalism, "Women's Asia," 34–116, discusses the ways in which decorating appropriated Asian themes at the turn of the century.

28. Woll, *Black Musical Theater*, 178.

29. R. Kearney demonstrates through extensive newspaper and documentary research that this phenomenon grew out of a racially nationalist celebration of Japanese trouncing of the Russians in the imperial battle over dominance in Asia (*African American Views of the Japanese*, 15).

30. Kearney, *African American Views of the Japanese*, 15.

31. FTCLC. White American versions of *The Mikado*, performed in the British/Japanese manner, continued through the early part of the century. White units of the Federal Theater performed traditional versions of *The Mikado* in San Francisco, Philadelphia, and New York between 1935 and 1939 that received lukewarm reviews and little critical (or scholarly) attention.

32. Poiger's research on swing music in Germany indicates the ways swing and jazz signified blackness as Americanness. See "Taming the Wild West."

33. *The Mikado*, published reviews file, FTCLC.

34. For more on memory in performance, see Roach, *Cities of the Dead*, 1–7. See also Conquergood, "Performing as a Moral Act," 1–13; Conquergood, "Between Experience and Meaning," 26–59.

35. Conquergood addresses reproduction and continuity in performance in "Between Experience and Meaning," 26–59, and "Performing as a Moral Act," 1–13. In both essays he discusses the tensions that stem from processes of becoming an oppressed other through performance.

36. In *The Black Atlantic* Gilroy contemplates how trades of culture and, at times, of black bodies, served as a marker of various stages of modernity as well as of the racial and national hybridity of Western systems of domination. I see the performance of *The Mikado* as an instantiation of the symbolic trade of racial identities to establish national power.

37. The *Chicago Defender*, for one, ran multiple stories announcing the opening.

38. Ben Burns, "WPA Negro Unit Swings 'The Mikado' at the Great Northern Theater," *Daily Record* (Chicago), 27 September 1938, published reviews file, FTCLC.

39. Nahum Daniel Brasher, "'The Mikado' Rates as Season's Best, Reviewer Pleased with Singing and Acting of Cast," *Chicago Defender*, 1 October 1938, published reviews file, FTCLC.

40. Program notes on *The Swing Mikado*, WPA Department of Information, NA.

41. Swing *Mikado* admission receipts record, NA.

42. John Cambridge, "Swing 'Mikado' Is New Federal Theater Triumph," *Daily Worker* (New York), 2 March 1939.

43. John Lyons, "Skimming the Cream," *Loyola News*, 12 October 1938, published reviews file, FTCLC.

44. *The Mikado* production title file, FTCLC.

45. Interview with Duncan Whiteside, Research Center for the Federal Theater Project, SCAGMU.

46. A Federal Theater employee interviewed by the George Mason Federal Theater archive speculated that this man's son, who danced a bit during rehearsals, was Sammy Davis Jr. Another up-and-coming star rumored to be associated with this production is Eartha Kitt, who was supposedly in the chorus. Interview with Duncan Whiteside, Research Center for the Federal Theater Project, SCAGMU.

47. Woll asserts that *The Swing Mikado* launched a new genre in black musical theater by combining popular music with classic operetta, inspiring additional black versions of *The Mikado*, tropical revues, and updated versions of other plays, including *A Midsummer Night's Dream* in 1939 and *Carmen* in 1943 (*Black Musical Theater*, 178–75).

48. *The Mikado*, production title file, FTCLC. The production report for *The Mikado* includes director (Harry Minturn), set design (Clive Rickabaugh), music (Edward Wurtzebach), lighting (Oscar Ryan), prop and costume (John Pratt) notes that describe the production in detail. There are no notes from the dance (Sammy Dyer and Hazel Davis) and vocal (Viola Hill) directors. The details provided below, unless otherwise noted, are drawn from this file.

49. "Swing Mikado's Songs Hailed by Lovers of Gilbert and Sullivan: Swing Copies and Orchestrations Now Available for Harry Minturn's Successful Swing Production," *Music World Almanac*, vol. 10, no. 9, Radio City, New York.

50. Interview with Duncan Whiteside, technical director of the Great Northern Theater 1938–39, by Karen Wickre for the Research Center for the Federal Theater Project, 13 August 1978, SCAGMU.

51. Ben Burns, "WPA Negro Unit Swings 'The Mikado' at the Great Northern Theater," *Daily Record* (Chicago), 27 September 1938, published reviews file, FTCLC.

52. Katherine Irvin, "All Colored Cast Scores in Swing Version of 'Mikado,' First Nighters Acclaim WPA 'Swing' Opera," *Chicago Sunday Bee*, 2 October 1938, published reviews file, FTCLC. By noting the absence of "oriental features," Irvin

recognizes that the opera no longer looked like it was set in Japan, though she, like several other observers, noted the Japanese influence on its culturally hybrid appearance.

53. *The Mikado*, production title file, FTCLC.

54. Ashton Stevens, "'The Mikado' Just a Twith of Swing in This WPA Ethiopera," *American* (Chicago), 26 September 1938, published reviews file, FTCLC.

55. *The Mikado*, playbills file, FTCLC.

56. C. J. Bulliet, "Negro 'Mikado' Is Season's Major Hit: Tom-Tom Mikado Frenzied Theater," *Chicago Daily News*, 19 January 1939, production title file, FTCLC.

57. Hubert Odishaw, "New Version of 'Mikado' Has Harlem-Congo Swing," *Daily Northwestern* (Chicago), 4 October 1938, published reviews file, FTCLC.

58. Most of the principals hailed from musical colleges and conservatories, many having won contests and awards in their fields. Program notes on *The Swing Mikado*, WPA Department of Information, NA.

59. Richard Lockridge, "The New Play: 'The Mikado,' Partly in Swing, Opens at the New Yorker Theater," *The Sun* (New York), 2 March 1939.

60. Fraction's reviews took a dive after the show moved to New York. It is very likely that a change in his performance can be attributed to the death of his wife during this period.

61. Claudia Cassidy, "Negro's 'The Mikado' Doesn't Need Its Swing to Score Federal Theater Success," *Journal of Commerce* (Chicago), 26 September 1938, published reviews file, FTCLC.

62. C. J. Bulliet, "Negro 'Mikado' Is Season's Major Hit: Tom-Tom Mikado Frenzied Theater," *Chicago Daily News*, 19 January 1939, published reviews file, FTCLC.

63. C. J. Bulliet, "Negro 'Mikado' Is Season's Major Hit: Tom-Tom Mikado Frenzied Theater," *Chicago Daily News*, 19 January 1939, published reviews file, FTCLC.

64. "Cooper Okays WPA Theater," *New York Amsterdam News*, 18 March 1939.

65. Nahum Brascher, "The Mikado Rates as Season's Best," *Chicago Defender*, 1 October 1938.

66. And these "GilbertandSullivanites" *did* attend. One reviewer commented that such "boresome folks" were present at the showing he attended. One person "spoiled [his] evening by sitting right behind [him], breathing the whole into his neckshave." Ashton Stevens, "'The Mikado' Just a Twith of Swing in This WPA Ethiopera," *American* (Chicago), 26 September 1938. Stevens called the unswung parts "all the old mildewed stage business," setting himself up in contrast to the avid followers.

67. Harry Minturn and Edward Wurtzebach (musical director for the FTP in Chicago), production title file, FTCLC. The swing arranger was Charles Levy,

a member of the Federal Music Project's arranging staff. The musical director added two numbers to the list of songs changed to swing time, Yum Yum and Nanki-Poo's duet "Were You Not to Ko-Ko Plighted" and the finale in act two. Encores were requested most frequently for "Flowers That Bloom in the Spring," the lovers' duet, and "Here's a How-de-do," sung by the three nobles Pish-Tush, Pooh-Bah, and Ko-Ko.

68. It is unclear what production this script comes from. While changes in the script indicate the swing version, the cast list cannot be matched with any of the casts of Federal Theater productions for which programs exist in federal archives and collections. The name on the front of the script is John Tate. The only location noted is in the alteration of one of Ko-Ko's lines, from "I never even killed a blue-bottle" to "I never even killed a Jersey-mosquito." *The Mikado*, play scripts file, FTCLC. A portion of a script at the National Archives from a Seattle production, one not found in Library of Congress collections, shows similarities to the John Tate script.

69. Baily, *The Gilbert and Sullivan Book*, 267.

70. *The Mikado*, playbills file, FTCLC. Language connoting sexuality here normalizes the original style as "straight," correct, and mainstream. The homoeroticized description of the swing version as "gay" and "weird" further removes the performance from dominant culture while fostering a leering fascination with marginalized sexual spectacle.

71. Claudia Cassidy, "Negro's 'The Mikado' Doesn't Need Its Swing to Score Federal Theater Success," *Journal of Commerce* (Chicago), 26 September 1938, published reviews file, FTCLC.

72. Lloyd Lewis, "Mikado Malayed," *Chicago Daily News*, 26 September 1938, published reviews file, FTCLC.

73. Ben Burns, "WPA Negro Unit Swings 'The Mikado' at the Great Northern Theater," *Daily Record* (Chicago), 27 September 1938, published reviews file, FTCLC.

74. Fraden, *Blueprints*, 17, 191, 194.

75. Publicity report, *The Mikado*, production title file, FTCLC.

76. "Exclusive to 'Pic' Magazine," Federal Theater Publicity Department, WPA, 20 March 1939, NA.

77. Transcript of interview with Don Farran by John O'Conner for the Research Center for the Federal Theater Project, George Mason University, 3 January 1976, SCAGMU. *The Hot Mikado* starring Bill Robinson played at the World's Fair. Swing music and jazz dance, based in the Federal Theater production, were paraded as emblematic of Western culture.

78. Fraden, *Blueprints*, 8. See also arguments about the emblematic status of racial blackness in America in Saxton, *The Rise and Fall of the White Republic*; Roediger, *The Wages of Whiteness*.

79. For further investigation of the development of swing music and swing dancing, see Stowe, *Swing Changes*; Dinerstein, *Swinging the Machine*. See also Hazzard-Gordon, *Jookin*.'

80. For more on the way swing dancing was seen as emblematic of a society on the verge of cultural and technological change, see Dinerstein, *Swinging the Machine*.

81. For more on these concepts in modernist representation see Lemke, *Modernist Primitivism*. Lemke conducts an excellent literature review of scholarship on modernism, culture, and representation.

82. Actually four youngsters, at least two from Brooklyn College, "eluded the corps of ushers and shagged, jitterbugged and jumped down the aisle" during the "Flowers That Bloom in the Spring" number at the end of the second act. They were later identified as Evelyn Zamichow, Sidney Margoshes, Francis Schacht, and Paul Gordon. WPA Department of Information, NA.

83. Goldberg, *Racist Culture*, 78–80, 90–97, 148–68.

84. Baily, *The Gilbert and Sullivan Book*, 7–8, 447.

85. C. Williams, "Parody, Pastiche, and the Play of Genres," 1.

86. Woll, *Black Musical Theater*. Woll's discussion of black musical theater through the twentieth century shows the development of comedic strategies that took advantage of and were sometimes the unfortunate product of a racist environment. From blackface and "coon songs" to the black Federal Theater's "new form" of musical theater, these strategies exploited various structures of expression to entertain.

87. For more on the relationship between black performance styles and pressure from mainstream institutions and black audiences, see Watkins, *On the Real Side*; Levine, *Black Culture and Black Consciousness*; Sampson, *Blacks in Blackface*; Ellison, *Shadow and Act*.

88. For discussions of performance stereotypes of black men in popular culture see Woll, *Black Musical Theater*; Ely, *Adventures of Amos and Andy*.

89. Marchetti, *Romance and the "Yellow Peril."*

90. For more on the use of black blackface performance and its challenges to supremacist racial structures, see Knight, *Disintegrating the Musical*; E. Smith, *Bert Williams*; Lhamon, *Raising Cain*.

91. Census records from 1920, 1930, and 1940 do not clarify the racial identity of Edward Fraction.

92. Work on minstrelsy in the tradition of Roediger, *The Wages of Whiteness*; Lott, *Love and Theft*; and Rogin, *Blackface, White Noise*, explain how blackface performance produces racial whiteness and racial otherness and thus (re)enforces a relationship of power between blackness and whiteness, black people and white people.

93. Play script, WPA Federal Theater Collection, MPARR.

94. An ironic, self-critical performance of the exotic does appear in later Afri-

can American culture. One example is the tom-tom number in the film *Stormy Weather*. This ironic self-criticism is possible, but it just does not occur here, where the exotic prevails.

95. "Chronological Report on Swing Mikado Incident," National Archives and Records Administration, Record Group 69, box 15, Washington, D.C. The Federal Theater technically was not supposed to compete with private theater. For many very good reasons, however, the Federal Theater in Chicago refused to release the show to private producers. Reasons included the show's local popularity, months of sold-out seats, and the protection of the cast.

96. "Chronological Report on Swing Mikado Incident," Record Group 69, box 15, Washington, D.C, NA.

97. Transcript of interview with Don Farran by John O'Conner for the Research Center for the Federal Theater Project, 3 January 1976, SCAGMU.

98. Vallillo, "The Battle of the Black *Mikados*," 153–57.

99. *New York Amsterdam News*, 25 March 1939. Articles comparing the two shows and debating whether two versions of the same production could be successful simultaneously were carried in New York newspapers during March and April 1939.

100. Vallillo, "The Battle of the Black *Mikados*," 154–55.

101. Vallillo, "The Battle of the Black *Mikados*," 157.

102. Transcript of interview with Don Farran by John O'Conner for the Research Center for the Federal Theater Project, 3 January 1976, SCAGMU.

103. For more on American representations of imperial lands, see Kaplan, "Romancing the Empire."

104. Fanon, "On National Culture," 45.

105. In this sense *The Swing Mikado* more closely follows the unspecific, abstract representational structure of *Utopia, Limited* (1893), a Gilbert and Sullivan play whose subject matter and aesthetics treat empire as plot. Similarly to *The Mikado*, *Utopia, Limited* dramatizes race-based negotiations of national identity in a manner that reinforces notions of Western superiority and power, only more so. *Utopia, Limited*, a less successful play, specifically treats the importation of British culture to an island colony. Gilbert and Sullivan operas were directly concerned with empire and its corporate nature. Carolyn Williams opines that *The Mikado* exposed the performativity of national identity in using a Japanese cover to treat British culture ("*Utopia, Limited*," 221–47). Williams argues that *Utopia*'s island costumes and dramatization of an imperial presence on the periphery instantiates a certain hybridity of cultures and fluidity of government systems. Her analysis ultimately ignores the unequal operation of power in a neutral "hybridity." She calls *The Mikado*'s representations a culturally hybrid product of a "museum culture of foreign tourism at home" (225). Williams leaves the cultural politics of this "museumifying" and tourism unscrutinized. Discussion of the implications of pervasive orientalism for national identity is absent

283
....

NOTES TO CHAPTER THREE

from this argument. For her, *The Mikado* and *Utopia, Limited* are examples of the potentially "unstable" nature of national identity, not a production of national identity through an othering that helps to reinforce it. The "Utopian" Islanders impeccably mimic the British court, a copy rendered perfectly on the bodies of the Islanders (British actors) through exquisite detail in the costumes and structure of the court scene. In this case the Savoy company dresses up as an oriental island culture that carefully and successfully dresses up as British. They actually play themselves displaced, othered, and returned home again in a theatrical reenactment of the politics of imperial representation. The import and export of culture, and the reflection of this trade on the integrity of home, became a recurring theme in Gilbert and Sullivan's more direct engagements with imperialism. The preservation of national identity, its strength and resonance through various forms of appropriation, masking, repetition, and contact, remained the question at the core of *The Mikado* as well. Williams sees *Utopia* as dramatizing the failure of a traditional system of empire owing to its capacity to blur the boundaries between the culture of the imperial state and the colonized one. The play deflates British arrogance of cultural superiority by asserting that British culture can be fully appropriated and impeccably performed. Gilbert and Sullivan's joke here is typically double-edged, as it hits both British cupidity in exporting its culture wholesale and the unoriginality of mimicry. The racial paranoia concerning the national performance of the colonized more closely resembles American fears of incorporation of the "copying" colonized other into the national body, rather than some faith in the intelligence and integrity of subject nations residing in the hope of assimilation. If exotic "savages" are indeed good colonial pupils, they might become the society that schools them (the supposed intent of civilizing missions), undermining their claim to global superiority and imperial right. A baseline of the opera's comedy is at the spectacle of the racial, colonized other devouring the parent nation. In *Utopia, Limited*'s layered performance of others' performance of self the exoticism of the island articulates a xenophobic fear of the other. The ideological work performed by its images of languid noble savages justifies the imperial effort. The comedy of reflexive appropriations lampoons as well as enacts the fear of the alien other becoming indistinguishable from the imperial nation. In *The Swing Mikado* black Americans play the role of the incorporated other in a metaperformance that acts out national imperial desire in a display of yet another's otherness.

106. Salman, "In Our Orientalist Imagination," 221–32.

107. Vergara, *Displaying Filipinos*, 19, 20. In *Facing West* Drinnon describes how hatred of Native Americans, foundational to westward expansion, served as a foundation for imperial policy in Asia and the Pacific.

108. Theodore Roosevelt, "The Strenuous Life," speech before the Hamilton Club, Chicago, 10 April 1899; Rudyard Kipling, "The White Man's Burden," *McClure's Magazine*, 12 February 1899.

109. Vergara, *Displaying Filipinos*, 7–17.

110. Vicente Rafael discusses Filipino identity, race, and U.S. colonization in "White Love," 185–218. Histories of U.S.-Filipino relations generally jump in their focus from war and U.S. annexation during the colonial period at the turn of the century to the invasion and occupation by the Japanese during the Second World War. During the interwar period, the Philippines served as a node in the establishment of U.S. global trade routes and relationships and a coaling station for U.S. shipping and held geographically strategic significance for security and military concerns. The continuation of these relationships seems to have persisted with a fair amount of stability through the Depression era. These historical phenomena do little to clarify the possible meanings behind the strong suggestion of Filipino identity in *The Swing Mikado*.

111. Rafael, "White Love," 198.

112. Amy Kaplan touches on homogenization of island identities in "Black and Blue," 228–29. Newspaper cartoons at the turn of the century characterized Islanders, Chinese, Japanese, and Negroes in a similar manner. Interestingly these cartoons bear a resemblance to the primitivist minstrel forms characteristic of the Jazz Age that graced newspaper descriptions of *The Swing Mikado*: black figures with exaggerated limbs and facial features.

113. Balce, "Filipino Bodies, Lynching, and the Language of Empire" 43–60.

114. Karnow, *In Our Image*, 130, 138.

115. Karnow, *In Our Image*, 11–20, 49, 197. Karnow's analysis of the American presence in the Philippines, however, concurs with imperial ideology of the time that the U.S. was actually "uniquely benign," a "sentimental imperialist" that employed "benevolence" in the "mission" of "civilizing" the Philippines. Michael Salman critiques the imperialism of these arguments in "In Our Orientalist Imagination," 221–26, 228.

116. In different ways Rafael, Karnow, and Salman illustrate and explore these characteristics of U.S. imperialism in the Philippines.

117. "Sentimental Imperialists: America in Asia," episode 9 of *The Pacific Century*, produced by Peter Bull and Alex Gibney (PBS, 1992).

118. M. Wright, *Revolution in the Philippines?*, 4, 5.

119. Fred Cordova surveys the plight of Filipino immigrants to the United States in *Filipinos*.

120. Espiritu, *Home Bound*, 26–29.

121. Claudia Cassidy, "Negro's 'The Mikado' Doesn't Need Its Swing to Score Federal Theater Success," *Journal of Commerce* (Chicago), 26 September 1938, published reviews file, FTCLC.

122. C. J. Bulliet, "Negro 'Mikado' Is Season's Major Hit, Tom-Tom Mikado Frenzied Theater," *Chicago Daily News*, 19 January 1939, production title file, FTCLC.

123. "Mikado in Swing: A Classic Gets Its Pace Lifted," Record Group 69, box

157, entry 877, NA. This is an article from a New York paper that discusses the show shortly after its opening. The source and writer are unavailable.

124. For more on African American anticolonial resistance, see Plummer, *Rising Wind*; Von Eschen, *Race against Empire*.

125. Little, *Disciples of Liberty*, 112–25.

126. Little, *Disciples of Liberty*, 119.

127. Newspaper and organizational evidence serve as the foundation for catalogues of diasporic and anti-imperialist sentiment in black internationalist movements in Edwards, *The Practice of Diaspora*; R. Kearney, *African American Views of the Japanese*; Von Eschen, *Race against Empire*.

128. See Plummer, *Rising Wind*.

129. Allen, "When Japan Was 'Champion of the Darker Races,'" 23–46.

130. Both Gallicchio, *African American Encounter with Japan and China*, and R. Kearney, *African American Views of the Japanese*, investigate African American perceptions of Japan's imperial invasion of China.

131. Gallicchio, *African American Encounter with Japan and China* 92, 102–21; Allen, "When Japan Was 'Champion of the Darker Races,'" 23. Both Allen and R. Kearney, *African American Views of the Japanese*, chart the development of the image of Japan as the "Champion of the Darker Races."

132. Gallicchio, *African American Encounter with Japan and China*, 71–72, 91–92; Plummer, *Rising Wind*, 70–71. See also Mullen and Watson, *W. E. B. Du Bois on Asia*.

133. Denning, *The Cultural Front*, 11–13; Gallicchio, *African American Encounter with Japan and China*, 91.

134. In this aesthetic combination of extremely leftist and rightist concerns, the performance approaches Benjamin's articulation of a cultural fascism (one not necessarily connected to statism), especially in its tapping of mass pleasure through exoticism and swing. See Benjamin, "The Work of Art in the Age of Mechanical Reproduction."

135. Roach, *Cities of the Dead*, 14–17.

4. LENS/BODY

1. Fusco, *English Is Broken Here*. Through the interactive performance of a fake pair of caged natives studying the visitors, Fusco and Peña were able to develop a "reverse ethnography" of viewers and interlocutors. They found overwhelmingly that the desire to assume, believe, and act upon the existence of the caged "savage" revealed "that colonialist roles have been internalized quite effectively" and persistently in the U.S. (46).

2. For studies that explore and critique hierarchies in anthropological methodologies and representations, see Trouillot, "Anthropology and the Savage Slot"; di Leonardo, *Exotics at Home*. Di Leonardo engages America's histo-

ries of producing otherness, national selfhood, and power through ethnographic discourses.

3. For more on Katherine Dunham and Zora Neale Hurston as anthropologists, see Aschenbrenner, "Katherine Dunham" 140, 141; Mikell, "Feminism in Black Culture in the Ethnography of Zora Neale Hurston," 58.

4. Hurston, *Tell My Horse*.

5. See Hurston, *Tell My Horse*, chapters 3, 6, 7, 12, 14.

6. This concept was first proposed by Dwight Conquergood and is used by E. Patrick Johnson in articulating the roots of black performance studies.

7. A large body of scholarship exists addressing the development and historiography of anthropology. Some useful texts include Stocking, *Race, Culture, and Evolution*; Stocking, *Romantic Motives*; Fox, *Recapturing Anthropology*.

8. F. V. Harrison and Harrison, "Introduction," 14; Du Bois, *Black Folk, Then and Now*, ix; Willis, "Skeletons in the Anthropological Closet," 121–52.

9. F. V. Harrison and Harrison, "Introduction," 3; Willis, "Skeletons in the Anthropological Closet,"121–52.

10. Hymes, "The Use of Anthropology," 152.

11. L. D. Baker, *From Savage to Negro*, 26–53, 65–73.

12. Du Bois, *The Philadelphia Negro*; F. V. Harrison and Harrison, "Introduction," 12–13; Muller, "Du Boisian Pragmatism and 'The Problem of the Twentieth Century,'" 319–37; L. D. Baker, *From Savage to Negro*, 111, 110, 113.

13. Stocking, "The Basic Assumptions of Boasian Anthropology." Stocking documents the persistence of Darwinian conventional wisdom charting the hierarchy of human races. See Stocking, *Race, Culture, and Evolution*, 113.

14. Hymes, "The Use of Anthropology," 27; Willis, "Skeletons in the Anthropological Closet," 121–52; Boas, *Race, Language, and Culture*, vi. The notion of the primitive in culture was not adequately challenged until the late 1960s, with the publication of arguments like Willis's and Caulfield's, and even then some anthropological scholarship still reflected biologism (Willis, "Skeletons in the Anthropological Closet," 122, 124, 126). Willis cites pioneering work by Stanley Diamond in 1964 that examines the "primitive concept as a construction," while not, however, challenging the ethnographic validity of anthropology. See Diamond, *Primitive Views*, 151. Willis holds that any possibility of a primitive ceased to exist with the imperial development of the world as marketplace and the institution of colonial governments and regulatory forces. This means that after the advent of global capitalism the existence of primitives, that is humans without contact with modernity, became purely an imaginary and ideological project of imperialism.

15. Willis, "Skeletons in the Anthropological Closet," 126.

16. Caulfield, "Culture and Imperialism," 182–212. Caulfield argues that acknowledging the pervasive impact of imperialism on culture must coexist with efforts to reinvent, change, and develop a usable anthropology.

17. Herskovits, *The Myth of the Negro Past*. Herskovits used data collected in West Africa, Haiti, and Jamaica during the 1930s. His research on black Americans' relationship to Africa constituted a major methodological and theoretical development in anthropology with regard to concepts of acculturation, dispersal, and retention. He used a diffusion model to trace the transmission of black culture to the New World and asserted that New World black cultures were primarily rooted in African ones, establishing a model of black cultural manifestation as either "remainders" or the result of acculturation (adaptation to "dominant" or European modes). In one stroke he demonstrated a linear past linking black culture to Africanisms, combating notions regarding the totalizing effects of slavery and blacks' lack of culture even as it simultaneously denied Africans in the Americas a distinctive cultural identity. Put simply, African American culture became a manifestation of remainders and acculturation. The significance and meaning of *Myth*'s content and scholarly and cultural intervention have been the subject of lively debate over the past half-century—a debate that has challenged the validity of anthropological interpretation of culture at its core. F. V. Harrison and Harrison, "Introduction," 12–13. See also Szwed, "American Anthropological Dilemma," 153–81. Thus questions of African American culture and identity lie at the heart of debates concerning disciplinary methodology and identity.

18. For more on ethnographic subjectivity, see Willie Baber's discussion of the life and work of the noted black anthropologist St. Clair Drake in Baber, "St. Clair Drake," 53.

19. L. D. Baker, *From Savage to Negro*, 127–187; F. V. Harrison and Harrison, "Introduction," 5, 10, 12.

20. L. D. Baker, *From Savage to Negro*, 162.

21. Michael Kearney argues that anthropology's function as a discipline was to differentiate between self and other, a process that was both scientific and cultural ("Borders and Boundaries of State and Self at the End of Empire," 52–74).

22. D. Hymes, "The Use of Anthropology," 49.

23. Baber, "St. Clair Drake," 208. This perspective was significantly different from Herskovits's argument regarding acculturation in 1941. An activist "politics of liberation," including a politicized concept of "homeland," constituted Drake's black diaspora.

24. For a discussion of the colonial imaginary, ethnographic display, and the black body in performance see Henderson, "Josephine Baker and La Revue Negre," 107–33. Henderson also explores the colonial connection between dance, feminized race, and primitivism.

25. Dunham, "Form and Function in Primitive Dance," 2, quoted in Aschenbrenner, *Katherine Dunham*, 50.

26. Pierre, "A Talk with Katherine Dunham," 75; Aschenbrenner, *Katherine Dunham*, 49.

27. Dunham, "The Negro Dance (1941)," 218; Dunham, *Dances of Haiti*, xxiv;

Dunham, *Island Possessed* (1994), 198. For more on the way dance contributes to racial and national identity formation, see Burt, *Alien Bodies*, 1–2.

28. Aschenbrenner, *Katherine Dunham*, 49–53.

29. Dunham, "Form and Function in Primitive Dance"; Pierre, "A Talk with Katherine Dunham," 75; Aschenbrenner, *Katherine Dunham*, 49–58.

30. Original editor's note that accompanied the original publication of Dunham, "The Negro Dance (1941)," 217.

31. Pierre, "A Talk with Katherine Dunham," 75. Jamaican histories that cover this period include Sherlock and Bennett, *Story of the Jamaican People*; Monteith and Richards, *Jamaica in Slavery and Freedom*. Economic and imperial histories include Rogozinski, *A Brief History of the Caribbean*; Langley, *The Banana Wars*; Hart, *From Occupation to Independence*.

32. Madison, "Performance, Personal Narratives, and the Politics of Possibility," 276–86.

33. The nodes of performance are addressed in Clark, "Performing the Memory of Difference in Afro-Caribbean Dance," 188–204. Clark shows Dunham's research-to-performance method to construct history and her choreography to apply engaged critique to the material she encountered.

34. For a specific example of postmodern anthropology at work, see Fabian, *Power and Performance*, xiii–xv, 3–15.

35. Conquergood distills "three principles that are the distinguishing qualities of a performance paradigm" of ethnography that Dunham displayed in her work: "(1) Process, (2) Embodiment, (3) Dialogue" ("Between Experience and Meaning," 26–59).

36. Aschenbrenner, "Katherine Dunham," 140–41.

37. For more on Dunham's life and work, see her autobiography, *A Touch of Innocence*; Beckford, *Katherine Dunham*.

38. Conquergood, "Performing as a Moral Act," 1–13. Conquergood explains, "Dialogical performance is a way of having an intimate conversation with other peoples and cultures. Instead of speaking about them, one speaks to and with them. The sensuous immediacy and empathic leap demanded by performance is an occasion for orchestrating two voices, for bringing together two sensibilities. At the same time, the conspicuous artifice of performance is a vivid reminder that each voice has its own integrity" (10).

39. Melville Herskovits, *Film Study of West Africa* (1931) and *Haitian Valley Film Study* (1934), NMNH. Herskovits studied under Franz Boas. He also supported, and some go so far as to say supervised, Dunham's research in Jamaica and Haiti.

40. Jackson, "An Ethnographic Filmflam," 32–42.

41. Rony, *The Third Eye*, 9–10.

42. Melville Herskovits, *Haitian Valley Film Study* (1934), NMNH.

43. Melville Herskovits, *Film Study of West Africa* (1931), NMNH.

44. Rony, *The Third Eye*, 8.

45. Rony, *The Third Eye*, 5.

46. Aschenbrenner, *Katherine Dunham*, 15.

47. Pierre, "A Talk with Katherine Dunham," 75; Aschenbrenner *Katherine Dunham*, 49.

48. Katherine Dunham fieldwork films, "L'Ag'Ya, Jamaica and Martinique, 1936, video clip #18, 19, 20"; "Traditional Dance, Jamaica and Martinique Fieldwork, 1936, video clip #25"; "Traditional Dance, Trinidad Fieldwork, 1936, video clip #13," MDLC. See also http://www.loc.gov.

49. "Katherine Dunham on Her Anthropological Films, video clip #34," MDLC.

50. This relationship prefigures John Jackson's observation of the ways black Harlemites positioned themselves as participants in the making of video ethnographies by expecting a level of reciprocity between the filmmaker and themselves. See Jackson, "An Ethnographic Filmflam."

51. Katherine Dunham fieldwork films, "Urban social dance, Jamaica and Martinique, 1936, video clip #20," MDLC.

52. Katherine Dunham fieldwork films, "Urban social dance, Jamaica and Martinique Fieldwork, 1936, video clip #21," MDLC.

53. In the films available it appears that Dunham is less intrusive than her predecessor, Zora Neale Hurston, who at times positioned and posed filmic subjects or appeared herself before the camera within the ethnographic frame (Rony, *The Third Eye*, 203–11). Hurston made two sets of ethnographic films in the United States, one between 1927 and 1929 and another sometime during the mid-1930s (MPLC). Rony examines the way that Hurston's trickster-like appearance with the subjects in the church films undermines the typical objectification inherent in ethnographic film. The participation, direct gaze, and posing of Hurston's subjects act not as data collection but as an editorial presentation of an ethos, of beauty, and of community character. Dunham's display of ethnographic subjectivity in her filmmaking is more disciplinary and less playful than Hurston's but maintains some of this intersubjective impact. Hurston's gazing back in film acts similarly, however, to Dunham's dancing of Western dances for a Jamaican polity. Both performances posit the irony of their own bodies as ethnographer and subject in ethnographic performance. While their work shows how performance culture appropriated anthropological methodologies to construct black racial identities, these black anthropologist artists also show how anthropological practice could use performance to accomplish black ethnographic subjectivity.

54. Benston, "The Aesthetic of Modern Black Drama," 61–78.

55. This position is akin to Kirin Narayan's "shifting identifications amid a field of interpenetrating communities and power relations" ("How Native Is a Native Anthropologist?," 671–86).

56. Clark and Wilkerson, *Kaiso!*, 103–4; Clark, "Katherine Dunham's Tropical Revue," 147–52.

57. Madison, "Performance, Personal Narratives, and the Politics of Possibility," 276–86.

58. The films were made much later than the period under discussion here, but serve as a good example of the rigorous training of the body.

59. Films on Dunham technique include "Yonvalou, video clip #62"; "Contractions, video clip #46"; "Progressions: Dunham Walk-Slow, video clip #56"; "Advanced 2nd Position Plié with Back Leg Lift in Fourth Position, video clip #52," MDLC.

60. Quoted in Orme, "The Negro in Dance as Katherine Dunham Sees Him," 59–62.

61. Aschenbrenner, *Katherine Dunham*, 63–65.

62. For a history of Dunham's training in dance, see Perpener, *African American Concert Dance*, 133–36. Dunham wrote accounts of her travels and research, including *Journey to Accompong*, about her experience in Jamaica, and *Dances of Haiti* and *Island Possessed* (1969), about her work in Haiti. She rarely receives the credit she deserves as a skillful writer. Her lyrical prose in *Journey to Accompong* and *Island Possessed* is neither dry nor that of a distanced observer, but rather rich and active.

63. See Perpener, *African American Concert Dance*, 128–60; Manning, "Modern Dance, Negro Dance, and Katherine Dunham," 487–505. For more on black dance, see Myers and Reinhart, *African American Genius in Modern Dance*; Myers, *The Black Tradition in Modern Dance*; Malone, *Steppin' on the Blues*; Emery, *Black Dance*.

64. Dunham's choreography and dancing were featured in Hollywood films, including a short devoted to her own company, Warner Brothers' *Carnival of Rhythm*, directed by Stanley Martin (1941; DVD, Warner Home Video, 2007); Paramount Pictures' *Star Spangled Rhythm*, directed by George Marshall (1942; DVD, Universal Home Entertainment, 2003); Universal Pictures' *Pardon My Sarong*, directed by Erle Kenton (1942; VHS, MCA/Universal Home Video, 2000); Twentieth Century Fox's *Stormy Weather*, directed by Andrew L. Stone (1943).

65. Claudia Cassidy, "About the *Ballet Fedre*," *Journal of Commerce* (Chicago), 29 January 1938. *Ballet Fedré* opened on 27 January 1938 and played initially for a limited engagement of ten days at Chicago's Great Northern Theater. The show was extended six additional days after its slated closing date of 2 February.

66. *Ballet Fedré* production title file, FTCLC; Clark, "Katherine Dunham's Tropical Revue," 148–49.

67. Publicity report, "Katherine Dunham to Open with Ballet Ferde [*sic*] in Loop," *Chicago Defender*, 29 January 1938.

68. The score was by Robert Sanders of the University of Chicago Music Department. Clive Rickabaugh, the set designer for *Ballet Fedré*, and Edward Wurtzebach, the orchestra conductor, both worked on *The Swing Mikado*. Duncan Whiteside designed *Ballet Fedré*'s lighting.

69. Clark, "Katherine Dunham's Tropical Revue," 147–52. Clark's article provides a comprehensive and detailed description of *L'Ag'Ya*'s appearance, story, and structure as it appeared as a portion of *Tropical Revue* that premiered in 1942. Clark reconstructs the dance through firsthand observation and interviews with Dunham and her collaborators. Clark's seminal analysis shows the significance of Dunham's research and the traditional dance forms she uses in the ballet. For the most part descriptions of the ballet that appear in monographs that postdate Clark's article rely on her excellent work.

70. In considering the migration and trade of the dance form(s) of the tango from its earliest stages as black symbolic, community-based, resistant, kinesthetic expression to its international, interracial, intercultural appropriations, Marta Savigliano explains the trade of power in dance practice ("Fragments for a Story of Tango Bodies," 199–232).

71. Savigliano, "Fragments for a Story of Tango Bodies," 213.

72. "Cooper Okays WPA Theater," *New York Amsterdam News*, 18 March 1939.

73. Eugene Stinson, "Review of Ballet Fedré," *Chicago Daily News*, 3 February 1938.

74. Claudia Cassidy, "About the *Ballet Fedre*," *Journal of Commerce* (Chicago), 29 January 1938, emphasis added.

75. Cecil Smith, "Federal Dance Gives First Program," *Chicago Tribune*, 28 January 1938.

76. Clark, "Katherine Dunham's Tropical Revue," 149. Sally Ann Ness explores the nonlinear narrative of movement in Filipino dance in *Body Movement Culture*, 98–153.

77. For a discussion of the way dance as a community experience contributes to a sense of identity, see Tomko, *Dancing Class*.

78. For further investigation of the relationship between a sense of nationalism and modern dance, see Manning, *Ecstasy and the Demon*; Manning, *Modern Dance*; Franko, *Dancing Modernism*.

79. Robert Pollak, "All-Negro Folk Ballet Steals Federal Show," *Chicago Daily Times*, 28 January 1938.

80. Clark, "Katherine Dunham's Tropical Revue," 150.

81. Clark, "Katherine Dunham's Tropical Revue," 150.

82. My references to the practice of vaudun and voodoo in this chapter follows Dunham's terminology in an attempt to separate the serious consideration of a system of religious belief from exoticized representations of that belief. Neither Dunham nor the performances refer to "voodoo" in their reference to the "animistic religion in Haiti; originally Dahomean pantheon of spirits"

(Aschenbrenner, *Katherine Dunham*, 7). I use the term "voodoo" to invoke the exoticizing gaze that dispenses with any concern for religious or social content, but appropriates vaudun as spectacle or savagery.

83. Clark, "Katherine Dunham's Tropical Revue," 150.

84. The zombie king's headdress seems to be the same headpiece used for the Mikado's costume in *The Swing Mikado* several months later. *Ballet Fedré*, photographic prints file, FTCLC.

85. Clark, "Katherine Dunham's Tropical Revue," 148. The aesthetic that Clark reconstructs derives from the two decades of performance that followed this first showing. The zombie king's costume changed after the performance in 1938. His appearance became an opportunity to more decisively implicate a Western cultural power. In later versions of the ballet, including in *Tropical Revue* (1943), he wears "the remnants of the colonial era—a black tattered suitcoat, tophat and tie" as he presides over the ritual. His decaying colonial costume signals both the influence and the symbolic passing of the colonial era. Both representations of the voodoo overlord imply an understanding of imperial relationships: in the former the possibility of his voodoo power as represented by Americans capitulates to exoticism; in the latter the performance critiques the colonial perspective that produced exoticism in the first place.

86. Clark, "Katherine Dunham's Tropical Revue," 150.

87. Clark, "Katherine Dunham's Tropical Revue," 151.

88. Clark, "Katherine Dunham's Tropical Revue," 151.

89. Clark, "Katherine Dunham's Tropical Revue," 151.

90. Eugene Stinson, "Review of Ballet Fedré," *Chicago Daily News*, 3 February 1938.

91. Eugene Stinson, "Review of Ballet Fedré," *Chicago Daily News*, 3 February 1938.

92. Katherine Dunham, "Jamaica and Martinique Fieldwork, 1936, video clip #19," MDLC.

93. Katherine Dunham, "Katherine Dunham on Ag'Ya, video clip #36," MDLC.

94. Kaye Dunn, "L'Ag'Ya of Martinique," *Esquire*, November 1939, reprinted in Clark and Wilkerson, *Kaiso!*, 46. Dunham used "Kaye Dunn" as a pen name.

95. Katherine Dunham, "Ag'Ya fight from L'Ag'Ya, Katherine Dunham Company 1947, video clip #29," MDLC.

96. Katherine Dunham, "Ag'Ya fight from L'Ag'Ya, Katherine Dunham Company 1947, video clip #29," MDLC.

97. Diawara, "Englishness and Blackness," 830–44.

98. Clark, "Katherine Dunham's Tropical Revue," 149, 151.

99. Jane Desmond writes, "While the notion of 'appropriation' may signal the transfer of source material from one group to another, it doesn't account for the changes in performance style and ideological meaning that accompany the transfer. Concepts of hybridity or syncretism more adequately describe the com-

plex interactions among ideology, cultural forms, and power differentials that are manifest in such transfers" ("Embodying Difference," 41).

5. ETHNOGRAPHIC REFRACTION

1. *The Devil's Daughter*, directed by Arthur H. Leonard (Sack Amusement Enterprises, 1938). An alternate title for this film was *Pocomania*, a term that might be translated as "a little crazy" and that was used for practices of vaudun. See Hurston, *Tell My Horse*, 3.

2. Grossberg, "Bringin' It All Back Home," 20, quoted in Madison, "Performance, Personal Narratives, and the Politics of Possibility," 278.

3. Madison, "Performance, Personal Narratives, and the Politics of Possibility," 278.

4. For discussions of race, performance, and authenticity, see Johnson, *Appropriating Blackness*; Jackson, *Real Black*.

5. Fatimah Rony explains that even popular film repeated racist assumptions and relationships and offered new ethnographic material that dehumanized, fetishized, and sometimes bestialized a nonwhite other outside of Western civilization with the effect of establishing a normalized, typically white, Western subjectivity (*The Third Eye*, 7).

6. Audience responses to Coco Fusco and Guillermo Gomez-Peña's performance piece "Two Undiscovered Amerindians" demonstrates the mutually reinforcing relationship between abjection and objectification and the belief in obtaining an unmitigated truth about "savage" cultures *because* they are on display. See Fusco, *English Is Broken Here*, 37–64. The relationship between savagery or primitivism and ethnographic display is circular: one provides evidence of the other.

7. "The Devil's Daughter," *Motion Picture Herald* 137, no. 10 (1939), 27. The unidentified reviewer identifies the informal dance piece as "Sweet Charlie, a native conga dance performed by the Lynsted Market dancers."

8. Geertz, *The Interpretation of Cultures*, 413–53. Geertz claims that the best discussion of cockfighting was published in the early 1940s by Bateson and Mead in *Balinese Character*. Dunham uses the term "cockfight" metaphorically in some of her discussions about men's dance dating from the mid- to late 1930s. Although Geertz's famous discussion of the Balinese cockfight materialized in print in 1973, the animism, cultural significance, social interaction, virtual competition, and gendered implications surrounding the cockfight have remained, in one capacity or another, of interest in the field.

9. This cockfight might also be seen as an oblique performance of interracial conflict in the pitting of a black rooster against a white one. This gesture recognizes the larger structure of global racial dynamics than those treated in the film.

10. A documentary specificity seems to look at a culture in a way that delineates its particularity. Here the ethnographic display elaborated native authenticity through anthropologically canonical images of native dance and the cockfight. See Ruby, *Picturing Culture*.

11. Desmond, "Invoking 'the Native,'" 84–85, 88.

12. "The Devil's Daughter," *Motion Picture Herald* 137, no. 10 (1939), 74; "The Devil's Daughter," *Film Daily* (New York), 76, no. 116 (1939), 6.

13. Promotional poster, Margaret Herrick Library, AMPAS.

14. Rony, *The Third Eye*, 7.

15. Rony, *The Third Eye*, 7.

16. Diawara, "Englishness and Blackness," 830–44.

17. Sampson, *Blacks in Black and White*, 20.

18. "The Devil's Daughter," *Motion Picture Herald* 137, no. 10 (1939), 74; "Today's Motion Pictures," *The Daily Gleaner*, 24 February 1940, The National Library of Jamaica, Kingston, Jamaica. Jamaican Research Provided by Terri Francis.

19. The interaction with locals that gets coded into the film is significantly less participatory than that seen in Katherine Dunham's practice.

20. Desmond, "Where Is 'The Nation'?," 81–110. Desmond identifies the possibility of mutual constructions of meaning occurring in the incidence of identities (like nation) being produced through other categories of identity (such as sex and gender).

21. Promotional poster, Margaret Herrick Library, AMPAS.

22. "Censors Reluctantly Pass 'Pocomania,'" *Daily Gleaner*, 17 February 1940, National Library of Jamaica, Kingston. Jamaican research provided by Terri Francis.

23. For a further exploration of racial sincerity and realness, see Jackson, *Real Black*.

24. For theories of the cultural impact of representation, see Morley and Chen, *Stuart Hall*; R. Williams, *The Sociology of Culture*; Higgins, *The Raymond Williams Reader*; Harvey, *The Condition of Post-Modernity*.

25. Desmond, "Embodying Difference," 84–85, 88.

26. Coco Fusco and Guillermo Gomez-Peña's performance "Couple in a Cage" offers a similar fake of savage primitive identities produced by a colonial gaze whose consequences proved quite real. Their performance acts as commentary on the constructedness of aboriginal shows and displays of native bodies and their effect throughout five hundred years of global colonial history. The ethnographic viewing practices of audiences in the late twentieth century reveal entrenched colonial attitudes and imperial desire. See Fusco, *English Is Broken Here*, 37–64.

1. *Stormy Weather* is in the genre of segregated cabaret films from the period, such as *Hallelujah!*, directed by King Vidor (MGM, 1929; DVD, Warner Home Video, 2006); *Harlem Is Heaven*, directed by Irwin Franklin (Sack Amusement Enterprises, 1931); *Cotton Club Revue* (1938); and *The Duke Is Tops*, directed by William L. Nolte and Ralph Cooper (Million Dollar Productions, 1938; later released as *Bronze Venus*, 1943).

2. Bogle, *Toms, Coons, Mulattoes, Mammies, and Bucks.*

3. Cripps, *Making Movies Black*, 85.

4. Bogle, *Toms, Coons, Mulattoes, Mammies, and Bucks*, 50, 132.

5. Cripps, *Making Movies Black*, 35–101.

6. Cripps, *Slow Fade to Black*, 377.

7. Cripps, *Slow Fade to Black*, 336.

8. Bogle, *Toms, Coons, Mulattoes, Mammies, and Bucks*, 136.

9. Cripps, *Slow Fade to Black*, 174.

10. For a history of black support of the Second World War, see Von Eschen, *Race against Empire.*

11. Bogle, *Toms, Coons, Mulattoes, Mammies, and Bucks*, 136.

12. Though describing a period about five years later, Mary Dudziak identifies strong international pressure (partly a result of the NAACP's international organizing) as the force that drove federal interest in changing the global perception of U.S. racism. See Dudziak, *Cold War Civil Rights*, 43–66.

13. Cripps, *Making Movies Black*, 52–55.

14. Cripps, *Slow Fade to Black*, 376–77.

15. *Stormy Weather* production file, Margaret Herrick Library, AMPAS.

16. Cripps, *Making Movies Black*, 95.

17. Bogle, *Toms, Coons, Mulattoes, Mammies, and Bucks*, 132.

18. Richard Dyer discusses Lena Horne's vocal style in "Singing Prettily."

19. Chude-Sokei, *The Last "Darky."* Chude-Sokei argues that minstrelsy permitted entry into Americanness through the literal black mask in performance and through blackness as a mask of nation.

20. Arthur Knight analyzes this blackface scene in *Disintegrating the Musical*, 110–19.

21. Lemke, *Primitivist Modernism*, 4.

22. "Danse Africaine" in Hughes, *Weary Blues.*

23. Pagan, *Murder at the Sleepy Lagoon*, 11, 98–125.

24. Kelley, *Race Rebels*, 165–67; Mercer, "Black Hair/Style Politics," 49.

25. The song was written in 1933 by Harold Arlen, a Jewish songwriter with the stature and credits of his friend George Gershwin, reportedly for Ethel Waters when she headlined at Harlem's Cotton Club. It has been understood as a blues tune of lost love that decries Depression-era poverty.

26. For more on dance from the period, see Manning, *Modern Dance, Negro Dance*. Ramsay Burt describes the cityscape and African origins of Dunham's choreography in the "Stormy Weather" scene as forms of modernism (Burt, *Alien Bodies*, 154–59).

27. Clark, "Performing the Memory of Difference in Afro-Caribbean Dance," 188–204.

28. Clark and Wilkerson, *Kaiso!*, 85–88; Horne and Schickel, *Lena*.

EPILOGUE

1. J. Baldwin, *The Devil Finds Work*, 28–34.

2. "New Movie, a Western Drama!," *Chicago Defender*, 1 October 1938.

3. Hurston, "Thirty Days among Maroons," 272. Originally published in *New York Herald Tribune Weekly Book Report*, 12 January 1947.

4. Dunham, *Island Possessed* (1994), viii.

5. Stepto, *Blue as the Lake*, 3–35.

6. R. Wright, *American Hunger*, 113.

....

BIBLIOGRAPHY

ABBREVIATIONS OF ARCHIVES AND LIBRARIES

AMPAS   Academy of Motion Picture Arts and Sciences, Margaret Herrick Library, Los Angeles, California

FTCLC   Federal Theater Collection, Library of Congress, Washington, District of Columbia

MDLC   Music Division, Library of Congress, Washington, District of Columbia

MPARR   Music and Performing Arts Reading Room, Library of Congress, Washington, District of Columbia

MPLC   Motion Pictures Reading Room, Library of Congress, Washington, District of Columbia

NA   National Archives, Washington, District of Columbia

NMNH   Human Studies Film Archives, National Museum of Natural History Smithsonian Institution, Washington, District of Columbia

SCAGMU   Special Collections and Archives, George Mason University, Fairfax, Virginia

NEWSPAPERS AND PERIODICALS

Chicago Defender
Daily Worker
Herald Tribune
Motion Picture Herald
New Leader
New York Amsterdam News

New York Daily News
New York Post
New York Sun
New York Times
Sunday Worker
Variety

Adubato, Robert A. "A History of the WPA's Negro Theater Project in New York City, 1935–1939." Ph.D. diss., New York University, 1978. Accessed at Research Center for the Federal Theater Project, SCAGMU.

Allen, Ernest, Jr. "When Japan Was 'Champion of the Darker Races': Satokata Takahashi and the Flowering of Messianic Black Nationalism." *Black Scholar* 24, no. 1 (1994), 23–46.

Allmendinger, Blake. *Imagining the African American West.* Lincoln: University of Nebraska Press, 2005.

Anderson, Benedict. *Imagined Communities: Reflections on the Origin and Spread of Nationalism.* New York: Verso Books, 1991.

Appiah, Anthony. *In My Father's House: Africa in the Philosophy of Culture.* New York: Oxford University Press, 1993.

Aschenbrenner, Joyce. "Katherine Dunham: Anthropologist, Artist, Humanist." *African American Pioneers in Anthropology,* edited by Ira Harrison and Faye Harrison, 137–53. Chicago: University of Illinois Press, 1999.

———. *Katherine Dunham: Reflections on the Social and Political Contexts of Afro-American Dance.* New York: Congress on Research in Dance, 1981.

Auerbach, Erich. *Mimesis: The Representation of Reality in Western Culture.* 1946. Princeton: Princeton University Press, 1953.

Baber, Willie. "St. Clair Drake: Scholar and Activist." *African American Pioneers in Anthropology,* edited by Faye V. Harrison and Ira E. Harrison, 191–212. Chicago: University of Illinois Press, 1999.

Baily, Leslie. *The Gilbert and Sullivan Book.* 1952. London: Spring Books, 1966.

Baker, Houston. *Modernism and the Harlem Renaissance.* Chicago: University of Chicago Press, 1989.

Baker, Lee D. *From Savage to Negro: Anthropology and the Construction of Race, 1896–1954.* Berkeley: University of California Press, 1998.

Balce, Nerissa S. "Filipino Bodies, Lynching, and the Language of Empire." *Positively No Filipinos Allowed: Building Communities and Discourse,* edited by Antonio Tiongson, Ricardo Gutierrez, and Edgardo Gutierrez, 43–60. Philadelphia: Temple University Press, 2006.

Baldwin, Davarian. *Chicago's New Negroes: Modernity, the Great Migration, and Black Urban Life.* Chapel Hill: University of North Carolina Press, 2007.

Baldwin, James. *The Devil Finds Work: An Essay.* New York: Dial Press, 1974.

Bateson, Gregory, and Margaret Mead. *Balinese Character: A Photographic Analysis.* New York: New York Academy of Sciences, 1942.

Bean, Annemarie. "Black Minstrelsy and Double Inversion circa 1890." *African American Performance and Theater History: A Critical Reader,* edited by Harry Elam and David Krasner, 171–91. New York: Oxford University Press, 2001.

Beckford, Ruth. *Katherine Dunham: A Biography*. New York: Marcel Dekker, 1979.

Bederman, Gail. *Manliness and Civilization: A Cultural History of Gender and Race in the United States, 1880–1917*. Chicago: University of Chicago Press, 1995.

Benjamin, Walter. "The Work of Art in the Age of Mechanical Reproduction." *Reading Images: Readers in Cultural Criticism*, edited by Julia Thomas, 62–75. New York: Palgrave, 2001.

Benston, Kimberly W. "The Aesthetic of Modern Black Drama: From Mimesis to Methexis." *The Theatre of Black Americans: A Collection of Critical Essays*, edited by Errol Hill, 61–78. New York: Applause, 1987.

Bhabha, Homi. *Location of Culture*. New York: Routledge, 1994.

Blassingame, John W. "The Press and American Intervention in Haiti and the Dominican Republic, 1904–1920." *Caribbean Studies* 4, no. 2 (1969), 27–43.

Boas, Franz. *Race, Language, and Culture*. New York: Macmillan, 1940.

Bogle, Donald. *Toms, Coons, Mulattoes, Mammies, and Bucks: An Interpretive History of Blacks in American Films*. 1973. New York: Continuum, 1998.

Bond, Frederick W. *The Negro and Drama*. College Park, Md.: McGrath, 1969.

Bontemps, Arna. *Black Thunder*. Boston: Beacon Street Press, 1936.

Brockett, Oscar G. *The Theater*. New York: Holt, Rinehart, and Winston, 1965.

Brooks, Daphne Ann. *Bodies in Dissent: Spectacular Performances of Race and Freedom, 1850–1910*. Durham: Duke University Press, 2006.

Brown, Jayna. "Black Patriarch on the Prairie: National Identity and Black Manhood in the Early Novels of Oscar Micheaux." *Oscar Micheaux and His Circle: African-American Filmmaking and Race Cinema of the Silent Era*, edited by Pearl Bowser, Jane Gaines, and Charles Musser, 132–46. Bloomington: Indiana University Press, 2001.

Brown, Lorraine, ed. *Liberty Deferred and Other Living Newspapers of the 1930s Federal Theatre Project*. Edited by Tamara Liller and Barbara Jones Smith. Fairfax, Va.: George Mason University Press, 1989.

Burt, Ramsay. *Alien Bodies: Representations of Modernity, "Race" and Nation in Early Modern Dance*. New York: Routledge, 1998.

Butler, Judith. *Bodies That Matter: On the Discursive Limits of "Sex."* London: Routledge, 1993.

Cannadine, David. "Gilbert and Sullivan: The Making and Un-Making of a British 'Tradition.'" *Myths of the English*, edited by Roy Porter, 12–32. Cambridge: Polity Press, 1992.

Canning, Charlotte. "'The Most American Thing in America': Producing National Identities in Chautauqua, 1904–1932." *Performing America: Cultural Nationalism in American Theater*, edited by Jeffrey D. D. Mason and J. Ellen Gainor, 91–105. Ann Arbor: University of Michigan Press, 1999.

Caulfield, Mina Davis. "Culture and Imperialism: Proposing a New Dialectic." *Reinventing Anthropology*, edited by Dell Hymes, 182–212. New York: Pantheon Books, 1972.

Chude-Sokei, Louis. *The Last "Darky": Bert Williams, Black on Black Minstrelsy, and the African Diaspora*. Durham: Duke University Press, 2006.

Clark, VèVè. "Katherine Dunham's Tropical Revue." *Black American Literature Forum* 16, no. 4 (1982), 147–52.

———. "Performing the Memory of Difference in Afro-Caribbean Dance: Katherine Dunham's Choreography, 1938–1987." *History and Memory in African-American Culture*, edited by Geneviève Fabre and Robert O'Meally, 188–204. New York: Oxford University Press, 1994.

Clark, VèVè, and Margaret B. Wilkerson, eds. *Kaiso! Katherine Dunham: An Anthology of Writings*. Berkeley: Institute for the Study of Social Change, CCEW Women's Center, University of California, 1978.

Coffman, Elizabeth. "Uncanny Performances in Colonial Narratives: Josephine Baker in Princess Tam Tam." *Paradoxa: Studies in World Literary Genres* 3 (1997), 379–94.

Cohen, Lizabeth. *Making a New Deal: Industrial Workers in Chicago, 1919–1939*. Cambridge: Cambridge University Press, 1995.

Colin, Paul. *Josephine Baker and La Revue Nègre: Paul Colin's Lithographs of Le Tumulte Noir in Paris, 1927*. New York: H. N. Abrams, 1998.

Conquergood, Dwight. "Between Experience and Meaning: Performance as Paradigm for Meaningful Action." *Renewal and Revision: The Future of Interpretation*, edited by Ted Colson, 25–59. Denton, Tex.: Omega, 1986.

———. "Performance Studies: Interventions and Radical Research." *TDR* 46, no. 2 (2002), 145–56.

———. "Performing as a Moral Act: Ethical Dimensions of the Ethnography of Performance." *Literature in Performance* 5, no. 2 (1985), 1–13.

Cook, David. *A History of Narrative Film*. New York: W. W. Norton, 1990.

Cordova, Fred. *Filipinos: Forgotten Asian Americans. A Pictorial Essay 1763–circa 1963*. Dubuque, Iowa.: Kendall/Hunt, 1983.

Craig, E. Quita. *Black Drama of the Federal Theater Era: Beyond the Formal Horizons*. Amherst: University of Massachusetts Press, 1980.

Cripps, Thomas. *Making Movies Black: The Hollywood Message Movie from World War II to the Civil Rights Era*. New York: Oxford University Press, 1993.

———. *Slow Fade to Black: The Negro in American Film, 1900–1942*. 1977. New York: Oxford University Press, 1993.

Cronon, William. *Nature's Metropolis: Chicago and the Great West*. New York: W. W. Norton, 1991.

———. *Uncommon Ground: Rethinking the Human Place in Nature*. New York: W. W. Norton, 1996.

Debo, Annette. "Interracial Modernism in Avant-Garde Film: Paul Robeson and H. D. in the 1930 Borderline." *Quarterly Review of Film and Video* 18, no. 4 (2001), 371–83.

302

Denning, Michael. *The Cultural Front: The Laboring of American Culture in the Twentieth Century*. New York: Verso Books, 1996.

Desmond, Jane. "Embodying Difference: Issues in Dance and Cultural Studies." *Everynight Life: Culture and Dance in Latin/o America*, edited by Celeste Frasier Delgado and Jose Esteban Muñoz. Durham: Duke University Press, 1997.

———. "Invoking 'the Native': Body Politics in Contemporary Hawaiian Tourist Shows." *TDR* 41, no. 4 (1997), 83–109.

———. "Where Is 'The Nation'? Public Discourse, the Body, and Visual Display." *East-West Film Journal* 7, no. 2 (1993), 81–110.

Diamond, Stanley, ed. *Primitive Views of the World*. New York: Columbia University Press, 1964.

Diawara, Manthia. "Black Spectatorship: Problems of Identification and Resistance." *Black American Cinema*, edited by Manthia Diawara, 211–20. New York: Routledge, 1993.

———. "Cultural Studies / Black Studies." *Borders, Boundaries, and Frames: Cultural Criticism and Cultural Studies*, edited by Mae Henderson, 202–11. New York: Routledge, 1995.

———. "Englishness and Blackness: Cricket as Discourse on Colonialism." *Callaloo* 13, no. 4 (1990), 830–44.

di Leonardo, Micaela. *Exotics at Home: Anthropologies, Others, American Modernity*. Chicago: University of Chicago Press, 1998.

Dinerstein, Joel. *Swinging the Machine: Modernity, Technology, and African American Culture between the World Wars*. Amherst: University of Massachusetts Press, 2003.

Dolan, Jill. "Geographies of Learning: Theatre Studies, Performance, and the 'Performative.'" *Theatre Journal* 45 (1993), 417–41.

Domingo, W. A. "Gift of the Black Tropics." *The New Negro*, edited by Alain Locke, 341–49. New York: Simon and Schuster, 1992.

Dorinson, Joseph, and William Pencak, eds. *Paul Robeson: Essays on His Life and Legacy*. Jefferson, N.C.: McFarland, 2002.

Drake, St. Clair, and Horace R. Cayton. *Black Metropolis: A Study of Negro Life in a Northern City*. 1945. Chicago: University of Chicago Press, 1993.

Drewal, Margaret. *Yoruba Ritual: Performers, Play, Agency*. Bloomington: Indiana University Press, 1992.

Drinnon, Richard. *Facing West: The Metaphysics of Indian Hating and Empire Building*. Norman: University of Oklahoma Press, 1997.

Du Bois, W. E. B. *Black Folk, Then and Now*. New York: Henry Holt, 1939.

———. "Criteria of Negro Art." *The Portable Harlem Renaissance Reader*, edited by David Levering Lewis, 100–105. New York: Penguin Books, 1994.

———. *The Philadelphia Negro*. Philadelphia: University of Pennsylvania Press, 1899.

————. *The Souls of Black Folk.* 1903. Boston: Bedford Books, 1997.

Dudziak, Mary. *Cold War Civil Rights: Race and the Image of American Democracy.* Princeton: Princeton University Press, 2000.

Dunbar, Paul Laurence. *Lyrics of a Lowly Life.* 1899. New York: Arno Press, 1969.

Duncan, Whiteside. Interview by Karen Wickre, Research Center for the Federal Theater Project, SCAGMU, 13 August 1978.

Dunham, Katherine. *Dances of Haiti.* 1947. Los Angeles: Center for Afro-American Studies, University of California at Los Angeles, 1983.

————. "Form and Function in Primitive Dance." *Educational Dance* 4, no. 10 (1941), 2–4.

————. *Island Possessed.* Chicago: University of Chicago Press, 1994.

————. *Island Possessed.* New York: Doubleday, 1969.

————. *Journey to Accompong.* New York: Henry Holt, 1946.

————. "The Negro Dance (1941)." *Kaiso! An Anthology of Writings by and about Katherine Dunham,* edited by VèVè Clark and Margaret B. Wilkerson, 217–26. Berkeley: University of California Press, 1978.

————. *A Touch of Innocence.* New York: Harcourt Brace, 1959.

Dunn, Kaye. "L'Ag'Ya of Martinique." 1939. *Kaiso! An Anthology of Writings by and about Katherine Dunham,* edited by VèVè Clark and Margaret B. Wilkerson, 201–7. Berkeley: University of California Press, 1978.

Dyer, Richard. "Crossing Over." *Heavenly Bodies: Film Stars and Society,* 64–136. New York: Routledge, 2003.

————. "Singing Prettily: Lena Horne in Hollywood." Paper presented at Imitating Life: Women, Race, Film, 1932–2000, conference at Princeton University, 2000.

Edwards, Brent Hayes. *The Practice of Diaspora: Literature, Translation, and the Rise of Black Internationalism.* Cambridge: Harvard University Press, 2003.

Elam, Harry, Jr. "The Black Performer and the Performance of Blackness: *The Escape; or A Leap to Freedom* by William Wells Brown and *No Place to Be Somebody* by Charles Gordone." *African American Performance and Theater History: A Critical Reader,* edited by Harry J. Elam Jr. and David Krasner, 288–305. New York: Oxford University Press, 2000.

Ellison, Ralph. *Shadow and Act.* New York: Random House, 1964.

Ely, Melvin Patrick. *The Adventures of Amos and Andy: A Social History of an American Phenomenon.* New York: Free Press, 1991.

Emery, Lynne. *Black Dance: From 1619 to Today.* Salem, N.H.: Ayer, 1988.

Espiritu, Yen Le. *Home Bound: Filipino American Lives across Cultures, Communities, and Countries.* Los Angeles: University of California Press, 2003.

Everett, Anna. *Returning the Gaze: A Genealogy of Black Film Criticism, 1909–1949.* Durham: Duke University Press, 2001.

Fabian, Johannes. *Power and Performance: Ethnographic Explorations through*

Proverbial Wisdom and Theater in Shaba, Zaire. Madison: University of Wisconsin Press, 1990.

Fanon, Frantz. "On National Culture." *Colonial Discourse and Post-Colonial Theory: A Reader*, edited by Patrick Williams and Laura Chrisman, 36–52. New York: Columbia University Press, 1994.

———. *The Wretched of the Earth*. New York: Grove Weidenfeld Press, 1991.

Farmer, Paul. *The Uses of Haiti*. Monroe, Me.: Common Courage Press, 1994.

Fenin, George, and William Everson. *The Western: From Silents to Cinerama*. New York: Orion Press, 1962.

Flanagan, Hallie. *Arena: A History of the Federal Theater*. New York: Noble Offset Printers, 1940.

Fox, Richard G., ed. *Recapturing Anthropology: Working in the Present*. Santa Fe, N.M.: School of American Research Press, 1991.

Fraden, Rena. *Blueprints for a Black Federal Theater, 1935–1939*. London: Cambridge University Press, 1994.

France, Richard. "The 'Voodoo' Macbeth of Orson Welles." *Yale/Theater* 5, no. 3 (1974), 66–78.

Franko, Mark. *Dancing Modernism / Performing Politics*. Bloomington: Indiana University Press, 1995.

Fusco, Coco. *English Is Broken Here: Notes on Cultural Fusion in the Americas*. New York: New Press, 1995.

Gaines, Kevin. *Uplifting the Race: Black Leadership, Politics, and Culture in the Twentieth Century*. Chapel Hill: University of North Carolina Press, 1996.

Gallicchio, Marc. *African American Encounter with Japan and China: Black Internationalism in Asia, 1895–1945*. Chapel Hill: University of North Carolina Press, 2000.

Garvey, Marcus. "Africa for the Africans (1923)," and "The Future as I See It (1923)." *The Norton Anthology of African American Literature*, 2nd edition, edited by Henry Louis Gates Jr., and Nellie McKay, 997–99. New York: W. W. Norton, 2004.

Gates, Henry Louis, Jr. *The Signifying Monkey*. Oxford: Oxford University Press, 1988.

Geertz, Clifford. *The Interpretation of Cultures: Selected Essays*. New York: Basic Books, 1973.

Gibney, Alex. "Sentimental Imperialism: America's Cold War in Asia." *The Pacific Century*. Public Broadcasting Service, 1992.

Gilbert, W. S. *The Mikado*. New York: Boni and Liveright, 1917.

Gill, Glenda E. *White Greasepaint on Black Performers*. New York: Peter Lang, 1988.

Gilroy, Paul. *The Black Atlantic: Modernity and Double Consciousness*. New York: Verso, 1993.

———. "'. . . to be real': The Dissident Forms of Black Expressive Culture." *Let's*

Get It On: The Politics of Black Performance, edited by Catherine Ugwu, 12–33. Seattle: Bay Press, 1995.

Goldberg, David Theo. *Racist Culture: Philosophy and the Politics of Meaning.* Cambridge, Mass.: Blackwell, 1993.

———. *The Racial State.* Malden, Mass.: Blackwell, 2002.

Goodwin, Marvin E. *Black Migration in America from 1915 to 1960: An Uneasy Exodus.* Lewiston, N.Y.: E. Mellen Press, 1990.

Goodyear, Frank Henry, III. "Constructing a National Landscape: Photography and Tourism in Nineteenth-Century America." Ph.D. diss., University of Texas at Austin, 1998.

Gottlieb, Peter. *Making Their Own Way: Southern Blacks' Migration to Pittsburgh, 1916–1930.* Urbana: University of Illinois Press, 1996.

Gould, Stephen Jay. "The True Embodiment of Everything That's Excellent." *American Scholar* 69, no. 2 (2000), 35–45.

Grossberg, Lawrence. "Bringin' It All Back Home: Pedagogy and Cultural Studies." *Between Borders: Pedagogy and the Politics of Cultural Studies*, edited by Henry Giroux and Peter McLaren, 1–25. New York: Routledge 1994.

Grossman, James R. *Land of Hope: Chicago, Black Southerners, and the Great Migration.* Chicago: University of Chicago Press, 1991.

Gunning, Tom. "Aesthetics of Astonishment." *Viewing Positions: Ways of Seeing Film*, edited by Linda Williams, 114–33. New Brunswick: Rutgers University Press, 1994.

———. "Tracing the Individual Body: Photography Detectives and Early Cinema." *Cinema and the Invention of Modern Life*, edited by Leo Charney and Vanessa Schwartz, 15–45. Berkeley: University of California Press, 1995.

Habermas, Jürgen. "Modernity—An Incomplete Project." *The Anti-Aesthetic: Essays on Postmodern Culture*, edited by Hal Foster, 3–16. Seattle: Bay Press, 1983.

Harrison, Alfertdeen, ed. *Black Exodus: The Great Migration from the American South.* Jackson: University of Mississippi Press, 1991.

Harrison, Faye V., and Ira E. Harrison. "Introduction: Anthropology, African Americans, and the Emancipation of a Subjugated Knowledge." *African American Pioneers in Anthropology*, edited by Faye V. Harrison and Ira E. Harrison, 1–36. Chicago: University of Illinois Press, 1999.

Hart, Richard. *From Occupation to Independence: A Short History of the Peoples of the English-Speaking Caribbean Region.* Sterling, Va.: Pluto Press, 1999.

Harvey, David. *The Condition of Post-Modernity.* Cambridge, Mass.: Blackwell, 1996.

Hazzard-Gordon, Katrina *Jookin': The Rise of Social Dance Formations in African-American Culture.* Philadelphia: Temple University Press, 1990.

Heermance, J. Noel. *Charles W. Chesnutt, America's First Great Black Novelist.* Hamden, Conn.: Archon Books, 1974.

Henderson, Mae G. "Josephine Baker and La Revue Negre: From Ethnography to Performance." *Text and Performance Quarterly* 23, no. 2 (2003), 107–33.

Herskovits, Melville. *The Myth of the Negro Past.* 1941. Boston: Beacon Press, 1958.

Higgins, John, ed. *The Raymond Williams Reader.* Oxford: Blackwell, 2001.

Horne, Lena, and Richard Schickel. *Lena.* Garden City, N.Y.: Doubleday, 1965.

Horton, James O., and Lois E. Horton. "Violence, Protest, and Identity: Black Manhood in Antebellum America." *Free People of Color,* edited by James Horton, 80–97. Washington, D.C.: Smithsonian Press, 1993.

Houseman, John. *Run-Through.* New York: Simon and Schuster, 1972.

Huggins, Nathan. *Harlem Renaissance.* New York: Oxford University Press, 1971.

Hughes, Langston. "The Negro Artist and the Racial Mountain." *The Portable Harlem Renaissance Reader,* edited by David Levering Lewis, 91–95. New York: Penguin Books, 1994.

———. *The Weary Blues.* New York: Alfred A. Knopf, 1926.

Hurston, Zora Neale. *Mules and Men.* 1935. Bloomington: Indiana University Press, 1978.

———. *Tell My Horse: Voodoo and Life in Haiti and Jamaica.* 1938. New York: Harper and Row, 1990.

———. "Thirty Days among Maroons." 1947. *Kaiso! Writings by and about Katherine Dunham,* edited by VèVè Clark and Sarah E. Johnson, 271–73. Madison: University of Wisconsin Press, 2005.

Hutcheon, Linda. *A Theory of Parody: The Teachings of Twentieth-Century Art Forms.* New York: Methuen, 1985.

Hymes, Dell. "The Use of Anthropology: Critical, Political, Personal." *Reinventing Anthropology,* edited by Dell Hymes, 3–82. New York: Pantheon Books, 1972.

Jackson, John, Jr. "An Ethnographic Filmflam: Giving Gifts, Doing Research, and Videotaping the Native Subject/Object." *American Anthropologist* 106, no. 1 (2004), 32–42.

———. *Real Black: Adventures in Racial Sincerity.* Chicago: University of Chicago Press, 2005.

James, C. L. R. *Black Jacobins: Toussaint L'Ouverture and the San Domingo Revolution.* 1938. New York: Vintage Books, 1989.

Johnson, E. Patrick. *Appropriating Blackness: Performance and the Politics of Authenticity.* Durham: Duke University Press, 2003.

Jules-Rosette, Bennetta. *Baker in Art and Life: The Icon and the Image.* Urbana: University of Illinois Press, 2007.

Kaplan, Amy. "Black and Blue on San Juan Hill." *Cultures of United States Imperialism,* edited by Amy Kaplan and Donald E. Pease, 219–36. Durham: Duke University Press, 1993.

———. "Manifest Domesticity." *American Literature* 70, no. 3 (1998), 581–606.

———. "Romancing the Empire: Embodiment of American Masculinity in the Popular Historical Novel of the 1890s." *Postcolonial Theory and the United*

307

States: Race, Ethnicity, and Literature, edited by Amritjit Singh and Peter
    Schmidt, 220–43. Jackson: University Press of Mississippi, 1996.
Kapur, Sudarshan. Raising Up a Prophet: The African American Encounter with
    Gandhi. Boston: Beacon Press, 1992.
Karnow, Stanley. In Our Image: America's Empire in the Philippines. New York:
    Random House, 1989.
Katz, William Loren. Black People Who Made the Old West. Trenton, N.J.: Africa
    World Press, 1992.
————. The Black West. Garden City, N.Y.: Anchor Books, 1973.
Kazacoff, George. Dangerous Theatre: The Federal Theatre Project as a Forum for
    New Plays. New York: P. Lang, 1989.
Kearney, Michael. "Borders and Boundaries of State and Self at the End of Em-
    pire." Journal of Historical Sociology 4, no. 1 (1991), 52–74.
Kearney, Reginald. African American Views of the Japanese: Solidarity or Sedition?
    New York: State University of New York Press, 1998.
Kelley, Robin D. G. Freedom Dreams. Boston: Beacon Press, 2002.
————. Race Rebels: Culture, Politics, and the Black Working Class. New York:
    Free Press, 1994.
Keyssar, Helene. The Curtain and the Veil: Strategies in Black Drama. New York:
    Burt Franklin, 1981.
Knight, Arthur. Disintegrating the Musical: Black Performance and American Musi-
    cal Film. Durham: Duke University Press, 2002.
Kornweibel, Theodore, Jr. "Seeing Red": Federal Campaigns against Black Mili-
    tancy, 1919–1925. Bloomington: Indiana University Press, 1998.
Krasner, David. Afterword to African American Performance and Theater History:
    A Critical Reader, edited by Harry Elam and David Krasner, 345–50. New
    York: Oxford University Press, 2001.
————. "Black Salome." African American Performance and Theater History: A
    Critical Reader, edited by Harry Elam and David Krasner, 192–211. New York:
    Oxford University Press, 2001.
Lacan, Jacques. "The Mirror Stage as Formative of the I Function as Revealed
    in Psychoanalytic Experience." Ecrits: A Selection. New York: W. W. Norton,
    1977.
Langley, Lester D. The Banana Wars: United States Intervention in the Caribbean,
    1898–1934. Wilmington, Del.: SR Books, 2002.
Lavie, Smadar, and Ted Swedenburg. Introduction to Displacement, Diaspora,
    and Geographies of Identity, edited by Smadar Lavie and Ted Swedenburg,
    1–26. Durham: Duke University Press, 1996.
Lawrence, E. P. "The Banned Mikado: A Topsy Turvy Event." Centennial Review
    18 (Spring 1974), 160–69.
Lemann, Nicholas. The Promised Land: The Great Black Migration and How It
    Changed America. New York: Vintage Books, 1992.

Lemke, Sieglinde. *Primitivist Modernism: Black Culture and the Origins of Trans-atlantic Modernism*. New York: Oxford University Press, 1998.

Levine, Lawrence. *Black Culture and Black Consciousness: Afro-American Folk Thought from Slavery to Freedom*. New York: Oxford University Press, 1978.

Lhamon, W. T. *Raising Cain: Blackface Performance from Jim Crow to Hip Hop*. Cambridge: Harvard University Press, 2000.

Limerick, Patricia Nelson. *Something in the Soil: Legacies and Reckonings in the New West*. New York: W. W. Norton, 2000.

Little, Lawrence. *Disciples of Liberty: The African Methodist Episcopal Church in the Age of Imperialism, 1884–1916*. Knoxville: University of Tennessee Press, 2000.

Locke, Alain, ed. *The New Negro: Voices of the Harlem Renaissance*. 1925. New York: Touchstone Books, 1997.

Lott, Eric. *Love and Theft: Blackface Minstrelsy and the American Working Class*. New York: Oxford University Press, 1993.

Lowe, Lisa. *Critical Terrains: French and British Imperialisms*. Ithaca: Cornell University Press, 1991.

———. *Immigrant Acts: On Asian American Cultural Politics*. Durham: Duke University Press, 1996.

Loy, R. Phillip. *Westerns and American Culture: 1930–1955*. London: McFarland, 2001.

Madison, D. Soyini. "Performance, Personal Narratives, and the Politics of Possibility." *The Future of Performance Studies: The Next Millennium*, edited by Sheron Dailey, 276–86. Annandale, Va.: National Communication Association, 1998.

Malone, Jaqui. *Steppin' on the Blues: The Visible Rhythms of African American Dance*. Chicago: University of Illinois Press, 1996.

Manning, Susan A. *Ecstasy and the Demon: Feminism and Nationalism in the Dances of Mary Wigman*. Berkeley: University of California at Los Angeles, 1993.

———. "Modern Dance, Negro Dance, and Katherine Dunham." *Textual Practice* 15, no. 3 (2001), 487–505.

———. *Modern Dance, Negro Dance: Race in Motion*. Minneapolis: University of Minnesota Press, 2006.

Marchetti, Gina. *Romance and the "Yellow Peril."* Berkeley: University of California Press, 1993.

Marks, Carole. *Farewell—We're Good and Gone: The Great Black Migration*. Bloomington: Indiana University Press, 1989.

Martin, Wendy. "'Remembering the Jungle': Josephine Baker and Modernist Parody." *Prehistories of the Future: The Primitivist Project and the Culture of Modernism*, edited by Elazar Barkan and Ronald Bush, 310–25. Stanford: Stanford University Press, 1995.

Mathews, Jane D. *The Federal Theater, 1935–1939: Plays, Relief, and Politics*. New York: Octagon Books, 1980.

McClintock, Anne. *Imperial Leather: Race, Gender, and Sexuality in Colonial Conquest*. New York: Routledge, 1995.

McCloskey, Susan. "Shakespeare, Orson Welles, and the 'Voodoo' *Macbeth*." *Shakespeare Quarterly* 36, no. 4 (1985), 406–16.

McElrath, Joseph R., Jr., ed. *Critical Essays on Charles Waddell Chesnutt*. New York: G. K. Hall, 1999.

McKay, Claude. *Harlem: Negro Metropolis*. New York: E. P. Dutton, 1940.

Melosh, Barbara. *Engendering Culture: Manhood and Womanhood in New Deal Public Art and Theater*. Washington, D.C.: Smithsonian Institution Press, 1991.

Mercer, Kobena. "Black Hair / Style Politics." *New Formations* 3 (1987), 49.

Micheaux, Oscar. *The Conquest: The Story of a Negro Pioneer*. Lincoln, Neb.: Woodruff Press, 1913.

——. *The Homesteader: A Novel*. 1917. College Park, Md.: McGrath, 1969.

Mikell, Gwendolyn. "Feminism in Black Culture in the Ethnography of Zora Neale Hurston." *African American Pioneers in Anthropology*, edited by Ira Harrison and Faye Harrison, 51–69. Chicago: University of Illinois Press, 1999.

Miller, Angela. *Empire of the Eye: Landscape Representation and American Cultural Politics, 1825–1875*. Ithaca: Cornell University Press, 1993.

Mitchell, Lee. *Westerns: Making the Man in Fiction and Film*. Chicago: University of Chicago Press, 1996.

Mitchell, Loften. *Black Drama: The Story of the American Negro in the Theater*. New York: Hawthorne Books, 1967.

Monteith, Kathleen E. A., and Glen Richards, eds. *Jamaica in Slavery and Freedom: History, Heritage and Culture*. Kingston, Jamaica: University of the West Indies Press, 2002.

Morley, David, and Kuan-Hsing Chen, eds. *Stuart Hall: Critical Dialogues in Cultural Studies*. London: Routledge, 1996.

Mudimbe, V. Y. *The Invention of Africa: Gnosis, Philosophy, and the Order of Knowledge*. Bloomington: Indiana University Press, 1988.

Mullen, Bill V., and Cathryn Watson, eds. *W. E. B. Du Bois on Asia: Crossing the World Color Line*. Jackson: University of Mississippi Press, 2005.

Muller, Nancy Ladd. "Du Boisian Pragmatism and 'The Problem of the Twentieth Century.'" *Critique of Anthropology* 12, no. 3 (1992), 319–37.

Munich, Adrienne Auslander. "'Capture the Heart of a Queen': Gilbert and Sullivan's Rites of Conquest." *Centennial Review* 28, no. 1 (1984), 23–44.

——. "Queen Victoria, Empire, and Excess." *Tulsa Studies in Women's Literature* 6, no. 2 (1987), 265–81.

Myers, Gerald. *The Black Tradition in Modern Dance*. Durham, N.C.: American Dance Festival, 1988.

Myers, Gerald, and Stephanie Reinhart. *African American Genius in Modern Dance*. Durham, N.C.: American Dance Festival, 1993.

Naison, Mark. *Communists in Harlem during the Depression*. Urbana: University of Illinois Press, 1983.

Narayan, Kirin. "How Native Is a Native Anthropologist?" *American Anthropologist* 95, no. 2 (1993), 671–86.

Nenno, Nancy. "Femininity, the Primitive, and Modern Urban Space: Josephine Baker in Berlin." *Women in the Metropolis: Gender and Modernity in Weimar Culture*, edited by Katharina von Ankum, 145–61. Berkeley: University of California Press, 1997.

Ness, Sally Ann. *Body Movement Culture: Kinesthetic and Visual Symbolism in a Philippine Community*. Philadelphia: University of Pennsylvania Press, 1992.

North, Michael. *The Dialect of Modernism: Race, Language, and Twentieth-Century Literature*. New York: Oxford University Press, 1994.

O'Conner, John, and Lorraine Brown. *Free, Adult, Uncensored: The Living History of the Federal Theater*. Washington, D.C.: New Republic Books, 1978.

Oehling, Richard. "The Yellow Menace: Asian Images in American Film." *The Kaleidoscope Lens: How Hollywood Views Ethnic Groups*, edited by Randall Miller, 182–206. Englewood, N.J.: Jerome S. Ozer, 1980.

O'Neill, Eugene. *The Emperor Jones*. New York: Boni and Liveright, 1921.

Orme, Frederick L. "The Negro in Dance as Katherine Dunham Sees Him." 1938. *Kaiso! An Anthology of Writings by and about Katherine Dunham*, edited by VèVè Clark and Margaret B. Wilkerson, 191–94. Berkeley: University of California Press, 1978.

Pagan, Eduardo. *Murder at the Sleepy Lagoon: Zoot Suits, Race, and Riot in Wartime L.A.* Chapel Hill: University of North Carolina Press, 2006.

Painter, Nell Irvin. *Exodusters: Black Migration to Kansas after Reconstruction*. Lawrence: University of Kansas Press, 1986.

Perpener, John O., III. *African American Concert Dance: The Harlem Renaissance and Beyond*. Chicago: University of Illinois Press, 2001.

Phillips, Kimberley L. *Alabama North: African American Migrants, Community, and Working Class Activism in Cleveland, 1915–1945*. Urbana: University of Illinois Press, 1999.

Pierre, Dorathi Bock. "A Talk with Katherine Dunham." *Kaiso! An Anthology of Writings by and about Katherine Dunham*, edited by VèVè Clark and Margaret B. Wilkerson, 248–50. Berkeley: University of California Press, 1978.

Plummer, Brenda Gayle. "The Afro-American Response to the Occupation of Haiti, 1915–1934." *Freedom's Odyssey: African American History Essays from Phylon*, edited by Alexa Benson Henderson and Janice Sumler-Edmond, 313–34. Atlanta: Clark Atlanta University Press, 1999.

———. *Haiti and the United States: The Psychological Moment*. Athens: University of Georgia Press, 1992.

311

————. *Rising Wind: Black Americans and U.S. Foreign Affairs, 1935–1960*. Chapel Hill: University of North Carolina Press, 1996.

Poiger, Uta. "Taming the Wild West: American Popular Culture and the Cold War Battles over East and West German Identities, 1949–1961." Ph.D. diss., Brown University, 1995.

Rafael, Vicente. "White Love: Surveillance and Nationalist Resistance in the U.S. Colonization of the Philippines." *Cultures of United States Imperialism*, edited by Amy Kaplan and Donald Pease, 185–218. Durham: Duke University Press, 1993.

Rampersad, Arnold. "Langston Hughes and Approaches to Modernism in the Harlem Renaissance." *The Harlem Renaissance: Revaluations*, edited by Amritjit Singh, William S. Shiver, and Stanley Brodwin, 49–72. New York: Garland, 1989.

Reed, Christopher Robert. *The Chicago NAACP and the Rise of Black Professional Leadership, 1920–1966*. Bloomington: Indiana University Press, 1997.

Reid, Mark. *Redefining Black Film*. Berkeley: University of California Press, 1993.

Renda, Mary. *Taking Haiti: Military Occupation and the Culture of U.S. Imperialism, 1915–1940*. Chapel Hill: University of North Carolina Press, 2000.

Revitt, Paul. "Gilbert and Sullivan: More Seriousness than Satire." *Western Humanities Review* 19 (1965), 19–34.

Roach, Joseph. *Cities of the Dead: Circum-Atlantic Performance*. New York: Columbia University Press, 1996.

Robeson, Paul. "Paul Robeson on Negro Race." *Paul Robeson Speaks: Writings, Speeches, Interviews, 1918–1974*, edited by Philip Foner, 98–100. Secaucus, N.J.: Citadel Press, 1978.

————. "Primitives." *Paul Robeson Speaks: Writings, Speeches, Interviews, 1918–1974*, edited by Philip Foner, 109–13. Secaucus, N.J.: Citadel Press, 1978.

Robeson, Paul, Jr. *The Undiscovered Paul Robeson: An Artist's Journey, 1898–1939*. New York: John Wiley, 2001.

Robinson, Cedric. *Black Marxism: The Making of the Black Radical Tradition*. Chapel Hill: University of North Carolina Press, 2000.

————. *Black Movements in America*. New York: Routledge, 1997.

Roediger, David. *The Wages of Whiteness: Race and the Making of the American Working Class*. New York: Verso, 1991.

Rogin, Michael. *Blackface, White Noise: Jewish Immigrants in the Melting Pot*. Berkeley: University of California Press, 1996.

Rogozinski, Jan. *A Brief History of the Caribbean: From the Arawak and the Carib to the Present*. New York: Meridian, 1994.

Rony, Fatima Tobing. *The Third Eye: Race, Cinema, and Ethnographic Spectacle*. Durham: Duke University Press, 1996.

Roosevelt, Theodore. *The Strenuous Life: Essays and Addresses*. New York: Century, 1900. Bartleby.com.

Rose, Phyllis. *Jazz Cleopatra: Josephine Baker in Her Time*. New York: Vintage Books, 1991.

Ross, Ronald Patrick. "Black Drama in the Federal Theater, 1935–1939." Ph.D. diss., George Mason University, Federal Theater Archives, 1972.

Rothel, David. *The Singing Cowboys*. South Brunswick, N.J.: A. S. Barnes, 1978.

Ruby, Jay. *Picturing Culture: Explorations of Film and Anthropology*. Chicago: University of Chicago Press, 2000.

Said, Edward. *Orientalism*. New York: Vintage Books, 1979.

Salman, Michael. "In Our Orientalist Imagination: Historiography and the Culture of Colonialism in the United States." *Radical History Review* 50 (Spring 1991), 221–32.

Sampson, H. T. *Blacks in Black and White: A Source Book on Black Films*. Metuchen, N.J.: Scarecrow Press, 1995.

———. *Blacks in Blackface: A Sourcebook on Early Black Musical Shows*. Metuchen, N.J.: Scarecrow Press, 1980.

Sanders, Leslie Catherine. *The Development of Black Theater in America: From Shadows to Selves*. Baton Rouge: Louisiana State University Press, 1988.

Savigliano, Marta E. "Fragments for a Story of Tango Bodies (on Choreocritics and the Memory of Power)." *Corporealities: Dancing Knowledge, Culture and Power*, edited by Susan Foster, 199–232. New York: Routledge, 1996.

Saxton, Alexander. *The Rise and Fall of the White Republic: Class Politics and Mass Culture in Nineteenth Century America*. New York: Verso, 1990.

Schechner, Richard. *Performance Theory*. New York: Routledge, 2003.

Schmidt, Hans. *The United States' Occupation of Haiti, 1915–1934*. New Brunswick: Rutgers University Press, 1971.

Schuyler, George. "The Negro-Art Hokum." *The Portable Harlem Renaissance Reader*, edited by David Levering Lewis, 96–99. New York: Penguin Books, 1994.

Schwartz, Bonnie Nelson. *Voices from the Federal Theatre*. Foreword by Robert Brustein. Madison: University of Wisconsin Press, 2003.

Scott, William. *Sons of Sheba's Race: African-Americans and the Italo-Ethiopian War, 1935–1941*. Bloomington: Indiana University Press, 1993.

Seabrook, W. B. *The Magic Island*. Illustrated with drawings by Alexander King and photographs by the author. New York: Harcourt, Brace, 1929.

Shakespeare, William. *Macbeth*, edited by Carol Chillington Rutter. New York: Penguin Books, 2005.

Shannon, Magdaline W., and Jean Prince-Mars. *The Haitian Elite and the American Occupation, 1915–1935*. New York: St. Martin's Press, 1996.

Sherlock, Philip, and Hazel Bennett. *Story of the Jamaican People*. Kingston, Jamaica: Ian Randle, 1998.

Sherron, Jane de Hart. *The Federal Theater, 1935–1939: Plays, Relief, and Politics*. New York: Octagon Books, 1980.

Sitkoff, Harvard. *A New Deal for Blacks: The Emergence of the Civil Rights as a National Issue.* New York: Oxford University Press, 1978.

Sklaroff, Lauren Rebecca. "Ambivalent Inclusion: The State, Race, and Official Culture." Ph.D. diss., University of Virginia, 2003.

Slotkin, Richard. *Gunfighter Nation: The Myth of the Frontier in Twentieth Century America.* New York: Atheneum, 1992.

Smith, Eric. *Bert Williams: A Biography of the Pioneer Black Comedian.* Jefferson, N.C.: McFarland, 1992.

Smith, Geoffrey. *The Savoy Operas: A New Guide to Gilbert and Sullivan.* London: Robert Hale Limited, 1983.

Smith, Henry Nash. *Virgin Land: The American West as Symbol and Myth.* New York: Vintage Books, 1957.

Sproul, Robert M. "Modus Operandi: Carnival Poetics in W. S. Gilbert's Savoy Operas." Ph.D. diss., UMI Dissertation Abstracts International, 1996.

Stansfield, Peter. *The Exile. Hollywood, Westerns and the 1930s: The Lost Trail.* Devon: University of Exeter Press, 2001.

Stedman, Raymond William. *Shadow of the Indian: Stereotypes in American Culture.* Norman: University of Oklahoma Press, 1982.

Steen, Shannon. "Racing American Modernity: Black Atlantic Negotiations of Asia in the 'Swing' Mikadoes." *AfroAsian Encounters: Culture, History, Politics,* edited by Heike Raphael-Hernandez and Shannon Steen, 167–87. New York: New York University Press, 2006.

Stephens, Michelle Ann. *Black Empire: The Masculine Global Imaginary of Caribbean Intellectuals in the United States, 1914–1962.* Durham: Duke University Press, 2005.

Stepto, Robert B. *Blue as the Lake: A Personal Geography.* Boston: Beacon Press, 1998.

Stewart, Jacqueline. *Migrating to the Movies: Cinema and Black Urban Modernity.* Berkeley: University of California Press, 2005.

———. "Negroes Laughing at Themselves?: Black Spectatorship and the Performance of Urban Modernity." *Critical Inquiry* 29, no. 4 (2003), 650–77.

Stewart, Jeffrey C. "Paul Robeson and the Problem of Modernism." *Rhapsodies in Black: Art of the Harlem Renaissance,* edited by Susan Ferleger Brades, Roger Malbert, and David A. Bailey, 90–101. Berkeley: University of California Press, 1997.

Stocking, George. "The Basic Assumptions of Boasian Anthropology." *Delimiting Anthropology: Occasional Inquiries and Reflections,* 24–48. Madison: University of Wisconsin Press, 2001.

———. *Race, Culture, and Evolution: Essays in the History of Anthropology.* New York: Free Press, 1968.

———. *Romantic Motives: Essays on Anthropological Sensibility.* Vol. 6, *History of Anthropology.* Madison: University of Wisconsin Press, 1989.

Stowe, David W. *Swing Changes: Big Band Jazz in New Deal America.* Cambridge: Harvard University Press, 1994.

Studlar, Gaylyn. *This Mad Masquerade: Stardom and Masculinity in the Jazz Age.* New York: Columbia University Press, 1996.

Szwed, John F. "An American Anthropological Dilemma: The Politics of Afro-American Culture." *Reinventing Anthropology,* edited by Dell Hymes, 153–81. New York: Pantheon Books, 1972.

Tichi, Cecelia. *Shifting Gears: Technology, Literature, Culture in Modernist America.* Chapel Hill: University of North Carolina Press, 1987.

Tomko, Linda. *Dancing Class: Gender, Ethnicity, and Social Divides in American Dance, 1890–1920.* Bloomington: Indiana University Press, 1999.

Tompkins, Jane. *West of Everything: The Inner Life of Westerns.* New York: Oxford University Press, 1992.

Torgovnick, Marianna. *Gone Primitive: Savage Intellects, Modern Lives.* Chicago: University of Chicago Press, 1990.

Trouillot, M. R. "Anthropology and the Savage Slot: the Poetics and Politics of Otherness." *Recapturing Anthropology: Working in the Present,* edited by Richard G. Fox, 17–44. Santa Fe, N.M.: School of American Research Press, 1991.

Vallillo, Stephen M. "The Battle of the Black *Mikados.*" *Black American Literature Forum* 16, no. 4 (1982), 153–57.

Vandercook, John W. *Black Majesty: The Life of Christophe, King of Haiti.* New York: Harper and Brothers, 1928.

Vergara, Benito M., Jr. *Displaying Filipinos: Photography and Colonialism in the Early 20th Century.* Quezon City: University of the Philippines Press, 1995.

Von Eschen, Penny. *Race against Empire: Black Americans and Anti-Colonialism, 1937–1957.* Ithaca: Cornell University Press, 1997.

Walker, Lewis, and Ben C. Wilson. *Black Eden: The Idlewild Community.* East Lansing: Michigan State University Press, 2002.

Watkins, Mel. *On the Real Side: Laughing, Lying, and Signifying—The Underground Tradition of African-American Humor.* New York: Simon and Schuster, 1994.

Watkins-Owens, Irma. *Blood Relations: Caribbean Immigrants and the Harlem Community, 1900–1930.* Bloomington: Indiana University Press, 1996.

Weinstein, Brian, and Aaron Segal. *Haiti: The Failure of Politics.* New York: Praeger, 1992.

White, Shane, and Graham White. *Stylin': African American Expressive Culture, from Its Beginnings to the Zoot Suit.* Ithaca: Cornell University Press, 1999.

Williams, Carolyn. "Parody, Pastiche, and the Play of Genres: The Savoy Operas of Gilbert and Sullivan." *The Victorian Comic Spirit: New Perspectives,* edited by Jennifer Wagner-Lawlor, 1–21. Aldershot: Ashgate, 2000.

———. "*Utopia, Limited*: Nationalism, Empire and Parody in the Comic Operas of Gilbert and Sullivan." *Cultural Politics at the Fin de Siecle*, edited by Sally Ledger and Scott McCracken, 221–47. Cambridge: Cambridge University Press, 1995.

Williams, Linda. *Hard Core: Power, Pleasure, and the "Frenzy of the Visible."* Berkeley: University of California Press, 1989.

Williams, Raymond. *The Sociology of Culture*. Chicago: University of Chicago Press, 1999.

Willis, William S., Jr. "Skeletons in the Anthropological Closet." *Reinventing Anthropology*, edited by Dell Hymes, 121–52. New York: Pantheon Books, 1972.

Witham, Barry B. *The Federal Theatre Project: A Case Study*. New York: Cambridge University Press, 2003.

Woll, Allan. *Black Musical Theater: From Coontown to Dreamgirls*. Baton Rouge: Louisiana State University Press, 1989.

Wright, Martin, ed. *Revolution in the Philippines? A Keesing's Special Report*. Chicago: St. James Press, 1988.

Wright, Richard. *American Hunger*. New York: Harper and Row, 1977.

Yoshihara, Mari. "Women's Asia: American Women and the Gendering of American Orientalism, 1870s–WWII." Ph.D. diss., Brown University, 1997.

INDEX

Page numbers in italics refer to illustrations.

Baldwin, James, 256
Ballet. *See* Dance; *specific works*
Ballet Fedré (Chicago Federal The-
ater), 185
Bataan (film), 237
Bean, Annemarie, 14
Beard, Matthew "Stymie," 59
Belonging. *See* National belonging
Belton, Robert, 38

Benedict, Ruth, 177
Birth of a Nation (film), 21
Black activism, 15–17
Black diaspora: aesthetic of, 203;
anthropology and, 24, 167, 171, 172;
dance and, 188, 191, 199–200; feminized formation of, 219; identity
and, 185, 227, 259; performance
and, 23, 165, 172, 213, 226; transnationalism and, 178, 259; utopias
of, 25, 201
Black Empire (theater production),
109
Blackface: black minstrelsy and, 14,
139, 144–45, 241–42; references
to, 137, 139–40, 144–45, *146*; white
minstrelsy and, 15, 132, 137, 230
Black filmmaking: assimilation and,
57; Depression-era, 3, 21–22, 23; as
modernity, 56–57; national belonging and, 56; racism and, 20, 22, 236;
regulation of, 22; westerns, 28–30,
40–41. *See also specific films*
Black identity: expansionism and,
28–29, 30, 42, 51, 57, 68; FTP and,
19, 70, 134; masculine, 74; na-
tional/racial, 4–5, 17, 73, 110–14;
Native Americans and, 42–43;
performing, 12–15; power and, 3–4,
6; representations of, 204; resistance and, 110–14. *See also* American identity
Black Jacobins (James play), 91

*Black Mikado or the Town of Kan-Ka-
Kee, The* (theater production), 123
Black minstrelsy, 14
Blackness: Americanness and, 2, 7, 21,
40, 87, 144, 235, 237; backwardness
and, 74; belonging and, 2; colonial
fantasies of, 9; compared to whiteness, 198; conflated African and
West Indian, 11–12; cultural power
and, 7; dance and, 174; diasporic,
109; embodiment and, 2, 13; exoticized, 76, 79, 150, 157; global, 6, 17;
immigrants and, 54; modernity
and, 8–10, 21, 140, 198, 232; performance and, 2, 5, 11, 12–15, 144–45,
259; as spectacle, 88; stereotypes,
42, 153; symbolic use of, 8, 15, 54,
64, 139, 144; transnational, 17,
111–12, 200. *See also* Black identity;
Primitivism
Black patriotism, 17, 25, 235, 236, 237,
238, 239, 246, 248, 253, 254
Black performance. *See* Performance
Blue as the Lake (Stepto), 257, 267n15
Blue Network (NBC), 149
Boas, Franz, 167, 169, 170
Bogle, Donald, 232–33, 236
Bontemps, Arna, 94
Bronze Buckaroo (film), 58
Brooks, Clarence, 58, 59
Brown, Ada, 230
Buffalo Soldiers, 17
Bulliet, C. J., 132–33, 155–56
Burroughs, Eric, 81–83

Cabin in the Sky (Dunham show),
185
Calloway, Cab, 228, 230, 239, 246, 254
Carter, Jack, 79, 88, 105, 216, 258
Casablanca (film), 239
Cassidy, Claudia, 189
Caulfield, Mina Davis, 170

319

320

and, 8–12, 73–74, 242–43; racism
and, 245
Moorish Science Temple of America,
161
Moreland, Mantan, 67, 257
Morely, Mrs. J. O., 36
Murray, N. B., 58
Mussolini, Benito, 112, 113

324

326
....

STEPHANIE LEIGH BATISTE is a
performer and an associate professor in the
Department of English and in the Department
of Black Studies at the University of California,
Santa Barbara.

Library of Congress Cataloging-in-Publication Data
Batiste, Stephanie Leigh
Darkening mirrors : imperial representation in
Depression-era African American performance /
Stephanie Leigh Batiste.
p. cm.
Includes bibliographical references and index.
ISBN 978-0-8223-4898-6 (cloth : alk. paper)
ISBN 978-0-8223-4923-5 (pbk. : alk. paper)
1. African Americans — Race identity — 20th century.
2. African American theater — History — 20th century.
3. African Americans in motion pictures — History —
20th century. 4. African Americans in popular
culture — History — 20th century. 5. African American arts — 20th century. I. Title.
E185.625.B375 2012
305.896′073 — dc23   2011027451